THE WOMAN JESUS LOVED

NAG HAMMADI
AND
MANICHAEAN STUDIES

FORMERLY

NAG HAMMADI STUDIES

EDITED BY

J.M. ROBINSON & H.J. KLIMKEIT

XL

THE WOMAN JESUS LOVED

MARY MAGDALENE IN THE NAG HAMMADI LIBRARY AND RELATED DOCUMENTS

BY

ANTTI MARJANEN

E.J. BRILL
LEIDEN · NEW YORK · KÖLN
1996

The paper in this book meets the guidelines for permanence and durability of the Committee on Production Guidelines for Book Longevity of the Council on Library Resources.

BT
1391
.M37
1996

Die Deutsche Bibliothek – CIP-Einheitsaufnahme

Marjanen, Antti:
The woman Jesus loved : Mary Magdalene in the Nag Hammadi Library and related documents / by Antti Marjanen. - Leiden ;
New York ; Köln : Brill, 1996
   (Nag Hammadi and Manichaean studies ; 40)
   ISBN 90-04-10658-8
NE: GT

ISSN   0929-2470
ISBN   90 04 10658 8

PRINTED IN THE NETHERLANDS

TABLE OF CONTENTS

PREFACE

This book is a slightly revised version of my dissertation accepted by the Theological Faculty of the University of Helsinki in January 1996. Although writing a dissertation is often a lonely undertaking, it never takes place fully alone. This is very true with my work as well. Several people have in various ways contributed to its completion.

More than fifteen years ago Prof. Günter Wagner (Baptist Theological Seminary, Rüschlikon, Switzerland) gave me the first impetus towards the study of the Gnostic Mary Magdalene by introducing me to the secrets of the Coptic language and the Nag Hammadi Library.

After I left Rüschlikon and returned to Finland Prof. Heikki Räisänen (University of Helsinki) welcomed me warmly among his students even though I chose to work on a subject which was not closely linked with his own primary scholarly interests. Although he frequently offered his comments on the various drafts of my work with a remark "I do not really know much about this matter," his critique was most helpful, especially from the viewpoint of methodology. The accuracy and consistency of argumentation demanded by a professor is the best gift a student can ever receive.

Special thanks are due to Prof. Karen L. King (Occidental College, Los Angeles) who became involved in my writing process in its final, most productive phase. She read the entire manuscript and made numerous, perceptive comments and suggestions, which both forced and persuaded me to rethink several aspects of the work and inspired new discoveries as well. Her excellent mastery of sources, creativity of thought, and expertise in the area of Gnosticism could not but impress me time and again.

With great appreciation I mention my two closest colleagues, Dr. Risto Uro (University of Helsinki) and Dr. Ismo Dunderberg (University of Helsinki), who not only read the manuscript and made many valuable comments about it, but with whom I also tested out many of my preliminary ideas. Because of and during these discussions, some of these ideas were discarded forever, but many were refined to become useful parts of the final product.

There were also others who read and commented on sections of the dissertation in its various stages. In particular, I refer to Prof. Lars Aejmelaeus (University of Helsinki), in whose New Testament seminars I was able to present and get feedback about my work at its early phase, and Prof. Dieter Lührmann (University of Marburg), who kindly agreed to read a preliminary version of the chapter on the *Gospel of Mary* and made several useful suggestions.

The discussions I had with my former fellow-students and present colleagues, including Dr. Markku Kotila, Dr. Matti Myllykoski (University of Helsinki), and Prof. Kari Syreeni (University of Uppsala), deepened my understanding of the historical study of early Christian texts and thus gave me firmer ground to work on Gnostic Mary Magdalene traditions.

Furthermore, I wish to express my special gratitude to Prof. James M. Robinson, Director of the Institute for Antiquity and Christianity, Claremont, California, who not only kindly invited me to stay and work for five weeks at the Institute in Fall 1994 but also recommended my work to be accepted in the series *Nag Hammadi and Manichaean Studies*. I am likewise indebted to Jon Ma. Asgeirsson, Associate Director of the Institute, who took care of all the practical arrangements which my visit in Claremont involved. He was also willing to enter into many fruitful conversations about our common interest — Gnosticism. In addition, he read the entire manuscript and made several valuable suggestions for its improvement.

I also want to thank Prof. Sasagu Arai and Dr. Siegfried Richter who sent me a copy of their respective articles otherwise inaccessible to me.

The major responsibility of revising my English was painstakingly born by my friend and fellow-Rüschlikoner Rev. Gary Denning. At an early stage of the work Rev. James and Mary Tiefel corrected my language as well.

I received financial aid from several sources. On two occasions I was able to work in a research project sponsored by the Finnish Academy. In addition, the University of Helsinki granted me a scholarship which allowed me to work three months without other obligations in the final phase of the study. I was also supported by grants from the Olly and Uno Donner's Foundation and Alfred Kordelin Foundation.

Of several individuals who in non-academic, yet important ways made it easier for me to pursue my work I wish to thank my mother Linnea Marjanen and my brother Markku Marjanen. Special thanks are likewise due to my friend, engineer Risto Huhtala, who at one point of the process solved the lack of space in our home by constructing a separate study chamber for me.

Finally, I dedicate this book to my wife, Solveig, and our children, Katja, Jani, Patrik, and Jenna. Without them the work would probably have been accomplished earlier. Yet, with them my life has been so much richer that I do not mind.

In a train between Helsinki and Hyvinkää, April 1996.

Antti Marjanen

CHAPTER ONE

INTRODUCTION

1. *Survey of Research*

Although Mary Magdalene is not one of the most studied biblical personages, she has still been an object of inquiry from the very beginning of the study of early Christian texts. Three major areas of interest have dominated the exegetical and theological discussion about her: Mary Magdalene and the four anointers of the New Testament gospels, Mary Magdalene in Gnostic writings, and Mary Magdalene from women's studies perspectives. While the New Testament episodes have been in the foreground from the pre-critical era into the period of modern exegesis, i.e., from the third century until our own, the last hundred years have witnessed increased scholarly attention given to Gnostic writings, with women's studies gaining momentum within the last two decades. The present study of Mary Magdalene focuses on these more recent areas of interest. Nevertheless, the New Testament connections are briefly introduced in order to give perspective to the presentation.

1.1 *Mary Magdalene and the Four Anointers*

When the early church fathers began to study Mary Magdalene pericopes of the New Testament, the most burning issue for them was to decide what the relationship of Mary Magdalene was to the four anointment accounts of the New Testament (Mark 14,3-9; Matt 26,6-13; Luke 7,36-50; John 12,1-8). There is no need here to go into details of this discussion.[1] Suffice it to say that since the sixth century the most common, but from a modern exegetical perspective, untenable view in this matter was that Mary Magdalene, Mary of Bethany (John 12,1-8), and the anonymous anointers in Mark 14,3-9 (Matt 26,6-13) and Luke 7,36-50 were one and the

---

[1] For a detailed survey of patristic interpretations, see Holzmeister 1922, 402-422.556-584.

same person.[2] The notion had its starting-point in an assumption that Mary Magdalene who is mentioned in Luke 8,2 is identical with the woman in Luke 7,36-50. A further harmonizing corollary of this identification was that Mary Magdalene and all the other anointers were merged as well. In the late Middle Ages this interpretation gained such a dominant position in the Western Church that those who disagreed with it risked being condemned by the church.[3] In the Greek Orthodox Church the situation was different. All three women, Mary Magdalene, Mary of Bethany, and the anointer of Luke 7,36-50, were seen as distinct persons, and Mary Magdalene was not linked with the incident of anointment at all.[4]

It was not until historical-critical exegesis began that there developed a greater variance in the Western tradition of interpretation. Most of the Protestant exegetes adopted the "Eastern" line of interpretation, whereas Roman Catholic scholars continued to abide by the traditional conception. Only in our century have Catholic interpreters begun to question more widely the identification of Mary Magdalene with any of the anointers.[5] The long history of interpretation during which Mary Magdalene has primarily been seen in light of the anointers, especially of the prostitute in Luke 7, has nevertheless left its traces on the picture drawn of her even in modern times. Even if scholars nowadays very seldom see Mary Magdalene in Luke 7, in more popular — both religious and secular — interpretations of the New Testament texts she is frequently considered to be a penitent woman with a notori-

---

[2] The untenableness of this interpretation was already shown by Sickenberger (1925, 63-74) and Burkitt (1930-31, 157-159). Recent attempts, such as Feuillet 1975, 357-394, to revive this traditional view have not brought out anything substantially new to the treatment of this question.

[3] Haskins 1993, 250-251.

[4] Haskins 1993, 26.406 n. 55.

[5] Modern Catholic exegesis of Luke 7,36-50 is well represented by the comment of Fitzmyer (1981, 688): "In Western Church traditions, at least since the time of Gregory the Great, Mary of Bethany has been conflated with the sinner of Galilee, and even with Mary Magdalene, 'out of whom seven demons had come' (8:2). There is, however, no basis for this conflation in the NT itself, and no evidence whatsoever that the 'possession' of Mary Magdalene was the result of personal sinfulness."

ous past.[6] Sometimes this notion has also crept into the mind of a modern New Testament scholar.[7] Typical of the portrait composed throughout the centuries of Mary Magdalene from the New Testament gospels is that her assumed role as a loose, but contrite woman has overshadowed the part she played in the Easter narratives.[8] In later legends and sermons she is much better known as Luke's penitent sinner than as "apostle to the apostles."[9] It was actually women's studies perspectives which brought the Easter texts into a focus in the discussion about the canonical Mary Magdalene.[10]

1.2 *Mary Magdalene, New Coptic Manuscripts, and Women's Studies Perspectives*

A new viewpoint to the personage of Mary Magdalene was opened by the discoveries of the two new Coptic manuscripts in the course of the eighteenth and the nineteenth century. In them, for the first time, the ancient writings *Pistis Sophia*, the *Gospel of Mary*, and the *Sophia of Jesus Christ* were brought to light. All three works were revelation dialogues which showed their readers how some second and third century Christians viewed the risen Lord, his disciples, and his female followers, including Mary Magdalene. Earlier the conception of an extra-canonical Mary Magdalene within Christian tradition was based on three rather brief references of the heresiologists to her connections with some

---

[6] Classic examples of this are Kazantzakis' book *The Last Temptation of Christ* and Scorsese's film based on it as well as Webber's and Rice's rock opera *Jesus Christ Superstar*, but see also Grassi & Grassi (1986, 58-67) who claim to make their popular presentation of Mary Magdalene "in accord with the information modern biblical study has given" (1986, vi).

[7] Kümmel (1976, 213) refers to Ethelbert Stauffer who in his popular book *Jesus war ganz anders* (1967) insists that Mary Magdalene was a charming lady whom Jesus had received into his company in order to protect her from sinking deep again into her earlier wanton behavior.

[8] Haskins 1993, 16.58-97.

[9] The term is used of Mary Magdalene who brings the message of resurrection to the twelve. It was most likely coined by Hippolytus (see Bauer 1967 [1909], 263; Haskins 1993, 65); for its use in later sermons and religious illustrations, see Haskins 1993, 220-222; Schüssler Fiorenza 1979, 209.

[10] Haskins 1993, 392.

Gnostic groups[11] and on medieval legends.[12] The new texts revealed the existence of another Mary Magdalene tradition.

Among the first to discover a new Mary Magdalene was Carl
Schmidt who in his studies of *Pistis Sophia*[13] and the *Gospel of
Mary*[14] paid attention to Mary Magdalene who assumes a leading
role among the disciples as a receiver, an interpreter and a transmitter of the teachings of the Risen Jesus. Schmidt also noticed
that in both of these writings a conspicious tension prevails between Mary Magdalene and the male disciples of Jesus. Peter in
particular experiences her as a rival who threatens his and the
other disciples' authority. Following Harnack, Schmidt suggested
that the tension possibly reflects a discussion about the role of
women in Christian communities. Other sholars who studied these
same writings made similar observations but on the whole this
perspective did not attract great attention.[15] Still, the main interest
in Mary Magdalene continued to concentrate on the canonical texts
and on the old question of the relationship of Mary Magdalene to
the four anointers of the New Testament.[16]

In the 1970's the situation changed decisively. That was caused
by two factors. First, the publication of the Nag Hammadi Library,
begun in the late 50s and completed in the form of a facsimile

---

[11] According to Origen, Celsus knew of a tradition which considered
Mary Magdalene (Μαριάμμη) as an originator of a Gnostic group
(*Contra Cels.* 5,62); Hippolytus connects Mary Magdalene (Μαριάμμη)
with the Naassenes, who claim to derive their teachings from James
through her (*Ref.* 5.7,1; 10.9,3); Epiphanius refers to the *Great Questions
of Mary* (*Pan.* 26.8,2-3), which he attributes to the Gnostics or to the
Borborites, according to which the Risen (?) Jesus once took Mary
Magdalene aside on the mountain and revealed her a special secret (for
the analysis of the text, see the chapter below "Mary Magdalene in the
Great Questions of Mary").

[12] For medieval legendary material, see Malvern 1975, 71-99; Haskins 1993, 98-228.

[13] Schmidt 1892, 452-455.

[14] Schmidt 1896, 839-846.

[15] E.g. Harnack 1891, 16-17; Zscharnack 1902, 160-161; Bauer 1967
[1909], 438.448-449. With regard to Mary Magdalene, Bauer's inferences
are indeed somewhat confused; on the one hand, he regards the Mary of
the *Gospel of Mary* as the mother of Jesus (1967 [1909], 448), on the
other hand, she is seen as Mary Magdalene who has received a special
revelation from the Savior (1967 [1909], 438).

[16] See e.g. Holzmeister 1922, 402-422.556-584; Sickenberger 1925,
63-74; Burkitt 1930-31, 157-159.

edition during the 70s,[17] offered four new sources in which Mary
Magdalene is depicted in a way different from that of the canonical gospels but somewhat similar to that of the *Gospel of Mary*
and *Pistis Sophia*. The *Gospel of Thomas*, the *Dialogue of the
Savior*, the *First Apocalypse of James*, and the *Gospel of Philip* all
give Mary Magdalene a significant role.[18] Second, not only was
the number of sources multiplied, but also a new and third perspective to Mary Magdalene texts was introduced. During the last
two decades religious texts dealing with women have been studied
more than ever before under the presupposition that they provide
information about attitudes towards women prevailing in the religious circles where the texts originated and were read, even the
socio-historical circumstances under which the female audience of
the texts lived.

A representative example of the new women's studies perspectives is Elisabeth Schüssler Fiorenza's book *In Memory of Her*.[19]
Although published not more than twelve years ago, it has already
become a classic in showing how a feminist perspective can be
utilized to enrich the historical-critical study of Christian origins.[20]
Schüssler Fiorenza's starting-point is the thesis that early Christian
women have had a more important role in shaping the history of
early Christianity than the first impression of the extant sources
enables us to see. Most sources available to us are so patriarchal
and androcentric that the actual contributions of women have been

---

[17] The Nag Hammadi Library was discovered in Upper Egypt near
the modern Nag Hammadi in 1945. It consists of 13 codices which
contain more than 50 tractates. Most of the tractates are Gnostic, some
non-Gnostic but obviously capable of being submitted to a Gnosticizing
interpretation. For a concise general introduction to the library and the
contents of its writings, see J.M. Robinson 1988.

[18] Earlier in 1930, the discovery of a Manichaean library originating
in Medinet Madi in Egypt (see Schmidt & Polotsky 1933, 6-10) already
increased the number of the extra-canonical texts where Mary Magdalene
appeared. For Mary Magdalene in Manichaean texts, see the *Psalms of
Heracleides* in the *Manichaean Psalm-book* (Allberry 1938, 187.192.
194).

[19] Schüssler Fiorenza 1983. The book contains several themes and
aspects which Schüssler Fiorenza has dealt with in earlier articles; for
references, see pp. XXV n. 15; 36 n. 2; 65 n. 24.

[20] Other good examples of the new perspective are Schüssler Fiorenza 1980, 60-90; Schottroff 1980, 91-133; see also the studies in
Moxnes 1989, 1-163.

silenced or hidden behind the gender rhetoric.[21] The task of a feminist inquiry is to exercise a hermeneutics of suspicion, i.e., to go beyond the patriarchal control of the texts and to find the evidence which either directly or obliquely provides affirmation of women.

Thus the marginalization of women is not to be understood as an authentic presentation of historical reality but it is rather an ideological construction reflecting early Christian patriarchalism which defeated more "egalitarian" tendencies. With this understanding in mind, Schüssler Fiorenza maintains that the few early Christian texts which show that the early Christian movement was inclusive of women's active and equal participation in its life, even in leadership, do not speak about rare exceptions to the rule but rather hint at a much wider female activity. Based on these observations, she delineates a new reconstruction of Christian origins where a special emphasis is laid on women's contributions, on the one hand, and on their suppression by patriarchal views and structures, on the other. Although Schüssler Fiorenza herself does not focus very much on Mary Magdalene, the methodological framework she develops has greatly influenced further studies examining both the canonical and the extra-canonical — especially those which are traditionally styled Gnostic — Mary Magdalene texts.

The study of Mary Magdalene which claims to be the first to take full account of both *Pistis Sophia* and the *Gospel of Mary* as well as the texts of the Nag Hammadi Library is that of Marjorie Malvern.[22] In reality, the work, which deals with the transmission and transformation of the Magdalene myth from the New Testa-

---

[21] With regard to the topic of the present study, it is important to notice that Schüssler Fiorenza warns scholars about generalizing conclusions according to which patriarchal and androcentric attitudes can be found in certain kinds of texts ("orthodox") while others ("Gnostic") are free from them. She emphasizes (1983, 56; 66 n. 37) that all of the early Christian texts are basically products of a patriarchal culture and therefore all of them "must be tested *as to how much* they preserve and transmit the apostolic inclusivity and equality of early Christian beginnings and revelation."

[22] Malvern states in her preface (1975, XI): "I also examine, as does no scholar to date, the prominent place given the fictionalized Mary Magdalene in second-century Gnostic writings." In light of this statement, it is no wonder that she does not list Schmidt's works in her bibliography.

ment texts through medieval legends, art, and plays to a modern rock opera, *Jesus Christ Superstar*, confines itself mainly to the two writings, i.e., to the *Gospel of Mary* and *Pistis Sophia*, which were known already before the Nag Hammadi find.[23] The two Nag Hammadi texts mentioned by her, the *Gospel of Thomas* and the *Gospel of Philip*, receive hardly any treatment.[24] Other Nag Hammadi writings and related documents which refer to Mary Magdalene are not discussed at all. Bearing in mind that no critical edition or English translation of the *Dialogue of the Savior* existed in the early seventies, it is understandable that Malvern does not pay attention to that writing. There is no excuse, however, for not mentioning the *First Apocalypse of James*, the *Sophia of Jesus Christ*, the *Great Questions of Mary*, and the *Manichaean Psalmbook*. All of these writings could have been available to Malvern.

Malvern's conclusions concerning Mary Magdalene's position are rather farfetched and do not find support in the texts. She insists that both in the *Gospel of Mary* and in *Pistis Sophia* Mary Magdalene is pictured as the feminine counterpart for Christ, the man-god. In the *Gospel of Mary* it is achieved, Malvern argues, by attributing to her the role of "the 'prophetess' proclaiming to the disciples revelations secretly given her by the 'true prophet'," i.e., Christ.[25] Malvern derives the notion of Mary Magdalene being Jesus' companion and counterpart from the *Gospel of Philip* and the idea of the prophetess and the true prophet from the *Pseudo-Clementine Homilies* (3,17-25)[26] and uses them as interpretative keys to the *Gospel of Mary* without giving any reason for her course of action. Especially the analogy between Mary Magdalene and the prophetess in the *Pseudo-Clementine Homilies* appears

---

[23] Malvern 1975, 30-56.

[24] Malvern (1975, 30) derives the notion of Mary Magdalene as being Jesus's companion from the *Gospel of Philip* and utilizes it as an interpretative key to the *Gospel of Mary* but does not clarify what it means in the context of the *Gospel of Philip* itself. The *Gospel of Thomas* (especially logion 114) is mentioned by Malvern only to illustrate the ambivalence toward women expressed in Early Christian texts (37-38).

[25] Malvern 1975, 40.

[26] Malvern (1975, 40) actually thinks her source is an apocryphon called "The True Prophet." No such writing exists. The text she refers to is a section of the *Pseudo-Clementine Homilies*. Its name owes its origin to the translator of the text in Schneemelcher 1989, 479 (for the English translation, see Schneemelcher & Wilson 1992, 531).

strange, because in the *Pseudo-Clementine Homilies* the prophetess
is a negative, earthly counterpart for the male and heavenly true
prophet.

In *Pistis Sophia*, according to Malvern, Mary Magdalene ab-
sorbs the feminine attributes of the (Pistis) Sophia, goddess of
wisdom, and is thus presented as the female divine counterpart of
Christ.[27] Again, Malvern's claim remains unfounded. Regardless
of what one thinks of Malvern's characterization of Pistis Sophia
as a goddess of wisdom, which in itself is a problem,[28] it is clear
that there is nothing in the writing which justifies the kind of
identification which Malvern sees between Pistis Sophia and Mary
Magdalene.

The next to draw scholarly attention to the Gnostic Mary
Magdalene was Elaine Pagels. Although her treatment of Mary
Magdalene consists of only a few pages in her popular but seminal
book, *The Gnostic Gospels*,[29] it has had a great impact on later
studies on this topic. Pagels' basic thesis is simple but challenging:
the Gnostic texts which give Mary Magdalene a dominant role
among the followers of Jesus and display the competition between
her and the male disciples, especially Peter, are used as a weapon
of polemics. In her view, these Gnostic writings "use the figure of
Mary Magdalene to suggest that women's activity challenged the
leaders of the orthodox community, who regarded Peter as their
spokesman."[30] They serve to speak on behalf of those Gnostic
women who despite the "orthodox"[31] opposition sought to gain

---

[27] Malvern 1975, 55.

[28] Malvern's interpretation of Pistis Sophia is a result of assimilating
freely features of various female figures who do not seem to have any
direct connection to each other, such as Helen, the Sophia of the *Sophia
of Jesus Christ*, the Mother Goddess of the Eleusinian mysteries and the
Sophia of Jewish Wisdom.

[29] Pagels 1981, 76-81.

[30] Pagels 1981, 77.

[31] Being aware of the problematic nature of this term, I have decided
to use it for want of anything better. For the sake of variety, the terms
"ecclesiastical" and "mainstream" Christianity are employed too. The
terms refer to those second and third century Christians whose doctrinal
and pragmatic decisions lead to the formation of the Catholic Church of
the Constantinian era. Obviously, the border-line between orthodox and
non-orthodox, even between orthodox and Gnostic Christians vacillates.

positions of authority in Christian communities.[32] According to Pagels, this aspiration is found especially in the *Gospel of Philip*, the *Dialogue of the Savior*, the *Gospel of Mary*, and *Pistis Sophia*.

For Pagels, the emerging egalitarian pattern reflected in these writings is not relativized by the fact that in certain Gnostic Mary Magdalene texts the feminine is undeniably spoken of with contempt (*Dialogue of the Savior*) or the masculine is used to symbolize what is divine and the feminine what is merely human (*Gospel of Thomas*, *Gospel of Mary*). In the case of the former, the target is not woman, but the power of sexuality, in the case of the latter, the authors of the texts simply employ language patterns familiar in their environment. Although not showing enough regard to the complexity of the way the sources picture Mary Magdalene, Pagels' thesis opened a new perspective worth exploring into the figure of Mary Magdalene in the second and third century Gnostic texts.

All the extant extra-canonical and non-patristic writings containing Mary Magdalene traditions — with the exception of the *First Apocalypse of James* — are for the first time introduced by François Bovon in an article written in 1984. In his survey of those texts which he calls Gnostic, Bovon includes the *Gospel of Thomas*, the *Gospel of Mary*, the *Sophia of Jesus Christ*, *Pistis Sophia*, the *Dialogue of the Savior*, the *Gospel of Philip*, the *Great Questions of Mary*, the *Manichaean Psalm-book*. In addition, he presents the *Acts of Philip*, which in itself is not a Gnostic writing, but which, in his view, serves as an indication of the survival of Gnostic Mary Magdalene traditions.[33] Besides surveying all of the early Christian, non-patristic Mary Magdalene passages, Bovon also introduces some general hypotheses which seek to explain the origin and popularity of Mary Magdalene traditions among what

---

[32] A similar idea was put forward already by Zscharnack (1902, 161; Zscharnack, to be sure, states somewhat ambiguously that Peter in *Pistis Sophia* represents on the one hand the ecclesiastical Christians' view of women, on the other hand he is one of the twelve Gnostic disciples) and later by Wilson (1968, 102-103) but only Pagels' popular book brought this thesis to the awareness of a wider audience. Cf. also Krause 1981, 57.

[33] Bovon 1984, 50-62, esp. 53-58. In addition, Bovon covers in his article the evidence of the canonical gospels, *Epistula Apostolorum*, the *Gospel of Peter*, and the *Secret Gospel of Mark* (50-53).

he calls heterodox marginal Christian groups in the second and third centuries.[34]

First, those Mary Magdalene passages which emphasize her status as a companion of Jesus seem to reflect, according to Bovon, the influence of pagan mythological accounts which speak of divine dyads. Jesus and Mary Magdalene are thus a Christian adaptation of the mythical dyads in the same way as Simon Magus and Helen. Second, novels from late antiquity have also had an impact on Mary Magdalene traditions. Like the apocryphal acts, those Mary Magdalene passages which present her as Jesus' companion reveal romantic traits most easily traceable to the love stories of the Hellenistic period. Third, the importance of Mary Magdalene in the writings of second century Christian groups serves to legitimate the claims of women to have active roles in these communities. Correspondingly, the jealousy which the male apostles in many writings show towards Mary Magdalene because of her privileged role express the resistance of men to women's aspirations either in these particular communities or among ecclesiastical Christians.[35]

According to Bovon, all these hypotheses help us understand the development and the use of Mary Magdalene traditions in the second and third centuries. Yet he thinks that they do not adequately explain the great interest which the authors of so many second and third century writings took in her. The ultimate reason for choosing Mary Magdalene to be the companion of Jesus and the ideal believer in many second and third century writings is, for Bovon, her historical role as a witness to an appearance of the Risen Jesus, clearly reflected in the Gospel of John but omitted by other early Christian traditions such as 1 Cor 15,5-8. Without this experience she could hardly have enjoyed such popularity as a spiritual authority.[36]

Since Pagels' book supplied an interesting thesis for the use of Mary Magdelene passages and Bovon's article contained a good inventory of almost all the extant extra-canonical, non-patristic Mary Magdalene passages and some tentative reflections on their

---

[34] Bovon 1984, 56-57.

[35] As Bovon (1984, 56) himself acknowledges, this hypothesis owes its origin to Harnack (1891, 17) and Schmidt (1892, 455).

[36] Bovon 1984, 51-52.57.

origin and use, they provided a new starting-point for the study of Mary Magdalene in Gnostic and other extra-canonical writings. At the end of the eighties and at the beginning of the nineties at least four scholars have accepted the challenge.[37] In all of them, an attempt is made to take account both of the new sources and of women's studies perspectives.

1.3 *Four Recent Interpretations of the Gnostic Mary Magdalene: Price, Schmid, Haskins, and Koivunen*

In his provocative article, Robert M. Price[38] asserts that the historical Mary Magdalene, after having experienced an appearance of the Risen Jesus and thus having received credentials for apostleship in the sense of Acts 1,2-3 and 1 Cor 9,1, "became the apostle of an egalitarian, celibate christianity."[39] For Price, some second and third century Gnostic traditions preserved the memory that the historical Mary Magdalene "claimed a privileged disciple relationship with Jesus both before and after the resurrection, that she received unique revelations after the resurrection, and that these revelations included female equality with males based on the transcendence of sexuality in a spiritual union with Christ."[40] The Gnostic texts which picture a conflict between Mary Magdalene and the male disciples reflect thus an actual, historical controversy about Mary Magdalene's apostolic status.

According to Price, the information in the Gnostic texts is obliquely confirmed by the canonical writings which "reacted to her radical gospel by minimizing and distorting her role in the ministry of Jesus and the early Christian community..."[41] While in the Gospel of John an independent and historically authentic tradition (John 20,1.11-18) presents her as the first and the only witness to the appearance of the Risen Jesus, the evangelist modi-

---

[37] In addition to those special studies of Mary Magdalene which treat more than one writing, three commentaries on the *Gospel of Mary* have appeared; see Pasquier 1983 (which was issued already one year before Bovon's article); King 1992; King 1995. Cf. also De Boer 1988.

[38] Price 1990, 54-76.

[39] Price 1990, 57.

[40] Price 1990, 76.

[41] Price 1990, 67-73; the quote is taken from page 57.

fies the exclusiveness of this appearance account by making it the first in a series. A similar procedure is adopted in the so-called longer ending of the Gospel of Mark (16,9-10). In the following stages, the significance of the tradition orally known to New Testament authors is gradually disparaged further by making Jesus' revelation to Mary Magdalene simply repeat what the angel had already said (Matt 28,9-10); then by implying that Mary Magdalene did not actually see the Risen One (Luke 24,1-12); later by indicating that not only did she not see Christ but also that she disobeyed the commandment of the angel in the tomb (Mark 16,1-8); after that by creating another entirely different empty tomb story in which Mary Magdalene had hardly any role at all (John 20,2-10); and finally by omitting her altogether as is the case in the traditional list of resurrection appearances in 1 Cor 15,3-8. In addition, the orthodox polemic against Mary Magdalene tried to undermine her apostolic credibility by emphasizing her demon-possession (Luke 8,2; Mark 16,9) and by identifying her with the sinner of Luke 7,36-38.

Price's reconstruction of the historical Mary Magdalene reflected directly in the second and third century Gnostic texts and indirectly by the canonical writings is intriguing but contains too many major methodological problems to be plausible. First, the way Price sees the canonical witnesses to the events of Easter morning as reactions to the historically authentic and orally transmitted Mary Magdalene tradition found in John 20,1.11-18 is problematic. To be sure, he states that the canonical texts he uses to reconstruct the anti-Mary Magdalene trajectory were not written in the order in which he considers them, but rather that the New Testament writers severally preserved various stages of the tradition which evolved in the order he reconstructs in his article.[42] Nevertheless, this reservation does not help much. It is not feasible that the tradition which must have reached its final stage already before or with the formulation of the list in 1 Cor 15 (if it is a conscious reaction against the Mary Magdalene tradition of John 20,1.11-18, as Price assumes) could have been accessible to the writer of the so-called longer ending of the Gospel of Mark in its second stage, to the author of the Gospel of Mark proper in its

---

[42] Price 1990, 66.

fifth stage, and to the Jerusalem Christians formulating the confession in 1 Cor 15 in its final stage.[43]

Second, it is difficult to maintain that all the canonical Easter stories and the list in 1 Cor 15 would have an anti-Mary Magdalene stance. If the abrupt ending of the Gospel of Mark can be seen as a critique of Mary Magdalene and the other women, the same conclusion cannot be drawn from the Gospel of Matthew. In that gospel Mary Magdalene and other women experience an appearance of the Risen Jesus and successfully fulfill the task of delivering his message to the eleven male disciples (28,10-11.16). Similarly, the fact that the appearance to Mary Magdalene is followed by other appearances, as in the Gospel of John and in the so-called longer ending of the Gospel of Mark, need not necessarily be explained as a disparagement of its significance. The other appearances may simply serve as a positive confirmation of Mary Magdalene's experience.

The omission of Jesus' appearance to Mary Magdalene in the Gospel of Luke (and perhaps in the traditional list of 1 Cor 15 as well) does not necessarily indicate a polemical tendency. Unless one makes a hypothetical assumption, as Price does, that the writer was aware of an oral tradition about the encounter between Mary Magdalene and the Risen Jesus and tries to suppress it, Luke can be seen as following his source, i.e., the Gospel of Mark. If so, it is worth noting that Luke's description of Mary Magdalene's and the other women's action is in a way less critical than Mark's. While in Mark they fail to announce the message of the young

---

[43] Instead of assuming that all the Easter materials of the New Testament derive from one uniform tradition which through editorial alterations of a polemical nature have engendered different versions, it is more feasible to think that at the beginning there were various "Easter experiences," which more or less independently sought to explain the Easter events. In his Finnish article, Uro (1995, 93-111) suggests that 1 Cor 15, Mark 16,1-8, Luke 13,34-35 (Q) each provide a reflection of an early interpretation of the Easter events. 1 Cor 15 can be traced through the so-called Hellenists back to Jerusalem where the appearances served to legitimize the leadership roles of spiritual authorities. The original Markan version (Mark 16,7 is redactional) has its starting point in an experience according to which Jesus "was taken away." It is possible that this tradition originated in the stories of women who had returned to Galilee. In the last redactional layer of Q, Jesus' departure is interpreted in light of a Jewish myth in which it is told how Wisdom could not find a dwelling among people and therefore returned to angels (cf. *1 Enoch* 42).

man, in Luke they do bring the news of the resurrection to the
male disciples. It is the latter who are unable to grasp it. On the
other hand, Luke's report does contain features which suggest that
he wants to show that faith in the resurrection of Jesus is not
based on the word of women but on the proclamation of men,
especially that of the apostles. Unlike the Gospel of Mark, in Luke
the women are not commissioned to announce the message of the
resurrection and when in any case they tell about it their testimony
is regarded as λῆρος ("non-sensical talk"; Luke 24,11) until it is
corroborated by male witnesses (24,12.33-34.48). Yet there is no
indication that all this should be taken as a special polemic against
Mary Magdalene. Rather, it serves Luke's overall tendency to give
a lot of space in his work for women but to draw up strict boundaries for their activities both in the circle of Jesus and in the early
church.[44] According to Luke, leadership is a male prerogative,
whereas women are seen as servants and/or financial supporters,
as the programmatic statement of Luke 8,3 implies (cf. also Acts
9,36; 12,12; 16,15.40).

Third, the reconstruction of the Mary Magdalene Christianity
made by Price is not based on a uniform testimony of all the
Gnostic Mary Magdalene texts but it is a compilation of elements
derived from different sources. Not all of the writings are encratic,
not all of them portray Mary Magdalene as the privileged disciple,
and only in the *Gospel of Philip* can the idea of her spiritual
marriage with Jesus find support. Not a single Gnostic text seems
to contain all the elements which in Price's view characterize the
form of Christianity started by the historical Mary Magdalene. On
the whole, Price's reconstruction of early Mary Magdalene Christianity seems to be a product by which features documented in
later writings are arbitrarily combined together and projected to an
earlier time. Price's study illustrates well what a precarious task it
is to employ second and third century texts to reconstruct biographical data about a biblical person of the first century.

A different approach to Mary Magdalene in the Nag Hammadi
texts and other related documents is presented by Renate Schmid
in her master's thesis, written under the guidance of Prof. Joachim

---

[44] For modern treatments of Luke's view of women, see Schaberg
1992, 275-292; Seim 1995, 728-762.

Gnilka at the University of Munich.[45] Unlike Price, Schmid does not use any space in her work to discuss whether Mary Magdalene passages included in the writings she calls Gnostic reveal anything about the historical Mary Magdalene. Rather, her primary goal is to see what role the authors of the writings give to Mary Magdalene in their own textual world.[46]

Schmid examines closely only three of the relevant sources: the *Gospel of Mary*, the *Gospel of Philip*, and *Pistis Sophia*. Mary Magdalene passages of four other writings, the *Gospel of Thomas*, the *Sophia of Jesus Christ*, the *Dialogue of the Savior*, and the *First Apocalypse of James* are simply quoted and occasionally receive a brief comment.[47] Taking into account the scope of the study this is understandable. Yet Schmid defends her approach by claiming that these texts provide very little material and no independent perspective for the discussion of the role of Mary Magdalene. This is an understatement as will be shown in the present study. Schmid also lacks knowledge of Coptic.[48] This not only causes her technical difficulties[49] but places restrictions on her text analyses as well.[50]

Compared to other recent studies of the Gnostic Mary Magdalene, the strength of Schmid's work lies in the fact that she seeks to interpret the meaning of Mary Magdalene passages within the

---

[45] Schmid 1990. The thesis was accepted already in 1988 and it was published two years later.

[46] Schmid 1990, 2-3.

[47] The *Acts of Philip* is omitted as a non-Gnostic writing which represents a different genre; it is also possible, according to Schmid, that Mary, the sister of Philip, which the text speaks about is not to be identified with Mary Magdalene of the Gnostic texts (92 n. 2). The *Great Questions of Mary* is not mentioned by Schmid at all.

[48] Schmid 1990, 97 n. 5.

[49] While discussing the meaning of the Coptic word for "man, human being," Schmid (1990, 14-15) suggests that it is spelled ⲚⲢⲰⳘⲈ.

[50] E.g. in the explication of *Gos. Phil.* 59,6-11, Schmid (1990, 25-27) does not discuss the linguistic problems the interpretation of the text involves. In *1 Apoc. Jas.* 40,22-26, Schmid (1990, 81-82) is not capable of dealing with the questions the reconstruction of the lacuna presupposes. Nor is the meaning of the phrase ⲈⲠⲦⲎⲢϥ in the *Dial. Sav.* 139,13 treated in the way it deserves. Schmid (1990, 80) simply thinks that ⲠⲦⲎⲢϥ is identical with the pleroma, as it is in many Gnostic texts; yet in the context of the *Dialogue of the Savior* this interpretation is highly unlikely as the use of this word and the word ⲠⲗⲎⲢⲰⳘⲀ in the *Dialogue of the Savior* demonstrates (see p. 85 n. 41 below).

context of the entire writing. For example, the significance of
praise aimed at Mary Magdalene is not overemphasized if a similar commendation is directed to other disciples elsewhere in the
writing. However, Schmid does not consistently carry through with
her methodological principle. In her analyses of the *Gospel of
Philip* and *Pistis Sophia* she does not deliberate thoroughly enough
how the positive treatment of Mary Magdalene's role is related to
many positive aspects which one can find in the authors' presentations of the male disciples.[51] The extremely positive picture
Schmid draws of the Gnostic Mary Magdalene would have become more nuanced if the Mary Magdalene passages had been
compared more often to texts where the authors of the writings
speak about the male disciples of Jesus and where they use feminine gender language. This kind of comparison could also have
given Schmid a better starting-point to assess what the Mary
Magdalene passages tell about the concrete situation of women in
the second and third century Gnostic communities. Now she
concludes with only a general remark that the picture of the perfect and perceptive Mary Magdalene must have been utilized to
support the self-consciousness of Gnostic women and to justify
their claims for authority.[52]

In her massive study of the Mary Magdalene myth, Susan
Haskins dedicates one chapter to the Gnostic Mary Magdalene.[53]
In her presentation, three aspects stand out. First, in agreement

---

[51] Although Schmid (1990, 38) cites Gaffron (1969, 215) who states
that despite the fact that in *Gos. Phil.* 63,37-64,5 the role of the archons
becomes the lot of the disciples they "im PhEv durchaus positiv geschil-
dert werden," she does not face this problem. After having analyzed the
Mary Magdalene passages in the *Gospel of Philip*, Schmid simply concludes: "Es liegt also eine äußerst positive Darstellung und starke
Heraushebung der M.M. aus dem Kreis der Jünger vor." In her analysis
of *Pistis Sophia*, Schmid (1990, 58-61) recognizes that there are texts
which seem to indicate that the task of preaching and transmitting the
mysteries is entrusted to the male disciples, but she does not take the text
at face value but thinks that those texts somehow include Mary Magdalene as well. Another main problem with Schmid's handling of *Pistis
Sophia* is that the source-critical division between *Pistis Sophia I-III* and
Pistis Sophia IV which she seems to accept (Schmid 1990, 44) does not
in any way affect her actual treatment of the text. When she pictures the
role of Mary Magdalene in *Pistis Sophia*, she deals with the text as if it
were uniform.
[52] Schmid 1990, 89.
[53] Haskins 1993, 33-57.

with Pagels, she thinks that the positive statements of the Gnostic writings about Mary Magdalene, such as her special relationship to the Savior (*Gospel of Philip, Gospel of Mary*), her leading role within the group of the apostles (*Gospel of Mary, Dialogue of the Savior, Pistis Sophia*), and her ability to receive visions and to have greater comprehension than Peter (*Gospel of Mary, Pistis Sophia*), as well as the references to tension between Mary Magdalene and Peter, all reflect a historical situation where the question of women's participation in Christian communities was still a matter of controversy.[54] This must have taken place long before the end of the second century, since by then all egalitarian tendencies "had been discarded in favour of a return to the patriarchal system of Judaism which had preceded them."[55] Unlike Pagels, she in fact seems to place the conflict already in the first century. While orthodox sources are either entirely silent about the debate or allude to it only indirectly, e.g., by discrediting the women's report of their Easter experience (the Synoptics) or by omitting the women from the list of those to whom the Risen One appeared (Paul), the Gnostic writings, in the figure of Mary Magdalene, have preserved an authentic memory of the debate.[56]

Haskins' claims remain on the same general level as those by Pagels. A detailed analysis of the texts will demonstrate that they do not show enough regard for the complexity of the evidence. In addition, Haskins' use of the second century Gnostic writings as a source for reconstructing first century history as well as the employment of the Synoptics and 1 Cor 15 as an indirect testimony to an anti-woman attitude contain problems similar to those already pointed out in Price's case.

Second, like Malvern, Haskins seeks to argue that in *Pistis Sophia* Mary Magdalene as *alter ego* of Pistis Sophia is linked to a long and unbroken tradition of feminine deities whose Christian counterpart is Pistis Sophia.[57] Haskins does not produce, however,

---

[54] Haskins 1993, 37-42.

[55] Haskins 1993, 42.

[56] In fact, Haskins (1993, 55) seems even to suggest, like Price, that the second century Gnostic traditions of Mary Magdalene could "reflect a surviving historical tradition from Christ's life excluded from the orthododox accounts of his ministry."

[57] Haskins 1993, 44-45.48.

any compelling arguments which would justify the identification
of Mary Magdalene with Pistis Sophia.

Third, Haskins observes that despite the positive view of Mary
Magdalene certain Gnostic writings have they also include views
which devalue women. Feminine gender language is employed to
symbolize that which is negative, like procreation, sexuality, and
a non-pneumatic life-style (*Dialogue of the Savior, Gospel of
Thomas*).[58] This was already recognized by Pagels, although she
explained it as a culturally bound phenomenon which did not
principally question the pro-female attitude of the Gnostics. Haskins interprets this somewhat differently. In her view, not even the
Gnostics can, in the final analysis, be described as pro-female,
because gender bias prevailed among them too. Pagels' and Haskins' observations are important, and their significance to the
characterization and use of Mary Magdalene in various writings
will be more thoroughly explored below.

The most recent study of the Gnostic Mary Magdalene texts is
the dissertation by Hannele Koivunen.[59] Actually, the work focuses
on the *Gospel of Mary*, but also other Mary Magdalene writings
are introduced, even though they are utilized only as secondary
background material and are not thoroughly analyzed.[60] Koivunen's methodological starting-point is semiotic. Concretely this
means that the *Gospel of Mary* is subjected to reading of the text[61]
on three different levels of signification: firstness, secondness, and
thirdness.[62] On the level of firstness, the sign system of the text is
examined as independent of anything else, i.e., the text is read as
it presents itself to a reader who tries to approach the text without
being bound to any cultural sign system or, since this is not entirely possible in practice, at least so that the reader is conscious "of

[58] Haskins 1993, 54.

[59] Koivunen 1994.

[60] In fact, the title of the work, *The Woman Who Understood Completely*, is a quotation taken from the *Dialogue of the Savior* (139,11-13).

[61] Strangely, the text which is being read is not the extant Greek
manuscripts (as a matter of fact, Koivunen is not even aware of P. Oxy.
3525) and the Coptic version of BG 8502, but the English translation(!)
made by MacRae & Wilson in J.M. Robinson 1988, 524-527. Koivunen
knows neither Greek nor Coptic.

[62] Koivunen 1994, 51-66.189-267. Koivunen's methodological framework is primarily based on C.S. Peirce's theory of the categories of
existence.

his ties to his own culture with its paradigm, the stock of signifi-
cations."[63]

On the level of secondness, the immediate impressions gained
through the first level reading of the text "are compared with the
interpreter's own sign systems."[64] Encounter between the sign systems of the text and those of the interpreter means that the interpreter chooses the relevant — both familiar and foreign — elements of the text and brings them into contact with the sign systems of his/her own culture gained through those Christian documents and interpretations which represent orthodox Christianity. In
this process of accepting, rejecting, and assimilating, the signifi-
cations of the interpreter's own culture are recoded and redefined.
In practice, in the second level reading of the text a comparison
between the characterization of Mary Magdalene in the *Gospel of
Mary* and in orthodox Christian documents — both in the canon
and in later patristic traditions — is undertaken. On the level of
thirdness, the *Gospel of Mary* is approached not only through its
own sign systems or those of the interpreter's own culture but
through the mythic interpretants, which are found in other Gnostic
sources.

What are the results of Koivunen's semiotic reading of the
Gospel of Mary? On the level of firstness the yield of reading is
scanty: "...much of the text is incomprehensible to a person who
has grown up in a Western Christian culture" but it still proves to
be "some kind of sacral text," since it contains the figures of the
Savior, Mary Magdalene, and Peter.[65]

On the second level of reading, when the sign systems of the
Gospel of Mary and those of the interpreter's own "orthodox"
Christian culture are compared, Koivunen becomes more concrete,
but at the same time her conclusions prove to be problematic and
confusing. Despite her ostensibly ahistoric approach, her claims
are surprisingly history-oriented. Based on her comparison between the *Gospel of Mary* and the Easter accounts of the canonical
gospels, Koivunen infers that behind the texts one can find two
early, mutually rivalling and contradictory conceptions of Christianity. One was represented by (the historical?) Peter and was

---

[63] Koivunen 1994, 57.
[64] Koivunen 1994, 193.
[65] Koivunen 1994, 193.

20 CHAPTER ONE

characterized by law and administration.[66] Its message was simple and concrete, since it was hearer-oriented and directed at great masses.[67] The other one was engendered by (the historical?) Mary Magdalene, "the most important apostle," and it emphasized the inner and pneumatic. It was egalitarian, speaker-oriented and belonged to a select and initiated circle.[68] In due course the Petrine version of Christianity got the upper hand of the Gnostic type of Christianity, by distorting the portrait of Mary Magdalene as "the woman who understood completely" and making her a whore. The significance of the second level reading of the *Gospel of Mary* is to see that the Christian icon of Mary Magdalene, which, in Koivunen's view, has been reduced to the figure of a whore, can and must be reinterpreted in light of the *Gospel of Mary*. On the level of thirdness, Koivunen finds confirmation for her thesis. Other Gnostic writings dealing with Mary Magdalene reflect the same early schism.

In her historical conclusions, Koivunen reaches an inference similar to that of Price. Unlike him, she does not even try to argue why a major first century ecclesiastical conflict has its only explicit witnesses in second and third century documents, whereas no tangible traces of it can be found in sources of the first century.[69] The information of the second and third century writings is simply projected back to the first century.[70]

---

[66] Koivunen 1994, 215-216.

[67] Koivunen 1994, 273.

[68] Koivunen 1994, 216.273.

[69] Without any arguments, Koivunen (1994, 210) simply states that the Gospel of Mary "reveals the profound contradiction between Mary Magdalene and Peter, which is supported by many other Gnostic texts. It *seems*, according to the Gospel of Mary, that the traditions represented by Mary Magdalene and Peter separated from each other very early..., which means before the canonical texts were written..." (italics mine).

[70] It is not only the main thesis which is problematic in Koivunen's book. It also contains a great number of contradictions (e.g. according to p. 28 *Pistis Sophia* was found by the Scottish explorer James Bruce in 1769 in Luxor, according to p. 173, it was acquired for the British Museum in 1785 from Dr. Askew who had bought in London; sometimes the Coptic *Gospel of Mary* is part of the Nag Hammadi Library [p. 31], sometimes it belongs to BG 8502 [p. 48]), rudimentary mistakes (Koivunen maintains e.g. that according to Valentinus the pleroma consists of eight pairs of aeons [p. 73], that *Ptolemy's Letter to Flora* was written in the fourth century [p. 27], and that Epiphanius' report of Jesus' and Mary Magdalene's encounter on a mountain in *Pan.* 26 is

The presentation of the four recent studies of the Gnostic Mary Magdalene texts demonstrates the attractiveness and importance of the topic. Nevertheless, none of them has paid sufficient attention to the complexity of the problems involved with these texts and the historical context they reflect. The process which Schmidt's observations set in motion and which Pagels' insights carried somewhat further is far from being completed.

2. *Definition of the Task and Approach*

2.1 *Task*

The purpose of the present study is to delineate the portrait and the significance of Mary Magdalene in those second and third century Christian texts which are either Gnostic or at least contain central theological, soteriological, anthropological, and cosmological emphases that have close parallels in Gnostic thought. It is beyond the scope of this study to enter into an extensive discussion about the precise definition of Gnosticism. A short presentation of central elements of Gnostic thought succinctly summarized by Pearson may suffice:[71]

> ... first, ... adherents of Gnosticism regard *gnosis* (rather than faith, observance of law, etc.) as requisite to salvation. The saving "knowledge" involves a revelation as to the true nature both of the self and of God; indeed, for the Gnostic, self-knowledge *is* knowledge of God. Gnosticism also has, second, a characteristic *theology* according to

---

taken from the *Little Questions of Mary* and not from the *Great Questions of Mary* [p. 178]), untenable claims (e.g. Koivunen asserts that besides Q there existed an independent Gnostic Q deriving from 50 C.E. [pp. 209.271.287] and, here misquoting Bianchi, that no obvious evidence of connections between the Demiurge and the Jewish Yahweh can be established [p. 75]), and misrepresentations of scholarly views (e.g. Koivunen says [p. 169] that, in Parrott's view, *Eugnostos* and the *Sophia of Jesus Christ* have been influenced by Sethian Ophites and *Eugnostos* also by Valentinianism, while Parrott says exactly the opposite; Koivunen claims also [p. 174] that Tuckett has speculated with the idea of a Gnostic Q, even if no such idea appears in his book). Examples such as these could be easily multiplied.

[71] Pearson 1990, 7-8. In his summary Pearson relies chiefly on the works of Kurt Rudolph and Hans Jonas.

which there is a transcendent supreme God beyond the god or powers
responsible for the world in which we live. Third, a negative, radically dualist stance vis-à-vis the cosmos involves a *cosmology*, according
to which the cosmos itself, having been created by an inferior and
ignorant power, is a dark prison in which human souls are held
captive. Interwoven with its theology and its cosmology is, fourth, an
anthropology, according to which the essential human being is constituted by his/her inner self, a divine spark that originated in the transcendent divine world and, by means of gnosis, can be released from
the cosmic prison and can return to its heavenly origin. The human
body, on the other hand, is part of the cosmic prison from which the
essential "man" must be redeemed. The notion of release from the
cosmic prison entails, fifth, an *eschatology*, which applies not only to
the salvation of the individual but to the salvation of all the elect, and
according to which the material cosmos itself will come to its fated
end.[72]

To be sure, Pearson's characterization of Gnosticism is a kind
of idealized version. Hardly any of the known Gnostic writings
contain all the elements which Pearson presents and in some of
them certain elements are strongly modified or even opposed.
Therefore, it is difficult to draw a clear line between Gnostic and
non-Gnostic writings. There is a significant "grey area" between
the two. Yet Pearson's definition is a useful starting-point in
attempting to categorize religious writings, although sometimes it
seems to be a matter of emphasis whether a writing is called
Gnostic with some non-Gnostic elements or non-Gnostic with
some Gnostic motifs. It is, however, important for the present
consideration that practically all important second and third century writings where Mary Magdalene appears have clear connections
with central elements in Gnostic thought pointed out by Pearson.[73]

---

[72] In addition to these five doctrinal points, Pearson also points out
that Gnosticism had social, ritual, ethical, experiential, and mythopoetical
dimensions. This is of course true, but apart from the Gnostics' strong
inclination to mythopoesis, these did not include common Gnostic features especially typical of that movement alone. For example, the pre-
dominantly ascetic and acosmic ethics of Gnosticism was not foreign to
ecclesiastical Christians either.

[73] The religious character of these writings and their relationship to
Gnostic thought are discussed in detail in the introductions to the analyses of Mary Magdalene texts in these particular writings.

In all of the Gnostic writings which contain and use Mary Magdalene traditions she is presented as a dominant figure among the followers of Jesus. It is conspicuous that in many of these sources her visible, positive role leads to some kind of controversy with the male disciples of Jesus. The primary interest of this study is to see what role Mary Magdalene assumes in the textual and symbolic world of a particular writing and what her characterization reveals about the author's views on women, especially about their possibilities to gain a position of authority. In addition, an attempt will be made to ask what Mary Magdalene passages can tell, if anything, about the attitudes towards women, the concrete circumstances of their lives, and leadership roles within the circles where the texts were read. Clearly, the texts displaying a conflict between Mary Magdalene and the male disciples need special attention when it is asked whether and what the texts can tell about the attitudes of the authors and the concrete situation of the audiences.

2.2 *Sources*

The text material analyzed in the present study offers no sources not at least mentioned in earlier studies. Out of the Nag Hammadi writings, the *Gospel of Thomas*, the *Sophia of Jesus Christ* (which appears also in the Berlin Codex), the *Dialogue of the Savior*, the *First Apocalypse of James*, and the *Gospel of Philip* are included. Other important sources are the *Gospel of Mary*, *Pistis Sophia*, the *Great Questions of Mary*, the *Manichaean Psalm-book*, and the *Acts of Philip*. Apart from the *Acts of Philip*, all of these writings are either Gnostic or contain central elements of Gnostic thought. The *Acts of Philip*, which in itself is not a Gnostic work, is treated since it utilizes and expands Mary Magdalene traditions employed and developed in Gnostic sources. Yet no special chapter is devoted to this writing, but its most important Mary Magdalene passages are taken up in the chapter dealing with the *Gospel of Thomas*, because the two documents contain similar motifs.

Common to all these Gnostic sources is the fact that they scarcely build on canonical Mary Magdalene traditions. The narrative elements of the canonical Easter accounts are used only in the *Manichaean Psalm-book* but even there the Johannine account is expanded and embellished by many such features which bring it into close contact with other sources listed above.[74] So that possible connections and differences between various Mary Magdalene traditions can be more easily assessed, the writings will be treated in a chronological order, and the text analyses will be preceded by a section where relevant introductory issues, including dating and provenance, are discussed.

There are three other writings which have been included when the second and third century extra-canonical, non-patristic portrait of Mary Magdalene is discussed: the so-called *Secret Gospel of Mark*, *Epistula Apostolorum*, and the *Gospel of Peter*.[75] Should they be considered in the present study as well? Clearly, in the case of the *Secret Gospel of Mark* no treatment of the text is necessary. The extant parts of the writing[76] do not display Gnostic traits and, more importantly, there is no indication that the unnamed woman[77] of the text whom some scholars have identified with Mary Magdalene[78] is she.[79] Nor are the other two writings

---

[74] See below pp. 207-208.

[75] Bovon (1984, 52-53) includes all of these writings in his presentation of the "heretical" Mary Magdalene (cf. also Collins 1992, 580). To be sure, *Epistula Apostolorum* is not regarded by Bovon as a heretical writing but, in Bovon's view, it does obliquely give information about the heretical picture of Mary Magdalene by polemicizing against it.

[76] The fragments of the writing are quoted in a letter which Clement of Alexandria is supposed to have sent to a Theodoros. The only, incomplete handwritten copy of the letter has been preserved on two and a half empty pages at the back of a seventeenth century printed edition of Ignatius' epistles found in the Greek Orthodox monastery of Mar Saba (for this, see M. Smith 1973). There is no agreement among scholars about the authenticity of this letter. For the discussion, see Merkel 1987, 89-92; Meyer 1990, 94-99. If the genuiness of the letter is granted, it is moreover unclear what the relationship of the fragments is to the canonical Gospel of Mark and how the fragments are to be dated; for various suggestions, see Merkel 1987, 89-92; Meyer 1990, 94-99; Sellew 1991, 242-257.

[77] The unnamed woman appears twice in the *Secret Gospel of Mark* (II,23; III,15; for the text, see M. Smith 1973, 446-453.). In the latter instance she is introduced as ἡ ἀδελφὴ τοῦ νεανίσκου ὃν ἠγάπα αὐτὸν ὁ ᾿Ιησοῦς.

[78] Bovon 1984, 52; Collins 1992, 580.

[79] The only fact in the description of the unnamed woman which coincides with what we know about Mary Magdalene in other early Christian sources is her linkage with Salome and the mother of Jesus (Mark 15,40; 16,1; John 19,25; *Gos. Phil.* 59,6-11; *1 Apoc. Jas.* 40,25; *PS I-III*; *Man. Ps. II* 192,21-24). Nothing else is reminiscent of Mary Magdalene. The fact that the unnamed woman in the *Secret Gospel of*

Gnostic. In addition, the personage of Mary Magdalene does not seem to become a subject of special reflection in *Epistula Apostolorum* and the *Gospel of Peter* in the same way as in the sources listed above. Yet one has to ask whether these writings contain an attempt to disparage the significance of Mary Magdalene which could be interpreted as a direct or an oblique criticism against Gnostic portraits of her, and which thus could throw light on the use of Mary Magalene in early Christian controversies.

Epistula Apostolorum[80] is a non-Gnostic or perhaps even anti-Gnostic revelation dialogue[81] which refers to Mary Magdalene as one of the women to whom the Risen Jesus appeared and who announced the message of the resurrection to the male disciples (9-11). The role of Mary Magdalene is viewed in the same way as in the Gospel of Matthew. *Epistula Apostolorum* only emphasizes the disbelief of the male disciples. This aspect recalls the Lucan Easter account (24,11; cf. also Mark 16,11).[82] There is, however, nothing in the text which could be seen as a polemical attack against the visible, positive role given to Mary Magdalene in many Gnostic texts.[83] The disbelief of the disciples is not employed to

---

Mark lives in Bethany and is a sister of a man whom Jesus loved in a special way and whom he raised from the dead seems to suggest that the most natural identification of the unnamed woman is either Martha or her sister Mary (cf. John 11). Martha is also brought together with Salome and the mother of Jesus in *PS I-III* (cf. also *1 Apoc. Jas.* 40,25-26; *Man. Ps. II* 192,21-24).

[80] The passages where Mary Magdalene appears are preserved both in an Ethiopic and a Coptic version (for the Ethiopic version, see Guerrier & Grebaut 1913; for the Coptic version, see Schmidt 1919). For the English translations, see Schneemelcher & Wilson 1991, 249-284, esp. 254-255.

[81] As a reason for writing the text, the author presents the wish that no one should follow Simon and Cerinthus (1; 7).

[82] Cf. also Matt 28,17, however.

[83] Bovon (1984, 53) has suggested that the Coptic version, which presents Martha as the first messenger to the male disciples instead of Mary Magdalene, has preserved the original reading. Thus the text deprives Mary Magdalene of the task given to her in the Easter accounts of the canonical Gospels and serves, according to Bovon, anti-Gnostic polemic. Bovon's thesis contains several problems. The very idea that the replacement of Mary Magdalene by Martha must be understood as a result of a conflict is in itself problematic. Many other reasons could be easily imagined. Besides, there is no unanimity about the textual relationship between the two versions. The priority of the Coptic version is in no way proven. In addition, even if Martha is granted a temporal

disparage her value as a messenger. Rather, it serves to underline the depth of doubt which prevailed among the disciples.

In the *Gospel of Peter*,[84] too, Mary Magdalene appears in the section which deals with the events of Easter morning. Together with other women, she comes to the grave of Jesus in order to lament his death and possibly to anoint his body (50-52). When the women come to the grave they find it empty, and a young man is sitting inside the grave and announces that Jesus has risen. As in the Gospel of Mark, the women flee in fear. With regard to the description of Mary Magdalene, the only essential difference between the Synoptic gospels, especially Mark, and the *Gospel of Peter* is that the latter introduces Mary Magdalene as μαθήτρια τοῦ κυρίου. How is this epithet to be understood? According to Bovon, μαθήτρια τοῦ κυρίου is to be seen as a honorific title which is conferred upon Mary Magdalene in recognition of her significant role among the most intimate followers of Jesus.[85] However, the usage of the word μαθήτρια in secular Greek and early Christian literature does not lend support to Bovon's claim. In those rare instances[86] where it appears, it does not seem to have any honorific connotation. It simply denotes a female pupil, as distinct from the male ones.[87] The same appears to be true with the epithet of Mary Magdalene in *Gos. Pet.* 50. It has hardly any

---

priority as a messenger to the male disciples in the Coptic version, the same task is entrusted to a Mary too. This Mary is not necessarily ⲘⲀⲢⲓⲀ ⲦⲀⲘⲀⲢⲐⲀ (II,2) but it can be ⲘⲀⲢⲓⲀ ⲦⲘⲀⲅⲆⲀⲖⲎⲚⲎ (II,2-3; III,6-7) as well. In that case, Martha's and Mary Magdalene's roles are identical.

[84] For the text, see Klostermann 1933.

[85] Bovon 1984, 53.

[86] For the use of the word in secular and early Christian Greek literature, see Rengstorf 1967, 460-461; Bauer & Aland & Aland 1988, 986. In addition to the occurrences in Greek Christian literature (Acts 9,36; *Acts of Paul* 2,9 [Hamburg Papyrus]), it appears also in Coptic writings (*2 Book of Jeu* 99,8; 105,23; *PS* 353,17).

[87] A good example is Acts 9,36-38 where both the feminine μαθήτρια (Acts 9,36) and the masculine μαθητής (Acts 9,38) are used to denote the followers of Jesus. To be sure, μαθήτρια has here a more technical meaning "female Christian," whereas μαθητής stands for a "male Christian" or a "Christian" in general. For Luke μαθητής (μαθήτρια) and Christian are clearly synonyms in Acts. This is seen most clearly in Acts 11,26. It is also worth noting that οἱ μαθηταί can be linked with a genitive attribute τοῦ κυρίου (9,1).

function other than to point out explicitly that there were also women among the disciples of Jesus.

If the title μαθήτρια is not taken as a special commendation of Mary Magdalene, could it then be seen as a reflection of a tendency to place the female followers of Jesus in their own category,[88] clearly inferior to that of the male followers?[89] And if so, is it done for polemical purposes? The text, at least in its extant form, does not give an unambiguous answer to this question. The fact that the encounter between the young man and the women in the grave (*Gos. Pet.* 50) ends with the women's flight can hardly be taken as a proof of an attempt to discredit Mary Magdalene and other women. Like the parallel text in Mark, it seems to underline

---

[88] It is at least obvious that the twelve (μαθηταί) are seen as a distinct group in the *Gospel of Peter* (59).

[89] Especially in later writings, the person of Mary Magdalene seems to be used to justify this kind of tendency. It gains its classic expression in the fourth century *Apostolic Church Order* 1.26,1-2 (for the Greek text, see Schermann 1914, 32) where the (frivolous?) smile of Mary Magdalene (if indeed the Mary of the text is Magdalene and not Mary of Bethany; it is most likely that the text derives from the period when Mary represents a "combination" of Magdalene and Mary of Bethany; see pp. 131-132 below) is presented by Martha as the reason why women should not be allowed to participate in the Eucharist. Mary corrects Martha's claim by pointing out that she did not smile but Jesus himself taught that it is unnecessary for women to take part in the Eucharist since τὸ ἀσθενὲς διὰ τοῦ ἰσχυροῦ σωθήσεται. In his polemic against the Collyridians, who seem to have admitted women to priestly tasks, Epiphanius (*Pan.* 79.7,1-4) criticizes this practice by showing that no biblical women, not even the women who followed Jesus from Galilee and assisted him with their own possessions (cf. Mark 15,40-41; Luke 8,2-3) assumed such a role. A more positive version of the same tendency is found in *Vita Beatae Mariae* 36,89-95 (for the Coptic text, see F. Robinson 1896, 28-37), where Mary Magdalene is appointed by Mary, the mother of Jesus, to be the leader of the female virgins among the followers of Jesus after her. They constitute clearly a group separate from the apostles; their task is defined in terms of preserving their sexual purity (28,23-25), whereas the apostles in addition to being virgins are given the assignment to preach the gospel (28,22). It is also worth noting that in *Vita Beatae Mariae* it is not Mary Magdalene (cf. John 20,11-18) but Mary, the mother of Jesus, who meets the Risen Jesus and receives the command to tell her brothers to go into Galilee in order that Jesus might appear to them (*Vita Beatae Mariae* 30,37-39; cf. Mark 16,7). In addition, she instructs the apostles how to preach the gospel! Clearly, the work reflects mariological emphases; in other words, Mary, the mother of Jesus, is given a very special role, whereas the other women, Mary Magdalene included, are removed further from the tasks connected with the role of the apostles.

general confusion which the crucifixion of Jesus has caused within
the circle of the disciples. Nor is the fact that in the *Gospel of
Peter* the women are not commanded by the young man to deliver
any special message to the male disciples (cf. Mark 16,7) scarcely
an indication of a conscious effort to decrease the significance of
Mary Magdalene among the followers of Jesus. Rather, the omission makes more understandable the sorrow and irresolution of the
twelve in *Gos. Pet.* 58,[90] unless it is simply due to the circumstances that the *Gospel of Peter* was dependent on a tradition
which did not contain the command of the young man at all
because that was added only later by Mark to serve his own
theological purposes evident already in 14,28.[91]

Together with the next episode where Peter, Andrew, and Levi
are said to have gone fishing (cf. John 21), *Gos. Pet.* 50-57, by
means of creating a contrast to what follows, anticipates the positive impact which the appearance(s) of Jesus most likely contained
in the missing end of the gospel is (are) supposed to engender
among the readers. Thus, the way Mary Magdalene and other
women are depicted in the text is more naturally explained by the
overall literary intentions of the author than by an attempt to
utilize the passage in a concrete controversy over the status of
Mary Magdalene in Christian communities.

2.3 Methodological Considerations

With regard to the examination of Mary Magdalene's role in the
textual worlds of the Gnostic writings dealing with her, there are
three aspects which have not received sufficient attention in previous studies or which have been overlooked altogether. Their
inadequate consideration has not only affected the way the portrait
of Mary Magdalene is drawn but also the conclusions scholars
have reached from the writings' attitudes towards women in general. It is exactly these three aspects which the present study at-

---

[90] If the text had contained the young man's explicit command
directed to the women, the reader could think that despite their fear at the
grave they could have tried to inform the twelve about their experience,
since *Gos. Pet.* 57 does not state that the women did not speak anything
to anybody (as it is said in Mark 16,8).

[91] So e.g. Koester 1990, 238-239.

tempts to bring to the center of its approach. In this way a nuanced and balanced view of the characterization of Mary Magdalene and the use of Mary Magdalene traditions in the second
and third century Gnostic writings will hopefully be achieved.

First, the fact that Mary Magdalene has a prominent position
in so many writings which display important Gnostic themes does
not provide justification to think that she has the same role in the
textual world of each work and that Mary Magdalene traditions are
in each case employed for a similar purpose. This is confirmed
already by a cursory reading of Mary Magdalene passages in
various writings. For instance, not all of them picture Mary Magdalene as a rival of the male disciples. Methodologically, this
means that the character and the use of Mary Magdalene traditions
utilized in each writing must be studied separately before any
general conclusions are drawn.

Second, the characterization and the statements of Mary Magdalene should not be examined in isolation. In all the texts Mary
Magdalene is pictured as one of Jesus' most intimate followers.
Therefore, everything that is said about her or she says herself
must be compared to the way other disciples, especially the males,
are viewed in texts. Only thus is the portrait of Mary Magdalene
and her significance as reflecting the authors' attitudes towards
women seen in proper perspective. In other words, if a text says
that Mary Magdalene has come to the world to "make clear the
abundance of the revealer" (*Dial. Sav.* 140,17-19), one should not
make her the most dominant disciple within the circle of Jesus'
closest followers before the text is carefully studied in light of
those passages where a similar task is entrusted to other disciples
as well (*Dial. Sav.* 126,8-10; 126,16-17; 142,21-24).

Third, in several Gnostic writings the positive characterizations
of Mary Magdalene are accompanied by statements in which
images of the feminine are used as negative symbols. This should
already make one cautious about assuming that the positive view
of Mary Magdalene should be taken as an automatic indication
that the authors of the writings consciously advocate and propagate
a general pro-woman attitude. In principle, a picture of Mary
Magdalene as an active interlocutor or as an exceptional interpreter
of the Savior's words may simply serve as an attempt to defend
the presentation of Mary Magdalene as a significant authority
behind the traditions used in a given writing. In any case, more

serious attention is to be paid to the relationship between pro-Mary
Magdalene attitudes and those passages where images of the
feminine have a pejorative connotation.

In many previous studies the important role granted to Mary
Magdalene by the Gnostic writings dealing with her and her
conflict with the male disciples have been straightforwardly interpreted as a direct reflection of women's role and position among
the Gnostic readers of these texts. It is also my conviction that
religious texts such as these mirror not only the attitudes of the
author but also the conceptions and the situation of the assumed
readers. Yet it is not unproblematic to move from the text world
to the real world of the first readers. There is no easy way to
know how the views presented by the characters of the text are
related to those of its audience.[92] Nor is it self-evident that every
text and all of its features have concrete correlations in the "real
life" of a given community. To illustrate the point, one can ask:
Does the positive treatment of Mary Magdalene in a given writing
mean that the first readers accepted her as a spiritual authority
whose example was also followed so that any woman among them
could be given a similar role? Or was it rather written as a challenge to a community where women's strivings for equality were
dismissed? Or is the reference to Mary Magdalene a simple histor-
icizing reminiscence which has no relevance at the time of the first
readers as far as gender roles are concerned? It is only through
examining the texts for clues about kind of context in which a
particular text would make sense and by seeing where it places
emphases, where it sees problems, where it locates conflict, and
where it presupposes agreements that the most probable option can
be found.

In the case of those writings which display a controversy
between Mary Magdalene and the male disciples (*Gospel of Thomas*, *Gospel of Mary*, and *Pistis Sophia*), it is difficult to avoid the
impression that they are speaking to a concrete conflict. Nevertheless, one has to ask whether the controversy in all instances is over
the position of women in general or only over the role of Mary
Magdalene within the tradition both the author of the writing and
its readers know but value differently. Moreover, does the contro-

---

[92] In his presentation of sociology of knowledge as a method of
interpretation, Tuckett (1987, 143-144) makes a similar comment.

versy reflect a conflict between Gnostic and orthodox Christians or a dispute within a Gnostic group? In previous Mary Magdalene studies, it was commonly assumed that the former was the case. Consequently, Peter, the most important rival of Mary Magdalene, is regarded as the symbol of the orthodox faction. That the Nag Hammadi Library contains writings which clearly place Peter in the camp of the Gnostics (*Apocalypse of Peter*, *Letter of Peter to Philip*)[93] forces one to leave open the possibility that a controversy text may also reflect an internal conflict among Gnostics, Mary Magdalene and Peter embodying different sides of the dispute. In each instance, the final solution of the question depends on a detailed analysis of a given text.

---

[93] Parrott (1986, 206-210) has sought to show that in these two writings Peter is not regarded as genuinely Gnostic but he is made to be secretly a Gnostic in order that the text might have been used in anti-ecclesiastical polemic. Parrott's distinction is strange and not convincing at all. Certainly, at least the *Apocalypse of Peter* contains anti-ecclesiastical tones but there is nothing in the text which would indicate that the author does not regard Peter as the real founder of the Gnostic community (71,15-21), whereas he knows that the Gnostic (conception of) Peter is slandered by the sons of this age, i.e., ecclesiastical Christians (73,10-23; for the translation, see Koschorke 1978, 32). For a more thorough evaluation of Parrott's thesis, see pp. 66-70 below.

CHAPTER TWO

MARY MAGDALENE
IN THE GOSPEL OF THOMAS

1. *Introductory Remarks*

The *Gospel of Thomas* is clearly the most studied and most debated of all the Nag Hammadi writings. As is well known, its relationship to the Synoptic gospels, its compositional character, its relationship to Gnostic thought, and its dating and place of composition are all controversial issues.[1] Since the last three questions bear on the treatment of the Mary Magdalene passages in the writing, I shall state my own position with regard to these matters.

The *Gospel of Thomas* consists of independent sayings, 114 in number according to the most common divisions of the text.[2] Since the writing contains doublets it is probable that it has been put together from two (or more) smaller sayings collections.[3] The principle by which logia were joined together is not very obvious. In some instances they were apparently connected by means of a catchword and/or because of a common theme.[4] Compositional patterns other than this can hardly be detected. This has led some scholars to conclude that in its present form the *Gospel of Thomas* was not even meant to be a unified document having any consistent outlook.[5] This inference is too sceptical. Despite the fact that no clear overall structure can be discerned, as is actually typical

---

[1] Overviews of pertinent problems in the study of the *Gospel of Thomas* are provided by Haenchen (1961-62, 147-178.306-338), Fallon & Cameron (1988, 4195-4251) and Riley (1994, 227-252).

[2] For the Coptic text of the gospel used in the present study, see Layton 1989a, 52-92. For the extant Greek fragments, see Attridge 1989, 95-128. The numbering of the logia follows that of Layton 1989a.

[3] At least the following doublets can be found: 56//80; 87//112; 55//101; 48//106.

[4] For examples of catchword associations, see Patterson 1993, 100-102; several of his examples, to be sure, do not seem to be quite as clear and intentional as he suggests.

[5] Recently, this has been most strongly stressed by Wisse 1988, 304-305.

of sayings collections such as the *Gospel of Thomas*, the principle for selecting material was hardly a random choice. Clearly, the writing contains motifs central to its theological profile which wind like a thread through the whole book. According to the *Gospel of Thomas*, spiritual persons come from the light, belong to the light, and are on their way back to it (18; 19; 49; 50; 77). If they come to know their real identity (3; 18; 67) and if they are ready to renounce the world (27; 56; 80; 110) and to live ascetic life without family ties (22; 49; 55; 75; 101), they may enter into the light, i.e., they will find the kingdom and will not taste death. Salvation is not only seen primarily as a future event, it is already materialized in the present life of a Christian, though as a state of existence unseen to the world (51; 113). The emphasis on the interiorization of faith is also seen in a critical attitude towards outward religious practices (6; 14; 27; 53; 89; 104).

Although the redactor of the sayings collection has selected material with his main theological emphases in his mind and has obviously viewed his writing as a theological whole, it is not self-evident that the meaning of individual logia has remained the same in the redaction process. Therefore, a modern interpreter has to exercise caution in expounding logia. Their meaning as well as the meaning of the individual parts may vary depending on whether they are interpreted in light of their assumed original context or within the framework of the entire gospel. This has to be borne in mind also when the two Mary Magdalene passages of the writing are analyzed. This observation is especially important with logion 114, since it has been suggested that the passage was not included in the gospel by a conscious choice of the redactor but was added only afterwards. The question will be treated more thoroughly below.

The issue of *Thomas'* relationship to Gnosticism has been strongly debated since the very beginning of Thomasine studies.[6] Although those who have defended the Gnostic character of the writing constitute a majority among scholars, the opposite view

---

[6]   In fact, the discussion started already before the entire gospel was known. After the discovery of P. Oxy. 1, 654, and 655 scholars debated whether the fragments were orthodox or heretical (see Grenfell & Hunt 1898, 2; 1904, 11-12).

has also found a significant number of supporters.[7] Conflicting opinions are not only due to the fact that the evidence within the *Gospel of Thomas* is judged differently. Clearly, disagreement on this matter depends also on the diversity of ways Gnosticism is defined. In the present study the starting point for the assessment is the definition presented in the Introduction.

Admittedly, there are features in the *Gospel of Thomas* which do not coincide very well with any definition of Gnosticism. It lacks all the mythological explanations of the origin of evil. No allusion to the Sophia myth or to the Demiurge as a creator can be discerned. In fact, the material creation can be described in positive terms (12) or even connected with the Father (89). On the other hand, salvation in the *Gospel of Thomas* is perceived in the same way as in many Gnostic writings. It is a result of one's knowing oneself (3; 70; cf. also 111) or, more precisely, one's divine origin in the realm of light (49; 50; 18; 19). Jesus' instruction in logion 50, which he gives his disciples who have to explain their identity, has its closest parallels in those Gnostic texts which describe the post-mortem ascent of the soul past archontic powers back to the realm of light.[8]

---

[7] For representatives of these two views, see Fallon & Cameron 4230-4232; Riley 1994, 229-232.

[8] Cf. *Gos. Mary* 15,1-17,7; *1 Apoc. Jas.* 32,28-36,1; *Ap. Jas.* 8,35-36; *Apoc. Paul* 22,23-23,28; *CH* 1,24-26; Iren., *Adv. haer.* 1.21,5; Epiph., *Pan.* 26.13,2; 36.3,1-6; cf. also *2 Book of Jeu* 127,5-138,4; *PS* 286,9-291,23. Whether *Gos. Thom.* 50 itself is to be seen as a description of the interrogation during the post-mortem ascent of the soul or a mystical experience of *visio Dei*, as De Conick (1996) has sought to show, or as simply a catechesis created to give the audience of the Thomasine Jesus answers to fundamental questions which occupied people's minds everywhere in antiquity (for references, see De Conick 1996, 43-63) is difficult to decide, although the non-identification of the interrogators with archontic powers, the fact that the interrogators are not portrayed as hostile figures as well as the lack of explicit evidence of a mystical *visio Dei* experience in the *Gospel of Thomas* seem to suggest that the third option is most likely. Yet as regards the questions and answers presented in *Gos. Thom.* 50, the Gnostic ascent passages clearly provide the closest parallels. Therefore, it is obvious that *Gos. Thom.* 50 reflects Gnostic thought (so also Meyer [1992, 12] who otherwise thinks "it is difficult to call the Gospel of Thomas a gnostic gospel without considerable qualification"). De Conick (1996, 62-63) denies the Gnostic character of *Gos. Thom.* 50, but fails to show why the Thomasine version should be seen as a non-Gnostic Christian formula whereas its closest, although later, parallels are Gnostic.

It is also worth noting that even though the event of creation is not exhibited in negative terms, both the material world and the physical body are. The cosmos is not only to be destroyed at the end of the age (111; 11), but it is decaying already in the present time (56; 80). For those who find themselves the cosmos is worthless (111). In other words, salvation does not only mean that one discovers oneself, God, and the kingdom, but also that one is granted sight of the valueless character of the world. The same is true of the body. It is a sheer burden to the soul, to the real self of a person (29; 87; 112).

The visible, real world is not only worthless and therefore to be rejected. It is also dangerous and threatening. The attachment to the world may deprive one of one's salvation (27). In logion 21 the cosmos is given an even more active role.[9] The second part of Jesus' answer contains a parable of the owner of a house. In the following application of the parable Jesus states: "You, then, be on your guard against the world. Arm yourselves with great strength lest the robbers find a way to come to you. For otherwise they shall find the profit you expect."[10] The translation of the last sentence is different from the most common recent renderings of the text.[11] The Greek word ⲭⲣⲉⲓⲁ is given a positive meaning "profit, good"[12] and the conjunction ⲉⲡⲉⲓ is understood elliptically "for (if it were different); for otherwise."[13] Thus the verbal expression ⲥⲉⲛⲁϩⲉ ⲉⲣⲟⲥ can be translated in its most natural sense: "...they shall find (it)." If this interpretation is correct the robbers are not trying to create difficulties for the owner of a house, i.e, for a disciple, but they are trying to steal the most valuable possession he has. In this way, the peculiar genitive expression ⲡⲉϥⲏⲉⲓ ⲛⲧⲉ ⲧⲉϥⲙⲛⲧⲉⲣⲟ (= "his house of his kingdom") also becomes more understandable. The interpretative secondary addi-

---

[9] For the text and the translation, see pp. 39-40 below.

[10] A similar translation is found in Wilson 1960, 73; Ménard 1975, 60; Blatz 1987b, 102.

[11] Lambdin (1989, 63) translates the ⲉⲡⲉⲓ-clause: "... for the difficulty which you expect will (surely) materialize." Layton (1987, 384) and Meyer (1992, 33) render the text: "... for the trouble you expect will come."

[12] For this usage of the word, see *Dial. Sav.* 134,8; *PS* 358,1.

[13] For this meaning, see Bauer & K. Aland & B. Aland 1988, 575.

tion, ⲚⲦⲈ ⲦⲈϥⲘⲚⲦⲈⲢⲞ,[14] clearly breaks the boundaries of the parable and brings an allegorical application to the text. Thus, it is not the house (and the goods) of his disciple which the Thomasine Jesus is worried about but the kingdom,[15] i.e., salvation which disciples carry within themselves and whose ultimate consummation is expected to take place in the future. It is that which is the target of the worldly intrusion. With this interpretation, one cannot avoid the impression that the robbers too are more than an element in the parable, and they acquire features of worldly or even archontic powers which seek to obstruct the return of disciples to the realm of light.

Even though the *Gospel of Thomas* has no explicitly dualistic conception of God[16] and it contains no mythological aspects typical of a Gnostic cosmogony, its connections with Gnostic thought can hardly be denied. Its negative view of the world and the human body, its emphasis on the divine origin of the self and on self-knowledge as the prerequisite for salvation as well as its reference to the ultimate dissolution of the visible world are all elements which are in concert with Gnostic theology. Conglomeration of these features within one writing implies that the *Gospel of Thomas*, as a collection presently known to us, can be identified

---

[14] So Wilson 1960, 73-74; Quecke 1963, 48. Cf. also King 1987, 73, who, to be sure, does not see any mythological implications in the text but thinks its message is "preparedness for effectively dealing with the activity of wicked persons."

[15] Despite a clumsy way of putting it (see Quecke 1963, 50), the Coptic text seems to translate a Greek version which has contained a *genitivus appositivus*.

[16] It is of interest, however, that like many Gnostic writings the *Gospel of Thomas* seems to prefer ⲈⲒⲰⲦ to ⲚⲞⲨⲦⲈ as the designation of the Divinity. In this sense ⲈⲒⲰⲦ occurs 20 times. In the Coptic version ⲚⲞⲨⲦⲈ is used only in two logia. In logion 30 it refers to non-Christian gods. In logion 100 it is not certain whether it is identical with the Father or it represents a non-Christian god, since unlike the Synoptic versions of the saying it ends with a phrase: ⲀⲨⲰ ⲠⲈⲦⲈ ⲠⲰⲈⲒ ⲠⲈ ⲘⲀⲦⲚ ⲚⲀⲈⲒϥ ("... and give me what is mine."). Wilson (1960, 59-60) and Hall (1990, 485) have suggested that in logion 100 ⲚⲞⲨⲦⲈ stands for the Demiurge; although this assertion cannot be ruled out it is hardly the most likely interpretation because nothing elsewhere in the writing points to any interest in the person or function of the Demiurge. Besides, in the Greek fragments of *Thomas* the expression ἡ βασιλεία τοῦ θεοῦ appears at least in logion 27 but probably also in logion 3. In other words, if the word "god" is at all employed in the sense of the Demiurge it can have taken place only at the Coptic stage of transmission of the gospel.

as Gnostic or at least it can be seen to be part of the trajectory which was moving towards Gnosticism.[17]

Despite the fact that all the extant manuscripts of the *Gospel of Thomas* have been discovered in Egypt, it is not likely that the writing was composed there.[18] It is more probable that it gained its present form in Syria,[19] perhaps in Edessa or in another bi-lingual city approximately in the same geographical area.[20] The main arguments for a Syrian provenance are:[21] 1) the *Gospel of Thomas* uses the name (Didymos) Judas Thomas which must have originated in an Aramaic-speaking community and is typical of the works deriving from Syria; 2) there are several significant connections between the *Gospel of Thomas* and the *Acts of Thomas* as well as other writings which appear to have been composed in Edessa or in its surroundings; 3) the *Gospel of Thomas* reveals several Aramaisms.

With regard to the dating of the *Gospel of Thomas*, scholarly opinions vary widely.[22] The two main reasons for such great variation are: First, those who regard *Thomas* as independent of the Synoptic gospels tend to date it in the first century, whereas

---

[17] Of course this does not mean that all the individual logia have a special Gnostic thrust in them, nor even that all are especially applicable to a Gnostic or Gnosticizing interpretation.

[18] Especially in the early phase of Thomasine studies some scholars suggested that the *Gospel of Thomas* was written in Alexandria; for references, see Riley 1994, 238.

[19] It is possible that the smaller collections or an earlier version which underlie the gospel known in its Coptic version may have originated in other locations; this is emphasized by Patterson 1993, 120.

[20] Edessa is by far the most common suggestion for *Thomas'* provenance; for references, see Lincoln 1977, 65; Fallon & Cameron 1988, 4227-4228. Desjardins (1992, 121-133) accepts a Syrian origin of the *Gospel of Thomas* but repudiates the thesis that the place of writing should be Edessa. Rather, he thinks the *Gospel of Thomas* originated in Antioch.

[21] The summary closely follows that of Klijn (1972, 70) who indeed argues not only for a Syrian but more specifically for an Edessene provenance of the *Gospel of Thomas*.

[22] As is well known, the earliest dating of the entire writing is offered by Davies (1983, 3.146-147) who maintains that the *Gospel of Thomas* was composed 50-70 C.E. and the latest by Drijvers (1982, 172-173) who thinks that it has to be situated around 200 C.E. Neither of these suggestions has found a large following. Still, scholarly estimates range from a date in the last quarter of the first century to the mid-second century.

those who think that its final redactor was either wholly or partly
dependent on the Synoptic gospels situate it in the second century.
Second, those who think that the logia which hardly originated
before the second century (e.g. 7[23] and 53[24]) should be considered
as rare interpolations made after the final redaction of the collection are in favor of an earlier dating, while those who see these
logia as signs of a wider compositional activity tend to regard
Thomas as a second century writing.

It is not possible to discuss here in any detail all the problems
relevant to the dating of the entire collection of sayings in its final
form before its first copies were made.[25] Nevertheless, one can
fairly safely conclude that the version of the *Gospel of Thomas*
which is presently known to us through the Nag Hammadi Library
is a result of a long process of collecting and editing which began
sometime in the first century and was mainly completed in the
middle of the second century. Whether the chief part of the redactional work, through which the writing not only got its literary
shape but its theological character as well, took place in the first
century or in the first half of the second is difficult to decide at
this stage and remains to be clarified. As to the dating of the two
logia where Mary Magdalene appears (21; 114), with respect to
logion 21 there seems to be no reason to assume that the saying
is any younger than the revelation dialogues which introduce her
as an interlocutor of Jesus (*Sophia of Jesus Christ*; *Dialogue of the
Savior*). On the contrary, the independent character of the logion
suggests that it may represent a somewhat earlier stage of development than the texts in which a doctrinal treatise and a series of
traditional sayings were turned into dialogues. In the case of
logion 114 the situation is different. As will be argued below, it
should be considered a post-redactional addition into the collection
and derives from the late second century.

---

[23] For the dating, see Jackson 1985, 172-173.212-213.

[24] Logion 53 seems to reflect a second-century dispute about circum-
cision between Jews/Jewish-Christians and Christians and has, in its use
of a rationalizing biological argument, a close parallel in Justin, *Dial.*
19,3; for an interesting rabbinic parallel (*Tanchuma* B 7 [18a]), see
Stroker 1989, 34.

[25] For a survey of scholarly views and some pertinent problems, see
Fallon & Cameron 1988, 4224-4227; Patterson 1993, 113-118.

2. *Analyses of Mary Magdalene Logia*

There are two logia in the *Gospel of Thomas* where a woman called ΜΑΡΙϨΑΜ is referred to (21; 114). There is no doubt that in both cases the same woman is meant. In neither instance is the identity of ΜΑΡΙϨΑΜ more closely specified. Nevertheless, the situation described in logion 114 makes it most probable that it is Mary Magdalene about whom the texts speak. The tension between Peter and ΜΑΡΙϨΑΜ in logion 114 has its parallel in the *Gospel of Mary* and in *Pistis Sophia* where the conflict between these two is a conspicuous, if not a central theme.[26] Apart from Mary Magdalene, no other Mary turns up in such a polemic context. The form of the name, which in Coptic texts is used of Mary Magdalene, but not of the mother of Jesus, also bolsters this conclusion.[27]

2.1 *Logion 21*

ΠΕΧΕ ΜΑΡΙϨΑΜ ΝΙⲤ ΧΕ ΕΝΕΚΜΑΘΗΤΗⲤ ΕΙΝΕ ΝΝΙΜ
ΠΕΧΑϤ ΧΕ ΕⲨΕΙΝΕ ΝϨΝϢΗΡΕ ϢΗΜ ΕⲨϬΕⲗΙΤ ΑⲨⲤⲰϢΕ
ΕΤⲰΟⲨ ΑΝ ΤΕ ϨΟΤΑΝ ΕⲨϢΑΕΙ ΝϬΙ ΝΧΟΕΙⲤ ΝΤⲤⲰϢΕ
ⲤΕΝΑΧΟΟⲤ ΧΕ ΚΕ ΤΝⲤⲰϢΕ ΕΒΟⲗ ΝΑΝ ΝΤΟΟⲨ ⲤΕΚΑ-
ΚΑϨΗⲨ ΜΠΟⲨΜΤΟ ΕΒΟⲗ ΕΤΡΟⲨΚΑΑⲤ ΕΒΟⲗ ΝΑⲨ ΝⲤΕϮ
ΤΟⲨⲤⲰϢΕ ΝΑⲨ
ⲆΙⲆ ΤΟⲨΤΟ ϮΧⲰ ΜΜΟⲤ ΧΕ ΕϤϢΑΕΙΜΕ ΝϬΙ ΠΧΕⲤϨΝΗΕΙ
ΧΕ ϤΝΗⲨ ΝϬΙ ΠΡΕϤΧΙΟⲨΕ ϤΝΑΡΟΕΙⲤ ΕΜΠΑΤΕϤΕΙ ΝϤΤⲘ-
ΚΑΑϤ ΕϢΟΧΤ ΕϨΟⲨΝ ΕΠΕϤΗΕΙ ΝΤΕ ΤΕϤΜΝΤΕΡΟ ΕΤΡΕϤϤΙ
ΝΝΕϤⲤΚΕⲨΟⲤ ΝΤⲰΤΝ ⲆΕ ΡΟΕΙⲤ ϨΑ ΤΕϨΗ ΜΠΚΟⲤΜΟⲤ
ΜΟⲨΡ ΜΜⲰΤΝ ΕΧΝ ΝΕΤΝΤΠΕ ϨΝΟⲨΝΟϬ ΝΔⲨΝΑΜΙⲤ
ϢΙΝΑ ΧΕ ΝΕ ΝⲗΗⲤΤΗⲤ ϨΕ ΕϨΙΗ ΕΕΙ ϢΑΡⲰΤΝ ΕΠΕΙ ΤΕ-
ΧΡΕΙⲆ ΕΤΕΤΝϬⲰϢΤ ΕΒΟⲗ ϨΗΤⲤ ⲤΕΝΑϨΕ ΕΡΟⲤ
ΜΑΡΕϤϢⲰΠΕ ϨΝ ΤΕΤΝΜΗΤΕ ΝϬΙ ΟⲨΡⲰΜΕ ΝΕΠΙⲤΤΗΜⲰΝ
ΝΤΑΡΕ ΠΚΑΡΠΟⲤ ΠⲰϨ ΑϤΕΙ ϨΝΝΟⲨϬΕΠΗ ΕΠΕϤΑⲤϨ ϨΝ
ΤΕϤϬΙΧ ΑϤϨΑⲤϤ ΠΕΤΕ ΟⲨΝ ΜΑΑΧΕ ΜΜΟϤ ΕⲤⲰΤΜ ΜΑ-
ΡΕϤⲤⲰΤⲘ

Mary said to Jesus: "Whom are your disciples like?"
He said: "They are like little children who have settled in a field which is not theirs. When the owners of the field come, they will say:

---

[26] *Gos. Mary* 17,16-18,10; *PS* 58,11-21; 162,14-21; 377,14-17.
[27] For the forms of the names, see pp. 63-64.

'Let us have back our field.' The children undress in their presence
in order to let them have back their field and to give it back to them.

"Therefore I say, if the owner of a house knows that the thief is
coming, he will begin his vigil before he comes and will not let him
dig through into his house of his kingdom to carry away his goods.
You, then, be on your guard against the world. Arm yourselves with
great strength lest the robbers find a way to come to you. For otherwise they shall find the profit you expect. Let there be among you a
person who understands.

"When the grain ripened, he came quickly with his sickle in his
hand and reaped it. Whoever has ears to hear let him hear."[28]

Although several of *Thomas'* logia are presented in the form of a
dialogue between Jesus and his disciples, there are only a few
logia where any of the interlocutors are mentioned by name. The
only exceptions are the male disciples Simon Peter (13; 114),
Matthew (13), Thomas (13; cf. also incipit) and the two women,
Mary Magdalene (21; 114) and Salome (61). Besides these, the
only other character of Early Christianity who is mentioned in the
writing is James the Just (12).

Clearly, James and Thomas have a special role in the *Gospel
of Thomas*. James is known to have been appointed to be the first
leader of the disciples after Jesus' departure. Thomas is seen as the
one who (after James?) not only had a special understanding of
Jesus but who also is the one thanks to whom the secret teachings
of Jesus can be handed on to later readers.[29] Simon Peter and

---

[28] The text is taken from Layton (1989a, 62) and the translation
follows that of Lambdin (1989, 63) with the exception of changes made
on the basis of the argumentation above; see p. 35. In addition,
Lambdin's "man of understanding" is changed to "person who understands."

[29] Although James' position as an authority was recognized by the
compiler of the *Gospel of Thomas*, he also relativizes it by placing logion
13 immediately after logion 12. While logion 12 emphasizes a leader-
centered organization among the disciples, logion 13 points out that the
disciples, having come to a full realization of Jesus' (and their own) real
character, have no need of any master (cf. also 108). It is tempting to see
in logia 12 and 13 a reflection of a development from the hierarchical
understanding of Christian leadership, connected with James, to the
notion of a "masterless" Christian self-identity, linked with Thomas.
Whether the tension between logia 12 and 13 can be used to reconstruct
two clearly datable historical phases within the life of Thomasine
Christians, as suggested by Crossan (1991, 427-428) and Patterson (1993,
117), is more uncertain however.

Matthew, on the other hand, are pictured as possessing a mistaken conception of Jesus (13). Their inability to understand is underlined by the fact that if they (and other disciples) heard one word of the secret revelation imparted by Jesus to Thomas they would try to stone the latter. In the case of Simon Peter, logion 114 still corroborates the negative picture the gospel wants to paint of him.

Mary Magdalene and Salome are not depicted as the ones who misunderstand, but as the ones who at least do not yet understand enough. They do not seem to have attained a level of perception similar to that of Thomas. Both of them are involved in a discussion which elucidates the nature of discipleship. The discussion between Jesus and Salome (61) gives the latter a chance to avow that she is his disciple, although Jesus' comment after her confession seems to suggest that she is not yet a "masterless" disciple in the sense of Thomas (13; cf. also 108) but only that she is challenged to reach the highest level of discipleship and become "equal(?)[30] ... filled with light." It looks as if one can be a disciple in one sense without being a disciple in the *Thomasine* sense. The same seems to be true in logion 21.

Logion 21 begins with Mary Magdalene's question about the characteristics of the disciples.[31] Clearly, the question implies that

---

[30] The translation presupposes an emendation of the Coptic text. Instead of ϵϥϣⲏϥ ("devastated") one should read ϵϥϣⲏϣ, a form of the verb ϣⲱϣ which appears also in line 43,29 and characterizes the Father or his realm. It is not fully clear how the qualitative form of the verb should be translated in this logion. According to Crum (1939, 606), the qualitative of ϣⲱϣ means "to be equal, level, straight." This meaning of the word is adopted e.g. by the translators of *editio princeps* (see Guillaumont *et al.* 1959, 35; cf. also Ménard 1975, 66). This interpretation of the verb is somewhat surprising in its context unless "being equal" is seen as a mysterious characterization of the disciple (and of the Father) in the same way that the "equality" is presented as a trait of the Father and the pleromatic entities in *Tri. Trac.* 67,36; 94,40 (cf. Iren., *Adv. haer.* 1.2,6). Especially in more recent translations, ϣⲏϣ is interpreted more in light of its present context and in light of Thomasine theology. Since the obvious opposite of ϣⲏϣ is to "be divided" and since the gospel emphasizes the ideal of oneness, Layton (1987, 391) suggests a translation "to be integrated" (so already Gärtner 1960, 122), Lambdin (1989, 75) "to be undivided," and Meyer (1992, 47) "to be whole." The problem with these translations is that, to my knowledge, no parallel of this kind of use of ϣⲏϣ has been found.

[31] In the *Sophia of Jesus Christ* Mary Magdalene also asks a question about the disciples (III/4 114,8-12). However, in *Gos. Thom.* 21 the focus of Mary's question is on the essence of discipleship, whereas in *Soph. Jes. Chr.* III/4 114,8-12 she seeks to know where the disciples come from, where they will go, and what their task is on the earth.

she wants and needs to get more information about this matter. Should this be understood to suggest that she in fact does not yet belong to the circle of disciples who collectively act as interlocutors but that she only deliberates whether she should and could join it? To answer this question in the affirmative would be too hasty a conclusion. It is rather that, like Salome, Mary Magdalene is a disciple in the ordinary sense of the word. Nevertheless, she still lacks understanding and needs to be exhorted to become ⲞⲨⲢⲰⳘⲈ ⲚⲈⲦⲒⲤⲦⲎⳘⲰⲚ ("a person who understands"; 21). In other words, she is urged to reach the higher stage of discipleship that could be characterized as "masterless" (13) or "Jesus-like" (108).[32]

Mary Magdalene's or Salome's lack of understanding should not be overemphasized. They are by no means the only ones who have to receive a word of exhortation or a special instruction. Jesus' response to Mary Magdalene in logion 21 shows that his conversation with her is no private affair. The parenetic section after the parable of the thief is not directed to Mary alone but obviously to all the interlocutors, i.e., to all the disciples. It is also worth noting that in logion 22 where all the disciples ask whether they enter the kingdom as children, i.e., as disciples (cf. 21), Jesus points out that belonging to the circle of disciples is no automatic guarantee of entering the kingdom.[33] A disciple must become a disciple of the highest level in the special Thomasine sense in order to obtain the kingdom and immortality. Therefore, the disciples as well as the later readers of the text need a special ability to hear, to understand, and to interpret the words of Jesus (1). Like

---

[32] Differently Perkins (1995, 558), who thinks log. 21 and log. 61 show that Mary Magdalene and Salome "are clearly disciples whose insight is similar to that of Thomas." In the case of Mary Magdalene, Perkins tries to prove her thesis by claiming that "the introduction to log. 21 coordinates it with log. 13. In the latter, Jesus tested his disciples by asking them to provide a simile or comparison that expressed what he was like. In the former, Mary poses the same challenge in reverse." Yet, the parenetic part of Jesus' reply indicates that Mary Magdalene is not testing Jesus' understanding but is seeking to be taught by him.

[33] As a matter of fact, being a disciple in the ordinary sense of the word is almost the same as having a dearth of understanding in the *Gospel of Thomas*. Out of the twelve questions they put to Jesus at least seven reveal an explicit lack of understanding or a full misunderstanding (6; 18; 43; 51; 52; 99; 113).

Thomas, they have to drink from the bubbling spring of Jesus' mouth as well (13; 108).

Although in the *Gospel of Thomas* the prototype of a spiritually advanced disciple is clearly Thomas and all the other disciples including Mary Magdalene are in need of deeper instruction, nonetheless it is significant that she is singled out as a spokesperson for the entire group of disciples. What is the reason for this? Does it simply reveal the influence of a developing tradition reflected in Gnostic revelation dialogues, according to which Mary Magdalene had an active role in the conversations during which Jesus gave special, esoteric teachings to his disciples? This is possible, although in the *Gospel of Thomas,* according to its own priorities, Mary Magdalene obtains a more modest role, and the discussions do not seem to take place after but prior to the death and resurrection of Jesus. Yet one can ask whether the use of a tradition fully explains the writing's interest in Mary Magdalene. Or does the reference to Mary Magdalene, especially when another female disciple, Salome, also has a visible role in the gospel, say something about the concrete need of the redactor to include logia dealing with women in his writing? We shall return to this question again when analyzing logion 114 and ask what it reveals about the attitudes of the writer towards women and the position of women among the audience of the gospel.

2.2 *Logion 114*

ⲡⲉϫⲉ ⲥⲓⲙⲱⲛ ⲡⲉⲧⲣⲟⲥ ⲛⲁⲩ ϫⲉ ⲙⲁⲣⲉ ⲙⲁⲣⲓϩⲁⲙ ⲉⲓ ⲉⲃⲟⲗ
ⲛ̅ϩⲏⲧⲛ̅ ϫⲉ ⲛ̅ⲥϩⲓⲟⲙⲉ ⲙ̅ⲡϣⲁ ⲁⲛ ⲙ̅ⲡⲱⲛϩ
ⲡⲉϫⲉ ⲓ̅ⲥ̅ ϫⲉ ⲉⲓⲥϩⲏⲏⲧⲉ ⲁⲛⲟⲕ ϯⲛⲁⲥⲱⲕ ⲙ̅ⲙⲟⲥ ϫⲉⲕⲁⲁⲥ
ⲉⲉⲓⲛⲁⲁⲥ ⲛ̅ϩⲟⲟⲩⲧ ϣⲓⲛⲁ ⲉⲥⲛⲁϣⲱⲡⲉ ϩⲱⲱⲥ ⲛ̅ⲟⲩⲡ̅ⲛ̅ⲁ̅
ⲉϥⲟⲛϩ ⲉϥⲉⲓⲛⲉ ⲙ̅ⲙⲱⲧⲛ̅ ⲛ̅ϩⲟⲟⲩⲧ ϫⲉ ⲥϩⲓⲙⲉ ⲛⲓⲙ ⲉⲥⲛⲁⲁⲥ
ⲛ̅ϩⲟⲟⲩⲧ ⲥⲛⲁⲃⲱⲕ ⲉϩⲟⲩⲛ ⲉⲧⲙⲛ̅ⲧ̅ⲉⲣⲟ ⲛⲙ̅ⲡ̅ⲏⲩⲉ

Simon Peter said to them: "Let Mary leave us, for women are not worthy of life."

Jesus said: "I myself shall lead her in order to make her male, so that she too may become a living spirit resembling you males. For every woman who will make herself male will enter the kingdom of heaven."[34]

Logion 114 is one of the most studied and debated logia in the entire gospel.[35] With regard to the interpretation of Mary Magdalene there are three sets of important questions which need to be discussed. First, is the train of thought in the comment of Jesus internally consistent? In other words, how can Jesus speak at the same time about Mary whom he will "make male" and about women who "make themselves male?" Is this a contradiction and if it is, can it be reconciled? Or is this only seemingly a problem due to a mistaken understanding of the syntax of Jesus' statement, as Schüngel has suggested?[36] This reasoning inevitably poses the question of how the structure of the comment is to be analyzed and what kind of translation can be based on this analysis.

Second, what is actually meant with "being made/making oneself male" and how is this event related to "making the two one ... so that the male not be male nor the female female" in logion 22 (cf. also 106)? Again we meet a contradiction. Is it real or only apparent? If it is real, how is it to be explained? In addition, the phrase "being made/making oneself male" forces one to ask what kind of views of women are reflected in the text and how they possibly mirror the situation of the Christians among whom the logion was narrated and read.

Unavoidably, this leads to a third set of questions about the conflict between Peter and Jesus over the position of Mary Magdalene among the disciples. Is the conflict only a narrative device which gives the author a chance to present his/her view on this matter or does the text reflect a real debate? Finally, were Peter and Mary Magdalene randomly picked out to be the protagonists of the text or does the fact that they were chosen say anything more concrete about the nature of the debate?

---

[34] The text and the translation are taken from Layton (1989a, 92) and Lambdin (1989, 93).

[35] For recent studies on this logion, see e.g. Rengstorf 1970, 563-574; Meeks 1973-74, 193-197; Dart 1978, 321-325; Buckley 1985, 245-272; Meyer 1985, 554-570; Lelyveld 1987, 138-143; Arai 1993, 373-376; Schüngel 1994, 394-401; De Conick 1996, 18-21.

[36] Schüngel 1994, 394-401.

2.2.1 *Syntax and Translation*

In a recent article Schüngel called attention to the fact that according to all existing translations of logion 114 Jesus appears to make
a contradictory statement.[37] On the one hand, he promises to make
Mary Magdalene male so that she may become a living spirit and
enter the kingdom of heaven. On the other hand, he states that
"every woman who will make herself male will enter the kingdom
of heaven." In other words, what Jesus seems to be doing for
Mary Magdalene, all the other women are supposed to do for
themselves. Schüngel thinks that this inconsistency is not actually
in the text but in the minds of the translators, because they have
not understood correctly the syntax of logion 114. Schüngel's own
analysis of the syntax differs from the consensus of opinion in
three points:[38] First, he interprets the first sentence of Jesus' answer after ЄICϨHHTЄ as a rhetorical question to which a negative
answer is expected. Second, the following ϢINA-clause should not
be taken together with what precedes but with what comes after.
Third, ЄЧЄINЄ after the ϢINA-clause is not a circumstantial
which modifies an indefinite antecedent (OYΠNЄYMA) but a
second present which begins the main clause. To these syntactical
observations Schüngel still adds one concerning the semantics of
the text. He argues that the word ϨOOYT ("male") in the comment
of Jesus should not be understood as a gender related term but it
has a connotation "männlich tüchtig" or "zum eigenen Leben
fähig."[39] Based on his analysis, Schüngel makes the following
English translation of the text:[40]

> Simon Peter said to them: Mary should leave us, for life is not for
> women!
>   Jesus said: Watch this! Is it me, who shall drag her in order that
> I might make her male? In order that she, too, may become a pneuma

---

[37] Schüngel 1994, 394.
[38] Schüngel 1994, 397-400.
[39] Schüngel 1994, 399.
[40] Schüngel 1994, 400.

that is alive, her pneuma is equal to that of you,[41] you who are male.
For every woman who makes herself male[42] does enter the kingdom
of heaven.

With his interpretation Schüngel not only tries to remove the
terminological contradiction of Jesus' word but also the offense
which the phrase "every woman who makes herself male" causes.
If logion 114 is understood in this way, it matches well, in Schüngel's opinion, the main thrust of the *Gospel of Thomas*. He thinks
Thomas' central emphasis is found in a challenge, directed equally
to women and men, to search for human growth and ethical inde-
pendence through a process of finding one's potentialities, capaci-
ties and limits.[43]

There is no possibility nor any need to assess here whether
Schüngel's thesis about *Thomas'* central message can be maintained. However, if his understanding of logion 114 can be accepted, both syntactically and semantically, it has some significance
for the interpretation of Mary Magdalene in this passage. According to Schüngel, Mary Magdalene herself becomes more clearly a
symbol of the human possibility of reaching salvation. This notion
is held by a religious minority, whereas Peter represents a male-
chauvinistic view of the ecclesiastical majority.

None of Schüngel's arguments which support his translation are
really convincing. The first argument that the beginning of Jesus'
statement should be understood as a rhetorical question to which
a negative answer is expected is not impossible but less likely than
an alternative interpretation according to which the sentence is a
mere statement.[44] The second assertion is obviously the most

---

[41] At this point Schüngel's English translation differs from his German version as well as from the Coptic original. The Coptic text cannot
be read to emphasize the similarity of Mary Magdalene's pneuma to
those of the male disciples. Rather the comparison points out that Mary's
pneuma does become male.

[42] It is surprising that ϩⲟⲟⲩⲧ is translated by Schüngel (1994, 399)
"male," even if he insists that the word no longer has a gender related
connotation.

[43] Schüngel 1994, 400.

[44] Usually a rhetorical question is introduced by ⲙⲏ (see Till 1978,
213-214). A good example of this is provided by the last clause of *Gos.
Thom.* 72. It begins with a negation ⲙⲏ which is followed by a second
present.

important one in Schüngel's argumentation but it is also most vulnerable. As claimed by him, a sentence can begin with a final ϢⲓⲚⲀ-clause, but only if the main clause, which is supposed to come before it, is left out through an ellipsis.[45] It is extremely unlikely that a main clause comes after a final ϢⲓⲚⲀ-clause. Therefore, it is much more probable that the ϢⲓⲚⲀ-clause must be joined to the preceding, not to that which comes after. Schüngel's third argument stands or falls together with the second. If the ϢⲓⲚⲀ-clause is read together with the preceding, ⲈϤⲈⲓⲚⲈ cannot but be a circumstantial which modifies the indefinite antecedent ⲞⲨⲠⲚⲈⲨⲘⲀ. With his fourth argument, according to which ϨⲞⲞⲨⲦ does not have a gender related connotation in logion 114 but only implies that a person is capable of controlling his/her own life, Schüngel creates alternatives which exclude each other even if they need not. It is evident that the word has a symbolic connotation which goes beyond its concrete meaning but this "something more" is clearly connected with the gender related character of the word. This "something more" represents human values or characteristics which can be defined as "male" but obviously not as "female." Therefore, it is difficult to find in logion 114 the egalitarian emphasis which Schüngel sees in it.

Based on these observations, it should be concluded that the translation presented by Schüngel is not plausible. The earlier renderings, represented for example by Lambdin's,[46] convey more correctly the meaning of the Coptic text. If this be accepted, the contradiction in Jesus' comment observed by Schüngel seems to remain. Yet perhaps the disagreement between "Jesus making Mary male" and "every woman making herself male" is not so great after all. Both of the texts emphasize the transformation of a woman. In the first case, as an answer to Peter's attack against Mary Magdalene, the role of Jesus in the process of transformation is stressed, whereas in the general application of Jesus' instruction the situation is seen more from the vantage point of a woman being made/making herself male.

---

[45] The two examples of a ϢⲓⲚⲀ-clause beginning a sentence which Schüngel (1994, 398) finds in the *Gospel of Thomas* are no examples at all. In the first case ϢⲓⲚⲀ is not final but temporal (22) and in the second the conjunction clearly follows the main clause (103).

[46] Lambdin 1989, 93.

2.2.2 *The Meaning of Being Made/Making Oneself Male*

There are basically three lines of interpretation as to the arduous question of the meaning of the phrase "being made/making oneself male." These solutions do not even necessarily exclude each other.[47] First, "being made/making oneself male" has been interpreted as a concrete impersonation of a male by a woman.[48] It took place by means of cutting hair short and accepting male dress. The act signified an extremely radical ascetic choice. A woman, transformed by appearance into a male, shut herself outside the ordinary female ways of life, such as marriage and child-bearing. Thus, it clearly meant a denial of all sexual life. Yet the apocryphal acts provide several examples of this kind of behavior. We read about this in connection with Thecla (*Acts of Paul and Thecla* 25.40), Mygdonia (*Acts of Thomas* 114), Charitine (*Acts of Philip* 44),[49] and perhaps also Maximilla (*Acts of Andrew* 9).[50]

With regard to making Mary Magdalene male, one text is especially instructive. In the fourth century *Acts of Philip*, from chapter VIII on including the so-called *Martyrdom of Philip* (94-148),[51] there appears a woman called Mariamne. In the *Acts of Philip* 95 the Savior says to her: σὺ Μαριάμνη ἄλλαξον σου τὴν ἰδέαν καὶ ὅλον τὸ εἶδος τὸ γυναικεῖον.[52] In the previous chapter Mariamne is introduced as a sister of Philip. It is worth noting, that she is given the responsibility of keeping a register of all the countries where the apostles were doing mission work. This detail

---

[47] For a similar classification of the solutions, see King 1987, 66.

[48] E.g. Patterson 1993, 154-155, although he also sees other factors involved in the use of the expression.

[49] For these names, see Patterson 1993, 154.

[50] Later the term "male" was also used to express the excellence of women ascetics. Torjesen (1993, 211) refers to John Chrysostom who praised the ascetic Olympias thus: "Don't say 'woman' but 'what a man!' because this is a man, despite her physical appearance" (*Life of Olympias* 3).

[51] For the text, see Lipsius & Bonnet 1891-1903, II/2 36-90.

[52] Lipsius & Bonnet 1891-1903, II/2 37. Bovon (1984, 58) refers to another version of the text where the transformation of Mariamne into a man is described somewhat differently. To my knowledge, the manuscript is still unedited. Bovon's French translation of the text runs as follows: "Quant à toi, Mariamné, change de costume et d'apparance: dépouille tout ce qui, dans ton extérieur, rappelle la femme, la robe d'été que tu portes, ne laisse pas la frange de ton vêtement traîner par terre..."

appears in an unedited version of the writing.[53] While Jesus divided various places among the apostles her brother Philip became unhappy and cried because of the place allotted to him. Then Jesus turned to Mariamne and asked her to follow and to encourage him. The *Martyrdom of Philip* (107-148), narrates how the same Mariamne together with Bartholomew, travelled with Philip and proclaimed the gospel with a strong ascetic emphasis. The prominent role which Mariamne assumes within the circle of disciples makes it probable that she is to be identified with Mary Magdalene, although she has gained new legendary features and possibly also Mary of Bethany has been integrated into her person.[54] If this is so the *Acts of Philip* may provide the first witness to the interpretation that making Mary male in logion 114 refers to a concrete male impersonation. Be that as it may, it is at least clear that sometime in the second century "making oneself male" could have been understood very concretely. It is not impossible that logion 114 provides an early indication of this practice.

The second way to look at logion 114 is to interpret it in light of the Platonic myth of the androgyne (Plato, *Symposion* 189de), as it is reflected in the interpretations of the creation stories of Genesis. De Conick, for example, thinks that "becoming male" in logion 114 means the restoration of the androgynous prelapsarian man. "Since Eve was taken from Adam's side, so she must reenter him and become 'male' in order to return to the prelapsarian state of Adam before the gender division."[55] According to De Conick, "becoming male" of logion 114 is not in contradiction with "neither male nor female" of logion 22. Both of them speak about a return to the pristine state of the androgynous prelapsarian man. The only difference is that while in the case of logion 114 the

---

[53] See Bovon 1984, 58.

[54] In the *Acts of Philip* 94 Mariamne is linked together with Martha.

[55] De Conick 1996, 18; see also Lelyveld 1987, 142. Buckley (1985, 245-272) also thinks that "becoming male" is to be seen as a restoration of the lost unity reflected in Gen 2, but she suggests that this is not the ultimate goal for a woman. It is only the first stage of a salvific process which is followed by the "living spirit" stage which corresponds to the "living soul" in Gen. 2 (a similar interpretation is advocated by Arai 1993). It is difficult to find support in the text for Buckley's two stage model. "Making Mary male" and "becoming a living spirit resembling you males" cannot be but synonymous expressions describing in two different ways the same stage of development.

prelapsarian androgynous state is understood in terms of the situation when woman was still concealed in man (Gen 2), in logion 22 it is seen in light of the time before the gender differentiation had taken place in Gen 1,27. In both logia "salvation is based on returning to Adam's Pre-Fall state before the division of the sexes, and subsequently before the tasting of the forbidden fruit, sexual intercourse."[56]

The third solution represented with great erudition by Meyer tries to see logion 114 within the conceptual framework of the contemporary culture where "female" represents that which is earthly, sensual, imperfect, and passive, while "male" symbolizes that which is transcendent, chaste, perfect, and active.[57] The transformation of "female" into "male" is then to be understood as a movement from that which is physical and earthly to that which is spiritual and heavenly.

If the first explanation of the phrase "being made/making oneself male" interprets it from the perspective of its concrete application, the second and the third attempt to give a theological and sociocultural motivation for it. In fact, all explanations seem to be plausible in their own way. Common among them is the ascetic connotation of the phrase.

Yet, there is one point in De Conick's and Meyer's interpretations which requires a critical comment. Their insistence that logia 114 and 22 say essentially the same thing[58] does not do justice to the clear terminological difference between them. Even if the aim of both logia is to stress the importance of returning to a prelapsarian state or the necessity of reaching a state of asexuality, it must be emphasized that in logion 114 the goal is not achieved by the removal of gender differentiation but by the transformation of female into male.[59] Thus, in logion 114 salvation is defined by employing the patriarchal language patterns of the contemporary

---

[56] De Conick 1996, 18. Unlike De Conick, Buckley (1985, 270) does not think that the return to the lost unity of Adam in Gen 2 should necessarily be interpreted as a reference to sexual abstinence. For her, the *Gospel of Thomas* is not an ascetic document.

[57] Meyer (1985, 563-567) provides plentiful evidence for this kind of use of categories "male" and "female" in antiquity.

[58] De Conick 1996, 18-20; Meyer 1985, 567.

[59] This was emphasized by Vielhauer (1964, 298) and Rengstorf (1966, 565-566).

culture. It is important to realize that it is not only Peter's statement which displays this but also Jesus' response. Although advocating Mary's and all women's right to attain salvation in terms equal to their male colleagues within the circle of disciples and the kingdom, Jesus does it by using a language which devalues women. In the *Gospel of Mary* the same thing is expressed somewhat differently. There Jesus does not make women "male" but he makes both women and men "human beings (ⲣⲱⲙⲉ)" (9,20; cf. 18,16). Admittedly, salvation is even here defined in terms of male-oriented language. Yet, ⲣⲱⲙⲉ does not have the same exclusive character as ϩⲟⲟⲩⲧ in *Gos. Thom.* 114.

Gos. Thom. 114 comes terminologically close to those Valentinian and Naassene texts which view salvation as a transformation of "female" into "male" (*Exc. Theod.* 21,3; 79;[60] Heracleon, *Fr.* 5; Hipp., *Ref.* 5.8,44-45).[61] It is noteworthy that when the parallels speak about the transformation of "female" into "male" they mean everybody, both men and women. Men too are "female," if their life is controlled by cosmic powers. Whether this is true in the symbolic world of logion 114 as well, is difficult to say. It is only the position of women which is at stake in this logion.

The peculiar language of logion 114 raises the question of its relationship to the rest of the gospel. Besides, the contradiction between "being made/making oneself male" and "neither male nor female" (logion 22) is not the only feature which gives logion 114 a special position among *Thomas'* sayings. Logion 114 begins with a disciple addressing other disciples. This is a literary device not found anywhere else in the entire writing. It is also noteworthy that logion 113 seems to form a thematic inclusion with logion 3 and could thus be a natural ending of the collection. Based on

---

[60] As Vogt (1985, 434-435) has pointed out, Clement of Alexandria who has preserved the *Excerpta ex Theodoto* can himself in his own text use a similar expression when he describes a woman who has been liberated from fleshly concerns. In *Strom.* 6.100,3 he speaks about this kind of woman as follows: καὶ μή τι οὕτως μετατίθεται εἰς τὸν ἄνδρα ἡ γυνή, ἀθήλυντος ἐπ' ἴσης καὶ ἀνδρικὴ καὶ τελεία γενομένη.

[61] The phenomenon of "making a woman male" is also known from other religious traditions. Arai (1993, 376) refers to Mahâyâna-Buddhism which "developed a theory of the transformation of the female into male, whereby a woman too can become a Buddha." In the mystical Islamic tradition of Sufism it is also said that one can receive instruction from a woman, because a woman who has become male in the way of God is no longer a woman (for the reference, see Hallenberg & Perho 1992, 35).

these arguments, Davies has suggested that logion 114 is a later expansion of the gospel.[62] If this is accepted logion 114 may have been attached to the gospel fairly late in the second century. The fact that the phenomenon and the phrase "making oneself male" has very close, almost verbal parallels, on the one hand, in the second and third century apocryphal acts, and on the other, among the late second century Valentinian and Naassene texts speaks for a fairly late origin of the logion itself.

If the secondary character of logion 114 is accepted, the discussion of the role of Mary Magdalene and women in general is placed in a new context. While in logion 21 and 61 Mary Magdalene and Salome have a relatively visible role among the disciples as the ones who seek a deeper understanding of Jesus' teaching, in logion 114 Mary Magdalene becomes the object of an attempt to exclude her from the circle of Thomasine disciples altogether. This suggests that logion 114 has been added to the collection in a situation when the role of women in the religious life of the community has become a matter of debate for some reason. The one responsible for adding the logion to the gospel is speaking clearly on behalf of women. He/she does it by creating a saying in which Jesus speaks for Mary Magdalene against Peter. Yet the editor of the text is either so bound by his tradition or so alienated from earlier terminology of Thomasine traditions that he/she no longer uses the "neither male nor female" -language of logion 22 but resorts to employing a new expression of "making female male," which inevitably devalues women.

2.2.3 Conflict Over the Position of Mary Magdalene

One question remains: does the fact that Peter has been chosen to be the antagonist of Mary Magdalene tell us anything about the nature of the debate reflected in the text? Before any attempt to answer the question can be made Peter's view of Mary Magdalene and women in general has to be more carefully analyzed. In the first part of his statement Peter expresses his wish that Mary Magdalene leave the group he himself represents. The second part

---

[62] Davies 1983, 152-153.155 (cf. also Dart 1978, 324). He also presents some arguments with regard to the terminology used in logion 114 but these are not very convincing.

gives the reason: "Women are not worthy of life." The second part of Peter's comment as well as the last sentence of Jesus' reply show that Peter does not want to exclude Mary Magdalene and other women just from a group of privileged persons such as apostles, leaders, and teachers. It is a matter of a much more basic decision. Peter maintains that neither Mary Magdalene nor any other woman should have any part in salvation and the kingdom of heaven. Where in the world can one find such a narrow, discriminatory view of women? For example, if Peter is seen as a representative of a Christian majority view, as has been suggested,[63] where can this kind of conception of women be documented?

Certainly, Clement of Rome can write to his colleagues in Corinth: "Let us guide our women toward that which is good ... let them make manifest the moderation of their tongue through their silence" (*1 Clem.* 21,6-7).[64] Similarly, the author of the Pastorals writes his well-known words: "Let a woman learn in silence with all submissiveness. I permit no woman to teach or to have authority over men; she is to keep silent ... Woman will be saved through bearing children, if she continues in faith and love and holiness, with modesty" (1 Tim 2,11-12.15). Yet neither of these writers who clearly belong to the most candid advocates of patriarchal tendencies comes close to the total exclusion of women from a Christian context recommended by Peter in *Gos. Thom.* 114. The problem is that nowhere in early Christian literature does one find an equally negative view of women.

In light of these observations, one wonders whether Peter's comment was even meant to be an exact documentation of any contemporary Christian view of women. Was it simply an exaggeration which underlines once again the greatness of the disciples' misunderstanding and correspondingly the importance of Jesus' correction, as is often the case in the *Gospel of Thomas* (cf. e.g. 51; 52; 89; 99; 104)? Or if it was meant to reflect a contemporary conception of women, was it presented in such a way — either unintentionally or polemically — that the particular people holding this view would not necessarily have recognized themselves in it? If that is the case and Peter's comment somehow does mirror a contemporary view of women, there are at least two

---

[63] Schüngel 1994, 400.
[64] The translation is taken from Lightfoot (1976 [=1891], 23).

possibilities for understanding Peter. Either he can function as a caricature of a major ecclesiastical view with its clear subordination of women or he can be seen as a mischaracterized representative of a developing ascetic perspective in which male celibates view the presence of women as threatening.

Since the first alternative appears to be quite modern, especially when the language used in the answer of Jesus despite its non-subordinationist implication does devalue women, the second is more probable. That is, Peter could be regarded as an archetype, although somewhat misrepresented and exaggerated, of those early Christian ascetics who stated: "Pray in the place where there is no woman" (*Dial. Sav.* 144,16).[65] It is worth noting that one version of the *Acts of Philip* portrays Peter as a man who "fled from all places where there was a woman" (142).[66] Some other, strictly ascetic writings link Peter with traditions according to which he eliminates the sexual threat of the female presence by causing a young woman to die[67] or to become paralyzed.[68] In light of these observations, logion 114 could perhaps reflect a conflict between two different encratic positions, one emphasizing that an ascetic group should not include people of both sexes and thus implying that spiritually inferior women should be excluded, the other, favored by the writer of the logion, insisting that both male and female ascetics should have the same right to fulfill their ascetic ideal within the same community.

Regardless of whether the conflict in logion 114 was a mere literary device or whether it mirrored a real, although somewhat mischaracterized debate over the position of women, either between those representing a mainstream view of the subordination of women and those Gnostics opposing it or between those holding two different ascetic conceptions, it is clear at least how the position of women is seen in the text world of the saying. It is unequivocally the answer of Jesus which reveals this. Although patriarchal in its language, it gives Mary Magdalene and other

---

[65] For this text, see pp. 88-91.

[66] See Lipsius & Bonnet 1891-1903, II/2 81.

[67] So in the *Pseudo-Titus Epistle*; for the translation of the text, see Schneemelcher 1989, 52-70, esp. 54-55.

[68] So in the *Act of Peter*; for the translation of the text, see J.M. Robinson 1988, 529-531.

women an equal position vis-à-vis salvation compared to their male companions. Yet with regard to terminology, the transition from "neither male nor female" -language to "being made/making oneself male" -language cannot be seen as a positive development from the vantage point of the female audience.

CHAPTER THREE

MARY MAGDALENE
IN THE SOPHIA OF JESUS CHRIST

1. *Introductory Remarks*

The *Sophia of Jesus Christ* is a typical Gnostic[1] revelation dialogue[2] which describes a conversation between the Savior and his disciples either after the resurrection or during a reappearance following his ascension. The former is the case with the *Sophia of Jesus Christ* as its beginning evinces. The writing is preserved for us in two Coptic manuscripts.[3] In addition to the Coptic manuscripts, there is a small Greek fragment (P. Oxy. 1081)[4] which corresponds to *Soph. Jes. Chr.* III/4 97,16-99,12 and to *Soph. Jes. Chr.* BG 88,18-91,15.[5]

There is general agreement among scholars that the source for the *Sophia of Jesus Christ* is *Eugnostos*, a Gnostic or a proto-Gnostic writing[6] which appears in two versions in the Nag Ham-

---

[1] Especially in its concluding section, which has no parallel in *Eugnostos* (see below), the writing contains typical Gnostic features, such as the defect of the female, the figure of Yaldabaoth and the rescue operation of the light drops slumbering in the ignorance.

[2] For Gnostic revelation dialogues, see Perkins 1980.

[3] One is included in the Papyrus Berolinensis 8502 (= BG), which was discovered in Egypt and purchased for the Berlin Museum in 1896, but the Gnostic writings of which were not published until 1955 (Till 1955; Till's edition was revised by Schenke in 1972). The other is found in the third codex of the Nag Hammadi Library. The critical edition was prepared by Parrott in 1991.

[4] The most recent edition of the fragment appears in Parrott (1991, 209-216).

[5] In the following the references to the Nag Hammadi version are without further specification. The references to the Papyrus Berolinensis 8502 version are preceded by the capitals BG. Both versions stem from a common Greek *Vorlage*. Variations are due to different translations; see Parrott 1991, 16.

[6] Parrott (1991, 16) does not actually find in *Eugnostos* or rather in its sources (Parrott sees two separate sources in *Eugnostos*) anything distinctively Gnostic. He places the only clear reference to Gnostic ideology in an editorial part in III/3 85,8. Yet, he can characterize the

madi Library (III/3 and V/1).[7] *Eugnostos* is written in the form of a letter which the author of the *Sophia of Jesus Christ* has turned into a revelation dialogue by adding the frame material at the beginning and at the end (90,14-92,5; 114,8-119,18) and by introducing the interlocutors, the Savior and four of his disciples as well as a female follower, ⲘⲀⲢⲒⲀⲘ(ⲘⲎ),[8] into the body of the letter. At the same time an originally non-Christian *Eugnostos* has been Christianized.[9]

The purpose of the *Sophia of Jesus Christ* has been conceived in two ways. Krause maintains that the tractate serves as an attempt to convince non-Gnostic ecclesiastical Christians to accept that Christ taught Gnosticism.[10] Perkins, on the other hand, has proposed that the writer of the *Sophia of Jesus Christ* has produced the Christianized version of *Eugnostos* to convert non-Christian Gnostics to Christian Gnosticism.[11] Perkins' proposition has been forcefully advocated by Parrott.[12] Perkins and Parrott have pointed out that, in the material the author of the *Sophia of*

---

writing as proto-Gnostic since "it provided a theoretical basis for later developments that led to classic Gnosticism, as *SJC* (= the *Sophia of Jesus Christ*) shows." A similar conclusion is drawn by Sumney (1989, 178-181) although he does not date *Eugnostos* as early as Parrott. To be sure, in some of the proto-Gnostic features of the first source in *Eugnostos*, Parrott (1987, 78-82) sees the influence of a speculative type of Judaism which he can call early Sethianism.

[7] So Doresse 1948, 143-146.150-156; Krause 1964a, 215-223; Parrott 1971, 397-406; Tardieu 1984, 61; Sumney 1989, 172-181. Till (1955, 54) and Schenke (1962, 264-267) represent the opposite view, but their position has been convincingly contested by Krause (1964a, 215-223) and Parrott (1971, 397-406).

[8] The Nag Hammadi version of the *Sophia of Jesus Christ* employs the longer variant of the name (98,10; 114,9) while the shorter form is found in BG (90,1; 117,13).

[9] As to the non-Christian character of *Eugnostos*, Parrott (1992, 669) summarizes the present state of research: "Although various suggestions have been made about evidence of Christian influence in the composition of *Eugnostos* [Wilson 1968, 115-116; Tardieu 1984, 66], none has been convincing and *Eugnostos* is generally considered non-Christian, except for what appears to have been a late modification of the concluding prophecy in Codex III *Eugnostos*." See also Parrott 1991, 4.

[10] Krause 1964a, 223. The same thesis was suggested already by Doresse (1960, 198). Krause gives no other reasons for his claim except the general assumption that all the Christianized Gnostic texts served the propagation of Gnostic ideas among non-Gnostic Christians.

[11] Perkins 1971, 176-177; 1980, 98.

[12] Parrott 1991, 4-5.

Jesus Christ inserted into *Eugnostos*, the traditional Gnostic features do not receive very much attention whereas the role of Christ is treated very thoroughly. This suggests that the intended audience was already familiar with traditional Gnostic doctrines but needed to be instructed on the significance of Christ in Christian Gnostic soteriology. This raises an interesting question. If the readers of the *Sophia of Jesus Christ* were already acquainted with *Eugnostos*, how could they allow their most basic document to be presented to them in a largely revised form? Could not everybody see this as an attempted fraud? Parrott rejects this criticism, asserting that *Eugnostos* itself prepares its readers for a new version of this document by anticipating its revision: "[Now all] that has just been [said to you] I spoke in [such a way that] you might preserve it [all], until the word that need not be taught comes forth among you, and it will interpret these things to you in knowledge that is one and pure" (V/1 17,9-15).[13]

Perkins' and Parrott's thesis is more likely than Krause's. However, there is one problem with it. It is very rare in antiquity that an author tries to convert a group of people by using a religious tractate.[14] Therefore, it seems more probable that the *Sophia of Jesus Christ* is not primarily a missionary writing, but is addressed to a (former) non-Christian Gnostic community (or to a part of it) which is moving towards a Christian Gnostic re-interpretation of its basic beliefs. Thus, the writing serves the community by justifying its new self-identity. In this way, it becomes an aetiology of the community's new Christian Gnostic existence.

---

[13] Parrott has pointed out that at the end of *Eugnostos* III/3 (90,4-11) the anticipation of a Christian revealer is even more clearly stated. This redactional clarification was probably made when *Eugnostos* and the *Sophia of Jesus Christ* were combined.

[14] Perkins' and Parrott's thesis (and so also Krause's) presupposes that missionary activity was carried on by means of written documents. There is not, however, much evidence of that. The most notable example of a missionary writing, the *Letter to Flora,* shows that this was not completely unusual. Yet in case of the *Letter to Flora,* the text is addressed to an individual, whereas the *Sophia of Jesus Christ* is clearly meant to be read by many readers, perhaps even by a community (118,6-8).

2. Date and Provenance

The *Sophia of Jesus Christ* furnishes no references to datable events. A *terminus ad quem* is provided by the Greek papyrus fragment (P. Oxy 1081) which is dated early in the fourth century.[15] There are, however, some features in the contents of the writing which suggest that the actual date of its composition must be much earlier than the extant manuscripts. Till has argued that although the *Sophia of Jesus Christ* no longer displays the same philosophical outlook as the *Apocryphon of John* and is thus later, it must be dated earlier than *Pistis Sophia* which, with its abstruse and excessive descriptions of transmundane beings and worlds, represents a late decadent stage of mythological gnosis that has hardly any connection with its philosophical roots found in the *Apocryphon of John*.[16] Since Till dates the *Apocryphon of John* in the middle of the second century and *Pistis Sophia* in the middle of the third, the *Sophia of Jesus Christ* was, according to him, written sometime between these two periods.[17]

Parrott wants to push the date of the *Sophia of Jesus Christ* earlier. Because the writing does not reveal any traces of the struggle between the ecclesiastical and Gnostic Christians and it lacks, in a conspicuous way, all the influence of the great Gnostic systems of the late second century, it must have been composed already in the first or in the early second century.[18] In addition, Parrott thinks that, if the *Sophia of Jesus Christ* was produced to

---

[15] Puech 1950, 98 n. 2. The cartonnage which have been used to support the leather cover of the fifth codex of the Nag Hammadi Library contains some material which can be dated in the late third or early fourth century (see Barns *et al.* 1981, 3). The cartonnage of the codex III is completely lost however (J.M. Robinson 1972-1984, Cartonnage: IX). Papyrus Berolinensis is dated in the fifth century (Till 1955, 7).

[16] Till 1949, 245-249; 1955, 56.

[17] Till 1949, 248-249. Tardieu (1984, 60-62) also thinks that the *Apocryphon of John* is earlier than the *Sophia of Jesus Christ*. He claims that the similarities between the two must be explained by positing the former as the source for the latter. Since he assumes that the final redaction of the *Apocryphon of John* took place at the beginning of the third century and since he holds that the *Sophia of Jesus Christ* no longer represents the creative period of Gnosticism but is a result of a plagiarizing tendency he dates the *Sophia of Jesus Christ* in the first half of the third century.

[18] Parrott 1991, 6.

persuade non-Christian Gnostics to accept Christian Gnosticism, this itself suggests an early date, "especially in view of the fact that it seems to be assumed that the intended audience knows little or nothing about Christ."[19]

The early dating of the *Sophia of Jesus Christ* is congruous with that of *Eugnostos*. Even if one would not go as far as Parrott who thinks that *Eugnostos* was written already in the first pre-Christian century,[20] it is evident that it represents an initial stage of Gnostic cosmological speculation. It is not yet influenced by the radical rejection of the world, a revolt against the Jewish God or Hebrew scriptures, and possibly not by the Fall of Sophia, either.[21] Even though all this is already included in the *Sophia of Jesus Christ*, the ignorance its author displays of the great second century Gnostic systems and the developing conflict between Gnostic and ecclesiastical Christians speaks for a date in the early part of the second century. The first century date is not likely since the writing seems to presuppose both the finished version of the Gospel of Matthew and possibly also that of the Gospel of John.[22]

---

[19] Parrott 1991, 5.

[20] Parrott 1991, 5. His main argument for this early dating of *Eugnostos* is the reference to "all the philosophers" (III/3 70,15) against whom the author of the text directs his polemic. From the description of their views, Parrott concludes that the philosophers can be identified as Stoic, Epicurean, and the theoreticians of Babylonian astrology. On the basis of this observation, he states: "The latest time when these could be thought of as 'all the philosophers' was probably the first century B.C.E." The problem with Parrott's argumentation is that he places too great an emphasis on the word "all." There is no compelling reason to assume that the writer of *Eugnostos* wanted to encompass, objectively speaking, all the possible contemporary philosophers and their views in his description but more probably those which were known to him and important for his argument.

[21] Sumney 1989, 173-177; see also Parrott (1991, 16) who says that the sources of *Eugnostos* he reconstructs cannot be considered classically Gnostic, but only proto-Gnostic. The question of the Fall of Sophia in *Eugnostos* is under debate. Good (1987, 26-29) and Sumney (1989, 176-177) insist that *Eugnostos* 85,8-9 should not be understood as a reference to the Fall of Sophia. Parrott (1991, 16) has the opposite view but even he sees the passage as a redactional insertion of a later Gnostic editor.

[22] See Tuckett 1986, 32-35. Tuckett has tried to show that the author of the *Sophia of Jesus Christ* is dependent on the Gospel of Luke as well. However, the allusions to the Gospel of Luke are so vague that no real case for any sort of dependence between it and the *Sophia of Jesus Christ* can be presented.

The depiction of the Savior's appearance in *Soph. Jes. Christ* 90,14-91,24 and the reference to the perpetual presence of the Savior with his disciples in 101,13-15 can hardly have been written without the knowledge of Matt 28,16-20, although its use may have been indirect.[23] The second part of the Savior's greeting in 91,20-23 (ϯΡΗΝΗ ЄΤЄ ΤⲰЄΙ ΤЄ ϯϯ ⲘⲘΟⲤ "my peace I give to you") is so peculiarly Johannine (see John 14,27; cf. also 16,33)[24] that its occurrence in the *Sophia of Jesus Christ* must be taken as an indication of Johannine influence on its author. Hence, it would not be until the second century that the *Sophia of Jesus Christ* was composed.[25]

Like most Gnostic writings, *Eugnostos* and the *Sophia of Jesus Christ* yield very few indications of their place of composition. However, there is one interesting detail in *Eugnostos* which provides a basis for attempting to determine their provenance. Parrott has called attention to the use of a 360-day year in *Eugnostos* (III/3 84,4-5). In his opinion, this reference is credible only in Egypt, because "from ancient times the Egyptians had calculated the year as having 360 days, divided into twelve months of thirty

---

[23] A strange combination of the Mount of Olives and the Mount of Galilee (*Soph. Jes. Christ* 91,20) seems to suggest that use of Matt 28,16-20 has been indirect, perhaps based on an oral tradition resultant from the finished version of the Gospel of Matthew. Luttikhuizen (1988, 164-166) has also argued against direct dependence of the *Sophia of Jesus Christ* on the Gospel of Matthew and assumes that the author of the *Sophia of Jesus Christ* was familiar with these Matthean traditions through earlier Gnostic traditions or revelation texts.

[24] εἰρήνη ὑμῖν/σοι is a common traditional Jewish or Christian greeting or farewell formula (see e.g. Judg 6,23; 1 Chr 12,18; Tob 12,17; Luke 24,36; Phil 1,2) but the phrase "my peace I give to you" appears, to my knowledge, nowhere else in Jewish or Christian literature before the Gospel of John (Luke 10,6/Matt 10,13 are no parallels to John 14,27 for there εἰρήνη stands for the act of greeting; the first real parallel is *Gos. Mary* 8,14-15); so also Schulz 1983, 192-193. The fact that it begins a clear interpretative expansion of a traditional greeting formula also points to its special Johannine character.

[25] It is argued in many recent Johannine studies that the final version of the Gospel of John presupposes the Synoptic gospels; see e.g. Dunderberg 1994. If this is true the Gospel of John can hardly be dated earlier than to 100 CE. As is well known the *terminus ad quem* is provided by P[52] which is traditionally dated in the second quarter of the second century although some scholars have recently claimed that it was copied around 170 (see Dunderberg 1994, 25).

days each, plus five epagomenal days."[26] Parrott correctly describes the Egyptian calendrical data. The major problem in his
argumentation is whether the occurrence of a 360-day year in a
writing must necessarily point to an Egyptian origin. This does not
seem to be the case. A 360-day year appears also in *A Valentinian
Exposition* (30,34-38) and it is also clearly presupposed in Irenaeus' description of the Marcosians (*Adv. haer.* 1.17,1).[27]

Although Valentinians certainly had connections with Egypt
neither *A Valentinian Exposition* nor the activities of Marcus are
to be placed in Egypt.[28] In addition, even if the 360-day year could
be taken as an indicator of the Egyptian origin of *Eugnostos* the
same cannot automatically be said of the *Sophia of Jesus Christ*.[29]
Namely, the very text which speaks of a 360-day year has been
omitted in the *Sophia of Jesus Christ*. This could even be interpreted to suggest a writing in a cultural context where a 360-day
year no longer makes sense, as was the case in all areas where the
Roman Julian calendar became dominant.[30] In any case, whatever
weight one can lay on the calendrical data in determining the
provenance of *Eugnostos*, it provides no help when one tries to
decide where the *Sophia of Jesus Christ* was written.

Another feature which Parrott uses to locate *Eugnostos* in
Egypt is the similarity between "a major Egyptian conception of
the deities of the *Urzeit* and the pattern of *Urzeit* deities...behind
the present text of *Eugnostos*."[31] The evidence Parrott brings forth
for his claim is not unassailable[32] but even if one assumes that

---

[26] Parrott 1991, 7.

[27] For the significance of the calendrical data in Gnostic literature,
see Przybylski 1980, 56-70.

[28] Pagels (1990, 105) thinks that *A Valentinian Exposition* "may be
placed in the milieu of one of the western, Italic traditions of Valentinian
theology". As is well known Marcus, on the other hand, was active in
Asia Minor and in Gaul when Irenaeus came to know him (*Adv. haer.*
1.13,7).

[29] Contra Parrott 1991, 7.

[30] This is in fact suggested by Przybylski 1980, 65-66.

[31] Parrott 1987, 82.

[32] Parrott (1987, 82-88; 1991, 9-16) thinks that in the first part of
Eugnostos (III/3 70,1-85,9), which he sees to be a separate source, there
emerge two distinctive patterns of the deities of the transcendental world.
In his view, both of them resemble an Egyptian conception according to
which there is one initial all-encompassing divinity who creates another
separate non-androgynous deity who produces four other divine beings

Parrott's thesis proves the Egyptian origin of *Eugnostos* this still does not help locate the *Sophia of Jesus Christ*. The text which speaks about the beings of the transcendental world in *Eugnostos* (III/3 71,13-83,2) has been revised in such a way that it no longer has any clear connection with the Egyptian pantheon. Among other things, the section which, in Parrott's opinion, best reflects the Egyptian conception of the deities of the *Urzeit* (III/3 82,7-83,2) has been left out altogether! The question of the provenance of the *Sophia of Jesus Christ* will be taken up again after the examination of the Mary Magdalene passages.

3. *Mary Magdalene as an Interlocutor of the Savior*

The name Mary appears twice in the *Sophia of Jesus Christ* (98,10; 114,9; BG 90,1; 117,13). In both instances she poses a question to the Savior. In neither of these passages is Mary introduced as Magdalene. However, this identification is most likely. In Gnostic revelation dialogues there are only two Maries who present questions to the Savior, Mary, the mother of Jesus, and Mary Magdalene. Since in all those Coptic texts where Mary is explicitly defined as the (virgin) mother of Jesus the name is without exception spelled ΜΑΡΙΑ[33] while the form of the name

---

each of whom have a single female consort. The problem with Parrott's thesis is that neither of the patterns in *Eugnostos* is really convergent with the Egyptian pattern. The first (III/3 71,13-82,6) contains only three androgynous deities, in the second all six deities are androgynous (III/3 82,7-83,2). Therefore, he has to assume that the first presentation of the divine beings has undergone a redaction by which a Jewish Sethian speculation of Gen 1-5 has been imposed on the original Egyptian pattern; and in the second one, which he regards as the more original of the two, the female consorts of the first two absolute divine beings remain unexplained.

[33] The mother of Jesus appears in the following Coptic texts of Gnostic origin: *Gos. Phil.* 55,23.27; 59,7.10.11; *2 Apoc. Jas.* 44,[22]; *Testim. Truth* 45,11; *PS* 13,18; 116,21.25.26; 117,7.21; 120,14.19.21; 123,5.6; 124,6.14.19; 125,15. Even in the Greek texts of the Church Fathers this spelling of the name is usual (see e.g. Iren., *Adv. haer.* 1.15,3; Hipp., *Ref.* 5.6,7; 5.26,29; 6.35,3-4; 6.35,7; 6.36,3-4; 6.51,1; 7.26,8; 7.33,1; 8.9,2; 10.14,9; 10.15,6; 10.16,2; 10.21,2; Epiph., *Pan.* 31.7,4). E.g. Hippolytos employs only once the spelling Μαριάμ when he refers to the views of the so-called Docetists (*Ref.* 8.10,6) but even there he is not quoting any source. But in all the other 19 references to Mary, the mother of Jesus, he, too, uses the spelling Μαρία. Only in one

used of Mary Magdalene is almost always ⲘⲀⲢⲓ(ⲁ)ⲀⲘ(ⲘⲎ),[34] it is most probable that ⲘⲀⲢⲓⲀⲀⲘ(ⲘⲎ) in the *Sophia of Jesus Christ* is Magdalene.

The dialogue described in the *Sophia of Jesus Christ* is introduced by a post-resurrection appearance story. The text begins by presenting the disciples of the Savior, the twelve men and the seven women,[35] who are gathered on a mountain located in Galilee and called "Divination and Joy." Before the disciples see the Savior they are said to be perplexed about "the underlying reality of the universe and the plan and the holy providence and the power of the authorities and about everything that the Savior is doing with them in the secret" (91,3-9). Then the Savior appears to them "not in his previous form, but in the invisible spirit" (91,10-11). As in most appearance stories the sight prompts amazement and fear among the disciples but the Savior calms them and asks them why they are so perplexed. Thus, the dialogue proper is initiated. It ends with a description of the great joy which the answers of the Savior have called forth in the disciples who become preachers of the gospel of God, the eternal Father, imperishable forever (BG 127,2-10).

The purpose of the dialogue is made clear by its framework. At the beginning the disciples are puzzled precisely by those questions to which a Gnostic message is supposed to respond. In the *Sophia of Jesus Christ* Gnostic revelation is supplied by the answers of the Risen Jesus, viz., the Savior. The material of *Eugnostos* is in some places supplemented by redactional sections which have an explicit Gnostic profile, such as *Soph. Jes. Christ* 106,24-

---

Greek manuscript of the *Protevangelium of James* (Papyrus Bodmer 5) the name of the mother of Jesus is spelled μαριάμμη (see Bovon 1984, 61 n. 47).

[34] The only exceptions are the *Gospel of Philip* and *Pistis Sophia I-III*. However, in the *Gospel of Philip* the mention of the three Maries (59,6-11) already presupposes the use of the same form of the name. Perhaps for this reason, Magdalene is called ⲘⲀⲢⲓⲀ in 63,32-34 as well. In *Pistis Sophia I-III* Mary Magdalene is most often called ⲘⲀⲢⲓⲀ or ⲘⲀⲢⲓⲀ ⲦⲘⲀⲄⲆⲀⲗⲏⲚⲎ but the name ⲘⲀⲢⲓⲀⲀⲘ, too, appears more than 20 times and ⲘⲀⲢⲓⲀⲀⲘⲘⲎ once as well (346,9). It is significant that in *PS I-III* the name Mary is never spelled ⲘⲀⲢⲓⲀⲀⲘ(ⲘⲎ) in those instances where it indisputably refers to the mother of Jesus.

[35] According to the Coptic text, the seven women are also said to be disciples of the Savior. Namely, both the twelve disciples and the seven women are the subject of the verb ⲚⲈⲢⲉ...ⲘⲀⲐⲎⲦⲉⲩⲉ (90,16-18).

108,16 as well as the last answer of the Savior (BG 118,1-
126,16).³⁶ The conclusion of the writing shows that the Gnostic
revelation of the Savior has found fertile soil among the disciples
who willingly receive the new gospel and become its proclaimers.
The author of the writing intends to say no more and no less than
that the post-resurrection encounter between the Risen Savior and
his disciples leads the disciples to convert to Christian Gnosticism.
This implies that the most genuine Gnostic teaching derives from
the Risen Jesus transmitted through the preaching of his disci-
ples.³⁷

4. Mary Magdalene and the Philip Group

The dialogue proper contains twelve questions put to the Savior
and twelve answers given by him. In spite of the introductory
scene, where it is said that the dialogue will take place between
the Savior and his twelve disciples as well as his seven female
followers (90,16-18), only some of the disciples are actively
involved in the conversation. Certainly, two questions are attributed to the entire group of disciples (105,3-4; 106,9; BG 100,3-4;
102,7-8) and one to the Holy Apostles (112,19-20; BG 114,12-13)
but the only disciples who pose questions so that their names are
mentioned are Philip, Matthew, Thomas, Mary Magdalene, and
Bartholomew. Like Mary, Philip (92,4; 95,19; BG 79,18-19; 86,6),
Matthew (94,1; 100,17; BG 82,19-20; 93,13), and Thomas (96,14;
108,17; BG 87,8; 106,11) put two questions each to the Savior
whereas Bartholomew appears only once as a questioner (103,22;
BG 98,8). Why do only five of the nineteen present questions?

The text does not give any direct answer to this question. All
the persons asking questions are introduced without any comment
whatsoever. Nor do the reactions of the Savior, if there are any,
reveal anything about the particular questioners. His comments are
always directed to the whole group of interlocutors. In 97,23-24,
in the midst of the answer to the inquiry of Matthew, the Savior

---

³⁶ Both sections refer to Yaldabaoth and his world of forgetfulness
(106,24-107,11; BG 119,1-120,3).
³⁷ Perkins (1980, 97) states: "In connection with the setting of the
work, the questions (of the disciples) assure the reader that true apostolic
preaching is the source of gnosis."

states: "I have addressed those who are awake." In response to
Thomas he can even give praise to the quality of the question
(108,19-23) but, again, it is addressed to all who participate in the
discussion. In fact, the interlocutors mentioned by name do not
seem to be very important as individuals but only as representatives of a larger whole. When the text describes the result of the
dialogue it is obvious that *all* nineteen disciples, not only the five
mentioned by name, have received the Gnostic instruction of the
Savior and do become the proclaimers of the new Gnostic gospel
(BG 127,2-10). With this observation, we return to our earlier
question but modify it somewhat: why were just the five questioners mentioned by name chosen to represent the whole group? And
why was Mary Magdalene one of them?

Parrott has developed an interesting thesis about the five questioners in the *Sophia of Jesus Christ*.[38] He claims that the author
of the text is dependent on the list of disciples in the Gospel of
Mark (3,16-19) and the other Synoptics (Matt 10,2-4; Luke 6,14-
16). In that list Philip, Bartholomew, Matthew, and Thomas constitute the second group of four after Peter, James, John, and
Andrew. Wanting to introduce his readers to Christian Gnosticism,
the writer of the *Sophia of Jesus Christ* selected the Philip group
to represent the disciples of the Savior in the dialogue, the purpose
of which is to highlight the position of Christ as the new revealer
of the saving knowledge and as the victor over the sinister powers
of the world. This choice is motivated by the fact that the first
four of the synoptic list of disciples, the Peter group, were already
so closely associated with a Judaistic, particularistic understanding
of Christ that they could not be used to introduce a more univer-
salistic, Gnostic interpretation of Christ which the author of the
Sophia of Jesus Christ aspired to present in his writing. In other
words, the Philip group, with the addition of Mary Magdalene,
was chosen to stand for the Gnostic disciples.

Seeking to support his thesis, Parrott examines all the relevant
revelation dialogues in order to show that the same distinction he
finds between the Peter and the Philip group in the *Sophia of
Jesus Christ* also exists in other writings.[39] After examining both
Gnostic and non-Gnostic tractates he concludes that early in the

---

[38] See Parrott 1986, 193-219.
[39] Parrott 1986, 203-213.

Christian Gnostic movement a group of disciples led by Philip "was chosen to be the bearers of the distinctive Christian-gnostic message, while at the same time another group was identified with the orthodox position."[40] At the beginning this division did not serve polemical purposes (e.g. in the *Sophia of Jesus Christ,* in his view) but later the Gnostic authors began to use the Peter group in the struggle against their non-Gnostic opponents. Hence, "in the gnostic revelation dialogues, Peter, Andrew, James, and John, at one time or another, are seen as being secretly gnostic, in an inferior position in relation to the gnostic disciples, as opposed to the active role of the female (gnostic) disciples of Jesus, or as converting to Gnosticism."[41] According to Parrott, the *Letter of Peter to Philip* is of special significance for his thesis since that writing speaks of the Peter group and the Philip group even if the members of neither of these groups are explicitly introduced (132,12-15; 133,12-13). While both the Peter and the Philip groups are portrayed as Gnostic, the Gnostic character of the Peter group, in Parrott's view, serves only as anti-ecclesiastical polemic. The Peter group itself is seen only as secretly Gnostic.[42]

The problem with Parrott's thesis is that he exaggerates the consistency with which the two groups of disciples are treated in the second century Gnostic and ecclesiastical revelation dialogues. As he himself observes, the Philip group is also included in the list of disciples in the ecclesiastical, anti-Gnostic *Epistula Aposto- lorum.*[43] And even if this is due to the desire of the ecclesiastical author to emphasize the totality of the apostolic witness, neverthe- less, it does show that the Philip group is not merely adopted by the Gnostics. Besides, the way Jesus' disciples are portrayed by other second century Christian writers also speaks against a clear- cut distinction between the ecclesiastical Peter and the Gnostic Philip group. In my view, already Papias' statement in which he refers to Andrew, Peter, Philip, Thomas, James, John, and Mat- thew, on an equal footing, as his authorities for the teachings of Jesus, undermines Parrott's claim (Eus., *Hist. eccl.* 3.39,4). More- over, Parrott fails to explain why those Gnostic texts where Peter

---

[40] Parrott 1986, 218.
[41] Parrott 1986, 218.
[42] Parrott 1986, 207-210.
[43] Parrott 1986, 210-211.

or another member of his group converts to Gnosticism or is seen
to be secretly Gnostic (e.g. *Ap. John.; Apoc. Pet.; Ep. Pet. Phil.*)
must be understood solely as expressions of anti-ecclesiastical
polemic and why they cannot demonstrate that a Gnostic group,
too, can appeal to the authority of Peter[44] or another member of
the Peter group (see e.g. *Ap. John* II/1 32,1-5). In addition, in
some Gnostic texts there is no doubt that a member of the Peter
group appears to be a Gnostic authority at least as prominent as
some members of the Philip group. For example, in *PS I-III* Jesus
says to his disciples: "I said to you once: 'In the place where I
will be, there will also be with me my twelve servers.' But Maria
Magdalene and John the Virgin will be superior to all my disciples" (232,24-233,2).[45]

With regard to the problematic character of Parrott's thesis, the
figure of Bartholomew is especially instructive. Among Gnostic
revelation dialogues he appears only in *Pistis Sophia IV* but he is
mentioned in two non-Gnostic revelation dialogues, *Epistula
Apostolorum* and the *Questions of Bartholomew*, the former of
which is even anti-Gnostic. In the latter he appears to be the
principal questioner. Parrott thinks that Bartholomew is used in
these non-Gnostic texts in a polemical way in the sense that his
being a "Gnostic" disciple is adopted by ecclesiastical authors to
show that "Gnostic" disciples, too, were in reality ecclesiastical
Christians.[46] However, there is nothing in those texts which would
confirm that suggestion. Whatever interpretation one gives to the
appearance of Bartholomew in *Epistula Apostolorum* and in the
Questions of Bartholomew, in the *Sophia of Jesus Christ* his
behavior does not diverge from that of his better known Gnostic
colleagues. Probably all this only shows that the distinction between the "ecclesiastical" and "Gnostic" disciples was not at all
unambiguous in the second and third century. In various groups

---

[44] For a Gnostic Peter, see Koschorke 1978, 27-35; Perkins 1980,
113-125; T.V. Smith 1985, 117-134. Parrott's attempts to deny that the
Basilidians claim to derive their teachings from a secret tradition of Peter
transmitted through Glaucias are also not very convincing (1986, 216-
217).

[45] Parrott (1986, 205) himself admits that here John "should probably
be included among the gnostic disciples."

[46] Parrott 1986, 211.

and geographical areas some disciples of Jesus like Bartholomew and Peter may have been conceived in different ways.

However, for the present consideration of the *Sophia of Jesus Christ*, the valid and important point in Parrott's analysis is the observation that the Philip group, or at least Philip, Matthew, and Thomas, seem to be dominant figures in some Gnostic revelation dialogues (*Thom. Cont & Dial. Sav:* Judas (Thomas), Matthew;[47] *Gos. Mary:* Levi (Matthew?); *PS I-III:* Philip, Thomas, and Matthew [71,18-23; 72,11-20]).[48] It is particularly significant that *Pistis Sophia I-III* is familiar with a tradition according to which these three disciples are given the task of recording all the words the Savior says and the things he does.[49] For the consideration of Mary Magdalene, it is important that apart from the *Book of Thomas the Contender* she also appears in the same Gnostic revelation dialogues with a visible role. This is well in line with the tendency adopted in the *Sophia of Jesus Christ*. We may conclude that in some, although not in all, Gnostic writings, Gnostic conviction (or conversion to Gnosticism) was more easily attached to Philip, Matthew, Thomas, and Mary Magdalene than to the members of the Peter group. This detail constitutes an important link between these particular writings. It is, however, too precarious to try to establish a case for a genetic theological or sociological connection between them on the basis of this single point alone. However, since apart from the *Book of Thomas the Contender* all the other writings of this group come under scrutiny in the present study, the question of their relatedness will be assessed again with some further questions in mind.

Whatever the fact that the authors of these Gnostic revelation dialogues have chosen a member or members of the Philip group and Mary Magdalene to represent the Gnostic disciples says about

---

[47] In the *Book of Thomas the Contender* ΜΑΘΑΙΑC in 138,2-3 could also be Matthias whose writings were known to church fathers (for references, see Puech & Blatz 1987, 306-309).

[48] It is interesting that Heracleon refers to the same group, viz., Matthew, Philip, Thomas, (and Levi), when he speaks of those disciples who have confessed their faith in acts and works which correspond to their faith but not in public by means of martyrdom (Clem. Al., *Strom.* 4.71,3-4).

[49] It is worth noting, however, that in *Pistis Sophia I-III* also other disciples, including Peter and John, represent the Gnostic standpoint. For this, see the chapter "Mary Magdalene in Pistis Sophia."

the precise relationship between these writings, it is not self-evident that the reasons for the choice are fully identical. It is best to
consider the motives of each writer separately. What, then, were
the motives of the author of the *Sophia of Jesus Christ*? If it is
true that the *Sophia of Jesus Christ* was written to establish the
new Christian self-identity of the former non-Christian Gnostics,
the most likely reason why only the Philip group and Mary Magdalene were mentioned by name is that in the context where
Eugnostos was read they were known to be disciples associated
with a Gnostic version of Christianity. So, the writer of the *Sophia
of Jesus Christ* made use of a tradition known to his readers.

It is of course possible, as Parrott also suggests,[50] that the
Sophia of Jesus Christ was written in the period when the Philip
group was not yet known to represent a Gnostic Christianity. In
that case they were chosen only because the more renowned
apostles, such as Peter, Andrew, and the Zebedees, were too
closely linked with ecclesiastical Christianity, at least in this
particular area. Even if the readers of *Eugnostos* were not necessarily fully aware of all Christian teachings, in general, and ecclesiastical emphases, in particular, they most likely knew the names
of the main religious heroes of non-Gnostic ecclesiastical Christianity. Peter, Andrew, and the Zebedees could no longer be introduced as the representatives of the Gnostic version of Christian
faith but the lesser known Philip group could. If this is the case it
is the author of the *Sophia of Jesus Christ* who gives the initial
impetus to the Gnostic career of the Philip group. This suits the
early second century dating of the writing. The Gnostic Philip
group is then adopted by some later Gnostic revelation dialogues
— whether this is a result of a direct dependence on the *Sophia of
Jesus Christ* or not, need not be decided here. Whether the tradition of the Philip group has in some stage of its use served polemical purposes remains open for discussion. It is most likely, however, that the author of the *Sophia of Jesus Christ* created a group
of Gnostic disciples merely for pragmatic reasons.

---

[50] Parrott 1986, 202.

5. *The Gnostic Mary Magdalene*

If the Gnostic Philip group is an invention of the author of the *Sophia of Jesus Christ* we have to ask what its implications are for our understanding of the Gnostic Mary Magdalene. Does the Gnostic Mary Magdalene derive from the author as well? There is one fact which seems to speak against this assumption. Compared with other members of the Philip group, Mary Magdalene, apart from being a Gnostic disciple, has another special function in the *Sophia of Jesus Christ*. Clearly, she also represents the seven Gnostic women (*Soph. Jes. Chr.* 90,17-18). Yet the group of seven female disciples is probably not a creation of the author of the *Sophia of Jesus Christ*. If the reconstruction of *1 Apoc. Jas.* 38,16 suggested by Schenke is correct, as is most probable, the idea of seven female disciples is also found in that writing.[51]

In the *First Apocalypse of James* the seven women are known, in the same way as in the *Sophia of Jesus Christ*, i.e., as disciples of Jesus. However, in the *First Apocalypse of James* they are not linked with the twelve disciples. In fact, the seven women are distinguished from the twelve and are depicted positively as persons being "strong by a perception which is in them" (38,22-23), whereas the twelve seem to be less advanced spiritually and in need of a deeper instruction, to say the least.[52] Since the relationship of the seven female followers of Jesus to his male disciples is described differently in the *Sophia of Jesus Christ* and in the *First Apocalypse of James*, and since no other special theological or thematic connections between the two exist, the idea of seven

---

[51] The reconstruction is found in Schenke 1966, 29. Schoedel (1979, 94-95) has the same though he gives credit for it to G.M. Browne. According to these authors, lines 38,16-18 read as follows: ⲧϣⲓⲛⲉ ⲙ̄ⲙⲟⲕ ⲉⲣ[ⲟϥ] ⲧ[ⲥⲁϣ]ϥⲉ ⲛ̄ⲥϩⲓⲙⲉ ⲛⲓⲙ ⲛⲉ ⲛ̄ⲧⲁⲩ[ⲣ̄ ⲙⲁ]ⲑⲏⲧⲏⲥ ⲛⲁⲕ. Neither Schenke nor Schoedel spell out any arguments for their view. Still this reconstruction proves most likely for the following reasons: First, the attribute of the word ⲥϩⲓⲙⲉ at the end of line 16 cannot actually be anything but a number. If it were some other attribute, the copula of the nominal clause as well as the pronominal suffix of the subsequent relative converter would not be in the plural but in the singular following the grammatical number of the main word ⲥϩⲓⲙⲉ and the demonstrative article attached to it. Second, the only possible number which fills the lacuna is the feminine form of the number seven (ⲥⲁϣϥⲉ).

[52] For the relationship of Mary Magdalene and the other women to the twelve in the *First Apocalypse of James*, see pp. 137-143.

women seems to derive from a common tradition earlier than either writing.⁵³ Both of these writers have then used the tradition in their own way. In addition, in both cases Mary Magdalene is only secondarily brought together with the seven women. In fact, the author of the *First Apocalypse of James* knows another tradition of Gnostic female followers of Jesus according to which there were four in number and one of them was Mary Magdalene (*1 Apoc. Jas.* 40,22-26).⁵⁴ This supports a suggestion that the tradition of the Gnostic Mary Magdalene antedates both the *First Apocalypse of James* and the *Sophia of Jesus Christ*.

To summarize the previous discussion, in the *Sophia of Jesus Christ* Mary Magdalene is portrayed as a female disciple of Jesus who, during a post-resurrection dialogue between him and his disciples, becomes convinced of his special Gnostic revelation. Together with Philip, Thomas, Matthew, and Bartholomew, she is selected to represent Gnostic converts since probably both the writer of the text as well as the readers are aware of a tradition according to which she was a Gnostic disciple. Thus, Mary Magdalene is made to represent seven Gnostic women who were known to accompany Jesus together with his twelve disciples. It is worth noting that the information the author of the *Sophia of Jesus Christ* gives the readers about Mary Magdalene is very scarce. It is of course possible that the author did not know anything more. But it is equally clear that neither did he/she feel it necessary to tell more, neither about Mary Magdalene nor about any other disciple mentioned by name. The main goal was to show that the most genuine form of Gnosticism was the Christian one taught by the Risen Jesus and transmitted through the preaching of his disciples, especially by the Philip group, to use the term coined by Parrott, and by Mary Magdalene.

In light of the visible role Mary Magdalene assumes in the *Sophia of Jesus Christ* both as an authoritative receiver and transmitter of the Gnostic message, the last answer of Jesus to his disciples, paradoxically given to a question posed by Mary herself,

---

⁵³ Since the *Sophia of Jesus Christ* and the *First Apocalypse of James* otherwise reveal no signs of dependence on each other, the fact that the former is dated some decades, perhaps even half a century earlier than the latter has no importance.

⁵⁴ For this, see the section "Mary Magdalene in the First Apocalypse of James."

is quite surprising. In that reply Jesus calls the future Gnostic Christians, who are going to emerge as a result of his disciples' preaching, a "male multitude" (BG 124,14-16). Maleness is in obvious contrast to femaleness, which is the source of deficiency (118,13-18; cf. BG 117,18-119,1). Salvation is also described as knowing "the words of the masculine Light" (108,4). Thus, the author of the *Sophia of Jesus Christ* adopts the pattern of gendered language typical of Mediterranean culture, in which the male represents that which is perfect, powerful, and transcendent and the female what is incomplete, weak, and mundane.[55] The same dichotomy of male and female gender imagery appeared already in *Gos. Thom.* 114, and, as will be shown later, it will also be met in the *Dialogue of the Savior* and the *First Apocalypse of James*. Just as in the *Dialogue of the Savior* (see below) and probably also in *Gos. Thom.* 114, maleness is connected with the ideal of sexual asceticism in the *Sophia of Jesus Christ*. Jesus' disciples are urged to remove themselves from "the unclean rubbing that is from the fearful fire" (108,11-13). No doubt, disengagement from the sexual passion is demanded.[56]

What impact could the apparent contradiction between the visible role granted to Mary Magdalene and the pejorative use of feminine gender language have on the first readers of the *Sophia of Jesus Christ*, especially on women? Since the same tension is found in the *Dialogue of the Savior* and in the *First Apocalypse of James* we shall return to this question in connection with the chapters dealing with these writings.

Before leaving the treatment of Mary Magdalene in the *Sophia of Jesus Christ* we return to the question of the writing's provenance. The examination of Mary Magdalene's role in the writing

---

[55] King (1995, 630 n. 14) cites Philo as a typical representative of his own time illustrating well how gendered imagery was utilized in antiquity (*Quaest. in Gen.* 4,15): "The soul 'has, as it were, a dwelling, partly men's quarters, partly women's quarters. Now for the men there is a place where properly dwell masculine thoughts (that are) wise, sound, just, prudent, pious, filled with freedom and boldness, and akin to wisdom. And the women's quarters are a place where womanly opinions go about and dwell, being followers of the female sex. And the female sex is irrational and akin to bestial passions, fear, sorrow, pleasure, and desire, from which ensue incurable weaknesses and indescribable diseases."

[56] So also M.A. Williams 1985, 157.

did not provide much new insight in this regard. Yet one factor
did surface which may help. The fact that the *Sophia of Jesus
Christ* and the *First Apocalypse of James* both employ the tradition of the seven Gnostic women, although probably independently
on each other, may indicate that they stem from places which are
situated relatively close to each other geographically. Based on the
mention of Addai (*1 Apoc. Jas.* 36,15; 36,22), the reputed founder
of eastern Syrian Christianity (especially Osrhoëne), Schoedel
seeks to locate the *First Apocalypse of James* in eastern Syria.[57]
Thus, the provenance of the *Sophia of Jesus Christ* could be
sought approximately in the same area. This is congruous with the
evidence that the New Testament material the writer of the text is
using derives from the Gospels of Matthew and John, which are
often located somewhere in Syria at large.[58] Admittedly, the basis
of the conclusion is not very strong but perhaps somewhat stronger
than that of the other suggestions.[59]

---

[57] Schoedel 1979, 67; see also the discussion on pp. 127-128. Two
other items in the *First Apocalypse of James* may suggest an eastern
Syrian origin: The name of the mountain in *1 Apoc. Jas.* 30,20-21,
Gaugelan, may be a somewhat corrupt Syriac form of Golgotha (see
Schoedel 1979, 80-81). Secondly, the four women mentioned in *1 Apoc.
Jas.* 40,24-26, Salome, Mary Magdalene, probably Martha (there is a
lacuna in the manuscript at this point), and Arsinoe, are brought together
also in the *Manichean Psalm-book II* (194,19-22; see also 192,21-24)
which most probably originated in Mesopotamia and which could easily
reflect influences of Syrian (Gnostic) Christian traditions.

[58] For the provenance of the Gospel of Matthew, see Meier 1992,
624; for the provenance of the Gospel of John, see Becker 1979, 50.

[59] Because the author of the *Sophia of Jesus Christ* has confused the
Mountain of Olives and the Mountain of Galilee (91,18-20), Tardieu
(1984, 349) has thought that the writing cannot have been composed in
Palestine or in Syria but rather in Egypt. Tardieu's point is worth attention but hardly forcible enough to disprove the theory of the Syrian
origin of the *Sophia of Jesus Christ*. It presupposes a geographical
knowledge which cannot necessarily be demanded from people of antiquity.

CHAPTER FOUR

MARY MAGDALENE
IN THE DIALOGUE OF THE SAVIOR

1. *Introductory Remarks*

The *Dialogue of the Savior* is a Gnostic revelation dialogue between the Lord and his disciples,[1] in which Matthew, Judas,[2] and
Mary are singled out by name. The only extant copy of the *Dialogue of the Savior* is the fifth tractate of the third codex of the
Nag Hammadi Library. The writing contains pages 120-147 of the
codex.[3] Some of the pages are heavily mutilated, none of them is

---

[1] Although the writing contains the idea of a cosmos created by the
Father or the First Word (129,20-21; 133,5-10; 144,8-10) it is to be
characterized as Gnostic. It is likely that the participation of the Father
in creating the world reflects the view of a cosmogony source used in the
writing (127,19-128,33; 129,16-131,15; 133,3-13). As a matter of fact, in
the third instance where the creation motif appears outside the source
(144,8-10), it is accompanied with a reference to the Sophia myth (so
also Krause 1977, 27; see also 140,12-14); for the identification of
Sophia with ⲦⲘⲁⲁⲨ ⲘⲠⲦⲏⲢϤ, see *Soph. Jes. Christ.* III/4 114,14-15.
Apart from these creation texts, the cosmos is seen as a place of deficiency (*Dial. Sav.* 139,15-18); it is impoverished (132,5) and evil (132,8-
9). Not only is the cosmos described as an obstacle which tries to prevent
a disciple from entering into the place of life (131,22-132,9), the body
has the same negative function (132,9-12; 134,11-14). A further typical
Gnostic feature is that salvation is granted only to the one who knows
his/her pleromatic origin and the wickedness of the cosmos and the body
(132,15-16; 134,11-24; 139,15-18). Even Koester & Pagels (1984, 15)
who have found traces of a non-Gnostic sayings tradition in the *Dialogue
of the Savior* admit that the writing itself provides an example of how
this tradition "was further developed within the horizon of gnostic
thought."
[2] Judas of the text is probably to be identified with Judas Thomas
found in the Syrian manuscripts of John 14,22; *Gos. Thom.* incipit; *Thom.
Cont.* 138,2. It is worth noting that in the *Acts of Thomas* 2 he is referred
to as "Judas who is also called Thomas." Cf. also the *Doctrine of Addai*
(for the text, see Howard 1981, 10); Eus., *Hist. eccl.* 1.13,11.
[3] The first critical edition of the text was prepared by Emmel (1984).
It also contains an English translation which is used in the present study
unless otherwise advised.

entirely intact.[4] Yet the main contents and literary character of the text is transparent.

It has been noted that the *Dialogue of the Savior* displays conspicuous differences in content and style. Whether this is due to the writer using various types of traditional material[5] or composing the work as an elaboration and expansion of an earlier dialogue[6] is difficult to decide. In this study there is no need to solve the entire question of the writing's literary unity. Yet it has to be asked whether this question has some bearing on our understanding of Mary in the writing.

Apart from one instance, the name Mary[7] appears exclusively in those parts of the dialogue which introduce the one presenting a question or a comment in the following direct speech. The only exception to this is at the beginning of the vision account (134,24-25) where Mary, together with Judas (Thomas) and Matthew, is secondarily brought to the text. The secondary character of Mary, Judas (Thomas), and Matthew is clearly seen in that originally the vision was evidently received by one person only (135,14-15;

---

[4] The manuscript has suffered some minor damage even after its acquisition by the Coptic Museum in Cairo. This was verified when the extant remains of the manuscript were compared with the photographs which were taken soon after its initial conservation (see Emmel 1984, 19-20). At least a part of the manuscript (the middle of pages 145-146) was separated from it already before it was purchased. Fortunately, the fragment belongs to a miscellaneous collection of papyri which was sold to the Beinecke Rare Book and Manuscript Library (New Haven, Connecticut). It was identified as part of the third codex of the Nag Hammadi Library by Stephen Emmel in 1980 (Emmel 1980, 53-60).

[5] Perkins 1980, 108.

[6] Koester & Pagels 1984, 1; this was already asserted in an earlier compositional analysis of the text, see Pagels & Koester 1978, 66-74. Cf. also Blatz 1987a, 246.

[7] The name appears in two different forms: ⲘⲀⲣⲓⲀⲘ (126,17-18; 134,25[?]; 139,8; 143,6; 144,5-6; 144,22; 146,1[?]) and ⲘⲀⲣⲓⲀⲘⲘⲎ (131,19; 137,3-4; 140,14-15; 140,19; 140,23; 141,12; 142,20). Bovon (1984, 55) has suggested that this is due to the employment of different sources. It is to be noted, however, that also in *Pistis Sophia I-III* two different versions of the name Mary can be used of Mary Magdalene within a single uniform passage. Therefore, Bovon's conclusion is by no means inevitable, and even if it could be sustained it has no bearing on the study of Mary Magdalene in the *Dialogue of the Savior*, because in the dialogue material where she only appears (see below) there are no indications that Mary Magdalene would be viewed differently in its various parts.

136,17).[8] This suggests that Mary has an essential part in the dialogue material but has not appeared in other possible sources at all. This does not, however, mean that the use of Mary has necessarily been confined to only one literary layer in the *Dialogue of the Savior*. If the dialogue form was not created by the author of the text but was already found in a source used by him/her, as Koester & Pagels have argued, it has to be asked whether the passages referring to Mary reveal any signs of a later redaction. And if they do, one must explore how views of Mary in the dialogue source and its possible redaction are related to each other. Are they in agreement or does the redactor of the text want to say something more about Mary than his/her source? We shall return to this question when Mary's comment in 139,8-13 is analyzed.

As in most of the Gnostic writings, the *Dialogue of the Savior* refers to no datable incidents. It is nevertheless most likely that it received its final form sometime in the second century.[9] Some parallels with the Thomas tradition[10] and the appearance of Judas (Thomas) as one of the main interlocutors of the Lord may suggest

---

[8] Pagels & Koester 1978, 67; Koester & Pagels 1984, 9. As to the grammatical subject of this section, a shift from singular to plural is also recognized by Perkins (1980, 107).

[9] Since the terms and phrases used by the author of the final text resemble those of the deutero-Pauline and catholic epistles, Koester & Pagels (1984, 16; see also Koester 1979, 554; 1990, 174-175) date the writing in the early decades of the second century C.E., before the period of the *Epistula Apostolorum* and Justin Martyr. The dialogue source which they assume to underlie the *Dialogue of the Savior* was nevertheless, in their view, composed earlier in the last decades of the first century. This dating is based on the claim that this source does not betray any traces of acquaintance with the canonical gospels and represents a stage of the dialogical elaboration earlier than the Gospel of John. The thesis has been rightly questioned by Tuckett (1986, 129-130) and Perkins (1993, 54-56) who have pointed out that at least Mary Magdalene's comment in 139,8-11 presupposes knowledge of Matthew's redaction (Matt 6,34; 10,10). In attempting to advocate the claim made by Koester & Pagels, Hills (1991, 43-58) has been forced to reconstruct such a complicated history of transmission of proverbial sayings that it is no longer credible.

[10] Some of the most notable examples are the combination of the "elect" and the "solitary (ⲘⲞⲚⲞⲬⲞⲤ/ⲘⲞⲚⲀⲬⲞⲤ)" (*Dial. Sav.* 120,26; *Gos. Thom.* 49) and the "place of life" (*Dial. Sav.* 132,7: ⲡⲘⲀ ⲘⲡⲰⲚⲈ; *Gos. Thom.* 4: ⲡⲧⲟⲡⲟⲥ ⲘⲡⲰⲚⲈ).

that the writing was composed somewhere in the region of East Syria.[11]

2. *Mary Magdalene as an Interlocutor of the Lord*

Nowhere in the entire *Dialogue of the Savior* is it explicitly mentioned that the Mary of the text is Magdalene. The form of the name makes this identification very likely, however. As noted earlier the longer version of the name, ⲘⲀⲢⲒⳁⲀⲘ(ⲘⲎ),[12] seems to be the one which is used of Magdalene in Gnostic writings, whereas the mother of Jesus is called ⲘⲀⲢⲒⳁ and any Mary other than these two is hardly possible in Gnostic revelation dialogues.[13] It is also worth noting that Mary Magdalene is closely associated with Judas (Thomas) and Matthew in other Gnostic texts as well. This is the case with both *Pistis Sophia I-III* (72,5-22) and the *Sophia of Jesus Christ*.

In the same way as in the *Sophia of Jesus Christ*, Mary Magdalene is one of the disciples of the Lord who enters into a dialogue with him. It is not impossible that the dialogue is thought to have taken place after the resurrection[14] but nowhere in the extant part of the writing is this stated.[15] At this time Mary Magdalene does not represent a group of women. Indeed, there is no reference to any other woman in the *Dialogue of the Savior*. Together with Judas (Thomas) and Matthew, Mary Magdalene functions as a spokesperson of the disciples who are also presented as a group

---

[11] Perkins 1980, 111.

[12] The fact that the name appears in two different forms in the writing (ⲘⲀⲢⲒⳁⲀⲘ and ⲘⲀⲢⲒⳁⲀⲘⲘⲎ) has hardly any significance. As Krause (1977, 24) has pointed out the same phenomenon can also be seen in *Pistis Sophia I-III* where Mary Magdalene is called ⲘⲀⲢⲒⳁ (ⲦⲘⲀⲅⳁⲀⲗⲎⲚⲎ), ⲘⲀⲢⲒⳁⲀⲘ, and ⲘⲀⲢⲒⳁⲀⲘⲘⲎ. The Coptic manuscript of the *Gospel of Mary* (BG 8502) uses the name ⲘⲀⲢⲒⳁⲀⲘ, whereas the Greek fragments of the writing (P. Oxy. 3525 and P. Ryl. 463) have the name μαριάμμη.

[13] See pp. 63-64.

[14] So Blatz 1987a, 245. The passages *Dial. Sav.* 139,6-7; 145,22-24 may imply that the Lord is about to ascend.

[15] This is emphasized by Koester & Pagels (1984, 1).

nine times.[16] Only once is their number, "the twelve disciples," explicitly mentioned (142,24-25).

There is nothing in the writing which would indicate that a tension prevails, to say nothing of a rivalry, between the disciples mentioned by name and the rest. It is typical that most of the replies of the Lord are directed to all the disciples even if only one has posed a question.[17] Thus, in the *Dialogue of the Savior*, Mary Magdalene is not played against the twelve but appears clearly to be on the same side with them.[18] The fact that she is acting as one of their representatives does imply, however, that together with Judas (Thomas) and Matthew, Mary Magdalene has a special position within the group of disciples in this writing. Why these three have been selected will be discussed later.

What is then the relationship of Mary Magdalene to the other two spokespersons for the disciples? Do they appear with equal authority, or is one of them to be regarded as more or less prominent than the others?[19] The number of the times Judas (Thomas), Mary Magdalene, and Matthew participate in the dialogue varies to some extent[20] but hardly enough to posit one having a dominant position in the dialogue over against the others.[21] Koester & Pagels

---

[16] In addition, once the question is posed by "they all" (137,11-12) and once by "they" (142,16).

[17] The only exceptions are: 125,2-3; 125,20 (but see 125,21-22); 132,10-12; 137,7-11; 140,1 (but see 140,5); 140,17-18; 146,4.

[18] This is to be said against Pagels (1978, 425) who seems to suggest that the *Dialogue of the Savior* displays a conflict between Mary Magdalene and the twelve, especially Peter (sic!).

[19] Haskins (1993, 40) is of the opinion that Mary Magdalene is clearly the most prominent among the three disciples. In her presentation of the Gnostic Mary Magdalene, she states: "Her dominant position is also clearly expressed in, for example, the *Dialogue of the Savior*, where she appears as the 'apostle who excels the rest,' superior to Thomas and Matthew..." It is typical of Haskins' presentation that the characterization of Mary Magdalene, which she puts in quotation marks, is not derived from the writing itself but represents her own interpretation.

[20] Mary Magdalene speaks 13 times, Judas (Thomas) 16 times to the Savior and three to Matthew, and Matthew 10 times. In addition, once either Judas or Matthew addresses the Lord but the lacuna in the text does not allow us to draw any firm conclusion in that case (128,12). For the same reason, the person speaking in 144,2 remains fully unknown.

[21] Pace Perkins (1980, 107) who claims that Judas (Thomas) is the most central figure among the disciples since he "speaks more than the others." Perkins' other arguments for the prominence of Judas are not very convincing either. Referring to Krause (1977, 24), Perkins maintains

have argued that some of the comments of Mary Magdalene "seem
to serve as summaries and as transitions to new topics."[22] With
this they imply that the author of the writing gives Mary Magdalene a special place among the three, making comments and asking questions.[23] Certainly, some of Mary's comments and remarks
may be of special importance,[24] but the same could be said of
those of the other interlocutors as well.[25] Of greater significance
would be the question of whether the two texts which have been
seen as special commendations received by Mary[26] should be
understood as an indication of her special standing in the text
world of the *Dialogue of the Savior*. One occurs as an answer of
the Lord (140,14-19), the other is a comment added to the statement made by Mary Magdalene (139,8-13).

2.1 *Analysis of 140,14-19*

ΠΕϪΕ ΜΑΡΙϨΑΜΜΗ ϪΕ ϪΟΟϹ ΕΡΟΕΙ ΠϪΟΕΙϹ ϪΕ ΕΤΒΕ ΟΥ
ΑΕΙΕΙ ΕΠΕΕΙΜΑ ΕϬΝ̄ϨΗΟΥ Η ΕϮΟϹΕ
ΠΕϪΕ ΠϪΟΕΙϹ ϪΕ ΕΡΕΟΥШΝϨ ΕΒΟλ Μ̄ΠΕϨΟΥΟ Μ̄ΠΜΗ-
ΝΥΤΗϹ

---

that Judas is singled out for a special praise by the Lord. This assertion
is problematic since the special praise which Krause finds in 128,2f., if
it is praise at all, is not directed to Judas alone but to all the disciples.
Moreover, Perkins insists that Judas alone was the original recipient of
the apocalyptic vision in 134,25-138,2 and has thus the focal role in the
Dialogue of the Savior. As Pagels & Koester have pointed out it is
indeed probable that originally the vision account mentioned only one
recipient but that this person was Judas it is impossible to demonstrate.
Besides, even if it were Judas it does not become evident, not at least in
the present form of the text, why this would give him a superior position
compared to Mary Magdalene and Matthew.
[22] Koester & Pagels 1984, 4.
[23] Koester & Pagels 1984, 7; see also Koester 1990, 186.
[24] Koester & Pagels (1984, 4-5) refer to 139,8-13; 140,23-141,2;
143,6-10.
[25] Cf. Matthew's comment in 144,17-21; the same function can be
attributed to the venerative act of Judas in 131,16-18.
[26] Price 1990, 58.

Mary said: "Tell me, Lord, why I have come to this place? For profit or for loss?"[27]
The Lord said: "You make clear the abundance of the revealer!"

The question Mary poses in 140,14-17 has to do with her present earthly existence as a disciple. Since Mary's question is formulated in such a way that it appears to relate to her lot alone[28] and the answer is directly addressed to her[29] and not to other disciples, it has been suggested that the answer is to be understood as a word directed to her alone,[30] and not to all the elect.[31] If the text is read in this way it can be seen to assert that it is exclusively Mary Magdalene who is entrusted with the task of revealing the gnosis imparted by the Lord.[32] If that is true one would have a strong

---

[27] This rendering of Mary's question (see the apparatus of Emmel 1984, 81) presupposes that the emphasis is in two options which she presents as alternative reasons of her coming "to this place (= to the world)." The Lord chooses neither of them but states that the reason for her coming is to "make clear the abundance of the revealer." Another, less likely translation of the text begins with an assumption that the main emphasis of the question is in the first part, i.e., the question of Mary Magdalene shows that she knows that one comes to the world either to profit or to forfeit but she wants to understand the reason for that ("Tell me, Lord, why I have come to this place to profit or to forfeit"; see Emmel 1984, 81). The Lord's response then affirms that everybody's spiritual status in the world is made evident by the revealer and in this way also everybody makes clear the abundance or the greatness (ϩⲞⲨⲞ) of the revealer. The problem with this interpretation is that the expression ⲞⲨⲰⲚϩ ⲈⲂⲞⲖ ⲘⲠⲈϩⲞⲨⲞ ⲘⲠⲒⲘⲎⲚⲨⲦⲎⲤ does not only characterize the task of those who profit but curiously enough that of those who forfeit as well. Nevertheless, if this interpretation is accepted, the first person singular in Mary's question and the second person singular in the Lord's reply can hardly be taken in their literal sense as reference to Mary alone. Rather, they are used as a rhetorical device as to include all people.

[28] See, however, the previous note. In *Soph. Jes. Christ.* III/4 114,11-12 Mary Magdalene presents a somewhat similar question but it concerns all the disciples.

[29] The predicate of the sentence is in the second person feminine singular.

[30] Krause 1977, 25.

[31] Although Koester & Pagels (1984, 14) think that the Lord's reply is directed to all the elect they also consider it to be significant that it is Mary who "asks the crucial question."

[32] Krause (1977, 25) does not draw this conclusion but it could be done on the basis of his observations. Krause himself seems to suggest that the Lord's reply is not a concrete answer to Mary but is a mere praise of a clever, analytic question. This is highly unlikely for two

argument to prove her superiority over the other spokespersons of
the disciples. But can this conclusion be sustained in light of the
writing as a whole? Is the fact that the reply of the Lord is addressed to Mary Magdalene an unequivocal indication that the
word is meant to her only?

As noted above, normally Mary Magdalene, Judas (Thomas),
and Matthew voice questions as representatives of all the disciples.
This is demonstrated by the fact that the answers are usually
directed to this larger group and not to the questioner alone.
Therefore, one could assume that in those cases where the reply
is exceptionally addressed to the persons having posed the question it is also exclusively intended for them. The clearest example
of this is the Lord's answer to Matthew in 140,1-4. After Matthew's question about the dying of the dead and the life of the
living the Lord states: "[You have] asked me about a saying [...]
which eye has not seen, [nor] have I heard it except from you."
Matthew is said to have presented a unique question and receives
the commendation he deserves. Even if the continuation of the
answer is directed to all the disciples it is clear that the words at
the beginning of the Lord's reply are meant for Matthew alone.
There is, however, another passage where this kind of answer,
seemingly addressed to only one person, does in fact appear to be
directed to all of the disciples. In 137,3-11 Mary Magdalene poses
a question and the Lord gives a reply in the second person singular.[33] The next question asked by all the disciples and the subsequent answer indicate that despite its grammatical form the first
response of the Lord was not meant to be to Mary alone.[34] Since
the latter passage is a good parallel to 140,14-19 it has to be
concluded that Mary Magdalene's possible superiority as the

---

reasons. First, if Krause is right Mary's question remains unanswered.
Second, the Lord's reply constitutes a good answer to Mary although he
does not choose any of the two alternatives offered by her.

[33] In 146,4-5, too, the Lord addresses Mary Magdalene in the second
person singular. Unfortunately, the text is so fragmented that no conclusion from its presice character can be arrived.

[34] *Dial. Sav.* 137,3-12 reads: "Mary [said, ' ...] ... see [evil ...] ...
them from the first [...] each other.' The [Lord] said, '[...] ... when you
see them ... [...] become huge, they will ... [...] ... . But when you see the
Eternal Existent, that is the great vision.' Then they all said to him, 'Tell
us about it!' "

revealer of the gnosis over the other disciples cannot be based on the grammatical form of the predicate in 140,18-19.

Another fact which speaks against the assumption that it is Mary Magdalene alone who is charged with the specified duty of revealing the gnosis is provided by those texts which emphasize that this task is not exclusively confided to certain persons but that its fulfillment presupposes certain qualities. In 126,5-8, when all the disciples ask the Lord to identify the one who seeks and the one who reveals, the Lord replies: "[It is] the one who seeks [who also] reveals..." (126,8-10). In the following response to Matthew's question, the Lord adds: "...it is the one who can see who also reveals" (126,16-17). Later during the dialogue the same theme is again taken up in 142,21 where the Lord refers to the earlier discussion and says: "I have told you [that] it is the one who can see who [reveals]." It is worth noting that it is Mary Magdalene's question which gives impetus to the answer of the Lord in 142,21. Yet he does not direct his answer to her alone but, while recalling his earlier answer to Matthew, now presents it to all the disciples. Both texts indicate that the special revelation communicated by the Lord is not a prerogative of one of the disciples, but it is open to any of them who seek and can see.[35] Based on these observations, it is difficult to say that the Lord's reply to Mary Magdalene in 140,18-19 should be understood as an indication of her extraordinary superiority in comparison with other major interlocutors or even other disciples of the Lord. The most one can say of that text is that it can serve as a demonstration that Mary Magdalene is seen as *one* of those who seek and can see, and thus can "make clear the abundance of the revealer."

---

[35] If the word of the Lord in 137,16-138,2 can be interpreted as is done by Emmel in his footnote (1984, 75), it is well in line with this conclusion. The word is spoken to all the disciples: "[Strive] to save him [who] can follow [me (*or* you)], and to seek him out, and to speak from within him, so that, as you seek him out, [everything] might be in harmony with you! I [say] to you, truly, the living God [dwells] in you..."

2.2 *Analysis of 139,8-13*

ΠΕΧΑC ΝϬΙ ΜΑΡΙϨΑΜ ΧΕ ϨΙΝΑΪ ΕΤΚΑΚΙΑ ΜΠΕϨΟΟΥ
ΠΕϨΟΟΥ ΑΥΩ ΠΕΡΓΑΤΗC ΜΠΩΑ ΝΤΕϤΤΡΟΦΗ ΑΥΩ ΠΜΑ-
ΘΗΤΗC ΝϤΕΙΝΕ ΜΠΕϤCΑϨ
ΠΕΕΙΩΑΧΕ ΑCΧΟΟϤ ϨΩC CϨΙΜΕ ΕΑCΕΙΜΕ ΕΠΤΗΡϤ

Mary said: "Thus with respect to 'the wickedness of each day,' and
'the laborer is worthy of his food,' and 'the disciple resembles his
teacher.' "
She uttered this as a woman who had understood completely.

The other text which has provided special stimulus to the discussion of Mary Magdalene's privileged position in the *Dialogue of
the Savior* is the brief remark in 139,11-13 which stresses her
ability to understand.[36] The statement follows Mary's comment in
which she presents an interpretation of the Lord's saying about the
path by which his disciple is supposed to leave the material world
and about the difficulty of finding it (139,4-7).[37] The statement
gains special emphasis because it is seen as an editorial comment
which discloses the final redactor's view of Mary Magdalene.[38]
Thus, one can assume that even if the basic dialogue (e.g. 140,14-
19) does not grant extraordinary status to her it may have been
given to her in the final layer of the text.[39]

---

[36] Pagels (1978, 425; 1981, 77) counts this text among those which
demonstrate that Mary Magdalene surpasses the rest of the disciples in
gnosis. See also Pagels & Koester 1976, 72; Haskins 1993, 40.

[37] For the interpretation of Mary's comment, see Hills 1991, 50-51.
The only problem with Hills' interpretation is that he wants to see the
third saying of Mary's comment ("the disciple shall resemble his teacher"; the translation is mine. The conjunctive has been used here independently; see Till 1978, 165) as an attempt to reassure the disciples that the
knowledge they have received from their teacher is sufficient for them.
In light of the Lord's answer, the third saying is rather to be seen as a
warning against false self-confidence: if it is difficult for the Lord to
reach the path to the pleroma (see also 145,22-24) it cannot be easy for
the disciples either.

[38] Koester & Pagels 1984, 4.

[39] Krause (1977, 25) has emphasized that the high esteem of Mary
Magdalene can already be seen in the fact that she formulates her comment by using Jesus' own aphorisms ("the wickedness of each day" [cf.
Matt 6,34c]; "the laborer is worthy of his food" [cf. Matt 10,10e]; "the
disciple shall resemble his teacher" [cf. Matt 10,25a; see also John
13,16]). This is true but does not provide any proof of Mary's superiority

The redactional nature of 139,11-13 is indeed evident. It is the only remark which interrupts the dialogue proper by commenting on the direct speech. All other commentaries on the questions and statements presented by Mary Magdalene, Judas (Thomas), Matthew, and other disciples are included in the direct replies by the Lord. A similar redactional insertion is found in 131,16-18, where the redactor of the text attaches a part of the cosmogony source to a section of the dialogue source by presenting Judas as praising the Lord.

If the remark in 139,11-13 is taken to be a redactional expansion of the dialogue source, the next question is whether the picture it gives of Mary Magdalene is really different from that in the dialogue source. Does the editorial comment exalt Mary Magdalene above other disciples of the Lord, even above those who together with her are explicitly mentioned as interlocutors of the Lord?[40]

The exact meaning of the editorial remark depends on how the term ⲠⲦⲎⲢϤ is understood. Three interpretations have been offered. When the text was first translated into English ⲠⲦⲎⲢϤ was taken as a technical term evidently referring here to τὸ πᾶν, the totality of the universe.[41] Thus the remark was rendered: "This word she spoke as a woman who knew the All."[42] In the revised translation the sentence gained a different meaning: "This word she spoke as a woman who had understood completely."[43] This translation presupposes that ⲈⲠⲦⲎⲢϤ is perceived as an independent prepositional phrase.[44] The third possible interpretation is found in the apparatus of Emmel's edition.[45] According to it, ⲠⲦⲎⲢϤ could mean "everything" and the editorial remark should

---

over the other two representatives of the twelve (to be sure, this is not asserted by Krause), since the commentary of Matthew in 144,17-21 is formulated according to the same principle although the saying of Jesus used by him does not derive from a canonical gospel ("destroy the works of womanhood" [cf. Gos. Eg. = Clem. Al., Strom. 3.63,2]).

[40] The question is answered in the affirmative by Schmid 1990, 80.

[41] In Gnostic texts, ⲠⲦⲎⲢϤ often denotes the pleromatic world also, but probably not in the Dialogue of the Savior (cf. 139,14.16-17).

[42] Attridge 1977, 235.

[43] Emmel 1984, 79; the same understanding of the text appears in Blatz 1987a, 251.

[44] For the meaning of ⲈⲠⲦⲎⲢϤ, see Crum 1939, 424.

[45] Emmel 1984, 79.

then be translated: "This word she spoke as a woman who had understood everything." In that case, ⲡⲧⲏⲣϥ is simply tantamount to ϩⲱⲃ ⲛⲓⲙ.

Since ⲡⲧⲏⲣϥ can denote the totality of the universe in the *Dialogue of the Savior* (144,11), the first interpretation of the editorial remark is not impossible. It is unlikely, however, because the reply of the Lord (138,22-139,7) and its commentary by Mary do not have to do with cosmology but are related to the ascent of the disciples. In that context, the redactor's possible reference to the knowledge of the universe does not really fit. The matter is different with the other two suggestions. Both of them are linguistically possible and suit the previous text well. Whether the preposition should be attached to the verb or to the noun is a matter of taste,[46] since both solutions result in an interpretation according to which Mary Magdalene has a perfect understanding of what the Lord has said.

As to the role of Mary Magdalene in the text world of the redactor, the significance of the perfect understanding ascribed to her in the editorial remark should not be exaggerated, however. If the redactor had wanted to enhance the importance of Mary Magdalene compared with that given to her in the dialogue source, he/she would probably not have used practically the same expression for describing her ability to comprehend the words of the Lord as that which is employed in the source when speaking about *all* the disciples. In 142,11-13 the Lord states to all the disciples: "You have understood all the things I have said to you..." That Mary herself in 141,12-14 — only two manuscript pages after the redactor has asserted that she "had understood completely/everything" — wishes "to understand all things, [just as] they are" relativizes the weight of the editorial remark even further. Especially in light of this passage, it seems probable that the editorial note after Mary's comment does not, in fact, try to do more than point out how this one comment of hers manifests a good insight. The placement of ⲡⲉⲉⲓϣⲁϫⲉ in a position of emphasis at the beginning of the sentence supports this suggestion. If that understanding of the editorial remark is correct it scarcely

---

[46] The fact that the prepositional phrase ⲉⲡⲧⲏⲣϥ ("completely") does not occur elsewhere in the *Dialogue of the Savior* does not mean that it could not be used in that sense here in this editorial remark.

says more about Mary Magdalene than the commendation of the Lord in 140,1-4 says about Matthew. Although the latter is a part of the dialogue source there is no reason to doubt that the redactor would not accept its emphasis. It clearly praises Matthew for his extraordinarily perceptive question. Since the redactor also grants Judas (Thomas) a special moment of understanding in 136,16-18, there is no reason to think that he/she wants to elevate any of the three above the others. It is of significance, however, that, together with Judas (Thomas) and Matthew, Mary Magdalene is portrayed as a disciple mentioned by name who shows a special understanding of the gnosis imparted by the Lord.

3. Why were Mary Magdalene, Judas (Thomas), and Matthew chosen?

There seems to be no polemical reason why Mary Magdalene, Judas (Thomas), and Matthew were chosen to represent the disciples of the Lord in the *Dialogue of the Savior*. No rivalry between them and the rest of the disciples can be detected. In contrast to some other revelation dialogues, such as the *Gospel of Mary* and *Pistis Sophia*, in the *Dialogue of the Savior* the interlocutors mentioned by name do not contend with each other. All the questions and comments presented to the Lord seem to serve the common good, i.e., revealing the Gnostic teaching of the Lord. Why then are the three disciples given the privilege of having their names recorded in a writing which contains the authoritative teaching of the Lord?

The answer to this question is similar to that in the *Sophia of Jesus Christ*. In both writings Mary Magdalene, Judas (Thomas), and Matthew are presented as prototypes of the Gnostic disciples. They are chosen for this task since both writings were obviously composed in a context where a tradition was developing or had developed whereby these very disciples[47] were said to have received a special Gnostic revelation after the resurrection.[48] As

---

[47] The *Sophia of Jesus Christ* still adds Philip and Bartholomew to the group.

[48] This does not yet mean that the special Gnostic disciples constitute a fixed group in the second and third centuries while another group of disciples exclusively represent the non-Gnostic orthodox position as

noted above in connection with the treatment of the *Sophia of Jesus Christ*, they are major tradition bearers in other Gnostic writings as well. In *Pistis Sophia I-III*, Mary Magdalene is the chief interlocutor of the Savior, and Thomas and Matthew together with Philip are made the "official" scribes of Jesus' words and deeds (71,18-23; 72,11-20). In addition, Thomas and Matthew[49] are the two to whom the secret teaching of the Lord is entrusted in the *Book of Thomas the Contender*. In the *Gospel of Mary* it is Mary Magdalene who conveys the secret revelation of the Savior.

The tradition of special Gnostic disciples who received the secret teaching of the Risen Christ is also known by Irenaeus who states that some Gnostics held that Jesus "instructed a few of his disciples, whom he knew to be capable of understanding such great mysteries, in these things, and was then received into heaven" (*Adv. haer.* 1.30,14). Unlike the testimony of Irenaeus and the *Gospel of Mary*, neither the *Sophia of Jesus Christ* nor the *Dialogue of the Savior* presuppose, however, that the disciples selected for this special task exclusively represent the Gnostic disciples while the rest of the disciples are left without the secret revelation or display an inadequate understanding of it or reject it altogether. This seems to indicate that in the *Sophia of Jesus Christ* and the *Dialogue of the Savior* the idea of special Gnostic disciples is only at its very infancy stage. When the idea of special Gnostic disciples begins to serve a polemical purpose, and whether there exists any direct connection between its non-polemical use and its polemical application in Mary Magdalene traditions, will be discussed later when all the relevant texts have been analyzed.

4. *Mary Magdalene and the Works of Womanhood*

In light of the prominent position Mary Magdalene has in the *Dialogue of the Savior*, it is at first sight surprising that when asked how the disciples should pray the Lord replies (144,16): "Pray in the place where there is no woman." In whatever way

---

Parrott (1986, 193-219) has argued. For the discussion about Parrott's thesis, see the chapter on the *Sophia of Jesus Christ*.

[49] In *Thom. Cont.* the name is spelled ΜΑΘΑΙΑC (138,2-3) and could thus also refer to Matthias in Acts 1,23.26 (cf. also Hipp., *Ref.* 7.20,1.5; Clem. Al., *Strom.* 2.45,4; 3.26,3; 4.35,2; 7.82,1; 7.108,1).

prayer is understood here it is apparent that the saying, if taken literally, would have placed very heavy restrictions on women, while they were participating in the religious life of the community which used the *Dialogue of the Savior*. But can the text be understood literally? One could imagine that the very presence of Mary Magdalene among the interlocutors of the Lord would render this kind of interpretation impossible.[50] But how, then, should the word of the Lord be conceived?

The following comment of Matthew clearly seeks to explicate the saying of the Lord (144,17-21). The correct understanding of "pray in the place where there is no woman" is provided by showing it to be synonymous with another saying of the Lord: "Destroy the works of womanhood."[51] The continuation of Matthew's interpretation explains what the "works of womanhood" are. They do not mean the activities of women in general, not even the participation of women in religious life, but they refer to that activity which is most clearly to be a duty of a woman, i.e., giving birth. In this connection, it is worth noting that in other ascetic (Gnostic) texts both sexual intercourse (*Thom. Cont.* 144,9: ⲥⲩⲛⲏⲑⲉⲓⲁ ⲛ̄ⲧⲙ̄ⲛⲧⲥ̅ϩⲓⲙⲉ[52]) and lust (*Zost.* 1,13) can also be characterized as "feminine" acts.

Since the destruction of the "works of womanhood," according to Matthew, results in ceasing reproduction, the most natural explanation of this expression is to see it as a demand for conti-

---

[50] It can, of course, be assumed that this kind of dominical saying may have circulated separately among early Christians. If that was the case and the word was taken literally it must have reflected an ascetic tendency according to which male celibates were instructed to avoid the presence of women; cf. the discussion of *Gos. Thom.* 114 in the chapter "Mary Magdalene in the Gospel of Thomas." Later fourth century biographical apophthegmas of the desert fathers offer evidence for the fact that female company, even the occasional presence of a woman, was held to be particularly distracting for male ascetics (for references, see Clark 1995, 37).

[51] So Emmel 1984, 89. Attridge (1977, 237) has translated the text differently. He thinks that the two sayings are joined together as two co-ordinate clauses, and the end of Matthew's comment thus explains both of the sayings. ⲝⲉ is, however, here clearly explanatory ("namely"), and shows that the second saying interprets the first.

[52] The most natural interpretation of ⲛ̄ⲧⲙ̄ⲛⲧⲥ̅ϩⲓⲙⲉ is to see it as a genitive attribute of ⲧⲥⲩⲛⲏⲑⲉⲓⲁ.

nence.[53] The phrase is interpreted in the same way by an ascetic (Gnostic?) group[54] to which Clement of Alexandria refers in *Stromata* 3.63,1-2. Clement states: "Those who are opposed to God's creation because of continence, which has a fair-sounding name, also quote the words addressed to Salome which I mentioned earlier. They are handed down, as I believe, in the Gospel of the Egyptians. For, they say: the Savior himself said, 'I am come to undo the works of the female', by the female meaning lust, and by the works birth and decay."[55]

The pejorative flavor of the term female/womanhood used in both of these texts is to be explained by the negative attitude which ascetic groups adopted towards sexual intercourse and procreation. Sex and birth were bad[56] because it was through them that souls were fettered in the prison of the body and subjected to the power of death.[57] The only way to resist this was to refrain from sex altogether. Yet one can ask why feminine terminology has been chosen for these pejorative expressions. Certainly, the most natural way to describe birth may indeed be to call it a "work of womanhood." But since it is probable that the expression refers not only to the act of delivery but also to that of conception

---

[53] Koester & Pagels (1984, 15) insist that "the 'dissolution of the works of womanhood' does not suggest a metaphysically motivated sexual asceticism, but speaks of the secret birth through the one who 'is coming forth from the Father' (96[145:10-13])." Although they may be right in pointing out that a heavenly figure coming from the Father will introduce a new kind of birth, i.e., a deliverance from the governors, this does not, however, mean that the exhortation to "destroy the works of womanhood" could not be understood as an encouragement to sexual continence. In light of the context as well as the commentary on the parallel in the *Gospel of Egyptians* this interpretation appears most likely; so also Wisse 1988, 301-302.

[54] Since the group described by Clement was opposed to God's creation it is possible that it was not only encratic but also Gnostic.

[55] The translation is taken from Schneemelcher & Wilson (1991, 209).

[56] For some Gnostic examples, see my study (Marjanen 1992, 165-166) in which the following passages are listed: *Testim. Truth* 30,1-11; *Orig. World* 109,16-25; Iren., *Adv. haer.* 1.24,2 (Satornilos); Hipp., *Ref.* 5.7,14; 5.9,11 (the Naassenes). Epiph., *Pan.* 45.2,1 could be added to this list if the followers of Severus are considered to be Gnostic (for a different view, see Wisse 1988, 307). For further references, see Koschorke 1978, 112-113.

[57] For Gnostic texts where this is explicitly spelled out, see *Testim. Truth* 30,1-11; *Orig. World* 109,16-25; Clem. Al., *Strom.* 3.45,1.

it can be asked why this work has to be regarded as "feminine."[58] The most sensible explanation is that here the author, while making use of two traditional sayings, also assumes a traditional understanding of feminine gender language as symbolizing that which is weak, deficient, and negative. The phenomenon has a close parallel in the *First Apocalypse of James* where femaleness is employed to describe the existence in the material world (41,17-19).

Once again it is to be stressed, however, that in both writings the pejorative use of feminine terminology does not prevent the authors from attributing a special place to women among the followers of Jesus. According to both writings, Mary Magdalene — in the *Dialogue of the Savior* as the only woman, in the *First Apocalypse of James* together with others — belonged to those who received special gnosis. Thus, the adoption of feminine gender language as a negative symbol does not seem to be a result of a deliberate attempt to disparage women but a reflection of a common cultural language pattern.[59] There is, however, a significant difference in the ways that feminine gender language is used in the two writings.[60]

The author of the *Dialogue of the Savior* can go so far as to say that the female protagonist of the writing, Mary Magdalene, too, can participate in the discussion of the obliteration of the "works of womanhood" without feeling personally touched by the topic any more than the male disciples (144,22-23). In the *First Apocalypse of James* femaleness is not to be obliterated but assimilated to the male element (41,15-19). In contrast to the *First Apocalypse of James*, where the author can make James be amazed "how [powerless] vessels have become strong by a perception (*or* gnosis) which is in them" (38,21-23) and can thus also question standard conceptions of femaleness prevailing in the contemporary culture and in its language patterns, in the *Dialogue of the Savior* no such criticism appears.

---

[58] According to ancient gender construction, "woman" was identified in terms of menstruation, child-birth, and sexuality.

[59] For a representative example, see p. 73 n. 55.

[60] For a more extensive presentation of the view of the *First Apocalypse of James*, see the section "Mary Magdalene and the Feminine Terminology as a Symbol of the Perishable" in the chapter "Mary Magdalene in the First Apocalypse of James."

If there were women among the ancient audience of the *Dialogue of the Savior*, as there probably were, they were exposed to a mixed message. On the one hand, they heard about Mary Magdalene, a prominent woman, who together with her two male colleagues played the most important part in a dialogue between Jesus and his disciples while he was imparting his most valuable teachings. On the other hand, while describing such behavior a Christian may not take part in, the text used metaphorical language which clearly and in an unqualified way devalued women.[61] If these women readers wanted to become or stay as members of the community which used the *Dialogue of the Savior*, they could not simply identify with a shrewd spiritual authority whom they met in Mary Magdalene, but they also had to face the challenge of negative gender language in order to appropriate the message of the text. How did they go about solving this dilemma? Did they protest and rebel? Or did they quietly comply with the fact that even if a woman could discuss matters of salvation, womanhood symbolized factors which prevented one from being saved? Or were they so accustomed to language patterns of their time that they overlooked the problem altogether?

There is no way to give certain answers to these questions. One thing is evident, however. If the women readers of the *Dialogue of the Savior* were aware of the contradictory character in its use of gender specific language, the heroine of the writing, Mary Magdalene, did not provide them with unambiguous guide to dealing with this dilemma. Although being a woman and a spiritual authority in the writing, she is made to accept uncritically, even to wish, that the works of womanhood be destroyed.[62] Thus, the

---

[61] Matthew's interpretation of the two traditional sayings (144,17-21: "Pray in the place where there is no woman" and "Destroy the works of womanhood") as a demand for celibacy serves only as an attempt to explain their meaning to contemporary readers and not to remove or to reduce the offense which the gender language employed in these sayings has to women readers.

[62] There is no indication in the text that Mary's comment in 144,22 (ⲥⲉⲛⲁϥⲟⲧⲟⲩ ⲉ[ⲃⲟⲗ] ⲁⲛ ⲱ̄ⲁⲉⲛⲉϩ) should be understood as a criticism or a protest. Irrespective of whether it be taken as a question ("Will they [= the works of womanhood] never be destroyed"; so Attridge 1977, 238; see also the apparatus of Emmel 1984, 89) or as a simple statement ("They will never be obliterated"; so Emmel 1984, 89), it expresses a fear that the works of womanhood might never be destroyed, thereby implying a wish that this not be so. In any case, the text makes it clear

women readers of the text had to consent to the fact that their most prominent female paragon gave her approval to the use of gendered imagery which emphasized women's inferiority and subordination typical of the dominant male construction of gender in Mediterranean society. Thereby Mary Magdalene herself was made to undermine the positive impact which her own role as a major interlocutor of Jesus might have had on furthering a new ideology of women's position in society and religious life.

---

that Mary Magdalene has nothing against the dissolution of the works of womanhood.

CHAPTER FIVE

MARY MAGDALENE
IN THE GOSPEL OF MARY

1. *Introductory remarks*

A good indicaton of the esteem Mary Magdalene enjoyed among Gnostics is the fact that an entire Gnostic Christian gospel is written in her name.[1] Admittedly, nowhere in the text is Mary, who has given the gospel its name, supplied with the epithet Magdalene. Even so, there is hardly any doubt that she is meant. With the exception of the mother of Jesus, no other Mary has such an important role in Gnostic writings that she could possibly have been introduced without any further specification.[2] Since the name

---

[1] Although the *Gospel of Mary*, at least in its extant form, undeniably lacks some of the typical features of Gnostic thinking, such as the Demi-urge and the Sophia myth, it does contain features which make it natural to categorize it as a Gnostic writing. Salvation is expressed in finding and following the divine presence in oneself (8,18-19) and in deliverance from adulterous attachment to matter (7,13-20), from desire and igno-rance (16,19-21), and from the world (16,21-17,1). Both matter (8,2-4) and the human body (15,7-8; ϩⲃⲥⲱ "garment" stands for the body [cf. *Gos. Phil.* 57,19-22]; the translation made by Wilson & MacRae 1979, 463 ["I served you as a garment, and you did not know me."] obscures this fact; the more dynamic translation by King [1992, 357] brings this out better: "You mistook the garment I wore for my true self.") represent that which does not originate from the heavenly sphere but belongs to the realm of darkness, desire, ignorance, and death. Although the *Gospel of Mary* does not refer to Yaldabaoth, the last four forms of the fourth power trying to prevent the soul moving from the material world to the realm of the light in *Gos. Mary* 16,8-12 have almost identical names with the authorities of Yaldabaoth in *Ap. John* BG 43,6-44,4 (Pasquier 1983, 81; for the lists of the archons of the planetary spheres, see also Welburn 1978, 241-254). In fact, the whole idea of the post-mortem ascent of the soul past archontic powers back to the realm of the light has its closest parallels in Gnostic texts (for the references, see the chapter "Mary Magdalene in the Gospel of Thomas" n. 8).

[2] In his evaluation of Tardieu's book (1984), Lucchesi (1985, 366) has maintained that one should take more seriously the possibility that Mary in the *Gospel of Mary* could be the mother of Jesus. His arguments to support his claim are not convincing. First, Lucchesi claims that it is a well-known feature in Christian tradition that the Risen Christ also appeared to his mother. This feature, however, occurs for the first time

of Mary is spelled ⲘⲀⲢⲒϨⲀⲘ in the Coptic version of the *Gospel of Mary* and μαριάμμη in the two Greek fragments (see below) it is most likely that the writing does not refer to the mother of Jesus but to Mary Magdalene.[3] In addition, the mother of Jesus does not turn up in situations where some kind of tension between the disciples and her is presented,[4] as is the case in the *Gospel of Mary* (see below).

It is furthermore stated in the *Gospel of Philip* that Jesus loved Mary Magdalene "more than [all] the disciples" (63,34-35). The same expression is used in the *Gospel of Mary* when one of Jesus' disciples, Levi, describes Jesus' relationship to Mary of that writing. He says: "He (Jesus) loved her more than us" (18,14f.).[5] The similarity of the statements suggest that the author of the *Gospel of Mary* is familiar with a tradition, utlized also in the *Gospel of Philip*, according to which Mary Magdalene was known to be a special favorite of Jesus.

---

in the writings of Ephraem Syrus (306-373; whether he depends at this point on Tatian's *Diatessaron* is not generally accepted; see Petersen 1985, 191; cf. however Bauer 1967 [1909], 263; Baarda 1994, 94-95) and Cyril of Jerusalem (310-386), later especially in Coptic writings connected with Jesus' disciple Bartholomew (see James 1975 [1924], 87.151.183; cf. also *Vita Beatae Mariae* 30,37-39) and in some pseudo-patristic Coptic texts (see Devos 1978a, 388; 1978b, 398-401). It is typical of these texts that the description of the appearance of the mother of Jesus resembles closely John 20,11-18, in which the Risen One appears to Mary Magdalene. Apparently, these texts represent a later development of the tradition. In them Mary Magdalene is replaced — possibly for apologetic or polemical reasons — by the mother of Jesus as the first witness to the resurrection. Secondly, Lucchesi insists that "dans nombre d'écrits à caractère apocryphe, subsistant en copte, c'est bien entendu la Vierge Marie qui, avec les Douze, est l'interlocutrice privilégiée de son Fils ressuscité lors derniers dialogues." The only apocryphal writings in which the mother of Jesus takes part in the post-resurrection conversation with the Risen One are the *Questions of Bartholomew* and *Pistis Sophia*. The situation in the *Questions of Bartholomew*, nevertheless, differs greatly from that in the *Gospel of Mary* (see below in the text). In *Pistis Sophia,* on the other hand, the mother of Jesus has an insignificant role compared with that of Mary Magdalene.

[3] For the use of the names, see the chapter on "Mary Magdalene in the Sophia of Jesus Christ" n. 33 and 34.

[4] Not even the *Questions of Bartholomew* (see Schneemelcher 1987, 425-437, esp. 429-432), provided it is Gnostic, can be seen in this light.

[5] The employment of the different verbs (ⲘⲈ in *Gos. Phil.* 63,34; 64,2.4 and ⲞⲨⲰⲰ in *Gos. Mary* 18,14) is probably due to the fact that the translators of the underlying Greek texts have selected divergent Coptic equivalents to render the original Greek word.

The Coptic *Gospel of Mary* is part of a manuscript,[6] Papyrus
Berolinensis 8502 (= BG), which was discovered in Egypt and
acquired for the Berlin Museum in 1896, but the Gnostic writings
of which were not published until 1955.[7] Unfortunately, of the
original 19 pages of the tractate pages 1-6[8] and 11-14 are missing.
The nine surviving pages are on the whole legible despite some
minor lacunae. In addition to the Coptic version, two Greek fragments of the *Gospel of Mary* have been discovered. One of them
(P. Ryl. 463)[9] corresponds to the sections 17,4-22 and 18,5-19,3
of the Coptic text and the other (P. Oxy. 3525) to the section 9,5-
10,14.[10] These Greek fragments were both found in Oxyrhynchus,
but they do not derive from the same manuscript as can be discerned by the dissimilarity in their script and format.[11] Both of the
fragments show such textual disagreements with the Coptic text
that they are best considered to be part of a version or versions
divergent from the *Vorlage* of the Coptic translation.[12] It is evident
that there were at least two different Greek versions of the *Gospel
of Mary* in circulation.

---

[6] The manuscript is mainly written in the Sahidic dialect but it also
contains   several features typical of the Subachmimic dialect; for further
details, see Till 1955, 18-20.

[7] Till 1955 (for the difficulties in the process of publication, see Till
1955, 1-2). A revised edition of the text was prepared by H.-M. Schenke
in 1972. For the *Nag Hammadi Studies* the text was edited by R.McL.
Wilson and G.W. MacRae in Parrott 1979, 453-471. That edition also
contains an English translation which is cited in this study unless otherwise noted.

[8] It is possible that 8 pages are missing. Schenke has suggested that
there may have been two further unnumbered pages at the beginning of
the manuscript (Till & Schenke 1972, 331).

[9] The text was edited for the first time by Roberts 1938, 18-23.

[10] As a matter of fact, P. Oxy. 3525 consists of two fragments but
one of them is so small that its precise contents and relationship to the
larger one or to the Coptic version cannot be clarified (see Lührmann
1988, 323). P. Oxy. 3525 was edited for the first time by Parsons (1983,
12-14). The most recent reconstruction and translation of the text is
found in Lührmann 1988, 323-325.

[11] Lührmann 1988, 322.

[12] Concerning the relationship between P. Ryl. 463 and the Coptic
text this was already pointed out by Roberts 1938, 20; see also Till 1946,
263; 1955, 24. With regard to the relationship of P. Oxy. 3525 to the
Coptic text a similar conclusion is drawn by Lührmann 1988, 336.

The *terminus ad quem* for the composition of the *Gospel of Mary* is provided by the Greek fragments.[13] On grounds of the paleographic analyses, P. Oxy. 3525 is dated by its editor in the third century,[14] P. Ryl. 463 more specifically in the first part of the third century or even earlier.[15] Since the latter contains textual problems owing to the copying of the text[16] and thus cannot be the autograph, the original text of the *Gospel of Mary* must have been written prior to it, but how much? If the gospel was composed in Egypt[17] the time difference between the date of writing and the production of the first copies — provided that P. Ryl. 463 was among them — does not need to be very long. If the place of writing was somewhere else it must have taken more time before

---

[13] Malvern (1975, 188 n. 13) and Haskins (1993, 409 n. 26) maintain that the last possible date of the *Gospel of Mary* can be deduced from the fact that Irenaeus knew the writing. This claim is surprising, since on the basis of Irenaeus' extant works such a statement cannot be verified. It is interesting that a similar suggestion was already made by Carl Schmidt, who was supposed to edit the Berlin Codex but who did not get the chance to complete his work. In his first presentation of the manuscript, based on his initial observations of the texts (1896, 839-846), he assumed that the codex contained three (!) writings: the *Gospel of Mary*, the *Sophia of Jesus Christ*, and the *Act of Peter*. Because some of the pages in the manuscript were misplaced (see Till 1955, 3) Schmidt had come to the conclusion that the *Gospel of Mary* and the *Apocryphon of John* formed one writing, the actual name of which was the *Gospel of Mary*. Since Schmidt found direct parallels between this writing and an anonymous Barbelo-Gnostic work cited by Irenaeus in *Adversus haereses*, he surmised that Irenaeus knew the *Gospel of Mary*. In reality, all the parallels were from that part of Schmidt's *Gospel of Mary* which is now known as the *Apocryphon of John*. Thus Schmidt's observations do not help to date the real *Gospel of Mary* but the *Apocryphon of John*. Schmidt's misconception was adopted by Harnack in his *Geschichte der altchristlichen Literatur* (1897, 712) and it has even survived in its second enlarged edition (1958, 713), which was published three years after the *editio princeps* of the *Gospel of Mary*(!). Since Malvern and Haskins do not document their claim, it is difficult to tell how they have come to this conclusion, but it may not be too far-fetched to think that they are still dependent on the *Wirkungsgeschichte* of Schmid's dating, even if they do not hold his view on the contents of the *Gospel of Mary*.

[14] Parsons 1983, 12.

[15] Roberts 1938, 20.

[16] For example, there is a dittography in 21,6, a mixture of two letters, which results in a comprehensible word, though unsuitable in its context in 21,7, and an omission of a negative in 21,13 (for the text, see Wilson & MacRae 1979, 468; Lührmann 1988, 327-330). All of these are best explained as copying errors.

[17] For this, see below.

a copy of the book reached Oxyrhynchus. At any rate, it is relatively safe to argue on the basis of the external evidence that the
Gospel of Mary should be dated before 200.[18]

In this connection it is interesting to note that practically all the
undisputed New Testament quotations in the *Gospel of Mary* are
derived from the gospels.[19] This may be an indication of a date
earlier than the end of the second century, since these writings
were widely disseminated already in the first half of the second
century, which is not true of other New Testament books.[20] Yet
the very fact that the *Gospel of Mary* is dependent either directly
or indirectly[21] on the gospels also indicates that it cannot be dated
very early in the second century. A date approximately in the
middle of the century is most likely.[22]

---

[18] This view represents a consensus among the scholars.

[19] The reference to "*my* peace" in *Gos. Mary* 8,14-15 is clearly a
typical Johannine trait (John 14,27; see p. 61). Luke 17,21-23, which
betrays traces of the Lucan redaction, is the obvious source of *Gos. Mary*
8,17-19. The warning in *Gos. Mary* 8,15-16 is most likely dependent on
the finished version of Mark (13,35) or Matthew (24,4). An echo of the
Matthean redaction may be found in the phrase the "gospel of the kingdom" (Matt 24,14; *Gos. Mary* 8,22). The hearing formula in *Gos. Mary*
7,8-9; 8,10-11 (cf. also 8,1-2) may also be dependent on the Synoptics,
although it is possible that it is a traditional proverbial saying which has
its own existence independent of them. It is also debatable whether the
theme of seeking and finding (*Gos. Mary* 8,20-21) has its roots in Luke
11,9.10 or Matt 7,7.8 or simply in a common Wisdom motif (cf. e.g.
Prov 8,17). Wilson (1956-57, 236-243) has found many other allusions
to the Gospels and to other New Testament writings as well. Apart from
the reference to ⲠⲢⲰⲘⲈ ⲚⲦⲈⲗⲒⲞⲤ ("the perfect human being") in *Gos.
Mary* 18,16, which may be an echo of Eph 4,13, they remain rather
vague. Pasquier (1983, 14-15) has tried to show that *Gos. Mary* 7,1-9,4
is an exegesis of Rom 7. However, for me the similarities between the
two look more accidental than the result of a deliberate exegetical reflection.

[20] By itself, this argument is, nevertheless, not conclusive because the
selective use of the writings of the New Testament may have been
caused by the nature of the *Gospel of Mary*.

[21] The author of the *Gospel of Mary* need not have had a direct
access to the gospels but may have been dependent on an oral tradition
resulting from the finished versions of the gospels.

[22] So also De Boer 1988, 95. King (1995, 628) dates the writing in
the first half of the second century since it "finds its life situation in the
early second century debates over women's leadership and the role of the
apostles."

The *Gospel of Mary* provides no clear clue about the location of its composition. Egypt has been suggested[23] as well as Syria.[24] Neither of the proposals have compelling force however.

2. *The Contents and Composition of the Writing*

Before a detailed analysis of the Mary Magdalene passages in the *Gospel of Mary* is undertaken a more general overview of the writing and the problems of its composition will be presented. The first surviving page of the gospel (p. 7) presents the conclusion of a dialogue between the Savior and his disciples. It is probable that the conversation has its setting in a postresurrection encounter between the Risen Jesus and his disciples just as in many other Gnostic revelation dialogues. The last questions which the disciples put to the Savior deal with the destiny of matter and the nature of sin. After he has answered these questions (7,3-8,11) the Savior says his farewells, gives his final encouragement and advice, and departs (8,14-9,5). The text, however, does not end with this but goes on depicting the perplexity of the deserted disciples. They are distressed and afraid till Mary Magdalene, who has not been introduced earlier in the extant part of the dialogue, stands up, comforts his male colleagues, and turns "their hearts to the good"[25] (9,14-22). Now the disciples begin to recall the words of the Savior and Peter asks Mary to tell the others such words which she knows and they have not heard. Then she proclaims to them a teaching which was imparted to her through a vision.

When Mary finishes her speech, of which approximately only half has survived (10,10-23; 15,1-17,7), she does not receive any commendation but is reprimanded by both Andrew and Peter. Andrew thinks that Mary's revelation discourse is doctrinally invalid and Peter calls into question whether the Savior can have

---

[23] So Pasquier (1983, 13-14), but her only argument is that all the extant manuscripts of the writing were discovered in Egypt.

[24] So Tardieu (1984, 25) on the grounds that there are similarities between the teachings of the *Gospel of Mary* and the school of Bardaisan, which flourished in Edessa at the end of the second century.

[25] Wilson & MacRae (1979, 461) have capitalized the word "good." I have used a small letter in order to avoid the impression that the word denotes the Savior. This is unlikely; for this, see below.

chosen a woman in order to communicate an important secret instruction to her (17,10-22).[26] After that Levi defends Mary against Peter, affirms her position as the special favorite of the Savior, and exhorts all the disciples to "put on the perfect human being" (18,16). In conclusion, it is reported that they "began to go forth [to] proclaim and to preach" (19,2).[27]

The somewhat complicated structure and contents of the writing have raised doubts about its literary coherence. Since the possible literary disunity of the text may have bearing on the interpretation of Mary Magdalene we have to deal with this question in some detail.[28] Till[29] and Puech[30] have concluded that the absence of Mary Magdalene in the first part of the writing indicates that the gospel was not originally a literary unity but consisted of two different works. The first was a dialogue between the Risen Jesus and his disciples (7,1-9,5) and the second a revelation discourse of Mary Magdalene in which she informs the male disciples of a vision during which she received a secret teaching from the Savior (10,1ff.).[31] While Mary Magdalene was the dominant figure in the second source she played no role in the first.

---

[26] For the comment of Peter, see below n. 74.

[27] The text of P. Ryl. 463 has here the singular: "Levi ... began to [preach.]" For the significance of this difference, see below.

[28] Schmid (1990, 18), for example, has suggested that the description of Mary Magdalene and Peter in *Gos. Mary* 17,10-19,5, which she regards as a secondary expansion of the writing, has been added only when there developed a historical conflict between the ecclesiastical and the Gnostic Christianity vis-à-vis the claims for authority put forward by certain women whom Mary Magdalene represents.

[29] Till 1955, 25-26.

[30] Puech 1959, 251-255. See also the revision of the article made by Blatz in Schneemelcher 1987, 313-314.

[31] Puech has strongly emphasized that it is not only the absence of Mary Magdalene in the first part of the writing which speaks for the disunity of the gospel but the claim the two sources make for the originality of form. The former resembles those dialogues during which the disciples present theological questions to the risen Savior, as he appears to them before his ascension or reappears after it from the heaven. This is a genre typical of Gnostic writings. The latter is "an account of a vision in the course of which the seer and the Revealer or Savior exchange questions and answers" (Puech 1959, 253). There is, nonetheless, no need to stress with Puech the dissimilarity of genre in the two parts of the writing. Both of them are in a dialogue form, even if in the former the dialogue takes place in the context of the Savior's appearance, in the latter during a vision.

The redactor of the gospel combined the two writings and provided a connection between the two by introducing Mary at the end of the first source.[32] In addition, Till insists that the redactional framework also contains the altercation among the disciples at the close of the entire gospel.

There are two major problems with this thesis. First, it is not at all evident that Mary Magdalene is introduced only in 9,12-14 for the first time in the writing. We are not told that that she "came there" or "entered into the room" but that she "stood up." In addition, even though the Greek verb ἀσπάζεσθαι can mean "to greet" or "to take farewell" (cf. *Gos. Mary* 8,12-13), its first perfect form in 9,13 need not be translated "she greeted," as if indicating that only now did Mary Magdalene appear among the disciples. It may denote "she embraced, kissed" as well (cf. *Gos. Phil.* 63,35-36; *PS* 338,16; 339,6). As a matter of fact, the Greek fragment P. Oxy. 3525 uses the verb κατεφίλησε,[33] which also has the meaning "she kissed."[34] Hence, it is far too precarious to

---

[32] A similar thesis of two sources behind the gospel is advocated by Wilson 1956-57, 236-243 (so also Wilson & MacRae 1979, 454-455), but he thinks that the redactional transition between the two sources is not confined to the introduction of Mary at the end of the dialogue between the Savior and the disciples but that it begins in 8,12. As a confirmation of his thesis Wilson points to the fact that the New Testament echoes seem to concentrate in the section after that particular line. Further, Wilson believes that the dialogue of the first part of the gospel was originally non-Christian, possibly Hermetic (between Hermes and Tat, for example), and was Christianized only by the final redactor of the gospel. Wilson's claim presupposes that the name of Peter and the hearing formula in 7,8-9 and 8,10-11 are redactional intrusions into the text. Wilson's argument seems too precarious since only a part of the first source of the *Gospel of Mary* has survived. Besides, even if the extant pages do not include any Christian elements beyond dispute, neither does it contain anything which a Christian Gnostic dialogue between the Savior and his disciples could not have. In addition, the dialogue does not take place between two interlocutors (7,14-15; 8,6-10) as is usually the case in the Hermetic dialogues.

[33] Whether this verb has been used together with a form of the verb ἀσπάζεσθαι, as Lührmann's reconstruction (1988, 324) of the lines 8 and 9 suggests ([...τότε ἀναστᾶσα Μαριάμμη καὶ ἀσπαζομένη] αὐτοὺς κατεφίλησε [πάντας καὶ λέγει...]), or instead of it, is impossible to say because of the fragmentary condition of the manuscript.

[34] What the exact purpose of this "embracing" or "kissing" may have been, it is difficult to say. If it is understood in the same way as in *Gos. Phil.* 63,35-36 (see the chapter "Mary Magdalene in the Gospel of Philip") it may imply that Mary Magdalene gave spiritual nourishment and consolation to other disciples. Cf. also *PS* 338,15-17 (see the follow-

assume on the basis of the extant section 7,1-9,12, where Mary
Magdalene is not mentioned, that she does not appear in the entire
first part of the writing.[35] Since that section mentions only one
disciple, Peter, by name, one cannot draw certain conclusions from
the role of various disciples at the beginning of the writing. Second, the bipartition of the writing is not really a reason to presuppose two separate sources behind the gospel. The two major
sections of the text (7,1-9,5 and 10,9-17,9) and the connecting
parts between them and at the end of the writing need not be seen
as two sources combined by redactional elements but as compositional units constituting the literary structure of the gospel.[36]

A different approach to the question of the writing's literary
unity has been proposed by Pasquier. Her point of departure is not
the compositional or genre analysis of the text but the tension in
the way the relationship between the male disciples and Mary is
described in various parts of the Gospel of Mary.[37] Because the
attitude of Peter to Mary Magdalene in 10,1-6, as he invites her to
tell the others the words of the Savior they have not heard, is
different from his hostility towards her in the debate on her teaching at the end of the gospel (17,18-22), Pasquier concludes that
these texts cannot belong to the same literary layer. Consequently,
since 9,20-10,6 is closely connected with the following revelation
discourse of Mary, she thinks that it was not originally the latter
which provoked Peter's objections in 17,16-22 but Mary's word
of encouragement after the departure of the Savior (9,14-20).

---

ing note).

[35] Cf. PS 338,15-17, which constitutes an interesting parallel to Gos.
Mary 9,12-14. In the passage Mary Magdalene asks the Savior's permission to respond to a question posed by Salome. When it is granted we
are reported that ⲁ ⲙⲁⲣⲓⲁ ϥⲟϭⲥ̄ ⲉⲣⲟⲩⲛ ⲡⲛ̄ ⲥⲁⲗⲱⲙⲏ ⲁⲥⲁⲥⲡⲁⲍⲉ
ⲙ̄ⲙⲟⲥ ⲡⲉⲭⲁⲥ ("...Mary sprang towards Salome, embraced her and
said"). The introductory formula of Mary's speech in PS 338,15-17 is
almost identical with Gos. Mary 9,12-14 and does not by any means
indicate that Mary has not been introduced into the narrative before that
moment.

[36] A somewhat different source theory is advanced by Fallon (1979,
131) who has suggested that the two parts of the Gospel of Mary originally belonged together and constituted a non-Christian apocalypse which
in the final version of the writing was broken up and complemented by
Christian frame material and insertions. However, the same criticism
applies to it as well.

[37] Pasquier 1983, 7-10.

Peter's invitation to Mary to recall the words of the Savior and her subsequent speech (9,20-17,[10]15)[38] are thus, according to Pasquier, a secondary addition to the original text.[39] In the pre-redactional version of the gospel, it is the theme of the androgynous unity as the goal of salvation (9,19-20) which provokes Peter's negative reaction to Mary's words.

Quite apart from the fact whether the tension in the text found by Pasquier is really as clearly discernible as we are given to understand, there is another problem in her hypothesis. Peter's objection in 17,16-22 cannot be a response to Mary's words in 9,14-20 since it necessarily presupposes Mary's revelation discourse (10,7-17,9). Peter's comment on the secret nature of Mary's revelation makes sense only as a reference to her words preceding her discourse (10,8: "What is hidden from you I will proclaim to you"), not to her short speech after the departure of the Savior.[40] This is realized by Schmid who, presupposing the same basic tension in the text as Pasquier, also suggests that 10,1-6 and 17,(10)16-22 do belong to different literary layers but that the latter is secondary to the former, not the opposite, as Pasquier assumes.[41] Yet even with this correction of Pasquier's thesis, Schmid has to face the question whether the tension in the text seen by Pasquier and herself is really so great that it warrants an assumption of a redactional expansion into the text.

Is the change in Peter's attitude to Mary Magdalene really due to a redactional correction or is it rather a plot development? Peter initially asks Mary to recount some teachings of Jesus which he and the other male disciples have not happened to hear (10,4-6). Instead Mary gives them an account of her secret vision challeng-

<hr/>

[38] According to Pasquier (1983, 9-10), this secondary addition, too, contains an earlier tradition, viz., Mary's revelation discourse (10,10-17,9).

[39] Unlike Till and Puech, Pasquier does not regard the dialogue between the Savior and the disciples in 7,1-9,5 as an independent source.

[40] The same is true with the remark of Andrew in 17,11-15. His words about that which "the Savior said" and about "these teachings" can hardly be understood as references to Mary's announcement in 9,14-20. They seem to presuppose Mary's revelation discourse (cf. especially 17,8-9). This is also admitted by Pasquier (p. 10 n. 39) who appears to have great difficulties in deciding whether the passage belongs to the pre-redactional stage of the text or to its secondary expansion.

[41] Schmid 1990, 18.

ing their position as the authoritative source and transmitters of the
Savior's teachings. Andrew and Peter attack Mary because of her
vision since it demonstrates not merely that the Savior loves her
more than other women (10,2-3), but more than the male disciples
as well (17,22; 18,14-15). In light of these observations, it is more
likely that the difference in the attitude of Peter to Mary reflected
in the text is not due to the inner inconsistency of the two sources
presumably used by the redactor[42] but to a development in the
text's plot.[43]

Now we turn to the texts which elucidate the role of Mary
Magdalene in the writing. Since the initial dialogue between Jesus
and his disciples as well as the extant end of the dialogue between
Jesus and Mary during her vision do not contribute to our understanding of Mary's role, the primary focus is on the sections 9,12-
10,16 and 17,7-19,5.

3. *Analysis of 9,5-10,16*

```
(5)    NTⲀⲢⲈϤϪⲈ NⲀÏ ⲀϤBⲰK NTOOY ⲆⲈ
(6)    NⲈYⲢⲀYⲠⲈI ⲀYⲢIⲘⲈ ⲘⲠϢⲀ ⲈY
(7)    ϪⲰ ⲘⲘOⲤ ϪⲈ NNⲀϢ NⲅⲈ ⲈNNⲀBⲰK
(8)    ϢⲀ NⲅⲈⲐNOⲤ NTNTⲀϢⲈOⲈIϢ N
(9)    ⲠⲈYⲀⲅⲅⲈⲗION NTⲘNTⲈⲢO ⲘⲠϢH
(10)   PⲈ ⲘⲠⲢⲰⲘⲈ ⲈϢϪⲈ ⲠⲈTⲘⲘⲀY Ⲙ
(11)   ⲠOY†ⲤO ⲈⲢOϤ NⲀϢ NⲅⲈ ⲀNON ⲈY
(12)   NⲀ†ⲤO ⲈⲢON TOTⲈ ⲀⲘⲀⲢIⲅⲀⲘ TⲰ
(13)   OYN ⲀⲤⲀⲤⲠⲀⲌⲈ ⲘⲘOOY THⲢOY
(14)   ⲠⲈϪⲀⲤ NNⲈⲤⲤNHY ϪⲈ ⲘⲠⲢⲢIⲘⲈ
(15)   ⲀYⲰ ⲘⲠⲢⲢⲀYⲠⲈI OYⲆⲈ ⲘⲠⲢⲢ ⲅHT
(16)   ⲤNⲀY TⲈϤϪⲀⲢIⲤ ⲅⲀⲢ NⲀϢⲰⲠⲈ
(17)   NⲘⲘHTN THⲢⲤ ⲀYⲰ NⲤⲢⲤKⲈⲠⲀ
(18)   ⲅⲈ ⲘⲘⲰTN ⲘⲀⲗⲗON ⲆⲈ ⲘⲀⲢⲠN
(19)   ⲤⲘOY ⲈTⲈϤⲘNTNOϬ ϪⲈ ⲀϤⲤB
(20)   TⲰTN ⲀϤⲀⲀN NⲢⲰⲘⲈ NTⲀⲢⲈⲘⲀ
(21)   ⲢIⲅⲀⲘ ϪⲈ NⲀÏ ⲀⲤKTⲈ ⲠⲈYⲅHT
(22)   [Ⲉⲅ]OYN ⲈⲠⲀⲅⲀⲐON ⲀYⲰ ⲀYⲢⲀⲢϪⲈ
(23)   [ⲤⲐⲀI] NⲢⲄYⲘ[N]ⲀⲌⲈ ⲅⲀ ⲠⲢⲀ NNϢⲀ
(24)                   [Ϫ]Ⲉ ⲘⲠ[ⲤⲰⲢ]
```

---

[42] The literary unity of the writing is also advocated or implied by
Tardieu 1984, 22; Lührmann 1988, 321-338; Luttikhuizen 1988, 158-168;
King 1995, 601-634.
[43] I owe this suggestion to Prof. Karen L. King.

(10,1) ΠΕϪΕ ΠΕΤΡΟС ΜΜΑΡΙϨΑΜ ϪΕ ΤСⲰ
(2) ΝΕ ΤⲚСΟΟΥΝ ϪΕ ΝΕΡΕΠСⲰⲢ ΟΥΑϢΕ
(3) ΝϨΟΥΟ ΠΑΡΑ ΠΚΕСΕΕΠΕ ΝϬ̇ΙΜΕ
(4) ϪⲰ ΝΑΝ ΝΝⲰϪΕ ΜΠСⲰⲢ ΕΤΕΕΙΡΕ
(5) ΜΠΕΥΜΕΕΥΕ ΝΑ̈Ι ΕΤΕСΟΟΥΝ ⲘⲘΟ
(6) ΟΥ Ⲛ̄ΑΝΟΝ ΑΝ ΟΥΔΕ ΜΠⲚСΟΤΜΟΥ
(7) ΑСΟΥⲰϢⲂ̄ ΝϬΙ ΜΑΡΙϨΑΜ ΠΕϪΑС
(8) ϪΕ ΠΕΘΗΠ ΕΡⲰΤⲚ †ΝΑΤΑΜΑ ΤΗΥ
(9) ΤⲚ ΕΡΟϤ ΑΥⲰ ΑСΑΡΧΕΙ ⲚϪⲰ ΝΑΥ
(10) ⲚΝΕΪϢϪΕ ϪΕ Α{Ϊ}ΝΟΚ ΠΕϪΑС ΑΙ
(11) ΝΑΥ ΕΠⲬС ϨΝ ΟΥϨΟΡΟΜΑ ΑΥⲰ ΑΕΙ
(12) ϪΟΟС ΝΑϤ ϪΕ ΠⲬС ΑΪΝΑΥ ΕΡΟΚ Μ̄
(13) ΠΟΟΥ ϨΝ ΟΥϨΟΡΟΜΑ ΑϤΟΥⲰϢⲂ ΠΕ
(14) ϪΑϤ ΝΑ̈Ι ϪΕ ΝΑΪΑΤΕ ϪΕ Ⲛ̄ΤΕΚΙΜ ΑΝ
(15) ΕΡΕΝΑΥ ΕΡΟΕΙ ΠΜΑ ΓΑΡ ΕΤΕΡΕΠΝΟΥС
(16) Μ̄ΜΑΥ ΕϤΜΜΑΥ ΝϬΙ ΠΕϨΟ

(9,5) When he had said this, he departed. But they (6) were grieved. They wept greatly (7) saying: "How shall we go (8) to the gentiles and preach (9) the gospel of the kingdom of the true (10) human being?[44] If they did (11) not spare him, how will (12) they spare us?" Then Mary (13) stood up, embraced[45] them all, (14) and said to her brethren: "Do not weep (15) and do not grieve nor be (16) irresolute, for his grace will be (17) entirely with you[46] and will protect (18) you. But rather let us (19) praise his greatness, for he has (20) joined us together[47] and made us into human beings."[48] When (21) Mary said

---

[44] Instead of the traditional translation "Son of Man" (Wilson & MacRae 1979, 461) this rendering has been chosen because it better corresponds to the way the Synoptic expression has been interpreted in the *Gospel of Mary*; see below (cf. also the translation by King [1992, 356]: the seed of true humanity).

[45] For this translation, see above.

[46] The last letter of the word ΤΗΡϹ is very uncertain, but Ϲ is the most logical restoration, since there is room for only one letter. Till's emendation (1955, 66) ΤΗΡ<Τ>Ⲛ "with you all" (cf. also King 1992, 356) is not necessary.

[47] P. Oxy. 3525 probably reads here συνήρτηκεν (Lührmann 1988, 325) "has joined together" and not κατήρτηκεν which would correspond to the Coptic ΑϤСⲂ̄ΤⲰΤ* "he has prepared." It is difficult to know which variant is original. Wilson & MacRae (1979, 461) follow the Coptic text, since they did not yet know the Greek version. King (1992, 356) translates according to the Greek version but mentions the other alternative in her apparatus.

[48] Wilson & MacRae (1979, 461) render the expression: "made us into men." Instead of "men" I prefer to translate "human beings" for two reasons. First, neither the Greek nor the Coptic version use the word

this, she turned their hearts (22) to the good, and they began (23) to
discuss the words (24) of the [Savior] (10,1) Peter said to Mary:
"Sister, (2) We know that the Savior loved you (3) more than the rest
of women. (4) Tell us the words of the Savior which you (5) remember[49] — which you know (6) (but) we do not, nor have we heard
them." (7) Mary answered and said: (8) "What is hidden from you I
will proclaim to you." (9) And she began to speak to them (10) these
words: "I,"[50] she said, "I (11) saw the Lord in a vision and I (12) said
to him: 'Lord, I saw you (13) today in a vision.' He answered and
(14) said to me: 'Blessed are you that you did not waver (15) at the
sight of me. For where the (16) mind is, there is the treasure.' ..."

The departure of the Risen Savior causes great perplexity among
the disciples. The challenge to go and preach the gospel to the
gentiles seems to be an insurmountable enterprise. The disciples
are afraid that they will be compelled to share the destiny of their
master and to undergo suffering and death.[51] This shows that they
have misunderstood the teaching of the Savior. In his last reply to
Peter's question (7,17-8,6) the Savior has tried to teach that the
deliverance from the body results in the removal of suffering and
death.[52] It is in this situation that Mary Magdalene intervenes and
assumes the dominant role among the disciples.

At first Mary tries to comfort and encourage her distressed
colleagues. Thus she assumes the role of the Savior. It is worth

---

which exclusively denotes "male persons," but the more comprehensive
word "human being," although in both languages the word may mean a
"male person" as well. Secondly, I want to show the difference between
this text and *Gos. Thom.* 114, where Jesus promises to make Mary
Magdalene ϩⲟⲟⲩⲧ and uses the Coptic word which exclusively stands
for "male."

[49] The phrase "...which you remember..." is missing in P. Oxy. 3525
but its equivalent "What is hidden from you and *I remember* I shall
[proclaim..." appears later in Mary's answer.

[50] As King (1995, 630 n. 28) has pointed out, P. Oxy. 3525 reads:
"When I *once* saw..." This seems to indicate that the Savior may have
appeared to Mary on more than one occasion.

[51] As pointed out by Pasquier (1983, 67), a similar fear of suffering
among the disciples following the ascension of the Risen Jesus is found
in *Ep. Pet. Phil.* 138,15-16. It is interesting that there it is Peter who
explains to others that since the Lord suffered they have to suffer too.
The perspective in the *Gospel of Mary* is somewhat different, as Mary's
consoling words show. The disciples are given a promise of protection.

[52] King 1995, 610.

noting that Mary exhorts the male disciples not to be ϨΗΤ ⲤΝⲀΥ[53] (*Gos. Mary* 9,15-16). The literal meaning of Ⲣ̄ ϨΗΤ ⲤΝⲀΥ is "to be double-minded." Its Greek equivalents are διψυχεῖν/δίψυχος εἶναι and διστάζειν,[54] and here it is used in the sense of "being doubtful, irresolute."[55] In Christian religious language double-mindedness stands for a religious commitment which is only half-hearted and compromizing, spiritually less advanced (*1 Clem.* 11,2; *Herm. Vis.* 6,7; 11,4; 22,4; *Herm. Man.* 39,5-6). In *Tri. Trac.* 119,20-24 the psychic race of men, those who, according to the Valentinian conception, are less capable of discerning the spiritual truths, are described as being "double according to their determination for both good and evil". Even if the characterization of the psychic ones has a different Coptic verb (ϨⲀΤⲢⲈ, 119,23) its similarity to the description of the disciples in *Gos. Mary* 9,15-16, as implied by Mary's encouragement, is striking. Even though the Valentinian anthropological terminology does not occur in the *Gospel of Mary* it is obvious that the way the disciples are described in the writing corresponds to the portrait of the psychic ones in Valentinianism. Compared to Mary Magdalene, they are less capable of perceiving Jesus' spiritual teaching.

In her exhortations Mary Magdalene tries to make other disciples aware of their potentialities for spiritual perception and growth.[56] She reminds her male colleagues that the Savior has prepared[57] them and made them into human beings (9,19-20).

---

[53] The idea of doubtful, irresolute disciples derives probably from Matt 28,17; so also Lührmann 1988, 326.

[54] The Greek verb which appears in P. Oxy. 3525 is διστάζειν; cf. also *Ap. John* BG 21,15 where Ⲣ̄ ϨΗΤ ⲤΝⲀΥ appears to be a translation of διστάζειν (*Ap. John* IV/1 3,2).

[55] So also Wilson & MacRae 1979, 461.

[56] So also van Cangh 1992, 2285.

[57] The Coptic text (9,19-20) has the verb ⲀϤⲤⲂ̄ⲦⲰⲦⲚ̄ which Wilson & MacRae (1978, 461) translate "he has prepared us". In P. Oxy. 3525 there is probably the Greek verb συνήρτηκεν (at least not κατήρ-τηκεν, the expected Greek equivalent of the Coptic version [Crum 1939, 323b]; see Parsons 1983, 13; Lührmann 1988, 325) which is to be rendered "he has united us together." Lührmann (1988, 332) has interpreted the Greek text to say that Mary assures the disciples that the Savior has united the male and the female element in them so that they have become perfect (androgynous) humans. This is one possible interpretation but not the only one. The word can have been used in a fully non-technical sense, too. In the latter case, it emphasizes the ideal of group unity (King 1995, 611).

"Making into human beings" is an obvious allusion to the word of the Savior in which he pointed out to the disciples that ⲠϢⲎⲢⲈ ⲘⲠⲢⲰⲘⲈ[58] is within them.[59] The way the sentence is used in its present context shows that, instead of drawing attention to himself, the Savior wants to show that salvation is to be found in discovering one's own true spiritual self.[60] The text implies a clear Gnostic reinterpretation. One's true spiritual self and the element of the divine are seen to be identical, and the discovery of this insight brings salvation. Yet the course of events described in the *Gospel of Mary* shows that the role of the Savior in the process of salvation is only preparatory. He points to the real spiritual nature within them, but it is up to them to find it.[61]

Mary's instruction is seen as turning the hearts of the disciples to the "good" (ⲠⲀⲄⲀⲐⲞⲚ, 9,21-22). Even this comment is not Christological. Since the neuter form of the Greek adjective is employed (cf. also *Gos. Mary* 7,17),[62] the word cannot denote the Savior.[63] There are two other possibilities for understanding the phrase "turning the hearts to the good." In its immediate context it can be perceived as a reference to Mary Magdalene's successful effort to remove the despair of the disciples. This interpretation does not, however, explain adequately the technical character of the term ⲠⲀⲄⲀⲐⲞⲚ.

Another, more likely explanation of the phrase is provided by the earlier reference to the "good" in 7,17-20. In that text the Savior says to his disciples that "the good came into your midst, to the (essence) of every nature, in order to restore it to its root." The "good" is something which grants people a possibility of overcoming the unfortunate mixture of their true nature with matter and thus of attaining the restoration to their proper origin. If the "good" is not the Savior, the closest alternative which can fulfill the function presented here is the gnosis taught by him.

---

[58] The text edition of Wilson & MacRae (1979, 458) contains a printing error on line 8,18. Instead of ⲠϢⲎⲢⲈ there is ⲚϢⲎⲢⲈ.

[59] So also Schmid 1990, 95 n. 20.

[60] Cf. Pasquier 1983, 61; King 1995, 611.

[61] Similarly King 1995, 611.

[62] The neuter form of the Greek adjectives in Coptic denotes non-humans (Stern 1971 [1880], 78; Till 1978, 55-56).

[63] Contra Pasquier 1983, 70 n. 91; Tardieu 1984, 226.

Although the "good" is not a common substitute for gnosis, this is not the only instance where it seems to have been used in that sense. In the *Tripartite Tractate* the conversion of the fallen Logos is described as a turning away from evil[64] "to the good (ⲡⲉⲧⲛⲁ-ⲛⲟⲩϥ)" (81,24-29). As a result of this experience the Logos begins to pray and remembers that he belongs to the pleroma, to which, later on, he is able to return. In the same writing the psychic race of humans is characterized as one which is "double according to its determination for both good (ⲡⲁⲅⲁⲑⲟⲛ) and evil (ⲡⲕⲁⲕⲟⲛ)" (119,23-24). In the following sentence it is said that those psychic ones who are of good disposition will attain salvation. The author of the *Testimony of Truth*, although influenced by many Valentinian ideas and probably originating in a Valentinian Gnostic group, criticizes the disciples of Valentinus saying that they "leave the good" (56,7).[65] In these texts the term "good" is another way of speaking about the gnosis of belonging to the divine realm.[66] In light of these observations, *Gos. Mary* 9,21-22 seems to describe Mary as making or at least trying to make her colleagues receptive to this gnosis.[67] The result of her encouragement is that they start recalling the teachings of Jesus.

When the disciples begin to discuss or argue[68] with each other about the words of the Savior[69] Mary does not seem to participate in that conversation. It is only when Peter asks her to share her

---

[64] In 77,22-25 the situation of the Logos may be characterized by division, self-doubt, forgetfulness and ignorance.

[65] Koschorke (1978, 153) thinks that the expression signifies "ein Ablassen vom (Streben nach der Gnosis des) Lichtreich(es)".

[66] In some of these passages it is not always clear whether the "good" stands for the realm of the light or for the knowledge of it. Perhaps, the distinction is not very clear either. The reality itself and the knowledge of it tend to assimilate.

[67] Another possible interpretation of the "good" is to see it as a reflection of the highest ontological being in the Platonic sense. Thus, the presence of the "good" in the material world would mirror some of the dualistic aspects of Middle Platonic ontology (cf. e.g. *Allogenes* 52,11-12.17). Yet, the idea of "the good's coming into the midst of the disciples" is not easily explained on the basis of this thesis.

[68] γυμνάζειν is here used in the same sense as in scholastic exercises of the Greek gymnasiums (Pasquier 1983, 70).

[69] A similar situation is described in *Ap. Jas.* 2,8-15, where the disciples not only try to remember what Jesus had said to them, in secret or openly, but they also put it in books.

recollections that she joins the discussion. Even if it is not questioned that Mary Magdalene herself can convey the words of the
Savior it must be one of the apostles — in fact, the most important one — who grants her the invitation to participate in the
process of preserving the authentic Jesus tradition. It is worth
noting that Peter's address to Mary begins with the word "sister,"
which in no other Gnostic writings appears in Peter's mouth.[70]

The reason why Mary Magdalene is also given a chance to
share those words of Jesus she has heard is that, according to
Peter, the Savior loved her more than the rest of women. The
same theme of love comes up again in the concluding altercation
among the disciples, indeed in a different form, as we are going
to see, and also in the *Gospel of Philip* (64,1-10). In Peter's mind,
Jesus' love for Mary shows simply that Mary was his female
favorite. Yet any sexual attachment is hardly involved. This is
shown by the concluding discussion of the writing where Levi
contrasts the love of Jesus for Mary with that of Jesus for his male
disciples in such a way that the sexual dimension is ruled out (see
below).

The text does not say explicitly whether the disciples are talking about the words of the earthly or the Risen Jesus.[71] On the
basis of Peter's comment in 17,18-20 it is at least evident that
Peter and the other disciples do not expect to hear about a secret,
personal vision, even if they consider it possible that Mary can tell
them something they have not heard. In any case, Mary does not
disclose any words of the earthly Jesus, unheard to others, but
reveals "what is hidden" from her fellow disciples altogether.[72]
Mary tells about a vision in which she has encountered the Savior

---

[70] Schmid 1990, 16.

[71] In P. Oxy. 3525 it is the ἀποφθέγματα of the Savior (line 14)
the disciples are trying to recall. The use of this Greek word may suggest
that it is exactly the "terse, pointed sayings" (the definition of the word
ἀπόφθεγμα in Liddell & Scott [1968, 226]) of the earthly Jesus which
is meant. In the *Apocryphon of James* a similar situation is depicted and
there the disciples are trying to remember the words of the earthly Jesus
(2,8-15).

[72] King (1995, 612) has suggested that only the Coptic text implies
that Mary's report contains something that is "hidden" from other disciples, whereas P. Oxy. 3525 only states according to her translation: "I
will rep[ort to you as much as] I remember that you don't know" (King
1992, 357). Yet ΠΕΘΗΠ ΕΡѠΤΝ may well be a rendering of ὅσα ὑμᾶς
λανθάνει, as the Sahidic translations of Mark 7,24 and Luke 8,47 show.

and received from him a special revelation pertinent to salvation. At the same time it becomes evident that the recollection of the words of Jesus was not what Mary expected or wished to happen as she turned the hearts of the disciples to the "good." Her obvious purpose was to encourage them to seek new revelations of spiritual truths, i.e., the gnosis. By communicating her own vision she wants to lead them to a new way.

The special spiritual status of Mary Magdalene is underlined by her "not wavering at the sight of Jesus" in 10,14-15. In ancient thought immovability was considered to be a spiritual virtue, since it illustrates one's "conformity to the unchanging and eternal spiritual world."[73] The fact that Mary's mind ($\nu o\tilde{\upsilon}\varsigma$) is directed to the "good" implies that she is able to partake in the treasure of a direct revelation from the Savior.

In the first part of the conversation among the disciples Mary Magdalene appears to be the disciple who really understood the message of the Savior. She tries to make evident to her colleagues too that salvation is found within oneself. Likewise, she tries to show that the reception of divine revelation is not limited to repeating the old teachings of the Savior but it means to be constantly looking for new ones, even in the form of visions. For Peter and the other disciples, Mary is simply the woman the Savior loved most. In that capacity she enters into the discussion of the words of the Savior, but only because Peter invites her to do it.

4. *Analysis of 17,7-19,5*

(17,7)	ΝΤΕΡΕΜΑΡΙϨΑΜ ϪΕ
(8)	ΝΑ̈Ι ΑΣΚΑ ΡⲰⲤ ϨⲰⲤΤΕ ΝΤΑΠⲤⲰⲢ
(9)	ⲰⲀϪΕ ΝⲘⲘⲀⲤ ⲰⲀ ΠΕΕΙΜⲀ
(10)	Α̅ϤΟΥⲰⲰⲂ ⲆΕ Ν̅Ο̅Ι ΑΝⲆⲢΕⲀⲤ ΠΕϪⲀϤ
(11)	Ν̅ΝΕⲤΝΗΫ ϪΕ ⲀϪΙ ΠΕΤΕΤΝ̅ϪⲰ
(12)	ⲘⲘΟϤ ϨⲀ ΠΡⲀ Ν̅ΝΕΝΤⲀⲤϪ[Ο]ΟΥ
(13)	ΑΝΟΚ ΜΕΝ ϯΡ̅ΠΙⲤΤΕΥΕ ⲀΝ ϪΕ
(14)	ⲀΠⲤⲰⲢ ϪΕ ΝΑ̈Ι ΕⲰϪΕ ΝΙⲤⲂΟΟΥ
(15)	Ε ΓⲀⲢ ϨΝ̅ΚΕΜΕΕΥΕ ΝΕ Α̅ϤΟΥⲰ
(16)	ⲰⲂ Ν̅Ο̅Ι ΠΕΤΡΟⲤ ΠΕϪⲀϤ ϨⲀ ΠΡⲀ

---

[73] King 1995, 612. Cf. also the seminal study of M.A. Williams (1985) on the theme of stability in late antiquity.

(17)   ⲚⲚⲈⲈⲒϨⲂⲎⲨⲈ ⲚⲦⲈⲈⲒⲘⲒⲚⲈ ⲀϤ
(18)   ⲬⲚⲞⲨⲞⲨ ⲈⲦⲂⲈ ⲠⲤⲰⲢ̅ ⲬⲈ ⲘⲎⲦ̣Ⲓ
(19)   ⲀϤϢⲀⲬⲈ ⲘⲚ̅ ⲞⲨⲤϨⲒⲘⲈ Ⲛ̄ⲬⲒⲞⲨⲈ
(20)   ⲈⲢⲞⲚ ϨⲚ ⲞⲨⲰⲚϨ ⲈⲂⲞⲖ ⲀⲚ ⲈⲚⲚⲀ̣
(21)   ⲔⲦⲞⲚ ϨⲰⲰⲚ Ⲛ̄ⲦⲚ̄ⲤⲰⲦⲘ̅ ⲦⲎⲢⲚ̅
(22)   ⲚⲤⲰⲤ Ⲛ̄Ⲧ<Ⲁ>ϤⲤⲞⲦⲠⲤ ⲚϨⲞⲨⲞ ⲈⲢⲞⲚ
(18,1) ⲦⲞⲦⲈ Ⲁ̣[Ⲙ]ⲀⲢⲒϨⲀⲘ ⲢⲒⲘⲈ ⲠⲈⲬⲀⲤ Ⲙ̄
(2)   ⲠⲈⲦⲢⲞⲤ ⲠⲀⲤⲞⲚ ⲠⲈⲦⲢⲈ ϨⲒⲈ ⲈⲔ
(3)   ⲘⲈⲈⲨⲈ ⲈⲞⲨ ⲈⲔⲘⲈⲈⲨⲈ ⲬⲈ Ⲛ̄ⲦⲀ̈Ⲓ
(4)   ⲘⲈⲈⲨⲈ ⲈⲢⲞⲞⲨ ⲘⲀⲨⲀⲀⲦ ϨⲘ̄ ⲠⲀ
(5)   ϨⲎⲦ Ⲏ ⲈⲈⲒⲬⲒ ϬⲞⲖ ⲈⲠⲤⲰⲢ̅ ⲀϤⲞⲨ
(6)   ϢϢⲂ Ⲛ̄ϬⲒ ⲖⲈⲨⲈⲒ ⲠⲈⲬⲀϤ ⲘⲠⲈⲦⲢⲞⲤ
(7)   ⲬⲈ ⲠⲈⲦⲢⲈ ⲬⲒⲚ ⲈⲚⲈϨ ⲔϢⲞⲠ ⲚⲢⲈϤ
(8)   ⲚⲞⲨϬⲤ Ⲧ̄ⲚⲀⲨ ⲈⲢⲞⲔ ⲦⲈⲚⲞⲨ ⲈⲔⲢ̅
(9)   ⲄⲨⲘⲚⲀⲌⲈ ⲈϨⲚ ⲦⲈⲤϨⲒⲘⲈ Ⲛ̄ⲐⲈ Ⲛ̄
(10)   ⲚⲒⲀⲚⲦⲒⲔⲈⲒⲘⲈⲚⲞⲤ ⲈϢⲬⲈ ⲀⲠ
(11)   ⲤⲰⲦⲎⲢ ⲀⲈ ⲀⲀⲤ ⲚⲀⲌⲒⲞⲤ Ⲛ̄ⲦⲔ ⲚⲒⲘ
(12)   ⲀⲈ ϨⲰⲰⲔ ⲈⲚⲞⲬⲤ ⲈⲂⲞⲖ ⲠⲀⲚⲦⲰⲤ
(13)   ⲈⲢⲈⲠⲤⲰⲦⲎⲢ ⲤⲞⲞⲨⲚ Ⲙ̄ⲘⲞⲤ ⲀⲤ
(14)   ⲪⲀⲖⲰⲤ ⲈⲦⲂⲈ ⲠⲀ̈Ⲓ ⲀϤⲞⲨⲞϢⲤ̄ Ⲛ̄ϨⲞⲨ
(15)   Ⲟ ⲈⲢⲞⲚ ⲘⲀⲖⲖⲞⲚ ⲘⲀⲢⲚ̄ϢⲒⲠⲈ Ⲛ̄ⲦⲚ̄
(16)   Ⲧ̄ ϨⲒⲰⲰⲚ ⲘⲠⲢⲰⲘⲈ ⲚⲦⲈⲖⲒⲞⲤ
(17)   Ⲛ̄ⲦⲚ̄ⲬⲠⲞϤ ⲚⲀ̣Ⲛ̄ ⲔⲀⲦⲀ ⲐⲈ Ⲛ̄ⲦⲀϤ
(18)   ϨⲰⲚ ⲈⲦⲞⲞⲦⲚ̄ Ⲛ̄ⲦⲚ̄ⲦⲀϢⲈⲞⲈⲒϢ
(19)   ⲘⲠⲈⲨⲀⲄⲄⲈⲖⲒⲞⲚ ⲈⲚⲔⲰ ⲀⲚ ⲈϨⲢⲀ̈Ⲓ
(20)   ⲚⲔⲈϨⲞⲢⲞⲤ ⲞⲨⲀⲈ ⲔⲈⲚⲞⲘⲞⲤ ⲠⲀ
(21)   ⲢⲀ ⲠⲈⲚⲦⲀⲠⲤⲰⲢ̅ ⲬⲞⲞϤ Ⲛ̄ⲦⲈⲢⲈ
(19,1) [   ]Ⲁ̣Ⲓ ⲀⲨⲰ ⲀⲨⲢ̄ⲀⲢⲬⲈⲒ Ⲛ̄
(2)   ⲂⲰⲔ [ⲈⲦⲢⲈⲨⲦ]ⲀⲘⲞ Ⲛ̄ⲤⲈⲦⲀϢⲈⲞⲈⲒϢ

(17,7) When Mary had said (8) this, she fell silent, since it was to this point that the Savior (9) had spoken with her. (10) But Andrew answered and said (11) to the brethren: "Say what you (wish to) say (12) about what she has said. (13) I at least do not believe that (14) the Savior said this. For certainly these teachings (15) are strange ideas." (16) Peter answered and spoke concerning (17) these same things.[74] He (18) questioned them about the Savior: "Did he really

---

[74] In the Greek fragment P. Ryl. 463 the comment which the Coptic version ascribes to Peter is included in the speech of Andrew. This is an obvious error of the copyist (so also Lührmann 1988, 328). This is indicated by the fact that after Mary's comment, which is almost completely missing because of a lacuna of approximately four lines (only the two last words τοῦ σωτῆρος have been preserved; perhaps for this reason Schmid [1990, 7] and Perkins [1992a, 583] think P. Ryl. 463 has included no reference to Mary's reaction), Levi addresses Peter and not Andrew. Therefore, the text in 21,11-12 has to be corrected together with

(19) speak with a woman without our (20) knowledge (and) not openly? Are we to (21) turn about and all listen (22) to her? Did he prefer her to us?" (18,1) Then Mary wept and said to (2) Peter: "My brother Peter, what do you (3) think? Do you think that I (4) thought this up myself in my (5) heart, or that I am lying about the Savior?" (6) Levi answered and said to Peter: (7) "Peter, you have always been (8) hot-tempered. Now I see you (9) contending against the woman like (10) the adversaries. But if the (11) Savior made her worthy, who are you (12) indeed to reject her? Surely (13) the Savior knows her (14) very well. That is why he loved her more (15) than us.[75] Rather let us be ashamed and (16) put on the perfect humanity[76] (17) and acquire it for ourselves as he (18) commanded us, and preach (19) the gospel, not laying down (20) any other rule or other law (21) beyond what the Savior said." When (19,1) [   ][77] and they began to (2) go forth [to] proclaim and to preach.[78]

After the revelation discourse of Mary the relatively harmonious atmosphere changes. Mary's account does not correspond to their expectations at all. Andrew's assessment — "these teachings are strange ideas" (17,14-15) — suggests that Mary's vision is to be regarded as doctrinally invalid since it is not in agreement with Jesus' instructions. Because of the fragmentary condition of the writing no comprehensive comparison between Jesus' and Mary's teaching is possible. Yet at least at some points Mary's account seems to relate fairly well to what Jesus said in those replies

---

Lührmann (1988, 328) as follows: περὶ τοιούτ[ω]ν πρα[γμά]των ἐξ-εταζόμενος <λέγει Πέτρος > ὁ σω[τὴρ] κτλ. The omission of λέγει Πέτρος can very well be explained by an oversight due to the similar endings in the words ἐξεταζόμενος and Πέτρος.

[75] The equivalent of the Coptic N̄ϨOYO EPON ("more than us") is missing in P. Ryl. 463. Is it a mistake of the copyist, or does the Coptic text contain an editorial expansion of the original text? The question will be treated below.

[76] "Humanity" here corresponds to the "human being" in Gos. Mary 9,20.

[77] Till (1955, 78) restores the lacuna [ⲖⲈⲨⲈⲒ ⲆⲈ ⲬⲈ Ⲛ]Ⲁ̈ⲓ and translates the Coptic text as follows: "Als [aber Lewi das gesagt hatte,] schickten sie sich an zu gehen..." Wilson & MacRae (1979, 469) disagrees with Till's suggestion, since "it seems to crowd the lacuna slightly and leaves the following 'and' unaccounted for."

[78] There is a significant difference between the Coptic text and P. Ryl. 463 at the end of the passage. The Greek text reads: [ταῦ]τα εἰπὼν ὁ Λευ[εὶς μὲ]ν ἀπ[ελθὼν] ἦρχεν κη[ρύσσειν τὸ εὐαγγέλι]ον.

which are recorded at the beginning of the extant part of the writing.[79] The ascent of the soul which Mary's vision describes is a concrete illustration of the restoration of the soul to its root (7,17-20). The right answers presented by the soul to the archontic powers are made possible by the true self-knowledge which Jesus' view of salvation emphasizes. The soul's dialogue with the third power about the dissolution of everything (15,21-16,1) seems to presuppose Jesus' prior teaching on that topic (7,3-8). Only on the basis of these observations, can one conclude that all the readers of the text did not find Andrew's objection justified. This raises an interesting question. Is it possible that the author of the text is speaking to a situation in which some people, to whom the Andrew of the text gives his voice, question the religious ideas represented by Mary Magdalene of the text on doctrinal grounds, whereas the author wants to defend these very ideas by demonstrating their affinity with Jesus' own teaching which the author has constructed? We shall return to this question later.

Peter's criticism is different. It it is not directed so much against the contents of the revelation as against the way it was received. That a message claiming to be revelatory is disclosed through a private, secret vision revealed to a woman, not openly, appears to be the reason why Mary's vision account cannot be approved by Peter. It is somewhat surprising that Mary's gender bothers Peter since it did not when he invited her to take part in the discussion among the disciples. The obvious explanation is that in the first place she appeared as a representative of women, who got invitation to speak from the leading male disciple, whereas after her special visionary revelation the situation changed completely. This is demonstrated by the last two sentences of Peter's protest. When they are read carefully one realizes that another, perhaps the most decisive cause for his agitation is advanced by him only here. By granting such a secret and important revelation to Mary Magdalene alone, the Savior proves, according to Peter, to prefer her over the rest of the disciples, including Peter himself. She is no longer the woman above women but the most beloved disciple. This is later explicitly confirmed by Levi. It is thus the privileged status of Mary as the receiver and mediator of the authoritative revelation which is further reason for Peter's irrita-

---

[79] This is cogently demonstrated by King (1995, 614-615) whose presentation I follow at this point.

tion. It is clearly the intention of the author to portray Peter as a jealous man who fears being replaced by Mary Magdalene.

Mary's reaction to Andrew's and Peter's criticism is sorrow and bewilderment. She cannot believe that her integrity and reliability as a witness can be questioned in such a way as is done by Andrew and Peter. An accusation of lying about holy things, implied by the comments of Peter and Andrew, if proven right, is known to be a matter of serious consequence. In the collection of the *Sentences of Sextus* (NHC 32,8-12 [367-368]) it is stated: "The one who speaks lies about God is lying to God; a person who does not have anything truthful to say about God is abandoned by God." Moreover, it is said: "A [believing] nature cannot be[come lover] of lies" (16,4-6 [169]). In light of sayings such as these, which certainly reflect general religious sentiments of the time, Andrew's and Peter's comments do not disqualify Mary only as a mediator of religious truths but as an adherent of a religious conviction as well.

Peter's annoyance at Mary is undeniably enhanced by Levi who characterizes him as hot-tempered and compares him to the adversaries. Especially the last point is interesting. It may contain a reference to the archontic powers which Mary has described in her vision account. At least in the Coptic version this seems evident since the plural form is used.[80] Thus Levi accuses "Peter of being allied with the Powers, who illegitimately attempt to entrap the soul."[81] In any case it is obvious that Levi sees Peter and Andrew as creating a front line between themselves and Mary. There is no doubt which side Levi takes in the battle. For him, there is no reason to question the reliability of Mary's revelation. The fact that the Savior knew Mary very well and loved her gives Levi the full guarantee of Mary's truthfulness.

At this point P. Ryl. 463 and the Coptic text deviate from each other in a significant way. The Greek text says: πάντως γὰρ ἐκεῖνος εἰδὼς αὐτὴν ἀσφ[αλ]ῶ[ς] ἠγάπησεν μᾶλλον ("For surely, knowing her very well, he loved her. Rather..."). The Coptic text reads: ΠΑΝΤШС ΕΡΕΠСШΤΗΡ СΟΟΥΝ ΜΜΟС ΑСΦΑ-ΛШС ΕΤΒΕ ΠΑΪ ΑЧΟΥΟϢϹ ΝϨΟΥΟ ΕΡΟΝ ΜΑΛΛΟΝ ("Surely the Savior knew her very well. *That is why* he loved her *more*

---

[80] So King 1992, 359; 1995, 615.
[81] King 1995, 615.

than us. Rather...”). There are two differences between the two versions. ⲈⲦⲂⲈ ⲠⲀⲒ between the two Coptic sentences makes it more explicit that the first sentence gives the reason for saying the second. Yet the causal character of the participle in the Greek text probably explains this variant and shows that it is merely translational. The other difference, the phrase Ⲛ̄ϨⲞⲨⲞ ⲈⲢⲞⲚ (“more than us”) at the end of the second Coptic sentence is not a variant rendering. Is it an editorial expansion made only after the text had been translated into Coptic or has the Coptic translation preserved an original reading which the copyist of P. Ryl. 463 has omitted due to an oversight? It seems more probable to me that the latter is the case.

The likely Greek equivalent of the Coptic ⲀⳞⲞⲨⲞⳉⲤ̄ Ⲛ̄ϨⲞⲨⲞ ⲈⲢⲞⲚ is ἠγάπησεν μᾶλλον αὐτὴν ἢ ἡμᾶς.[82] If the copyist of P. Ryl. 463 had a text like this, he/she may have easily skipped over the words αὐτὴν ἢ ἡμᾶς, since another μᾶλλον follows immediately. Provided this reconstruction is accepted, the superior position of Mary as the beloved disciple of the Savior is not only granted her by the Coptic translator of the text but it is part of the symbolic world of the original *Gospel of Mary*.

Thus Mary gains in the *Gospel of Mary* a position similar to that of the Beloved Disciple in the Gospel of John, James the Just in the *First* and *Second Apocalypse of James*, and Thomas in the *Gospel of Thomas*. In the *Gospel of Philip* Mary has a similar position but only during the time of the earthly Jesus as will be shown in the chapter “Mary Magdalene in the Gospel of Philip.” Especially in the Gnostic writings the beloved disciple plays the role of a paradigmatic figure who is in a special way equipped to receive authoritative revelations which provide the basis for the tradition each particular writing cherishes.

Levi’s comment “he loved her more than us” implies further that in the *Gospel of Mary* the love relationship between the Savior and Jesus was not regarded as that between man and woman but between a master and his most beloved disciple. Mary did not obtain a special position among the intimate followers of Jesus because she was a woman but because the Savior *knew she was the best choice for the task of receiving his special revelation and acting as the spiritual authority among his disciples*. This raises

---

[82] For a similar construction, see John 3,19; 12,43.

an inevitable question: *why* was Mary Magdalene chosen to play the leading part in the the *Gospel of Mary*?

The question is difficult to answer. One thing is at least clear. It is obvious that in Christian Gnostic texts all those followers of Jesus whose names are explicitly associated with an appearance of the Risen One have enjoyed a special popularity as authoritative figures. Mary Magdalene belongs to this group (John 20,14-18; Mark 16,9-11). As a matter of fact, the basic setting of the *Gospel of Mary* presupposes a special encounter between Mary and the Risen Jesus analogous to that of John 20,14-18 or Mark 16,9-11, in particular. However, this does not necessarily explain fully why the author of *Gospel of Mary* selected just her. There would have been other options, including at least Peter, James the Just, John, and Thomas. In addition, the Gnostic writers can also appeal to such spiritual authorities to whom the New Testament accounts do not attribute any appearance. An outstanding example is Philip (*Gos. Phil.* 73,8; 86,18-19; *PS* 71,18-23). Therefore, additional questions concerning Mary's choice may be raised. Can the *Gospel of Mary* (and possibly some other Gnostic texts also) reflect a knowledge of the historical role Mary Magdalene had in the early Christian movement which goes beyond what the New Testament traditions tell about her as the obvious leader of Jesus' female followers[83] and as the receiver of the Risen Jesus' appearance?[84] Was she a spiritual authority comparable to some of Jesus' male disciples? Or was Mary Magdalene selected to be the protagonist of the writing because it was written to an audience consisting mainly of women? Or was the author of the book a woman who wanted to give the leading role to a woman? These questions cannot but remain interesting questions. The lack of evidence prevents us from finding answers which could be backed up with sufficient degree of probability.

Before the *Gospel of Mary* ends Levi still admonishes Peter and others to be ashamed of what they said to Mary and exhorts

---

[83] The fact that all the lists of women in the canonical gospels, with the exception of John 19,25, place her first speak strongly for this assumption.

[84] This is with caution suggested by King 1995, 620. If this is accepted it does not mean that the whole idea of a controversy between Mary Magdalene and Peter is projected back to the first century as Price (1990, 54-76) and Koivunen (1994) have done.

them with words which although being somewhat different recall
the earlier instruction of the Savior (8,18-21) as Levi himself
notes: "...let us...put on the perfect humanity and acquire it for
ourselves as he commanded us..." (18,15-18; see also 9,19-20).
Once again the disciples are challenged to find their true humanity
and to experience salvation. An interesting parallel to this phrase
is provided by Gos. Phil. 76,22-33: "Not only will they be unable
to detain the perfect man, but they will not be able to see him, for
if they see him they will detain him. There is no other way for a
person to acquire this quality except by putting on the perfect light
[and] he too becoming perfect light. He who has [put it] on will
enter [into the kingdom]. This is the perfect [light, and it is neces-
sary] that we [by all means] become [perfect men] before we leave
[the world.]"[85] In the Gospel of Philip "putting on the perfect man
(light)" expresses in a symbolic way how the Gnostics can receive
deliverance from those powers by which they are imprisoned in
this world. It is therefore another way to formulate the Gnostic
notion of salvation. "Having put on the perfect man" the Gnostics
secure their access to the pleroma, to the perfect light. In the
Gospel of Philip this takes place in connection with a sacramental
act.[86] In the Gospel of Mary the expression lacks all the explicit
sacramental interpretations. This does not necessarily mean that the
possibility of a baptismal reference has to be excluded (cf. also
Gos. Phil. 75,21-24)[87] but it may indicate that the expression is to
be understood as a simple invitation to respond positively to the
challenge of salvation without having to concretize it through any
symbolic action.

Levi's final words recall the Savior's commission to go and
preach the gospel. No explicit response to his admonitions is
recorded. There follows only an abrupt ending, the form of which
is rather different in the two versions which are available. P. Ryl.

---

[85] The translation is taken from Isenberg (1989, 195.197) and the
language is exclusive. The perfect man corresponds to the perfect human
being in my translation of Gos. Mary 18,16.

[86] In 75,14-21 "receiving the perfect man" takes place in the Eucharist; in 75,21-24 "putting on the living man" is connected with baptism; in 70,5-9 "putting on the light" occurs through the sacrament of the
bridal chamber; in 85,24-27 "the perfect light" is poured upon a Gnostic
through the sacrament of anointment.

[87] So King 1992, 360.

463 reads: "When he had said this, Levi departed and began to [preach the gospel]." The Coptic text contains an unfortunate lacuna which prevents a precise comparison between the versions. Nevertheless, it is clear that according to the Coptic version it is not only Levi but "they" who began to go forth and preach. According to P. Ryl. 463 the words of Levi do not seem to have any positive result. Other disciples simply refuse to obey him and obviously go away, whereas Levi alone accepts the commission given by the Savior and nothing is said of Mary. But who are the "they" in the Coptic version? There seem to be two options: all the disciples who after Levi's speech repent and decide to comply with his exhortation or Levi and Mary Magdalene. On the basis of the literary context the first alternative is the most natural. At the end of his speech Levi is clearly addressing the whole group of disciples, and so the third person suffix pronoun seems to refer to them. Yet the tone of the disciples' altercation, even that of Levi's last speech, is so tense that it is not easy to imagine that Levi could have caused a reconciliation among them. Could it be possible that the "they" of the Coptic text would be a cumbersome correction by the translator wanting to include Mary Magdalene in Levi's company but still to leave out all the other disciples?

5. The Conflict Between Mary Magdalene and Peter, and the Question of Social Reality

The concreteness of the controversy described by the author of the *Gospel of Mary* suggests that he/she addresses a debate in which some Christians engaged themselves in the second century. The debate centers around the validity of the tradition claimed to be derived from Mary Magdalene. Other topics involved are the legitimacy of women's spiritual leadership and the role of private post-resurrection visions as a reliable source of revelation. Instead of entering into a direct theological argument about these matters the author presents his/her convictions "narratively in the tensions among the disciples."[88]

The fact that the revelation received by Mary Magdalene is cast in the form of a vision is in itself an indication that the *Gospel of*

---

[88] King 1995, 621.

Mary affirms the legitimacy of post-resurrection visions as a source of authoritative teaching. It is in fact possible that the writing polemicizes against those Christians who wanted to assign the stamp of validity only to those words of Jesus which were presented as memorized by and transmitted through the apostles.

The way Mary Magdalene and Levi are pictured, on the one hand, and Peter and Andrew, on the other, makes it evident what view the author of the *Gospel of Mary* holds concerning the position of Mary Magdalene as a spiritual authority and the legitimacy of women's spiritual leadership. While validating Mary's teaching and privileged status against accusations launched by Peter that the Savior would not have revealed a special revelation to a woman that he did not tell to them, the *Gospel of Mary* affirms the legitimacy of women's spiritual authority. For the author of the *Gospel of Mary*, Peter and Andrew stand for those Christians who confine the authoritative teaching to what is taught publicly by men. Mary and Levi, on the other hand, "represent those Christians who question the validity of any apostolic authority that challenges the truth of their own experience of the Living Lord; for them, apostolic authority is not based simply on being one of the Twelve or on gender but on spiritual qualifications. Women who have those qualifications may exercise legitimate authority."[89]

In a society and among Christians, where women most frequently are denied any leadership function, the *Gospel of Mary* furnishes a new perspective. As succinctly put by Karen King, it

> provides an important complement to texts such as 1 Tim 2:8-15, which demand the silence and submissiveness of women and forbid them to have authority over men. We can now see that the position of 1 Timothy is *but one side* of a debate in early Christian circles. The *Gospel of Mary* also provides evidence that texts such as 1 Timothy were written precisely because women were exercising leadership and exerting their authority over men. If some thought that such women were immodest, unseemly, insubordinate, and garrulous, Levi's mocking response to Peter shows that others may have viewed the opponents to women's legitimate leadership as jealous, proud, contentious, and foolish.[90]

---

[89] King 1995, 623-624.
[90] King 1995, 624.

One question remains to be asked. Are there indications in the text that the controversy which is enacted in the story of Mary Magdalene and Peter reflects disagreements between Gnostic and non-Gnostic, orthodox Christians, as is frequently suggested?[91] The *Gospel of Mary* does not give any explicit answer to this question but it provides some clues which make this conclusion likely. First, the warning not "to lay down any rules" and not "to give a law like the lawgiver" twice repeated in the writing (8,22-9,4; 18,18-20) seems to reflect a typical Gnostic polemic against non-Gnostic, orthodox Christians, who intermingle "the things of the law with the words of the Savior" (Iren., *Adv. haer.* 3.2,2) and "who set up their error and their law" against the pure thoughts of the Gnostics (*Apoc. Pet.* 77,25-27). Whatever the precise contents of the law in these texts it is worth noting that the law is connected by Gnostics with an orthodox position.

Second, in the second century a vision as a source of revelation seems to be typical of Gnostic circles,[92] whereas the non-Gnostic, orthodox groups question its validity.[93] Third, the accusation expressed by Andrew that Mary Magdalene's revelation is not in agreement with the teachings of Jesus, is a claim frequently used by orthodox Christians in their anti-Gnostic polemic. The attempt to show affinity between Mary's and Jesus' teachings also fits well in the context where a Gnostic writer charged by more orthodox Christians with doctrinal errors is trying to show that his/her message ultimately derives from Jesus. Fourth, if the abrupt ending of the writing can be interpreted to indicate that Levi alone, or perhaps along with Mary Magdalene, went to proclaim the gospel of salvation within, but that the other disciples did not, it may suggest that the latter are seen to represent a different conception of salvation, most probably more in line with orthodoxy.

---

[91] E.g. Perkins 1980, 133; Pagels 1981, 77; T.V. Smith 1985, 105; Schmid 1990, 18.

[92] Pagels 1978, 415-430.

[93] See e.g. *Apoc. Pet.* 75,2-7 in which the Savior criticizes ecclesiastical Christians who say that visions come from a demon. See also Koschorke 1978, 49-52. Cf. also *Ps.-Clem. Hom.* 17.16,6; 17.17,5.

CHAPTER SIX

MARY MAGDALENE
IN THE FIRST APOCALYPSE OF JAMES

1. *Introductory Remarks*

The *First Apocalypse of James* is usually neglected or treated very cursorily, when Mary Magdalene traditions are studied.[1] This is probably because the name Mary appears only once in the writing and this particular passage (40,22-26) is fragmentary and difficult to interpret. The present study will show that the passage should not be overlooked because of its fragmentary condition. Interpreted in the context of the entire writing, it reveals important aspects of Mary Magdalene's role in early Christian traditions. Before proceeding to analyze the text, a brief presentation of the *First Apocalypse of James* is necessary. In addition, the question of its date and provenance will be treated.

The *First Apocalypse of James* is a Gnostic writing[2] which contains a secret teaching imparted by the Lord to James. It is cast in the form of a Gnostic revelation dialogue with a description of the death and the resurrection of Jesus as its narrative framework.[3] At present, the text is known through a single Coptic[4] manuscript

---

[1] In her presentation of those Gnostic texts where Mary Magdalene appears, Koivunen (1994, 172), for example, uses less than one page to introduce the *First Apocalypse of James*. No reference to the *First Apocalypse of James* is made by Malvern 1975, 30-56; Bovon 1984, 52-55; Grassi & Grassi 1986, 116-129; Price 1990, 57-60; Haskins 1993, 33-57.

[2] Among Gnostic features of the *First Apocalypse of James* there are the dualistic separation between the realm of the supreme deity and the heavens of the archons (26,2-30), the technical use of the term gnosis (28,7), the description of the ascent of the soul (33,11-34,20), and the idea of the higher and the lower Sophia (35,5-17).

[3] Schoedel 1979, 65.

[4] The original language of the writing is most probably Greek; see Funk 1987, 255.

belonging to the fifth codex of the Nag Hammadi Library.[5] There is another Coptic version of the *First Apocalypse of James* which, for the time being, is neither published nor available for study.[6] This is unfortunate since the Nag Hammadi version is in some places very fragmentary,[7] and comparison with another manuscript[8] would be of great help in producing a more complete critical edition of the text.[9]

The dialogue between the Lord and James is divided in two parts. The first takes place prior to the death of Jesus (24,11-30,11), the second follows his resurrection (31,2-42,19).[10] Since both parts presuppose each other and the second follows the first as a natural sequence (25,2-7; 29,19-25; 32,28-33,5), the bipartition of the dialogue cannot be taken as a sign of literary non-uniformity in the writing.[11] Neither does the somewhat awkward change of the subject pronoun from the third person singular to the

---

[5] The ancient title of the text is the Apocalypse of James but modern scholarship has added the word "first" in order to distinguish it from another writing bearing the same title in the same Nag Hammadi codex. That writing is now commonly known as the *Second Apocalypse of James*. The identical name of the two writings shows that they were written independently. This conclusion is strengthened by the fact that the *First Apocalypse of James* circulated separately from the *Second Apocalypse of James* (see next note; see also Funk 1987, 256). This means that the *Second Apocalypse of James* provides no direct clues for interpreting the *First Apocalypse of James*.

[6] J.M. Robinson 1972-1984, Introduction 21. That version of *First Apocalypse of James* is part of a manuscript which contains a copy of the *Letter of Peter to Philip* as well as a previously unknown dialogue between Jesus and his disciples.

[7] The manuscript comprises lines 24,10-44,10 of the fifth codex of the Nag Hammadi Library. Pages 24-34 are relatively well preserved; only a few lines at the bottom of each page are partly lost. Pages 35-44 are severely damaged both at the top and the bottom of each page.

[8] According to Funk (1987, 255) the newly discovered, but unedited version of the *First Apocalypse of James* is in better condition than the Nag Hammadi version.

[9] The first edition of the text was published by Böhlig & Labib 1963, 29-54. The most recent edition of the text was prepared by Schoedel 1979, 65-103. The English translations of the text are taken from Schoedel's edition unless otherwise noted.

[10] A post-resurrection appearance of Jesus to James is mentioned also in 1 Cor 15,7; *Gos. Heb.* 7 [Jerome, *De viris inl.* 2]; *2 Apoc. Jas.* 50,5-10; cf. also *Ap. Jas.* 2,15-39.

[11] So also Fallon 1979, 133; for a rather complex source theory of the *First Apocalypse of James*, see Kasser 1965, 78-81.

first in 24,11; 25,12; 27,18 seem to justify a source theory. Rather, these passages show the author identifying so closely with James that at times the author assumes the part of an interlocutor in the dialogue even though most of the time he/she maintains the role of the narrator. It is only near the beginning when a reference is made to an earlier question which now seems to be missing (24,26-27) that we may have an indication of a redactional rearrangement or even a loss of materials.[12] Since the question of the possible dislocation of materials does not bear on the present subject matter it need not be dealt with here.

James, the protagonist of the writing, is the brother of the Lord. Admittedly, in his initial address the Lord appears to deny any consanguinity between James and himself. He says to James: "I have given you a sign of these things, James, my brother. For not without reason have I called you my brother, although you are not my brother materially (= ϩⲣⲁⲓ ϩⲛ̄ ⲑⲩⲗⲏ)" (24,13-16). However, there are two items elsewhere in the writing that prevent one from taking this denial of "material" relation between the Lord and James as an indication that someone else other than James the Just is meant. First, James is not a member of the twelve (42,20-24) and cannot thus be one of the Zebedees, the other James of early Christianity famous enough to be chosen as the principal character of an early Christian document. Second, James is called "the Just" (32,3). This epithet is used of James, the brother of the Lord, in other early Christian writings, both ecclesiastical and Gnostic.[13] Based on this evidence, the statement that James is not a brother of the Lord materially does not mean that some unknown James other than the brother of Jesus, the first leader of the Jerusalem church, should be regarded as the interlocutor of the Lord in the *First Apocalypse of James*. Rather, it emphasizes that the most

---

[12] Schoedel 1979, 65.

[13] Jerome, *De viris inl.* 2 (citing the *Gospel of Hebrews*); *Gos. Thom.* 12; *2 Apoc. Jas.* 44,13-14; 60,12-13; Origen, *Contra Cels.* 1,47; Eus., *Hist. eccl.* 2.1,2-5 (citing Clement of Alexandria); 2.23,3-7; 4.22,4 (citing Hegesippus); 2.23,20 (citing Josephus although the text is not found in his extant writings).

important dimension in the relationship between Jesus and James is not physical[14] but spiritual.[15]

2. *Date and Provenance*

While imparting the Gnostic revelation to James, the Lord also instructs him how to pass this message on and when to make it public (36,15-38,11). Although the text is quite fragmentary and some of its details remain obscure, it still gives a fairly good overall view of the transmission process which the revelation received by James is supposed to undergo. Before his martyrdom, just prior to the destruction of Jerusalem, James is assigned the task of conveying the revelation to Addai who is expected to write it down ten years later (or ten years after the destruction of Jerusalem). Because of the lacunae at the bottom of page 36 and at the top of page 37 the next stage(s) of the transmission process remain(s) unclear. The next connecting link which can be distinguished in the text[16] is a man called Levi.[17] He begets two sons the younger of whom receives the Gnostic message from his father and keeps it hidden until he is seventeen years old. Then he reveals it. Whether he still hands it on privately to someone or proclaims it publicly does not become clear because of the lacunae in the text. At any rate it is evident that either his proclamation or that of his listeners' marks the beginning of the public Gnostic mission.

The passage summarized here is important in two ways. First, while the long secret transmission process of the revelation impart-

---

[14] It is not entirely out of question that the text regards James as the first leader of the Jerusalem church but for some theological reason wants to reject the notion that Jesus had physical siblings.

[15] It is noteworthy that Origen can also argue that Paul regarded James as the brother of the Lord, "not so much on account of their relationship by blood, or of their being brought up together, as because of his virtue and doctrine" (*Contra Cels.* 1,47).

[16] Only the first two letters of the name are unequivocally preserved in the manuscript. Since the third letter is most probably Ⲩ the most likely restoration of the name is ⲗⲉⲩ[ⲉⲓ].

[17] In its extant form, the text does not reveal more closely who this particular Levi is. Perkins' suggestion (1980, 144) that he is Mary Magdalene's defender in the *Gospel of Mary* is interesting but remains a mere conjecture.

ed to James reflects an awareness of the relative lateness of Gnostic preaching[18] it also intimates a relatively late date of the writing
itself. The transmission is clearly assumed to have taken place, if
not in the distant past, at least clearly much earlier than the composition of the writing. Since the temporal end point of the transmission must be considered somewhere in the early part of the
second century, the actual writing of the text cannot be dated
earlier than towards the end of the second century.[19] How much
later the date of composition could be, is difficult to say. An
approximate *terminus ad quem* is provided by the material found
in the cartonnage used to support the covers of the fifth codex of
the Nag Hammadi Library. The dateable cartonnage of the codex
derives from the first half of the fourth century. Thus, this codex
cannot have been prepared much later than in the latter half of the
fourth century.[20] Since the Coptic translation of the text has a text
history behind it, as is shown by another, possibly different variant
of the Coptic text, it was probably made already in the third
century.[21] The Greek original is of course still earlier but how
much? Is it to be placed closer to the beginning of the period in
question, i.e., towards the end of the second century, or to the end
of that period, i.e., at the end of the third century, or somewhere
in the middle? It is not easy to answer this question. However,
there are some indications which speak for a late second century
date.

The idea of the seven Gnostic women (38,16-18)[22] has its only
known parallel in the *Sophia of Jesus Christ* (90,17-18). If the
Sophia of Jesus Christ is dated in the first half of the second
century, as argued above, it is natural that the *First Apocalypse of
James* which contains the same motif is not dated much later,
especially when no literary dependence between the two can be
established. Another fact which speaks for a second century dating
is that the instruction given to James for his ascent past the archontic powers (32,28-36,1) has a very close, almost verbatim
parallel in the Marcosian formulae taught to a dying Gnostic in
connection with a sacrament of extreme unction (Iren., *Adv. haer.*

---

[18] This is pointed out by Perkins 1980, 144.
[19] So also Schoedel 1979, 67; Funk 1987, 255.
[20] J.M. Robinson 1972-1984, Cartonnage XIX.
[21] Funk 1987, 255.
[22] For my reading of the text, see pp. 135-137.

1.21,5).[23] Certainly, Epiphanius also knows the same formulae (*Pan.* 36.3,1-6). Nevertheless, he is not using an independent tradition but has Irenaeus as his source even though he attaches the material to his presentation of the Heracleonites.[24] The writer of the *First Apocalypse of James* can hardly have depended on an anti-Gnostic work of Irenaeus but rather derives his material from a Valentinian tradition known both to him/herself and to Irenaeus in the latter half of the second century.

The second noteworthy feature in the description of the transmission process is the mention of Addai (ⲁⲇⲇⲁⲓⲟⲥ/ⲁⲇⲇⲉⲟⲥ). Unfortunately the fragmentary nature of the text does not permit us to know much about this Addai. The extant lines say only that he is supposed to write down the revelation received by James and obviously to hand it on to the next member of the chain of tradition (36,20-27). Although not connected with James in any other Christian writings, Addai is not an unknown personage in Early Christianity. Sources deriving from Osrhoëne and Adiabene, such as the excerpts of the *Abgar Legend* in Eusebius' *Historia ecclesiastica* (1.13),[25] the *Doctrine of Addai*, and the *Chronicle of Arbela*,[26] introduce him as the founder of Christianity in Edessa.[27] In

---

[23] This was pointed out by Böhlig & Labib 1963; see also Schenke 1966, 27.

[24] Epiphanius seems to know nothing else about Heracleon but his name (Irenaeus too only mentions him [*Adv. haer.* 2.4,1]); therefore, in all probability, he uses the material which is the last part of Irenaeus' account of the Marcosians to create his presentation of the Heracleonites.

[25] Eusebius speaks of Thaddaeus, one of the seventy chosen by Jesus (Luke 10,1; Eus., *Hist. eccl.* 1.12,3; cf. also Matt 10,3 according to which Thaddaeus is one of the twelve). According to the *Abgar Legend*, Thaddaeus (= Addai) is sent by Thomas (not by James!) to perform healings and to proclaim the gospel in Edessa. It is possible that Eusebius or the writer of the legend has renamed the disciple in order to underline the apostolic origin of Osrhoënean Christianity.

[26] Schoedel 1979, 67.

[27] Certainly, the legendary material attached to the person of Addai, such as his belonging to the seventy called by Jesus as well as his connections with the Apostle Thomas and the King Abgar, are probably of a late date as Bauer (1964 [1934], 6-17), Drijvers (1987, 391-393), and Lieu (1992, 35) have argued. By no means does this exclude the possibility of the historical Addai who brought the gospel to the areas of Osrhoëne and Mesopotamia. With this assumption, nothing is said of the exact orientation of his proclamation or of other possible early Christian missionaries in those regions. If Addai were a mere secondary invention created by Syriac-speaking Christianity to justify its claims for ancient

addition, local Christian traditions of Arbela in Adiabene and Karkā de Bēt Selōk in Bēt Garmai insist that he was the first one to proclaim the Christian Gospel in these cities as well.[28] If the Addai of the *First Apocalypse of James* is the same as the one in these Edessene and Mesopotamian documents the provenance of the writing could well be sought in Osrhoëne or in Mesopotamia.[29] There are two further items in the *First Apocalypse of James* which may suggest an origin in that area. The name of the mountain in *1 Apoc. Jas.* 30,20-21, Gaugelan, may be a somewhat corrupt Syriac form of Golgotha.[30] In addition, the four women mentioned in *1 Apoc. Jas.* 40,22-26, Salome, Mariam, probably Martha, and Arsinoe (there is a lacuna in the manuscript at this point; for the restoration of the text, see below) are also brought together in the *Manichaean Psalm-book II* (194,19-22; see also 192,21-24) which probably originated in Mesopotamia and which can easily reflect influences of Syrian (Gnostic) Christian traditions.

Before examining more closely the only text where the name of Mariam appears, one further question remains: can something be said about the orientation of the Gnostic thinking represented by the *First Apocalypse of James*? It was noted above that the instruction imparted by the Lord to James for the ascent of the

---

and worthy origin it is probable that instead of him a more famous and clearly apostolic authority would have been chosen. As a matter of fact, the attempts to turn him into Thaddaeus or to join him together with the Apostle Thomas indicate that Addai has been felt to be an insufficient initiator of eastern Syrian Christianity. Drijvers' suggestion (1982, 157-175, esp. 157-166; 1987, 391-392) that the *Abgar Legend* has its origin in the late third century anti-Manichaean polemics where a legend of an orthodox Addai is created to combat the Manichaean Addai or Adda(s), one of the most prominent disciples and missionaries of Mani, is ingenious but hardly plausible. The *Abgar Legend* does not betray such polemical tones as Drijvers' thesis presupposes.

[28] For the evidence, see Lieu 1992, 35.

[29] The eastern Syrian origin of the *First Apocalypse of James* is advocated by Schoedel (1979, 67), with some hesitation also by Funk (1987, 255).

[30] See Schoedel 1991, 157-158. Schoedel also reckons with the possibility that the name of a Syrian holy mountain, Gaugal, has had influence on how the name of Golgotha was spelled. Böhlig (1967, 133) suggested earlier that the mountain the text speaks of is Galgala near Jericho. This assumption, however, is highly unlikely as Schoedel has demonstrated (1991, 157).

latter has its closest parallel in a Valentinian version quoted by Irenaeus. This is not the only point in common between the *First Apocalypse of James* and Valentinianism. The idea of the higher and the lower (Achamoth) Sophia in *1 Apoc. Jas.* 35,5-36,9 indicates that the writer of the text is familiar with a developed form of Valentinianism.[31] The description of the Father as unnameable and ineffable (24,20-21) and the doctrine of the unification of the female and the male element in the ultimate redemption of a Gnostic (41,17-19) are also themes which, although not only peculiar to Valentinian thinking, are quite congruous with it.[32] Based on these observations it can be assumed that the writer of the *First Apocalypse of James* was a Valentinian Christian or at least wrote his work in a milieu penetrated by Valentinian ideas.[33]

3. *The List of Women in 40,25-26*[34]

The name ⲘⲀⲢⲒⲀⲘ occurs only once in the *First Apocalypse of James*. It is part of a list where several female names are mentioned (40,25ff.). The first two names are Salome and Mariam. The third name is lost, and only the four last letters (ⲒⲚⲞⲎ̅) of the fourth name are preserved. After line 26 the text is so heavily corrupt that it is not easy to know how many names the list comprised altogether. Nevertheless, the two extant letters at the end of line 27 do not appear to be part of a name since there is no horizontal line above them as is the case with the three visible names and, at least in the majority of instances, with the proper names in the fifth codex of the Nag Hammadi Library, in general. Schoedel has also pointed out that the combination of letter Ⲧ and letter Ⲕ, with a supralinear stroke over the latter, does not easily lend itself

---

[31] Funk 1987, 255.

[32] Schoedel 1979, 67.

[33] The majority of scholars maintain that the *First Apocalypse of James* was produced under some influence of Valentinian thought (for arguments, see Veilleux 1986, 9-10) but there are differences as to the degree of this influence; for this, see Desjardins 1990, 6-7.

[34] For the entire text of *1 Apoc. Jas.* 40,22-26 and its translation, see below.

to being part of a female name.[35] Thus, it is probable that the list ended somewhere in the middle of line 27 or already at the end of line 26 after the letters ⲒⲚⲞⲎ. In the former case it contained five names or six at most, in the latter only four.

Böhlig & Labib as well as Schoedel have assumed that the number of women was mentioned in the passage itself but the numeral indicating it has disappeared through damage to the manuscript at the beginning of line 25. The numeral which best fills the lacuna of the text is, in their view, [ϥⲦⲞⲞⲨ] (four).[36] This reconstruction, which also makes use of an interesting parallel in the *Manichaean Psalm-book II* (see below), is ingenious but nevertheless unlikely. It does not explain adequately why the demonstrative article at the end of the previous line is masculine when one would expect to find its feminine equivalent since it is attached to a numeral referring to women. There is, however, another fact which suggests that the list of women in the *First Apocalypse of James* consisted of four names. When the editors of the *editio princeps* sought to restore the list they paid attention to the fact that the *Manichaean Psalm-book II* contains two presentations of Jesus' female disciples which include Marihamme, Martha, Salome, and Arsinoe[37] (194,19-22; 192,21-24).[38] One of these has only these four names (194,19-22), the other one adds seven other women (192,25-193,3). If the fourth name of the list in the *First Apocalypse of James* is restored to read [ⲀⲢⲤ]ⲒⲚⲞⲎ, as it

---

[35] Schoedel 1979, 98-99. It is at least clear that no Greek female name is transcribed into Coptic in such a way that it contains a supralinear stroke. If the name was Egyptian, of course, it could have included a supralinear stroke. It is however extremely unlikely that the list of women would have contained an Egyptian name.

[36] Böhlig & Labib 1963; Schoedel 1979, 98; Veilleux 1986, 54; the translations of Kasser (1968, 174) and Funk (1987, 263) also presuppose this reading although both of them have added a question mark after it. Schoedel mentions in a footnote another possibility, namely [ⲤⲀⲱϤⲈ] (seven; cf. *1 Apoc. Jas.* 38,16; see also Kasser 1968, 174), but dismisses it as improbable in light of the context and the parallel in the *Manichaean Psalm-book II* 194,19-22.

[37] The name there is spelled ⲀⲢⲤⲈⲚⲞⲎ, but the difference is due to orthographical variation. A Manichaean Gospel fragment discovered in Turfan also refers to Arsinoe, spelled 'Arsani'ah. She is one of the myrrhophores; Mary Magdalene and Salome are the other two (Puech & Blatz 1987, 321).

[38] Böhlig & Labib 1963.

could well be, although other possibilities cannot be ruled out,[39] the three names out of four would be the same as in *Man. Ps. II* 194,19-22. The probability that the two lists were identical, apart from the order of the names, is further enhanced by the fact that [MN̄ MAPΘA MN̄ ᾱPC] fills the lacuna of line 26 very well. Given these considerations, the four names in the list of women in *1 Apoc. Jas.* 40,25-26 could be read as follows: C̄AⲖⲰMH MN̄ MAPIAM [MN̄ MAPΘA MN̄ ᾱPC]INOH.

4. *The Identity of Mary in 40,22-26*

Once more a writing refers to a Mary without specifying her identity. Could she be someone other than Mary Magdalene? At least the form of the name seems to exclude the possibility that the mother of Jesus is meant.[40] At this time, however, in addition to Magdalene still another woman can be forwarded as an alternative identification of Mary. If one of the persons in the list of women is Martha, as argued above, one can ask whether MAPIAM of the text could be her sister, Mary of Bethany (John 11,19; 12,3). There are two arguments which render this interpretation unlikely. First, in *Pistis Sophia I-III*, the only known Gnostic text where Martha indisputably appears besides the *Manichaean Psalm-book II*, she does not do it together with her sister but indeed with Salome and Mary Magdalene (and Mary, the mother of Jesus). Second, one of the lists of four women in the *Manichaean Psalm-book II* makes it explicit that Mary of the text is Mary Magdalene (192,21-22). It introduces her as "a net-caster...hunting for the eleven others that were lost." This presentation of Mary recalls the first psalm in the collection of the *Psalms of Heracleides* in the *Manichaean Psalm-book II* in which Mary Magdalene is entrusted with the task of going to the eleven and to be a messenger "to these lost orphans" (*Man. Ps. II* 187,12-13).[41]

Having stated that Mariam in *1 Apoc. Jas.* 40,25 is probably meant to be Mary Magdalene and not Mary of Bethany, it is

---

[39] Greek female names with the ending INOH are fairly common. Dornseiff & Hansen (1957, 60) list 17 possibilities.

[40] See pp. 63-64.

[41] See the section "Mary Magdalene in the Manichaean Psalm-book".

necessary to stress that the distinction between these two alternatives may not have been fully clear in the mind of the author.
Namely, even in *Man. Ps. II* 192,23 Martha is called the sister of
Mary Magdalene. If that can be taken concretely,[42] the text is
probably an early indication of the tendency typical of later Christian writings in which Mary Magdalene and Mary of Bethany tend
to be fused into one and the same person.[43] Thus, the portrait of
Mary Magdalene is complemented with features gained from that
of Mary of Bethany.

When the role of Mary Magdalene in the *First Apocalypse of
James* is assessed, the following questions are particularly significant: What is her relationship to James, to the seven women
mentioned in 38,16-17, and to the twelve male disciples (42,20-
24)? In addition, one must ask how the discussion about femaleness and maleness (41,15-19) is related to Mary Magdalene and
other women mentioned in the writing. Because of the fragmentary
nature of the *First Apocalypse of James* great caution is in order
when conclusions are drawn. Nevertheless, some significant observations can be made. We shall begin by looking at the passage
where the list of four women appears.

5. *The Relationship of Mary Magdalene to James*

ⲉϢⲱⲡⲉ ⲉⲕ[Ϣⲁ]ⲛⲭⲉ ⲛⲉⲓϢⲁⲭⲉ ⲛ̄ⲧⲉ ⲧⲉⲓ[ⲉⲥⲑ]ⲏⲥⲓⲥ ⲧⲱⲧ
ⲛ̄ϩⲏⲧ ⲙ̄ⲡⲉⲉⲓ[...] ⲥⲁⲗⲱⲙⲏ ⲙⲛ̄ ⲙⲁⲣⲓⲁⲙ [ⲙⲛ̄ ⲙⲁⲣⲑⲁ ⲙⲛ̄
ⲁⲣⲥ]ⲓⲛⲟⲏ

---

[42] In the same context the relationship of two other women is described similarly. Iphidama is presented as a sister of Maximilla (*Man.
Ps. II* 192,26-28). This characterization is most probably based on the
account of the *Acts of Andrew* in which both appear as main female characters and are introduced as sisters (338; see Schneemelcher 1989, 127).

[43] See Holzmeister 1922, 556-584. It is usual to date this phenomenon fairly late, that is to say in the time of Augustine or even in the time
of Gregory the Great. Holzmeister maintains the latter view. Differently
Grant (1961, 138) who assumes that already Origen identifies the two
women with each other (and with the anonymous anointer in Luke 7).
Man. Ps. II 192,21-23 does indicate that this phenomenon has begun
quite early. However, when one criticizes Holzmeister one has to take
into consideration that the *Manichaean Psalm-book II* was discovered
only after he had written his article.

"...When you speak these words of this [perception/knowledge], be persuaded by these [...:] Salome and Mary [and Martha and Ars]inoe..."[44]

The way the relationship between James and Mary Magdalene as well as the other three women is to be viewed in *1 Apoc. Jas.* 40,22-26 depends, first, on how one understands the meaning of the imperative form of the Coptic verb ⲦⲰⲦ Ⲛ̄ϨⲎⲦ (40,24) and, second, on how one reconstructs the lacuna at the beginning of line 25. In this writer's assessment, all the commentators of the text have taken ⲦⲰⲦ Ⲛ̄ϨⲎⲦ as a transitive verb. Accordingly, they have interpreted the text as the Lord's command to James to offer encouragement, comfort, or a word of persuasion to the women listed in the text.[45] Since they think that the list of women included four names, they fill the lacuna at the beginning of line 25 with the Coptic numeral ϥⲦⲟⲟⲩ. Despite its ostensible plausibility, this interpretation of the text contains difficult problems which render it unlikely.

First, together with Ⲛ̄ϨⲎⲦ the verb ⲦⲰⲦ has exclusively an intransitive meaning both in the infinitive and in the qualitative (e.g. Rom 4,21; 2 Thess 2,12; *1 Apoc. Jas.* 42,17; *2 Apoc. Jas.* 61,4; *Paraph. Shem* 46,4; *Treat. Seth* 52,15; *Teach. Silv.* 115,26; possibly *1 Apoc. Jas.* 38,13 as well).[46] Thus, Ⲛ̄ before the demonstrative article on line 24 is not an object marker but is used in the instrumental sense. The most plausible meaning of ⲦⲰⲦ Ⲛ̄ϨⲎⲦ Ⲛ̄ is therefore "to be persuaded/convinced by" or "to be satisfied with." The second problem with the interpretation presented above is that the reconstruction of the lacuna at the beginning of line 25 can hardly be the numeral ϥⲦⲟⲟⲩ. As noted previously, it does not explain adequately why the demonstrative article at the end of the previous line is masculine when one would expect to find its feminine equivalent since it is attached to a numeral referring to women. Therefore, another restoration of the text has to be sought.

---

[44] The text is taken from Schoedel 1979, 98. For the translation, see the discussion below.
[45] Schenke (1966, 29) translates it ⲦⲰⲦ Ⲛ̄ϨⲎⲦ: "tröste", Schoedel (1979, 99) and Veilleux (1986, 55): "encourage", and Funk (1987, 263): "überzeuge".
[46] See also the passages mentioned in Crum 1939, 438.

There is of course no way of knowing for certain how the
lacuna of approximately five letters at the beginning of line 25
should be filled. Nevertheless, the demonstrative article at the end
of line 24 shows that the lacuna must at least begin with a masculine noun. If James is supposed to be persuaded by or be satisfied
with something the women have said or say, the exhortation of the
Lord beginning at the end of line 24 could be restored as follows:
ⲦⲰⲦ ⲚϨⲎⲦ ⲘⲠⲈⲈⲒ[ⲰⲀϪⲈ Ⲛ]ⲤⲀⲖⲰⲘⲎ ⲘⲚ ⲘⲀⲢⲒⲀⲘ (...be
persuaded by the word of Salome and Mariam...)[47] or ⲦⲰⲦ ⲚϨⲎⲦ
ⲘⲠⲈⲈⲒ[ⲘⲚⲦⲢⲈ] ⲤⲀⲖⲰⲘⲎ ⲘⲚ ⲘⲀⲢⲒⲀⲘ (...be persuaded by this
testimony: Salome and Mariam...). Both of these suggestions are
conjectures but they are based on a grammatically unforced reading of the text. Yet in whatever way the lacuna is reconstructed it
is clear that the text is meant to read that James can learn something from Mary Magdalene and the other three women as he
speaks "these words of this [per]ception" (40,23-24). This observation raises another question. What is the actual task requiring
James to be instructed to seek advice or help from the four wom-
en?

In the context of the *First Apocalypse of James* the only three
acts of speaking which James is encouraged to undertake are his
answers before the three toll collectors during his ascent (33,5-11),
his communication of the revelation imparted by the Lord to
Addai (36,15-16), and his rebuke of the twelve (42,20-24). No
other speaking or proclaiming activity seems to be expected from
him. On the contrary, he is urged to keep silent (36,13-14). To
speak the "words of this perception" could very well refer to any
of these events. In all these instances James is to utilize the
knowledge he has gained through the special instruction of the
Lord. Thus, the "words of this perception" is tantamount to the
"words of this gnosis."[48] This means that the word ⲈⲤⲐⲎⲤⲒⲤ (=
αἴσθησις) is used here differently from Platonic philosophy where
it is the equivalent of a lower cognitive faculty and refers to the

---

[47] This restoration of the lacuna faces the problem that if the last
letter of the lacuna of line 25 had had a supralinear stroke above it, it
possibly would have been visible in the extant text.

[48] In fact, the lacuna at the beginning of line 24, which is reconstructed by Schoedel (1979, 98) to read [ⲈⲤⲐ]ⲎⲤⲒⲤ, could be restored
[ⲄⲚ]ⲰⲤⲒⲤ as well.

observation of the visible world by the senses.[49] However, the use of ЄСѲНСІС is well in agreement with those texts in the Nag Hammadi Library in which ЄСѲНСІС clearly stands for ГNШСІС, the ability to see beyond the material reality (*Paraph. Shem* 29,2.12; 40,17; *Teach. Silv.* 89,24; *Trim. Prot.* 36,12; cf. also *Apoc. Pet.* 74,3). Even in *1 Apoc. Jas.* 38,22-23 where it denotes an unusual human capacity which gives its owners a special strength, ЄСѲНСІС[50] seems to be equated with gnosis. Based on these considerations, it seems evident that Mary Magdalene and the other three women mentioned by name would be considered spiritual authorities who could provide guidance to James in the most important tasks the Lord entrusts to him.

In light of the evidence provided by the *First Apocalypse of James*, it is worth noting that there is also another source which brings together James and Mary Magdalene. Yet the way the relationship between them is described there is different from the testimony of the *First Apocalypse of James*. According to Hippolytus of Rome, there existed a second century Gnostic group, the Naassenes, who claimed to ground their teaching on the tradition derived from James, the brother of the Lord, *through* Mary Magdalene (*Ref.* 5.7,1). If Hippolytus accurately reflects the view of the Naassenes, it indicates that at least the writings of the two Gnostic groups regarded James and Mary Magdalene as significant links in the formation of Gnostic traditions even though the relationship of these two to each other is seen differently. There being no theological or thematic connections between the *First Apocalypse of James* and the doctrines of the Naassenes, it is evident that the two groups trace their roots back to James and Mary Magdalene independently of each other.

6. *Mary Magdalene and the Seven Female Disciples of the Lord*

Unfortunately, the passage which speaks of the seven female disciples of the Lord is badly damaged (38,16ff.). Virtually eight lines at the end of page 38 and at the beginning of page 39 are

---

[49] Zandee 1991, 134-135.

[50] In *1 Apoc. Jas.* 38,22-23 the word is partly damaged but ЄСѲ[НСІС] is the most likely restoration of the text.

completely missing. Thus, the answer of the Lord to the question
of James concerning them is not available to us. The part of the
answer which is preserved no longer seems to speak about the
women. This means that the extant text provides no explicit testimony connecting the seven women mentioned in 38,16-18 and the
four women named in the list of 40,25-26. Can one still think that,
from the vantage point of the author of the *First Apocalypse of
James*, the four women belong to the group of seven when only
four of them have been referred to by name? There are two reasons to think that this is indeed possible.[51]

First, the seven women are portrayed by James as powerless
vessels who "have become strong by a perception which is in
them" (38,22-23). It cannot be mere coincidence that the seven are
described as women of *perception* and that James is urged to seek
advice of the four women when he speaks the words of *perception*[52] (40,23-24). In light of this terminological connection, it
seems probable that all seven female disciples of the Lord are
spiritually equiped in a special way but Salome, Mary Magdalene,
Martha, and Arsinoe are introduced as the prime examples of the
group, as women from whom even James can learn. Second, there
is some evidence in the text that these four of the seven are not
the only women explicitly mentioned by name. The fragmentary
line of *1 Apoc. Jas.* 42,4 ends with three letters $\overline{NN\lambda}$, with a
stroke above them indicating that they are part of a proper noun.
As Schoedel has noted,[53] it was probably a female name, such as
Anna, Joanna, or Susanna. Especially the last two are well-known
women in Early Christianity (Lk. 8,3; 24,10). It is worth noting
that the section where this female name appears is part of the
answer to a question by James which is somehow related to the

---

[51] This does not mean that the two references to Jesus' female
disciples, the one referring to four women, the other to seven, could not
and did not represent two originally distinct traditions, as suggested by
their separate use in *Man. Ps. II* 194,19-22; 192,21-24; 192,25-193,3 (for
four women, see also 142,4-13). That the seven women in *Man. Ps. II*
192,25-193,3 are given names deriving from various second and third
century apocryphal acts is of course a secondary development; see below
the chapter "Mary Magdalene in the Manichaean Psalm-book."

[52] If the text is restored to read ΓΝWϹΙϹ, the connection between the
two texts is of course not equally explicit, although these two terms seem
to be more or less identical in the *First Apocalypse of James*.

[53] Schoedel 1979, 100.

role of ⲧϣⲟⲙⲧⲉ (= these three ones; *1 Apoc. Jas.* 41,20). ⲧϣⲟⲙⲧⲉ could very well refer to those three women from the list of seven who have not been mentioned by name in the Lord's response immediately preceding the question of James (40,9-41,19).[54] Because the manuscript is damaged just after the opening part of James' question we do not know anything else about these three except that, according to James, they have been reviled and persecuted.

If this understanding of the text is correct, the Lord has probably spoken of all seven women in his two answers. They are depicted as contemporaries of James and seem to have access to a perception or gnosis of deeper spiritual truths similar to that James himself gains through the dialogue with the Lord. Yet apparently, they do not belong to the chain of authoritative witnesses whose task it is to pass on the tradition which is imparted by the Lord to James. Nor is there any indication in the extant parts of the writing that the women were reckoned with the children of Him-who-is (36,10-11). This expression is used as a technical term to describe those Christian Gnostics who adhered to the traditions preserved in the *First Apocalypse of James* and whose prototype James was. Instead, the women — or at least four of them — serve as a kind of model for how James is supposed to go about his own mission. The author of the *First Apocalypse of James* recognizes them as spiritual authorities although their influence on the traditions contained in his writing and transmitted to his readers seems to be less direct than that of James, the brother of the Lord. They had become strong by a perception which was in them, but they did not share the same basic revelation as James.

7. *Mary Magdalene and the Twelve Male Disciples*

The relationship of Mary Magdalene (and the other women) to the twelve male disciples does not appear to be dealt with directly in

---

[54] Schoedel (1979, 101) has translated the beginning of James' question as follows: "Rabbi, into these three (things) then, has their [   ] been cast." The reason why he adds "(things)" after the number three remains obscure (cf. also Veilleux 1986, 57). Kasser (1968, 175) translates the same text: "*Rabbi!*... aux épines, *donc*, on a jeté leur *genre*." This translation is based on a false reading of the text. Apparently, Kasser has read ⲧϣⲟⲛⲧⲉ instead of ⲧϣⲟⲙⲧⲉ.

the *First Apocalypse of James*. While the writing expressly addresses the question of James' attitude to the twelve, it still gives
at least indirect information about Mary's role too. In the extant
parts of the writing there are two passages which mention the
twelve.[55] In 36,1-4 the text refers to some unspecified entities[56]
which are "a type of the twelve disciples." The other passage is
42,20-24.[57] It begins the final section of the writing after the
second dialogue between the Lord and James. It describes how,
after the conversation, James sought out the twelve in order to
speak with them. It is particularly 42,20-24 which sheds light on
the relationship between James and the twelve (as well as Mary
Magdalene and the other women). But 36,1-4 is also important
since it contains typology which reveals how the writer views the
twelve. Having suffered textual damages and containing words
difficult to explain, both passages have engendered diverse and
contradictory interpretations. Thus, the relationship between James
and the twelve (as well as Mary Magdalene and the other women)
in the *First Apocalypse of James* is a controversial issue.

Schenke maintains that in *1 Apoc. Jas.* 36,2-4 the twelve disciples are juxtaposed with the twelve aeons of the Valentinian
pleroma who are above the realm of Achamoth, the lower Sophia
(36,5-6). The same positive understanding of the twelve appears
in the interpretation of *1 Apoc. Jas.* 42,14-23. According to Schenke, James finishes his last comment to the Lord by saying that he
is going to go to the twelve male disciples and to the seven wom-
en in order that, having believed in the Lord, they might find
consolation in their sorrow. Then James goes to the twelve, supports, and comforts them.[58] Schenke's translation of the text is
based on the argument that the verb ϭⲟϩⲉ in 42,21 does not have
the connotation of reproving but that of supporting and comfort-

---

[55] The twelve in 25,26 do not refer to the disciples but to the archons
who rule over one hebdomad each (see 26,1-3.23).

[56] Because the text in 35,23-36,1 is very fragmentary one can present
only conjectures as to what these unspecified entities are; for suggestions,
see below.

[57] The twelve can hardly refer to the archons, even though they are
the object of a ϭⲟϩⲉ (for the translation of the word, see below) in the
same way as the archons in the prediction of the Lord in 30,1-4. The
rebuke of the Lord materializes in 34,19-20 and 35,19-25, not in 42,20-
24 where James is the actor.

[58] Schenke 1966, 29.

ing.[59] The logical conclusion to Schenke's observations is that in the *First Apocalypse of James* the twelve also received gnosis and, together with James and the seven women, joined authoritative witnesses to the secret revelation of the Lord, although the credit for encouraging them belongs to James.[60]

A different view of the relationship between the twelve and James (as well as Mary Magdalene and the other women) is advocated by Perkins. According to her, the twelve in the *First Apocalypse of James* are not compared with the aeons of the pleroma but with the twelve lower heavens of Achamoth. Consequently, the twelve are "given a lower status than that of the Gnostics, who are sons of the Father. ...This arrangement implies that those Christians who depend on the twelve for their tradition belong to the lower Sophia. They do not have any share in the knowledge of the Father brought by Jesus."[61] Perkins sees the final encounter between James and the twelve as a rebuke of the twelve (42,20-24). She thinks the episode reflects the same anti-apostolic tendency that is found in the *Apocryphon of James*, in which the twelve disciples explicitly reject gnosis.[62]

Schoedel also sees a correlation between the twelve and Achamoth. Unlike Perkins, however, he does not think that Achamoth is a totally negative figure in the *First Apocalypse of James*. Rather, "two types of beings arise from Achamoth: those not entirely alien of which ... Gnostics can say, 'they are ours' (34,8); and those whom she produces in ignorance" (35,13-17).[63] Since the twelve disciples seem to have a prototype at a higher level, Schoedel believes they could belong to those products of Achamoth who "are not entirely alien."[64] This means that although Schoedel acknowledges James' superiority to the apostles who, in

---

[59] According to Crum (1939, 380), both meanings are possible.

[60] This interpretation is not explicitly stated by Schenke (1966, 29) but his translation of the text leads to this kind of conclusion.

[61] Perkins 1980, 143-144.

[62] Perkins 1980, 144.

[63] Schoedel 1991, 169.

[64] Schoedel argues that the context of the typology presupposes that the prototype of the twelve disciples and the twelve pairs is a positive entity, such as the duodecad or the body of Truth in the pleroma, since the Lord has just described the ascent of James to the Pre-existent One.

his view, represent Catholic Christians,[65] their evaluation is relatively mild in the *First Apocalypse of James*.[66] According to
Schoedel, the writer of the text wants to point out the greater
adequacy of Gnostic teaching compared with that of the twelve.
Yet he does not regard the twelve as belonging to the sphere of
the archons but as standing midway between the Gnostics, represented by James in the first place and the women, and the Jews
whom the archons typify.

As these interpretations show, it is not easy to determine the
position of the twelve in the text world of the *First Apocalypse of
James*. At any rate, it is at least apparent that some tension between James (and thus the women also) and the twelve can be
attested in the text. It is most obvious in the passage which describes the meeting between James and the twelve after James has
finished his conversation with the Risen Lord (42,20-24). In light
of the use of COϨE or its derivatives elsewhere in the *First Apocalypse of James*,[67] it is difficult to interpret lines 42,21-22 in any
other way than that James sternly rebuked the twelve.[68] The most
natural rendering of the phrase ⲀϤⲚⲞⲨⲬⲈ [ⲈⲂⲞⲖ][69] ⲚϨ[Ⲏ]ⲦⲞⲨ
Ⲛ̄ⲞⲨⲦⲰⲦ Ⲛ̄ϨⲎⲦ [...]ⲞⲢⲞⲒⲀ[70] Ⲛ̄ⲦⲈ [Ⲟ]ⲨⲄⲚⲰⲤⲒⲤ (= "he cast [out]
from them assurance [concerning the way/pouring out] of gnosis"[71]) strengthens the impression even more that James sees the
twelve through critical eyes. But does his rebuke indicate that the

---

[65] Schoedel 1991, 167.

[66] Schoedel 1991, 172-173. Although Schoedel translates COϨE in
42,21 "to rebuke" he does not seem to infer from this that the Gnostic
James in this passage distances himself completely from the apostles who
for their part repudiate gnosis.

[67] In all the other instances both the verb and the noun derived from
it is used in the sense of expressing a rebuke. The object of the reproof
in each case is the archons (28,2.8.9; 30,2).

[68] Contra Schenke 1966, 29.

[69] The most likely reconstruction of the lacuna at the beginning of
line 42,23 is [ⲈⲂⲞⲖ]. Other possible adverbs, such as ⲈϨⲞⲨⲚ or ⲈϨⲢⲀⲒ,
do not make sense in this context when attached to the verb ⲚⲞⲨⲬⲈ and
the preposition ϨⲚ̄-.

[70] Kasser (1968, 175) fills the lacuna so that he translates it: "[un
grand (?) épan]chement." This translation seems to presuppose a reading,
such as: [ⲞⲨⲚⲞϬ Ⲛ̄Ⲁ]ⲠⲞⲢⲞⲒⲀ. Schoedel (1979, 100) restores the text:
[ⲈⲦⲂⲈ ϮⲠ]ⲞⲢⲞⲒⲀ, and renders it: "[concerning the] way"; see also Funk
1987, 263.

[71] The translation is mine.

twelve have to be seen as fierce antagonists who in fact belong to the camp of the archons, as Perkins insists? In its extant form the text does seem to suggest an interpretation, such as Perkins', but the fragmentary character of the following lines of the text compels us to be cautious in drawing final conclusions.[72] The text can also be understood to represent James' initial reprimand which is then followed by an invitation to leave an insufficient understanding of gnosis and to seek a deeper perception in the same way that James himself and the women have done. Certainly, James transmitted his own secret revelation imparted by the Lord only to Addai, still this does not necessarily imply that no genuine spiritual knowledge could be attained outside the transmission process James launched, although it explains the non-apostolic nature of the secret tradition the *First Apocalypse of James* reflects. The women, as a matter of fact, are a good example.

The reasoning above also finds some support in observations one can make concerning the relationship of Achamoth to the twelve in the *First Apocalypse of James*. The text in which the two are explicitly brought together is 35,23-36,6. The passage is a part of the Lord's speech in which he instructs James how to manage the ascent to the Pre-existent One and how to pass on this knowledge. It begins by describing how James comes to the end of his ascent. Following a lacuna of three lines, the Lord presents a typology which illustrates his view of the twelve. According to the text, some unspecified entities are a type of the twelve apostles and the twelve pairs. Unfortunately, the fragmentary condition of the text prevents drawing any firm conclusions about the character of these entities. They may belong to the realm of the Pre-existent One but not necessarily. The twelve pairs, which are juxtaposed

---

[72] T.V. Smith (1985, 109) has suggested that the final fragmented section of the writing (43,7-22) records "the reaction of the twelve to James' revelation: while some accept it, others assert that James 'is not worthy of life' (43:15)." In T.V. Smith's view, it is jealousy on the part of certain members of the twelve which then results in James' condemnation to death. The problem with T.V. Smith's interpretation is that there is nothing in the passage which would indicate that the twelve are the speakers in the text. Neither can this be argued on the basis of the reference to twelve in 42,20-24, since there is a lacuna of approximately 11 lines between the two passages. In the text which is now destroyed new persons (for example some Jews; cf. the descriptions of James' martyrdom in *2 Apoc. Jas.* 61,1-62,12; Hegesippus [Eus., *Hist. eccl.* 2.23,12-18]) could very well have been introduced into the text.

with the twelve, are somehow related to Achamoth, but again the text is so damaged that the precise relationship remains unclear. Schenke's notion — which sees the twelve in a positive light — that the unspecified entities are figures which can typify both the twelve and the duodecad of the Valentinian pleroma[73] and Perkins' conception — which sees the writer giving an extremely critical view of the twelve — are both merely good conjectures. Therefore, it is useful to leave *1 Apoc. Jas.* 35,23-36,6 and approach the question of the relationship between Achamoth and the twelve through those texts that illuminate the role of Achamoth in the cosmology of the *First Apocalypse of James*.

Schoedel's observation that Achamoth is an ambivalent figure is an important point of departure.[74] On the one hand, the fact that she is from the Pre-existent One is made visible in her activities. On the other hand, since her activities are undertaken without any co-operation with the realm of the Pre-existent One, in other words, without any male partner, she may also produce sheer failures. The duality in her character is well illustrated by the fact that she produces both those who "are not entirely alien" (34,2) and the twelve archons. This means that the linkage between Achamoth and the twelve need not require that the twelve be seen in a completly negative light in the *First Apocalypse of James*. In addition, Schoedel points out that in the Marcosian system (which also included the Valentinian account of the ascent discussed above) both the twelve apostles and the twelve pairs (symbolizing the zodiac[75]) are typified by the Valentinian duodecad or "the body of Truth," one aeon of the Valentinian pleroma.[76] With these two considerations in mind, Schoedel suggests, as we have seen above, that the twelve assume a middle position between the Gnostics, represented by James, and the archons. In other words, they are those who "are not entirely alien."

Although Schoedel's assertion concerning the role of Achamoth is correct, nowhere in the extant part of the *First Apocalypse of*

---

[73] Schenke overlooks the fact that the Valentinian duodecad is not actually twelve but six pairs (see Iren., *Adv. haer.* 1.1,2).

[74] Schoedel 1991, 166-173.

[75] Both the precise interpretation of the twelve pairs as well as their position in the typology of the text is rather speculative in Schoedel's argumentation (1991, 171-173).

[76] Schoedel 1991, 171-173.

James are the twelve identified with those who "are not entirely alien." However, this possibility of interpreting the ambivalence of the products of Achamoth cannot be ruled out, especially considering those Valentinian texts which presuppose a category of the psychic ones standing somehow in the middle between the pneumatic and the hylic ones. At any rate, Schoedel provides a necessary warning against that line of interpretation in which the twelve are pictured in completely negative terms because of their attachment to Achamoth (Perkins).

On the other hand, Schenke's overly positive view of the twelve, based on his unlikely reconstructions and translations of the text, is equally untenable. It is obvious that some sort of distinction between James (and thus the women also) and the twelve can be attested in the text. This is not only shown by the apparent connection of the twelve with the lower Sophia but also by the manner in which the Lord's teaching of his own identity and that of the imperishable Sophia as well as the children of Him-who-is (36,7-11) is contrasted with the way in which he speaks about the twelve (36,1-6). In addition, the twelve do not have the same perception as James and Mary Magdalene or the other women. They have to be rebuked and disillusioned, since they evidently have an insufficient conception of gnosis and faith. Attractive but undeniably hypothetical is an assumption that in the text world of the *First Apocalypse of James* the twelve belong to that crowd around James (30,27; see also 30,21) who are not granted a special personal revelation or gnosis from the Lord, directly as in the case of James and the seven women or indirectly as in the case of Addai and those after him. They are only following James, being dispersed just before the revelation was imparted to him.

8. *Mary Magdalene and Feminine Terminology as a Symbol of the Perishable*

In light of the positive role the author of the *First Apocalypse of James* attributes to Mary Magdalene and the other women, it is pertinent to ask what their relationship is to the discussion of the perishable character of the femaleness in 41,15-19. The text states that the female element not only symbolizes the perishable but that it is inferior to the imperishable male element, and its goal is to be

assimilated to the latter. At the beginning of the writing there is
another text which sheds light on the notion of femaleness. In
24,27-30 the Lord instructs James that "femaleness existed, but
femaleness was not [first].[77] And [it] prepared for itself powers and
gods." This is an apparent allusion to the creative activity of
Achamoth, the lower Sophia. Powers and gods evidently stand for
the archons who rule over the material world.

The *First Apocalypse of James* is not the only Gnostic text
which uses feminine terminology symbolically. In some Gnostic
texts femaleness is a negative metaphor for sexuality which results
in giving birth and fettering souls in the bondage of matter (e.g.
Dial. Sav. 144,17-21; *Zost.* 1,10-15; cf. also *Thom. Cont.* 144,8-
10).[78] However, there is no evidence in the *First Apocalypse of
James* that femaleness here would symbolize sexuality. The text
does not contain any expressly encratic emphases. On the contrary,
it refers to begetting two sons without any negative verdict (37,13-
14).

The interpretation of femaleness in the *First Apocalypse of
James* must start with the observation that there is an analogy
between perishableness and femaleness. That which is perishable
is female. With this consideration in mind, it seems safest to
conclude that femaleness represents the mode of worldly existence,
taken as a whole. Not even the children of Him-who-is can escape
the severe limitations life in the material world brings with it. This
is illustrated by the destiny of James himself. He has to undergo
seizure and sufferings (32,17-22; 33,2-5). This cannot be avoided
but he can take comfort from the fact that this does not actually
affect the destiny of his real self. What actually matters is the
knowledge that the children of Him-who-is and perhaps also those
"who are not entirely alien" will attain the imperishableness of
maleness although their existence in the present material world is
characterized by the perishableness of femaleness.

In light of the positive evaluation of Mary Magdalene and the
other women, it is somewhat surprising that feminine gender

---

[77] The text reads: ΝΕϹϢΟΟΠ [Ν]ϬΙ ΤΜΝΤϹϨΙΜΕ ΑΛΛΑ ΝΕϹⲢ
ϢΟ[.....] ΤΜΝΤϹϨΙΜΕ ΑΝ. The most likely restoration of the lacuna is [ΠΤ
ΝϬΙ]; see Schoedel 1979, 68.

[78] For the use of feminine terminology as negative metaphors, see
Wisse 1988, 297-307; Marjanen 1992, 139-142.

imagery can be used in this rather devaluing way. Yet this is not too surprising when the pejorative use of feminine gender language is seen in the wider context of Mediterranean culture, where the male represents what is perfect, powerful, and transcendent and the female what is incomplete, weak, and mundane.[79] The same understanding of femaleness is reflected in the comment of James, where he characterizes the seven women as "powerless vessels" (38,21-22).[80]

However, it is important to note that femaleness is not absolutely negative in the statements expressed by the author of the *First Apocalypse of James*. Even though women are described as "powerless vessels" in accordance with the dominant contemporary language pattern, they may, to the great amazement of James, become "strong by a perception which is in them" (38,21-23). Thus, the standard conception of femaleness is questioned. In addition, femaleness is not something which children of Him-who-is leave behind in the act of redemption, but it is elevated to a higher level of reality. In other words, femaleness is not to be rejected but to be assimilated or transformed into maleness.[81] Thus, the notion of femaleness the author of the *First Apocalypse of James* represents is somewhat different from that of those radically dualistic Gnostic texts, the prime example being *Zostrianos*, in which femaleness stands for sexually characterized material being which has to be entirely abandoned (cf. also *Dial. Sav.* 144,17-21).[82] The closest parallels to the notion of femaleness in the *First Apocalypse of James* are found in *Excerpta ex Theodoto* (21,3; 79). In these texts, too, femaleness stands for existence in the material world, weak and subject to cosmic forces, and the female

---

[79] For a representative example of this view, see p. 73 n. 55.

[80] Cf. 1 Pet 3,7.

[81] As Wisse (1988, 302) has noted, *1 Apoc. Jas.* 41,15-16 echoes 1 Cor 15,53.

[82] Although emphasizing more the devaluation of femininity common to both the *First Apocalypse of James* and the radically dualistic Gnostic texts such as *Zostrianos*, Wisse (1988, 302) acknowledges the same difference.

is the one who has not yet reached the ultimate redemption but who does it by becoming male.[83]

In the texts of *Excerpta ex Theodoto* and in the *First Apocalypse of James* the perishableness of femaleness is not only a problem of women but that of men as well. To use the terminology of the *First Apocalypse of James*, both women and men have to and can "attain to the male element." Therefore, it is no problem for the author of the *First Apocalypse of James* to acknowledge Mary Magdalene and the other women as significant spiritual authorities, equalling James, the author's own spiritual hero. Through gnosis women are able to negate standard conceptions of femaleness prevailing in the contemporary culture. The powerless vessels can become so strong that they even function as an example for James while he is fulfilling the task given by the Lord.

The juxtaposition of the significant role of Mary Magdalene as well as that of the other women and the devaluing use of feminine terminology raises the question of the circumstances of composition. Is this somewhat surprising combination a further example of an unreflected way of assimilating two ostensibly contradictory notions, a practice common in religious writings, or does it reveal something about the audience of the writing? If the author of the *First Apocalypse of James* has deliberately juxtaposed pejorative feminine terminology with significant female spiritual heroes, he/she may have tried to take into account those readers, possibly mostly female, who had difficulty accepting the use of femaleness as an inferior category over against maleness. Introducing Mary Magdalene and the other women to the writing, next to James, the main spiritual authority of the work, the author alleviates the negative connotation attached to femaleness.

---

[83] The same is true with *Gos. Thom.* 114 as well, although it is probable that there femaleness is also a symbol of sexual desire and seductiveness, whereas maleness represents sexual continence.

CHAPTER SEVEN

MARY MAGDALENE
IN THE GOSPEL OF PHILIP

1. *Introductory Remarks*

There are two passages in the *Gospel of Philip*[1] where Mary
Magdalene appears (59,6-11; 63,30-64,9).[2] Both are important for
our understanding of early Christian Mary Magdalene traditions,
since in both she is viewed from the perspective of having an
extraordinary relationship to Jesus. The latter passage also treats
her special role among his disciples.

Apart from *Pistis Sophia*, the *Gospel of Philip* is the only
Gnostic writing where Mary Magdalene appears with the explicit
characterization of her identity. In both instances where she is
introduced in the text she is provided with a reference to her place
of origin (59,6-11; 63,30-64,9).

The *Gospel of Philip* is a Valentinian text that was written
either at the end of the second century or at the latest at the beginning of the third.[3] The interest the author shows in Syriac words

---

[1] The text was apparently written in Greek but it is known only in
Coptic translation, attested by a single manuscript in the second codex of
the Nag Hammadi Library (Layton 1989a). The English translations of
the text used in this study follow those of Isenberg (1989) unless otherwise noted.

[2] The present study cites the passages of the *Gospel of Philip* according to page and line of the manuscript (Layton 1989a). This is done
because there is no standard system to divide and to number the text in
smaller units (the most common is that of Schenke 1959; 1987; but see
also Krause 1971; Layton 1987). An additional problem is that in older
literature, reference is frequently made not to the manuscript pages (51-
86) but to the plate numbers of an early photographic facsimile of the
text (99-134; so e.g. the editions and translations of Schenke [1959], de
Catanzaro [1962], Wilson [1962], and Till [1963]). Ménard (1967) and
Layton (1987) include both systems of numbering, but in Ménard's
edition the manuscript pages are for some reason numbered so that the
first page has the number 53 and the last 88.

[3] According to Wilson (1962, 3-5), this dating is supported by features common to the *Gospel of Philip* and in the Valentinian systems
described by Irenaeus and contained in the *Excerpta ex Theodoto*, paral-

and etymologies (63,21-23; 56,7-9; 62,6-17) and in Eastern sacramental practice and catecheses suggests that the writing was probably composed in Syria,[4] possibly in Edessa[5] or in Antioch.[6]
Despite its name, the writing does not resemble a narrative gospel,
nor does it represent a sayings gospel or a revelation dialogue.
Rather, it is a collection of excerpts of various literary types,[7] with
special emphasis on sacramental and ethical themes.[8]

It is characteristic of the composition of the *Gospel of Philip*
that the excerpts are loosely joined together, sometimes without
any apparent literary linkage at all. Even such passages which deal
with the same topics can be found scattered in diverse places
within the gospel. This does not, however, mean that the writing
is simply "a collection of stray notes without much connection."[9]
Although the arrangement of the material is rather exceptional,
leading many scholars to conclude that the writing displays no
continuity or progression of thought,[10] both the content and style

---

lels with the Apostolic Fathers, and the outward form of the New Testament citations (for the last argument, see also Stroud 1990, 68-81). In
addition, Gaffron (1969, 64.70) thinks that the use of non-canonical and
non-Gnostic dominical sayings besides the citations of the canonical Gospels and the differentiation between the ἀπόστολοι and the ἀποστολικοί
point to a date in the second half of the second century. See also note 6.
Isenberg (1989, 134-135) prefers to date the writing in the second half
of the third century but gives no compelling reason why this should be
the case.

[4] Schenke 1987, 151; Isenberg 1989, 134.

[5] Because of its bilingual milieu (Greek and Syriac), Edessa is advocated by Layton (1987, 325) and Schenke (1987, 151).

[6] Segelberg 1966, 205-223; 1967-68, 207-210; Krause 1971, 94;
Siker 1989, 285-288. It is of interest that both the *Gospel of Philip* and
Theophilus of Antioch (about 180 C.E.) insist that the name Christian
derives from the rite of chrism (*Gos. Phil.* 74,12-14; Theophilus, *Ad
Autolycum* 1.1,12).

[7] For the literary genre of the *Gospel of Philip*, see Isenberg 1989,
132; Schenke 1987, 152-153.

[8] Schenke 1987, 152; Isenberg 1989, 132.

[9] This appraisal was made by van Unnik (1963-64, 465).

[10] So e.g. Schenke 1959, 1; Grant 1960, 2; Segelberg 1960, 191; van
Unnik 1963-64, 465; Isenberg 1989, 133. Even Gaffron (1969, 21-22)
who opposes those scholars who regard the *Gospel of Philip* as a collection of material without any definite plan of composition (Segelberg) or
as a florilegium of certain Gnostic sayings and ideas (Schenke), must
admit that the author of the writing has not succeeded "seinen Stoff ge-
ordnet darzubieten." Similarly Wilson (1962, 9-10), who thinks that the
author of the text has organized his material as to spiral inexorably to-

of the work betray enough coherence that it still seems to reflect theological interests and religious language, even literary devices,[11] cherished, if not by a single author, at least by one religious community.[12] This insight is important methodologically. Even if the excerpts which deal with Mary Magdalene seem to be independent in their immediate contexts they cannot be studied separately from the rest of the writing. Their full meaning must be determined by examining relevant issues in the entire work.[13]

2. *Analysis of 59,6-11*

Gos. Phil. 59,6-11 can easily be isolated from its immediate literary context. The preceding excerpt (58,26-59,6) speaks of the contrast between the natural and the spiritual birth and concludes with the remark: "We receive conception from the grace which is in one another" (59,5-6). The pericope which follows 59,6-11 introduces a new theme. It deals with the "names" of the "Father," the "Son" and the "Holy Spirit" (59,11-18) and has no direct connection with the foregoing.

The excerpt 59,6-11 can be divided in two parts:

---

wards the supreme mystery of the bridal chamber, concedes that it is difficult to find a clear and logical structure or development in the writing. Ménard (1967, 3-6) has claimed that the linking words between the excerpts function as signs of continuity and progression of thought but his argumentation seems quite vulnerable in light of the absence of linking words in many instances.

[11] For the theological emphases of the writing, see Wilson 1962, 12-25; for the style of writing, see Gaffron 1969, 14-18.

[12] Whether the final form of the text derives from an author who "zwar Überlieferungen verschiedener Art und Herkunft zusammengetragen hat, diesen dann aber seinen ganz persönlichen Stempel aufgedrückt hat," as Gaffron (1969, 14) insists, or whether it is a product of a compiler-editor whose own contribution to the text is basically limited to more or less random selections of material from the teaching of an earlier catechist, as Isenberg (1989, 134) maintains, is of secondary importance for the present consideration.

[13] This methodological observation is presented by Desjardins (1990, 92) in his study of sin in the *Gospel of Philip*. A different view is adopted by Layton (1987, 326) who thinks that "individual groups of excerpts can profitably be studied in isolation, with comparison of other works or fragments of Valentinianism or of classic gnosticism."

(1) ΝΕ ΟΥΝ̄ ϢΟΜΤΕ ΜΟΟϢΕ ΜΝ̄ ΠΧΟΕΙϹ ΟΥΟΕΙϢ ΝΙΜ
ΜΑΡΙΑ ΤΕϤΜΑΑΥ ΑΥϢ ΤΕϹϹϢΝΕ ΑΥϢ ΜΑΓΔΑΛΗΝΗ
ΤΑΕΙ ΕΤΟΥΜΟΥΤΕ ΕΡΟϹ ΧΕ ΤΕϤΚΟΙΝϢΝΟϹ
(2) ΜΑΡΙΑ ΓΑΡ ΤΕ ΤΕϤϹϢΝΕ ΑΥϢ ΤΕϤΜΑΑΥ ΤΕ ΑΥϢ
ΤΕϤϨϢΤΡΕ ΤΕ

(1) There were three (women)[14] who always walked with the Lord:
Mary, his mother, and her sister and the Magdalene, the one who was
called his companion.
(2) For Mary is his sister, his mother and his companion.[15]

The first part of the passage states that among Jesus' most intimate
followers there were three women who accompanied him during
his entire earthly career.[16] ΟΥΟΕΙϢ ΝΙΜ ("always") may also
emphasize the special closeness of their relationship to him.[17] In
presenting the three women, the author of the text is evidently
dependent on the list of women in John 19,25.[18] He has edited the
tradition by leaving out the specific identification of the sister of
Jesus' mother and by introducing Mary Magdalene as "the one
who was called his companion."

The second part of the excerpt is an explanatory continuation
of the first. Yet it is not altogether clear whether it simply states
that all three women who were in a close relationship to Jesus had
the same name or, by referring to her three manifestations, it tries

---

[14] ϢΟΜΤΕ is a feminine form and indicates clearly that women are
meant.

[15] The translation is mine (cf. Krause 1971, 101) and deviates from
that of Isenberg especially in the second part (for the reasons, see below
p. 160). Isenberg renders: "His sister and his mother and his companion
were each a Mary." For various translations of the second part of the
text, see Klauck 1992, 2357.

[16] The beginning of the text may echo Mark 15,41.

[17] It is probably an overstatement, however, to think that this particular adverb implies that the three women were "closer to and more ardent
followers of Jesus than were the other (male) disciples" as Buckley
(1988, 214) has suggested.

[18] Recently, this has been most forcibly argued by Klauck 1992,
2343-2358. The fact that no unanimity prevails as to the exact number
of the women in John 19,25 does not affect the question of dependence
between John 19,25 and *Gos. Phil.* 59,7-8. The author of the *Gospel of
Philip* has obviously interpreted John 19,25 in such a way that it refers
to three women.

to define more clearly who Mary *really* is.[19] That the meaning of the text is not immediately clear is shown by various and often ambiguous translations of the text.[20]

When the portrait of Mary Magdalene in the *Gos. Phil.* 59,6-11 is considered two questions are of prime importance. First, what does it mean that Mary Magdalene is viewed as the "companion of the Lord"? Second, if the last part of the excerpt not only confirms that Mary Magdalene was one of Maries accompanying Jesus but tries to say something more, how does this affect our understanding of Mary Magdalene in the writing?

2.1 *Mary Magdalene as the Companion of the Lord*

In *Gos. Phil.* 59,6-11 itself, there is no explicit reason given for calling Mary Magdalene the ΚΟΙΝΩΝΟΣ of the Lord. It is simply stated. Apart from the *Gospel of Philip*, Mary Magdalene is nowhere introduced as the companion of the Lord. Neither is this epithet attributed to any other disciple in extant early Christian writings. Difficulty in interpreting the word is complicated by the fact that the Greek word κοινωνός may assume a wide range of meanings. Basically, it denotes a person engaged in "fellowship or sharing with someone or in something."[21] What a κοινωνός can share with his or her partner can take many forms, ranging from a common enterprise or experience to a shared business.[22] In the Bible, for example, κοινωνός can be used to denote a marriage partner (Mal 2,14; cf. also 3 Macc 4,6), a companion in faith (Philem 17; cf. also *Interp. Know.* 9,31-32), a co-worker in proclaiming the gospel (2 Cor 8,23), or a business associate (Luke 5,10).

In the *Gospel of Philip*, ΚΟΙΝΩΝΟΣ occurs only twice. Besides 59,9, it is also found in 63,32-33. Because of its fragmented condition however, the latter passage is rather obscure in its use of the word.[23] The text can be reconstructed to show ΚΟΙΝΩΝΟΣ

---

[19] Klauck 1992, 2354.

[20] For different translations of the text, see Klauck 1992, 2356-2357.

[21] Hauck 1966, 797.

[22] For the use of the group κοινων-, see Hauck 1966, 797-809.

[23] For the text, see p. 162-163.

as a characterization of either Mary Magdalene[24] or Sophia.[25] If it
is an epithet of Mary Magdalene the text says nothing more than
59,9, i.e., it merely states that she was known to be the companion
of the Savior[26] but does not specify this relationship any further.
Only if it refers to Sophia could it help us gain more insight into
the meaning of the word in 59,9. Yet there is no way to decide
with any degree of certainty which one of the two restorations is
more probable.[27] Therefore, 63,32-33 cannot be taken into consideration when interpreting ΚΟΙΝΩΝΟC in 59,9.

Even if the word ΚΟΙΝΩΝΟC is rare and ambiguous in the
Gospel of Philip, other words of the group κοινων- ($\overline{P}$ΚΟΙΝΩΝΕΙ,
ΚΟΙΝΩΝΙΑ) as well as their Coptic equivalent $_2$ΩΤ$\overline{P}$ appear
frequently in the writing and provide a basis for understanding
ΚΟΙΝΩΝΟC. Basically, these words are used in three ways. First,
the words are employed in a pejorative sense referring to adulterous intercourse. It is important to note, however, that in those

---

[24] Isenberg (1989, 166) reconstructs the lacuna in *Gos. Phil.* 63,34:
$\overline{MC}$[ΩP TE MA]PIA, and thus thinks that 63,32-34 constitutes an inde-
pendent nominal clause: "And Mary Magdalene is the companion of the
Savior."

[25] Schenke (1965, 328) fills the lacuna on line 33 as follows: $\overline{MПE}$-
[CΩТHP MA]PIA. According to that restoration it is Sophia who is both
the mother of angels and the companion of the Savior. A new sentence
begins with the name Mary Magdalene and continues on line 34.

[26] There is no reason to assume that the Savior is not meant to be
identical with the Lord in 59,7 (see the following note).

[27] The arguments which speak for Isenberg's reconstruction (see note
24) are: (1) the characterization of Mary Magdalene agrees with her presentation in 59,9; (2) ΑΥΩ (63,32) is used in its most common function,
i.e., to connect independent clauses. A slightly weak point in Isenberg's
restoration is the fact that in 63,33 CΩТHP is used in its abbreviated form
whereas in 64,3 it is in its full form. To be sure, the translator or the
copyist of the *Gospel of Philip* is not consistent in employing or not
employing abbreviated forms (for CTAΥPOC, see e.g. 73,12 and 73,15).
In Schenke's reconstruction (see note 25), both occurrences of the word
CΩТHP are in the same form. Yet he has to presuppose the use of ΑΥΩ,
as joining nouns or their equivalents, which is somewhat unusual although not impossible, not even in the *Gospel of Philip* (see Layton
1989a, 291). Schenke also has to explain why both Mary Magdalene and
Sophia can be called the companion of Jesus/the Savior. His solution is
that Sophia is the companion of the lower Savior and Mary Magdalene
that of the earthly Jesus. Thus Schenke posits (1959, 3) that the *Gospel
of Philip* contains a Valentinian doctrine of three different Christs (Hipp.,
Ref. 6.36,4). The problem with this thesis is that *Gos. Phil.* 63,30-64,9
does not seem to make any distinction between the earthly Jesus and the
Savior.

cases it is not the words themselves which suggest the negative connotation, but the context in which they appear.[28] Thus, the word KOINⲰNOC as well as its Coptic equivalent have no pejorative flavor themselves. Therefore they cannot stand for an illegitimate sexual partner since the context of the text does not imply anything like that.

Second, the words of the group κοινων- as well as their Coptic equivalents refer to the literal pairing of man and woman in marital (and sexual) relationship. Although the pairing is portrayed in literal terms, it always functions as a metaphor for a deeper, spiritual partnership.[29] This being the case, the second use of the words is closely related to a third, in which the words serve to describe the salvific experience of a Gnostic Christian. It takes place when unity with the divine realm is reestablished. This experience is depicted as union with an angelic counterpart in the pleroma or as its ritual anticipation with another Gnostic of opposite sex in the sacrament of the bridal chamber. In both cases similar terminology can be employed.[30]

In light of this evidence, there remain two alternatives to interpret KOINⲰNOC in 59,9. First, it may simply indicate that in the text world of the *Gospel of Philip* Mary Magdalene was seen as the marriage partner of Jesus. The fact that the other two Maries are Jesus' relatives gives some support to the idea that the companionship of Mary could be understood in terms of a family connection. On the other hand, according to the text, the connecting link between the three women of the text is, besides the com-

---

[28] In 78,18 ⲢKOINⲰNEI denotes an illicit intercourse because it takes place between a woman and her adulterer. In 61,10-12 it is stated that "every act of sexual intercourse (KOINⲰNIⲀ) which has occurred between those unlike one another is adultery." The latter text is probably to be seen as an attempt to express metaphorically how impossible it is for a non-Gnostic to reach the unification to the pleroma. Another case of the use of ⲢKOINⲰNEI as a negative metaphor is in 65,3-5 where it is said that the male unclean spirits "unite with the souls which inhabit a female form." This results in defilement of the souls of women. The text goes on to describe how the same can happen with the souls of men when they are sexually attacked by the female unclean spirits. It is only the union of the soul with its angelic counterpart in the pleroma or probably already in the sacrament of the bridal chamber which makes the soul immune to the attacks of the unclean spirits (65,23-36).

[29] 81,34-82,7 (ⲢKOINⲰNEI); 76,6-9 (ϨⲰⲦⲢ); cf. also 78,25 (ⲦⲰϨ).

[30] See e.g. 70,9-22; 58,10-14; 65,23-26.

mon name, not their possible kinship with Jesus but their belonging to his most intimate followers. The decisive argument against the assumption that the primary meaning of ΚΟΙΝΩΝΟC is "wife" is the fact that in all the other instances where the *Gospel of Philip* speaks about someone's wife it uses the usual word CϨIΜΕ (65,20; 70,19; 76,7; 82,1). The words ΚΟΙΝΩΝΟC or ϨΩΤϷ [31] are clearly reserved for a more specific usage in the writing. This observation fits well with the fact that the writer of the text is not primarily interested in a marital relationship as such, but in the close relationship it illustrates.

The second and most likely alternative for interpreting the word ΚΟΙΝΩΝΟC is to see it as spiritual consort.[32] In this case, Mary Magdalene is identified as the earthly partner of Jesus with whom he forms a spiritual partnership. This syzygy functions as the prototype which the readers of the *Gospel of Philip* try to imitate in the sacramental act of the bridal chamber.[33] Whether the partnership of Jesus and Mary Magdalene is seen by the author of the text as involving marital and sexual dimensions as well, is difficult to decide. The solution to this question depends largely on how one views the position of sexual intercourse in the *Gospel of Philip* in general. At the moment, there is lively scholarly debate concerning this matter.[34] Some think that the ethos of the *Gospel of Philip* is exclusively encratic, with the result that even in marriage "Christians lived together without sexual intercourse."[35] Others maintain that according to the *Gospel of Philip* "the Gnostic, who is 'from above,' experiences love and expresses it in

---

[31] The noun ϨΩΤϷ, which is the masculine equivalent of the word used of Mary Magdalene in 59,11, occurs only in 70,24.29 and there it stands for the partner of Adam's soul, i.e., the spirit, his mother, who was imparted to him.

[32] So e.g. Schenke 1959, 3; Grant 1966, 192; M.A. Williams 1986, 210; Buckley 1988, 215-217; Rudolph 1988, 232; Filoramo 1990, 176; Schmid 1990, 42; Koivunen 1994, 157.

[33] So also Buckley (1988, 217).

[34] For the discussion, see Pagels 1991, 442-454, esp. 442-446.

[35] M.A. Williams 1986, 206; so also Segelberg 1960, 198; Rudolph 1988, 232.

sexual union. The non-Gnostic, who is 'from below,' experiences nothing but lust."[36]

Such a strong polarization in scholarly opinion demonstrates clearly the enigmatic character of the problem. There seem to be no passages in the *Gospel of Philip* which would clearly support the assumption that the author writes in favor of celibacy[37] or endorses sexual intercourse (in the bridal chamber between the perfect ones)[38] or perhaps even requires marriage and sexual

---

[36] Grant 1961, 133. Cf. also Buckley (1988, 224-225) who insists that the earthly union is the prerequisite of the spiritual union in the bridal chamber. Presumably, she thinks that the earthly union may include sexual intercourse since the ritual of the bridal chamber may have this dimension as well. A similar view was advocated earlier by Pagels (1983, 169) who interpreted the standpoint of the *Gospel of Philip* in light of the Valentinian view recorded by Irenaeus (*Adv. haer.* 1.6,4), according to which those "who have experienced that 'mystery of syzygies' are enjoined to enact marital intercourse in ways that express their spiritual, psychic, and bodily integration, celebrating the act as a symbol of the divine pleromic harmony. But those who remain uninitiated are to refrain from sexual intercourse." In a later study Pagels (1991, 442-454) has revised her view; see below.

[37] Those defending this view refer most often to *Gos. Phil.* 82,4-8 as well as to 69,1-4 to prove their case (see e.g. M.A. Williams 1986, 206). The former text contrasts the "marriage of defilement" with the "undefiled marriage," which is "not fleshly but pure." The latter states that "a bridal chamber is not for the animals, nor is it for the slaves, nor for defiled women; but it is for free men and virgins." The problem with this thesis is that it is not altogether clear that the contrast between the two marriages in 82,4-8 is that of the ordinary marriage which has to be rejected and that of the celibate marriage which alone can be recommended. The genitive attribute ⲙ̄ⲡⲧⲭⲱ̄ϨⲘ̄ does certainly indicate that the ordinary, earthly marriage is of lesser value than its pleromic counterpart enacted in the bridal chamber. For all that, it does not necessarily follow that it is to be condemned. In 64,31-65,1 the "marriage of defilement" is depicted as an image of the pleromic marriage, not as a reprehensible action. With this theory it is also difficult to explain why the qualification that "every act of sexual intercourse which has occurred between those *unlike one another* is adultery" (61,10-12), is necessary if all intercourse is condemned.

[38] Those who advocate this view read the *Gospel of Philip* against the background of the description of the Valentinians by Irenaeus (Iren., *Adv. haer.* 1.6,4; 1.13,3), in which the Valentinians, being the perfect, are enjoined to take part in sexual union (in the bridal chamber) while the non-Valentinians should practice continence (see e.g. Grant 1961, 131-134). The problem with this, however, is that, according to Irenaeus, there were also some Valentinians who made an attempt to live in celibate marriage (*Adv. haer.* 1.6,3; cf. also John Chrysostom, *De virginitate* [*PG* 48,536ff.], mentioned in Vööbus 1958, 58). To be sure, Irenaeus emphasizes that they frequently failed. Whether this is true or not need not be

intercourse as prerequisites for entering the bridal chamber.[39] Having recognized this, Pagels has in her most recent treatment of the subject made a new attempt to cut the Gordian knot. She has suggested that the author of the *Gospel of Philip* is not in favor of any particular form of marriage or sexual practice but, like other Valentinians and many ecclesiastical Christians as well, was aware of various alternative models, yet refrained from exclusively advocating any one of them. The main concern was not the choice between the ordinary and the celibate marriage but "the quality of one's intention and the level of one's gnosis."[40] Pagels' interpretation is plausible in light of the comments made by Church Fathers on sexual practices among Valentinians and best justifies the ambiguity of the *Gospel of Philip* itself.

With Pagels' thesis we do not come far in clarifying whether the author of the text thought the partnership of Jesus and Mary Magdalene involved a marital and sexual dimension. Her interpretation makes a negative or a positive answer possible. But before the problem can be left undecided we still have to consider one detail in the description of the relationship between Jesus and Mary Magdalene which may have bearing upon its solution. In *Gos. Phil.* 63,34-37 it is said that "[the Savior loved[41]] her more than [all] the disciples [and used to] kiss her [often] on her [...]"

The explicit mention that the Savior loved Mary Magdalene in an exceptional way recalls *Gos. Mary* 18,14-15, where Levi states

---

decided here. It is of importance that Valentinians seem to have had various practices with regard to marriage and sexual behavior.

[39] This interpretation is most clearly represented by Buckley (1980, 571-572; 1988, 223-225). The most important evidence for this view is found by her in *Gos. Phil.* 65,1-26, where the female and male human being can delude the evil powers by acquiring male or female power, respectively. According to her, this takes place in the "mirrored bridal chamber," i.e., in the marriage of this world. The problem with Buckley's interpretation is that it is not at all clear that the "mirrored bridal chamber" stands for the earthly marriage in this context. It is more likely that it signifies the ritual of the bridal chamber as the earthly counterpart of the final union between the Gnostic and his/her angel in the pleroma (so Wilson 1962, 121-122; Gaffron 1969, 203-204).

[40] Pagels 1991, 442-454; the quotation comes from page 453.

[41] The translation follows Schenke's restoration (1965, 328). Isenberg (1989, 168) has filled the lacuna differently and renders the text: "[But Christ loved] her..." Both reconstructions are possible but Schenke's harmonizes better with the continuation of the text where the title ⲤⲰⲦⲎⲢ is used.

the same thing. Earlier in the writing, Peter had already referred to a special relationship between Jesus and Mary Magdalene, although he described it in a more limited way. In 10,1-3 he addresses Mary: "Sister, we know that the Savior loved you more than the rest of women." In the extant part of the *Gospel of Mary*, there is no hint that Jesus' love for Mary would contain any sexual aspect. Not even Peter's comment is to be perceived in such a way. When Peter says that Mary was the woman Jesus loved most, it is not love between a man and a woman he is addressing, rather he is referring to the position of Mary among the disciples of Jesus. Thus, Peter does not actually emphasize that Mary was Jesus' favorite woman *as a love partner* but that she was Jesus' favorite *only* among women, not among all the followers of Jesus. It is only Levi who acknowledges her position of superiority among all the disciples of the Savior. In light of Levi's statement, it becomes especially clear that the love characterizing Jesus' and Mary's relationship in the *Gospel of Mary* is that of a master and his most beloved disciple. In this way, Mary Magdalene seems to have a role in the *Gospel of Mary* similar to that the Beloved Disciple has in the Gospel of John or James in the *Second Apocalypse of James* (56,14-16).[42]

Could the Savior's love for Mary Magdalene in the *Gospel of Philip* be understood in the same way? Certainly, the common background of the love motif is evident.[43] Yet in the *Gospel of Philip* the concretization of Jesus' love for Mary Magdalene by

---

[42] For the function and background of the beloved disciple motif in early Christian writings, see Schenke 1986, 111-125. For the beloved disciple motif in the *Second Apocalypse of James*, see Funk 1976, 151-152.

[43] It is not easy to decide whether the idea of a beloved disciple or Jesus' love for Mary is primary in the development of this tradition. As Schenke's study shows (1986, 120-125), the beloved disciple motif has been quite wide-spread in Early Christian writings and may have been used independently by the authors of the *Gospel of Mary* and the *Gospel of Philip*. However, the fact that the beloved disciple motif is linked in these two writings with the same person, Mary Magdalene, and especially in contrast to all the other disciples, speaks for a connection between these writings, in particular when Jesus' love for Mary Magdalene is not mentioned anywhere else (unless Jesus' love for Mary of Bethany in John 11,5 is projected onto her).

means of kissing[44] has been seen as an indication that this love is not only that between a master and his most beloved disciple, but it can have sexual implications.[45] There are, however, several reasons why the latter interpretation of kissing is not very likely in the context of the *Gospel of Philip*.[46] First, in the only other passage where kissing is referred to (58,30-59,6)[47] it is used without concrete sexual implications as a metaphor[48] of spiritual nourishment which leads to spiritual procreation.[49] Second, in other contemporary religious writings there are plenty of examples where kissing functions as a metaphor for transmitting a special

---

[44] The fact that the direct object (ⲘⲘⲞⲤ) of the verb form ⲚⲈϤⲀⲤ-ⲠⲀϨⲈ is followed by a prepositional phrase (corresponding to the Greek dative) makes it likely that the verb does not have the meaning "to greet" but "to kiss." Out of all the suggested proposals to fill the lacuna after ⲀⲦⲈⲤ- in 63,36 (in his apparatus Layton [1989b, 168] lists ⲞⲨⲈⲢⲎⲦⲈ, ⲞⲨⲞⲟϬⲈ, ⲦⲈϨⲚⲈ, ⲦⲀⲠⲢⲞ) the last one is most probable in light of 59,2-6.

[45] Price (1990, 59-60) points out that kissing was often employed to stand for sexual intercourse although he himself thinks that in the context of the *Gospel of Philip* "the implied sexual intercourse is purely spiritual and metaphorical in nature." If the kiss is seen as part of the ritual of the bridal chamber, as it is done by Schenke (1959, 5) and Wilson (1962, 95-96), and the bridal chamber is perceived to involve a sexual dimension, kissing — that of the Savior and Mary Magdalene as well — could have an erotic character. However, both the relationship of the kiss to the ritual of the bridal chamber (any relationship between the two has been strongly contested by Gaffron [1969, 213-217]) as well as the possible carnal nature of the latter are highly debated issues (see above). To be sure, Schenke himself, for example, does not think that the bridal chamber involved sexual intercourse.

[46] It is worth noting that a kiss between a man and a woman does not necessarily have erotic implications in Jewish and Christian literature. It may also indicate kinship between those who kiss each other or it may serve as an outward sign of reconciliation; cf. Gen 29,11; *Joseph and Aseneth* 22,9; 28,14; the unerotic holy kiss mentioned in various New Testament letters did not probably take place only between people of the same gender but between men and women as well (see especially Rom 16,16).

[47] ϯ ⲠⲒ (59,4; cf. also the noun ⲠⲒ in 59,3) and ⲀⲤⲠⲀϨⲈ (63,36) are used synonymously.

[48] The metaphorical nature of kissing is confirmed by a similar use of "conceiving" and "begetting" in the same context (58,19-22; 59,4-6).

[49] Whether the kiss is a mere metaphor for begetting spiritual offspring through teaching (58,30-31) or whether it also assumed a concrete form in a ritual holy kiss is of secondary importance. In the latter case it has no sexual dimension either.

spiritual power.[50] It is of particular interest that in *Gos. Truth*
41,34-35 it is by means of kisses that the eschatological reunion
with the Father is established.[51] Third, the altercation between the
disciples and the Savior in *Gos. Phil.* 63,37-64,9[52] suggests that
kissing is not to be understood as an expression of sexual love.
The question of the disciples shows that the relationship between
Jesus and Mary Magdalene is viewed in such terms that also male
disciples can be jealous of the position of Mary.[53] In addition,
when the disciples ask why the Savior loves Mary more than them
he does not point to any sexual motives but to her spiritual capacity to see what he (= the light, 64,7) is conveying to her[54] (through
the word, i.e., a kiss, making her capable of producing spiritual
offspring).[55] Fourth, in *2 Apoc. Jas.* 56,14-16, which is the most
interesting parallel to *Gos. Phil.* 63,34-37, it is said that when the
Risen Lord wanted to reveal his most secret mysteries to James he
kissed him and called him his beloved. In that context it is fully
clear that kissing has no sexual connotation.[56] It is a symbolic act
which demonstrates James' privileged position. Moreover, it is
through embracing the Lord that James receives the most important revelation, i.e., he comes to understand who the Hidden One
is.

   Although there is no positive evidence that the author of the
Gospel of Philip advocated encratism, and although the author
regarded Mary Magdalene as the partner of the earthly Jesus, it is
very unlikely that their consortium was viewed in terms of a
sexual relationship. The reference to Jesus kissing Mary is best
explained as an indication of the privileged position Mary Magdalene holds as his most beloved disciple whose spiritual perception

---

   [50] *Joseph and Aseneth* 19,10-11; *Odes Sol.* 28,6-7; *Disc. 8-9* 57,26-
28; cf. also Stählin 1974, 144. To be sure, in *Joseph and Aseneth* 19,10-
11 it is the lovers who kiss each other but the spiritual motif of the kiss
is clearly emphasized in the passage.
   [51] Attridge & MacRae 1985, 132.
   [52] For the text, see pp. 162-163.
   [53] Schmid 1990, 36.
   [54] For the connection of *Gos. Phil.* 63,30-64,5 and *Gos. Phil.* 64,5-10,
see below.
   [55] Similarly King 1995, 631 n. 42.
   [56] Cf. also *PS* 125,4-5 where Jesus and the John the Baptist are said
to have kissed each other.

excels that of the others. In fact, kissing may very well be understood as a means by which a special spiritual power is conveyed to her.

2.2 *The Three Manifestations of Mary*

The problems with *Gos. Phil.* 59,6-11 can be condensed into one question: does the text simply state that Mary Magdalene was one of the three Maries who accompanied Jesus during his earthly career[57] or does it contain an allegorical commentary of the foregoing which shows that the three women mentioned above are in fact one and the same woman, a Mary?[58] Before a solution to this question can be considered, the syntax of 59,10-11 must be analyzed.

The text can be divided into three sentences:

(1) ⲘⲀⲢⲓⲀ ⲅⲀⲢ ⲦⲈ ⲦⲈϥⲤⲰⲚⲈ

(2) ⲀⲨⲱ ⲦⲈϥⲘⲀⲀⲨ ⲦⲈ

(3) ⲀⲨⲱ ⲦⲈϥϨⲰⲦⲢⲈ ⲦⲈ

All are nominal sentences. The first is ternary, and the latter two are binary. If the first sentence is taken separately it could be rendered either: "For Mary is his sister," or: "For his sister is Mary."[59] Nevertheless, in light of the two subsequent binary sentences, in which the copular pronoun ⲦⲈ is the subject, the first translation is most likely. Namely, in both binary sentences the antecedent of ⲦⲈ is Mary rather than the sister of the Lord.[60] Thus, the whole text is to be rendered as follows: "For Mary is his sister, (and she is) his mother, and (she is) his companion."

Based on these observations, it is evident that here the author of the text does not merely list all the Maries who belonged to Jesus' most immediate company. Rather, he discloses that there is

---

[57] So Wilson 1962, 97-98; Schenke 1987, 159; Layton 1987, 335; Isenberg 1988, 159; Schmid 1990, 25-27.

[58] Trautmann 1981, 273; Pagels 1983, 167; 1988, 202; Buckley 1988, 215; Klauck 1992, 2357.

[59] Polotsky 1987, 37.

[60] If "his sister" were the subject of the first sentence, the second and the third sentences would give additional information about her. It would be, however, very strange if the author of the text stated that the sister of Jesus, otherwise completely unknown in the *Gospel of Philip*, were at the same time his mother and his companion.

a Mary who plays three different roles in the life of the Savior. She is his sister, his mother, and his companion. Who, then, is this Mary and how can she assume all these roles? The triple function of Mary shows that no historical person is meant. She is to be seen as a mythical figure who actually belongs to the transcendent realm but who manifests herself in the women accompanying the earthly Jesus. The reason she is called Mary may simply be due to the fact that the three women whom the author of the *Gospel of Philip* links with the earthly Jesus are all Maries.[61]

The transcendent counterpart of the three manifestations is not entirely clear. The best solution seems to be that "the 'three Maries' (the Savior's virgin mother, his sister, and Mary Magdalene) serve as images of Christ's spiritual syzygos in her triple manifestation, respectively as holy spirit, Wisdom, and as his bride the church."[62] According to a common Valentinian understanding, the Holy Spirit is the female member[63] of the conjugal pair which she constitutes together with (the first) Christ (Iren., *Adv. haer.* 1.2,5).

---

[61] The third woman of the list in 59,8-9 could also be Mary according to John 19,25 be Mary if the text were read in such a way that it included three women. It is also possible, however, that the author of the *Gospel of Mary* was aware of a tradition according to which Jesus' sister was Mary (Epiph., *Pan.* 78.8,1; 78.9,6; see Wilson 1962, 97-98). This would explain why in 59,10 she is no longer introduced as the sister of Jesus' mother but as his sister. Provided this is a legitimate understanding of the text, Schenke's attempt to remove the contradiction between 59,8 and 59,10 by emending 59,8 to read ⲧⲉϥⲥⲱⲛⲉ proves unnecessary (1959, 9; 1987, 159; cf. also Buckley 1988, 214). Moreover, the change from the sister of Jesus' mother to his sister may also be due to the fact that the author of the text wants to emphasize that Jesus' relationship to his sister is a reflection of the Savior's syzygy with Sophia who in some Gnostic texts is called the sister of the Savior (see below).

[62] Pagels 1988, 202. Pagels developed her thesis already in an earlier study (1983, 163-167). See also M. A. Williams 1986, 210). A similar view is advocated by Buckley (1988, 212) although she does not think that the consortium of Jesus and Mary Magdalene could mirror that of Christ and the Church (225 n. 67). Indeed, she maintains that the author of the text wants to emphasize the full identity of the three female figures: the Holy Spirit, Sophia, and Mary Magdalene. They all appear as the female syzygos of Christ/Jesus and each can symbolize both his spiritual and earthly partner. Trautmann (1981, 273) also asserts that on a deeper level of understanding the three women represent one and the same person. However, she insists that it is Mary Magdalene who is the sister, the mother, and the companion of the Savior.

[63] The polemic passage *Gos. Phil.* 55,23-27 shows that the Holy Spirit is regarded by the author as feminine and can thus be characterized very well as the mother of the Savior.

It is with their consent that the whole pleroma produces the Savior, the second Christ (Iren., *Adv. haer.* 1.2,6), who becomes the bridegroom of Sophia as she returns from the intermediate place to the pleroma (Iren., *Adv. haer.* 1.7,1). In Valentinian systems she is nowhere called the sister of the Savior but some other Gnostics, whom Irenaeus introduces but does not identify,[64] maintained this view (Iren., *Adv. haer.* 1.30,12). In the final consummation, it is the Church, the pneumatic *ekklesia*,[65] that is the spiritual syzygos of Christ in numerous Valentinian texts.[66]

In the text world of the *Gospel of Philip* then, the spiritual consortium of Mary Magdalene and Jesus has its parallel with the syzygies of the Holy Spirit and Christ as well as Sophia and the Savior (the second Christ). At the same time it is viewed as the prototype of the union between Christ and his Church which materializes when the images (= the pneumatic elect) are united with their angels (= their pleromatic counterparts) (58,10-14).

3. *Analysis of 63,30-64,9*

ΤⲤⲞⲪⲒⲀ ⲈⲦⲞⲨⲘⲞⲨⲦ[Ⲉ ⲈⲢⲞ]Ⳡ ⳉⲈ ⲦⲤⲦⲒⲢⲀ ⲚⲦⲞⳞ ⲦⲈ
ⲦⲘⲀⲀ[Ⲩ ⲚⲚⲀⲅ]ⲄⲈⲖⲞⳞ ⲀⲨⲰ [Ⲧ]ⲔⲞⲒⲚⲰⲚⲞⳞ ⲘⲡⳞ[... ⲘⲀ]ⲢⲒⲀ
ⲦⲘⲀⲅ[ⲀⲀ]ⲖⲎⲚⲎ
ⲚⲈⲢⲈ ⲡ.[.....ⲘⲈ] ⲘⲘⲞ[Ⳟ Ⲛ]Ⲣ̅ⲞⲨⲞ ⲀⲘⲘⲀⲐⲎⲦ[ⲎⳞ ⲦⲎⲢⲞⲨ ⲀⲨⲰ
ⲚⲈⳠ]ⲀⳞⲡⲀⲊⲈ ⲘⲘⲞⳞ ⲀⲦⲈⳞ[......Ⲛ̅ⲢⲀⲢ] Ⲛ̅ⳞⲞⲡ ⲀⲡⲔⲈⳞⲈⲈⲡⲈ
Ⲙ̅[ⲘⲀⲐⲎⲦⳮ ..].ⲈⲢⲞ.[.].[..]ⲘⲀ
ⲡⲈⳉⲀⲨ ⲚⲀⳠ ⳉⲈ ⲈⲦⲂⲈ ⲞⲨ ⲔⲘⲈ ⲘⲘⲞⳞ ⲡⲀⲢⲀⲢⲞⲚ ⲦⲎⲢⲚ̅
ⲀⳠⲞⲨⲰϢⲂ Ⲛ̅ⳠⲒ ⲡⳞⲰⲦⲎⲢ ⲡⲈⳉⲀⳠ ⲚⲀⲨ {ⲡⲈⳉⲀⳠ ⲚⲀⲨ} ⳉⲈ
ⲈⲦⲂⲈ ⲞⲨ †ⲘⲈ ⲘⲘⲰⲦⲚ̅ ⲀⲚ Ⲛ̅ⲦⲈⳞⲢⲈ ⲞⲨⲂ̅ⲖⲖⲈ ⲘⲚ̅ ⲞⲨⲀ
ⲈⳠⲚⲀⲨ ⲈⲂⲞⲖ ⲈⲨⳢⲘ̅ ⲡⲔⲀⲔⲈ ⲘⲡⲈⳞⲚⲀⳠ ⲤⲈϢⲞⲂⲈ ⲈⲚⲞⲨⲈⲢⲎⲨ
ⲀⲚ ⳢⲞⲦⲀⲚ ⲈⲢϢⲀ ⲡⲞⲨⲞⲈⲒⲚ ⲈⲒ ⲦⲞⲦⲈ ⲡⲈⲦⲚⲀⲂⲞⲖ ⳠⲚⲀⲚⲀⲨ
ⲈⲡⲞⲨⲞⲈⲒⲚ ⲀⲨⲰ ⲡⲈⲦⲞ Ⲃ̅Ⲃ̅ⲖⲖⲈ ⲈⳠⲚⲀⳢⲰ ⳢⲘ̅ ⲡⲔⲀⲔⲈ.

---

[64] Foerster (1979, 474 n. 87) has pointed out that Theodoret believes them to be Sethians or Ophites (*Haer. fab.* 1.14). Although there are some similarities between Sethian ideas and those found in Irenaeus' description, the connection is so vague that Theodoret's remark seems to be based on a mere guess. In fact, Irenaeus' other Gnostics seem to have much more in common with the Valentinians he has just introduced above.

[65] In contrast to the *Gospel of Philip*, some Valentinians insist that the Church also includes the psychic Christians (*Exc. Theod.* 58,1; *Interp. Know.*).

[66] Pagels 1983, 164-167.

As for the Wisdom who is called "the barren," she is the mother [of the] angels and the companion of the [...] Mary Magdalene[.] [... loved] her more than [all] the disciples [and used to] kiss her [often] on her [...]. The rest of [the disciples ...]. They said to him: "Why do you love her more than all of ous?" The savior answered and said to them: "Why do I not love you like her? When a blind man and one who sees are both together in darkness, they are no different from one another. When the light comes, then he who sees will see the light, and he who is blind will remain in darkness."[67]

As to the role of Mary Magdalene in the *Gospel of Philip*, the present passage poses two important questions. First, what is her relationship to the Savior? Second, what is her relationship to the rest of the disciples of Jesus? Since the first question has already been dealt with in connection with the analysis of *Gos. Phil.* 59,6-11, we concentrate here only on the latter. Before that question can be answered it is pertinent to consider the extent of the passage which should be included in the analysis.

3.1 *Demarcation of the Text*

Since our interest lies in Mary Magdalene's relationship to the rest of Jesus' disciples, it is the extent of the discussion between the disciples[68] and the Savior, that concerns us. Simply put: does the answer of the Savior, beginning in 64,4, contain only the question in 64,4-5 or is the comparison between a blind and a seeing one to be included? Some scholars think this comparison constitutes a new and separate pericope,[69] similar to that in 63,5-11;[70] others

---

[67] The text is taken from Layton 1989a, 166.168. The translation derives from Isenberg (1989, 167.169) with the exception of the second line; for the ambiguity of the text at this point, see above n. 24, 25 and 27.

[68] Since the text is here very fragmentary it is not right away clear with whom the Savior is discussing. Till (1963, 28) has filled the laguna on line 63,37 as follows: ⲀⲠⲔⲉⲤⲉⲉⲡⲉ Ⲛ̄[Ⲛ̄(Ⲥ)Ⲣⲓⲟⲙⲉ ⲀⲨ. Since the disciples are mentioned two lines earlier (63,35) another restoration is, however, more likely: ⲀⲠⲔⲉⲤⲉⲉⲡⲉ Ⲙ̄[ⲘⲀⲐⲎⲦⲎⲤ ⲀⲨ (so Schenke 1959, 12; Ménard 1967, 70; Layton 1989a, 168).

[69] Schenke 1959, 12; Wilson 1962, 116; Till 1963, 29; Ménard 1967, 70-72; Gaffron 1969, 386 n. 111; Schmid 1990, 106-107.

regard it as an essential element of the Savior's reply.[71] If 64,5-9 belongs to the answer of the Savior, it provides an apparent interpretation of the relationship between Mary Magdalene and the rest of the disciples.

The chief argument favoring a separation of 63,30-64,5 and 64,5-9 is Schenke's form-critical observation of the similarity between 64,5-9 and 63,5-11. Admittedly, the parallelism between the two texts is obvious but it is hardly a cogent reason for considering 64,5-9 as an independent entity which cannot be attached to the foregoing. In addition, there are other factors which support taking 63,30-64,9 as a unity. First, if the Savior's answer terminates after the question in 64,4-5, the question of the disciples remains unanswered. Second, it is not typical of the *Gospel of Philip* that an excerpt ends with a cryptic counter question.[72] In two instances a passage concludes with a question (75,13-14; 77,6-7) but in both cases the question is clearly rhetorical and the answer is self-evident. Third, it is very common in the *Gospel of Philip* that the train of thought is expounded through a question–answer pattern. This is a stylistic device the writing frequently displays (56,32-57,7; 60,34-61,12; 76,17-22; 79,33-80,23), and there is no reason to assume that this could not be placed in the mouth of the Savior too. Based on these observations, it seems reasonable to assume that the answer of the Savior to the question of the disciples in 64,2 extends to line 64,9.

---

[70] This observation is made by Schenke 1959, 12.

[71] Layton 1987, 339; Isenberg 1989, 169; Price 1990, 59; King 1995, 631 n. 42; Krause (1964b, 182; cf. also 1971, 105), too, asserts that this possibility has to be taken into consideration.

[72] Gaffron (1969, 386 n. 111) has recognized the problematic nature of the question. However, he regards it as a stylistic device which has a parallel in the *Gospel of Ebionites* (Epiph., *Pan.* 30.22,4). That text presents a dialogue between Jesus and his disciples which, according to Gaffron, ends with a counterquestion of Jesus, similar to that of *Gos. Phil.* 59,4-5. Gaffron's parallel is not very useful. First of all, Jesus' question in the *Gospel of Ebionites* is clearly rhetorical and the expected answer is known by everybody. Second, there is no way to know whether Jesus' answer to the question of the disciples has ended with his counterquestion. Epiphanius may have quoted only a part of it (cf. Luke 22,15-16).

3.2 Mary Magdalene and the Rest of the Disciples

According to the reply of the Savior (64,4-9), Mary Magdalene's role as his favorite among the disciples is due to her special ability to grasp spiritual realities. Compared to her, others are blind disciples who do not perceive the luminous character of Jesus but remain in darkness. While Mary Magdalene is elevated to a very special rank in spiritual hierarchy, other disciples seem incapable of understanding. In the context of the *Gospel of Philip*, this characterization of the disciples appears astonishingly negative. There are other excerpts in which they are portrayed differently.

The passages which speak of the immediate followers of Jesus refer to them either as apostles or as disciples. In some cases the latter term is used of a group distinct from the apostles (59,27-28)[73] or of a group which may contain members of a later generation of Jesus' followers as well or exclusively (71,13-15; 81,1-3). In 55,29-30; 55,37; 58,3-10; 59,23; 59,27-28; 62,5-6; 67,24-25; 73,8; 74,17-18 there is no doubt that a reference is made to the disciples of the earthly Jesus. Many of these texts give quite a positive picture of them. In 59,27-28 they are depicted as the teachers of later disciples. In 62,6-17; 67,24-25; 73,8-19 the author refers to them as authoritative bearers of the tradition. If 81,1-14 characterizes Jesus' apostles they are seen as capable of distinguishing between people of various spiritual qualifications and as providing the complete instruction to those who are worthy of it. According to 74,17-18, the apostles are the link through whom the readers of the *Gospel of Philip* have received the anointment which the Father first gave to his son and the son to his apostles. Since the anointment is seen to bring with it "everything," the resurrection, the light, the cross, and the Holy Spirit, it is evident that the role the author of the *Gospel of Philip* here grants to the apostles is quite far from that of the blind ones. By contrast, they seem to be spiritual authorities par excellence.

The only text other than 63,30-64,9 where the apostles are clearly introduced in negative terms is 55,28-30.[74] In that text, the

---

[73] The same is true with the ⲀⲠⲞⲤⲦⲞⲖⲓⲔⲞⲤ in 55,30 and 66,29.

[74] Another passage which may present a somewhat negative picture of a disciple of Jesus is 59,23-27. At least a disciple who asks something of this world cannot be regarded as fully understanding. According to the

apostles and their followers cannot understand the real nature of the conception of the Virgin Mary. They believe that Mary conceived by the Holy Spirit which, according to the author of the writing, is impossible since the Holy Spirit is feminine.[75] Therefore, those apostles are called Hebrews, i.e., they are spiritually immature as 62,6 shows (cf. also 52,21-24).

How is this diversity in presentation of the apostles to be explained? Could it be due to the fact that the author is drawing material from many different and — at least with respect to this topic — mutually contradicting sources without noticing their conflicting character? There is no doubt that the material which is used in the *Gospel of Philip* has various derivations. However, this solution hardly presents a plausible answer to the problem. The apostles and the disciples have such a significant role in the *Gospel of Philip* that it would be rather strange if the author would refer to them in such an unreflective manner as this solution would presuppose.

There is another, more natural explanation for a dual character of the apostles. This is suggested by 58,5-10. The passage which contains these lines deals with Jesus who was able to adapt himself to the individual viewer's powers of comprehension. It ends with a description of an appearance of Jesus to his disciples on the mountain. In that encounter the disciples are said to be able to see Jesus in his greatness. The text indicates that the real character of Jesus was not always discernible to his disciples. Either the passage has to be understood to say that the disciples could perceive Jesus' real nature only on special occasions such as this particular appearance in glory or that the apostles completely lacked understanding until he revealed himself to them on the mountain. If the appearance on the mountain is seen to refer to the Transfiguration, the first interpretation is more likely. If the text speaks of the appearance of the Risen Jesus to the apostles it shows that the disciples were small, i.e., unbelievers (cf. 80,9-10), during their stay with the earthly Jesus but gained full understanding after the resurrection.

Lord, his mother, i.e., the Holy Spirit, can give him something which is far superior to things of this world (see Stroker 1989, 42).

[75] In 71,4-5 it is explicitly stated that it is the Father who united with the Virgin who came down.

Many scholars think that *Gos. Phil.* 58,5-10 refers to the Trans-figuration.[76] Ménard has called attention to the fact that in *Exc. Theod.* 4,1-3 the appearance of Jesus in glory is connected with the Transfiguration. According to that text, it is in the Transfigura-tion that Jesus revealed knowledge to his disciples. By means of this knowledge they and the later congregation can enter into the pleroma. The description of the appearance as ϩⲚ̄Ⲛ ⲞⲨⲈⲞⲞⲨ ("in glory") also recalls the Transfiguration story, especially in its Lukan form (Luke 9,32). On the other hand, there are many reve-lation dialogues in which the disclosure of Jesus' real nature and the ultimate mysteries occurs on a mountain after the resurrec-tion.[77] Even though the expression "in glory" is not used in the texts, in each of them the Risen One is portrayed as a glorious, transformed figure. The most notable examples of these appear-ance stories are found in the *Sophia of Jesus Christ*, the *Letter of Peter to Philip*, and *Pistis Sophia I-III*.[78] It is typical of these texts that only the post-resurrection revelation provides the disciples with the right understanding of Jesus and the knowledge he came to impart.[79] In *Pistis Sophia I-III*, and possibly also in the *Sophia of Jesus Christ*, this is due to the fact that the earthly Jesus did not teach the disciples concerning the deeper spiritual truths. This is the task of the Risen Savior (cf. also Iren., *Adv. haer.* 1.30,14).[80] In the *Letter of Peter to Philip* the situation is different. The Risen Lord gives no new revelation but repeats everything he has already said during his earthly ministry (135,4-8). However, because of their unbelief, the disciples were not capable of understanding it.

---

[76] Puech 1959, 193; Ménard 1967, 146; Layton 1987, 334. Wilson (1962, 92) regards it as one possibility but also insists that there are other possibilities as well since a mountain is a common place for revelation.

[77] So also Wilson 1962, 92.

[78] *Soph. Jes. Chr.* 90,14-91,12; *Ep. Pet. Phil.* 134,9-18; *PS* 4,12-9,22.

[79] In *1 Apoc. Jas.* 30,18-31,2, Jesus appears after his resurrection on a mountain. In that tractate, however, James who sees the revelation has been a disciple with understanding already before the death of Jesus. A post-resurrection appearance has only a complementary function. Yet it is of interest that the twelve are pictured as without understanding, at least during the period before the death of Jesus (42,20-24; see also the treatment of the text in this study).

[80] As Luttikhuizen (1988, 162) has noted, this is seen even more clearly in the *Apocryphon of John*, where the teaching of the earthly Je-sus is incomplete and provisional (II/1 1,26-29), whereas the Risen Savior gives John full and definitive instruction.

These revelation dialogues, which seem to have an access to a common tradition, furnish the best clue to the interpretation of *Gos. Phil.* 58,5-10. As in those texts so also in this particular passage from the *Gospel of Philip*, Jesus' appearance in glory on the mount seems to have taken place after his resurrection. Only on that occasion is the real nature of his person and teaching made transparent to his disciples for the first time, since they have now become great, i.e., their unbelief has been removed. Until then, they were blind, incapable of seeing and understanding in the same way as the disciples in the *Letter of Peter to Philip*.

In light of these observations, the duality of the apostles in the *Gospel of Philip* can be explained by assuming that, while the majority of the excerpts dealing with the apostles or the disciples view them from the perspective of their post-resurrection experience of the great Jesus, there are two or perhaps three excerpts which reflect the inadequate understanding of the disciples prior to the post-resurrection appearance of Jesus.[81] Apart from 55,28-30 and possibly also 59,23-27, *Gos. Phil.* 63,30-64,9 portrays the disciples who are blind and small, dazed by their unbelief. It is only Mary Magdalene, the favorite of the Savior, who is able to see what the others can see only after the resurrection. Thus, Mary Magdalene is introduced as a paragon of apostleship whose spiritual maturity is reached by other followers of Jesus only later. Considering this and the fact that she is presented as a spiritual consort of Jesus, it is surprising that in the context of the *Gospel of Philip* as a whole, Mary Magdalene personally does not gain any significant position as a transmitter of spiritual mysteries. As noted above, this seems to be the task of the whole group of the

---

[81] The distinction between the pre-resurrection and the post-resurrection apostleship also affects the author's conception of the apostolic tradition. The apostolic tradition the author wants to connect is the one which developed after Jesus had revealed his greatness to the disciples. There is, however, another conception of the apostolic tradition which the author of the text criticizes and which he finds among those Christians whom he calls Hebrews (55,28-30; Siker [1989, 277] has argued that in the *Gospel of Philip* a Hebrew is not an ethnic designation but refers to a non-Gnostic Christian). This apostolic tradition stems from a pre-resurrection experience of discipleship and reflects the same lack of understanding the disciples themselves had.

apostles.[82] Whether Mary Magdalene is counted among them is nowhere explicitly discussed, but is probably presupposed in 63,37-64,1. At any rate, after the appearance of the Risen Jesus to his disciples she no longer seems to hold any special role among the followers of Jesus.

The fact that the spiritual superiority Mary Magdalene exhibits over the rest of the disciples during the earthly ministry of Jesus does not result in elevating her to the spiritual authority in the *Gospel of Philip*, as in the *Gospel of Mary*, for example, may be explained as the author's attempt to emphasize the common apostolic origin of his/her teaching. The author wants to stress that it does not derive from a single authority but it represents the collective witness of all the apostles. The only other condition of the message is that it be revealed to the apostles after they are made great, i.e., after the resurrection of Jesus.

If this reconstruction of the author's intentions is correct, it raises a further question: Why does the author of the *Gospel of Philip* include in the writing a text where one of the disciples, Mary Magdalene, is portrayed in such a positive light while on the other hand the writing underlines a lack of understanding among the disciples before the resurrection? There is no easy answer to this question. The most plausible explanation is that the positive pre-resurrection portrayal of Mary Magdalene has to do with her role as Jesus' companion. To assign this role to a disciple without understanding would not suit the paradigmatic character the syzygy of Jesus and Mary Magdalene holds for the readers of the *Gospel of Philip*. Therefore, already before the post-resurrection appearance of Jesus, Mary Magdalene is granted a position superior to that of all the other disciples.

---

[82] The whole group of apostles remains rather vague. Only one of them, Philip (73,2), is mentioned by name. Levi appears in 63,26, but there is no certainty that he is considered to be an apostle.

CHAPTER EIGHT

MARY MAGDALENE IN PISTIS SOPHIA

1. *Introductory Remarks*

Pistis Sophia consists of conversations between the Risen Jesus and his disciples. Among the interlocutors of Jesus, Mary Magdalene assumes a very prominent role. In the entire writing, she presents more questions to Jesus than all the others together, and without exception her interpretations of Jesus' speeches gain an especially favorable reception. Indeed, *Pistis Sophia* is that Gnostic writing which, besides the *Gospel of Mary,* is most often used to delineate a portrait of the Gnostic Mary Magdalene.[1]

Pistis Sophia is known to us through a single manuscript, Codex Askewianus. It bears the name of an English manuscript collector, Dr. Askew, who purchased it from a bookseller in London in 1773. How and when the manuscript reached London is unknown to us. The text was issued for the first time around 80 years later.[2] The standard critical edition of the text was prepared by Carl Schmidt in 1925.[3] Since that time there have been no new editions of the text. The Coptic text of *Pistis Sophia* which is included in the *Nag Hammadi Studies* series reproduces Schmidt's text virtually unaltered except for some minor corrections.[4]

---

[1] Malvern 1975, 30-56; Haskins 1993, 33-57. Schmid (1990) adds the *Gospel of Philip* to these two writings.

[2] The editor of the text was M.G. Schwartze who also translated it into Latin. The publication of the text took place after Schwartze's death (for the earliest phases of Codex Askewianus, see Schmidt & Schenke 1981, XVI-XVII).

[3] A German translation of the text was published by him already in 1905. This and its later version (1925) have been re-edited by Till in 1954 and 1959. Till follows Schmidt's translations closely, giving his own alternative renderings in an appendix. The fourth edition of the translation was prepared by Schenke in 1981 (= Schmidt & Schenke 1981).

[4] Schmidt & MacDermot 1978b, VII. In the present study, the references to *Pistis Sophia* are made according to this work. The first number gives the page number of the Coptic text, the second number refers to the line. All the English translations of *Pistis Sophia* are taken from Schmidt

In its present form, *Pistis Sophia* is divided into four books. Already very early, it was realized that the fourth one was only secondarily attached to Books I-III.[5] Its independent character is most clearly shown by the beginning (353,1-5) which gives the subsequent dialogue a setting of its own. As will be noted below, there are also other differences between *Pistis Sophia I-III* and *Pistis Sophia IV*.[6] Thus, the two parts of *Pistis Sophia* will be treated separately when Mary Magdalene passages of the writing are examined.[7] Only at the end, after both portraits of Mary Magdalene have been presented separately, will comparison between the two be undertaken.

Among scholars there is agreement that both parts of *Pistis Sophia* stem from Egypt. This is attested by references to the Egyptian calendar and to Egyptian mythological names and concepts.[8] There is general agreement that both works of *Pistis Sophia* date from the third century.[9] It has been suggested that *Pistis*

& MacDermot (1978b) unless otherwise advised.

[5] According to Puech & Blatz (1987, 290), the first one to argue this was K.R. Köstlin in 1854.

[6] See also Perkins 1992b, 376.

[7] The composite character of *Pistis Sophia* is also recognized by Schmid (1990, 44). Curiously enough, she does not draw any conclusions from this. While presenting Mary Magdalene in *Pistis Sophia*, she deals with the writing as if it were an integrated unity (cf. also Koivunen 1994, 173.175-176).

[8] Schmidt & Schenke 1981, XXIII-XXIV. See also Harnack 1891, 101-103; Quispel 1961, 387.

[9] For the arguments, see Harnack 1891, 95-101; Leisegang 1950, 1817-1818. The *terminus ad quem* for *Pistis Sophia* is provided by the fact that the author wrote this work in a time when it was still possible for Christians to be lawfully persecuted (277,10-16). After 313 C.E this was no longer the case. The explicit references of *Pistis Sophia I-III* to the early third century writing, the *Books of Jeu* (*PS* 247,4-5; 349,16.23; 350,8), and the obvious dependence of *Pistis Sophia IV* on the same writing in its description of the mysteries (cf. Schmidt 1925, LIV-LXXXI), put the *terminus a quo* somewhere in the first half of the third century.

Sophia IV is earlier than *Pistis Sophia I-III*[10] but this cannot be settled with certainty.[11]

There is no doubt that both parts of *Pistis Sophia* are Gnostic works. They seem to presuppose a myth resembling that of the *Apocryphon of John*. The primary interest of *Pistis Sophia I-III* is not, however, to explain the origin of evil and the imprisonment of the soul in the world.[12]   Book I and the large part of Book II are concerned with the repentance and the deliverance of the fallen Sophia, here called Pistis Sophia. The rest of Book II contains Jesus' answers to various types of questions presented by the disciples, most of which have to do with the ranks to which souls may go according to the mysteries they have received. In Book III the central topics in the dialogue between Jesus/the Savior and the disciples are: how to preach gnosis to the world, to whom are the mysteries and the forgiveness of sins granted, and who are to go to the light? *Pistis Sophia IV* reveals the punishments of evil archons and shows the disciples access to the divine mysteries by which they can escape judgment. The final part of Book IV deals with the ultimate fate of various sinners, and the text concludes with a prayer to Jesus for compassion, spoken by the disciples in Amente. Philosophical speculation about the nature of the highest God and the soul's relationship to him, typical of many earlier Gnostic writings, is no longer traceable in *Pistis Sophia*.[13]

Because *Pistis Sophia* is such an extensive work and Mary Magdalene appears so often on its pages, it is not possible to examine every Mary Magdalene passage in detail in this study. Instead, we will try to sketch the picture of Mary Magdalene both in *Pistis Sophia I-III* and in *Pistis Sophia IV* under two headings:

---

[10] Schmidt 1925, XL-LXXXI; see also Quispel 1961, 387; Schmidt & Schenke 1981, XXIV.

[11] The dependence of *Pistis Sophia I-III* on the *Books of Jeu* is evident (see *PS* 246,20-21; 247,3-5; 349,23; 350,8); it is equally clear that the *Second Book of Jeu* serves as the source for the author of *Pistis Sophia IV* (see Schmidt 1925, LIV-LXXXI). However, the temporal priority of *Pistis Sophia IV* over against *Pistis Sophia I-III* can hardly be definitely decided on the observations Schmidt (1925, XL-LXXXI) presents.

[12] For an overview of the contents, see Schmidt & MacDermot 1978b, XIV-XVIII.

[13] Perkins 1980, 140.

The Position of Mary Magdalene Among the Disciples and *Mary Magdalene as Rival of the Male Disciples.*

2. *Mary Magdalene in Pistis Sophia I-III*

The name of Mary Magdalene is spelled in three different ways in *Pistis Sophia I-III.* The most common Coptic equivalent is ⲘⲀ-ⲣⲓⲀ,[14] sometimes with the epithet ⲘⲀⲅⲆⲀⲗⲎⲚⲎ[15] and more frequently without. In addition, the name is also spelled ⲘⲀⲣⲓ-ϩⲀⲘ[16] and once ⲘⲀⲣⲓϩⲀⲘⲘⲎ (346,9). Variety in the names has raised the question of literary unity in *Pistis Sophia I-III.*[17] It is not impossible that the writing is a result of a redactional process[18] but it is not very likely that the different versions of the name Mary Magdalene can be used to distinguish between various redactional layers of the text. This is shown by the fact that within one passage which gives the impression of being literarily coherent both the name ⲘⲀⲣⲓⲀ and ⲘⲀⲣⲓϩⲀⲘ can be juxtaposed (29,1-18; 52,14-56,13; 72,3-22; 123,6-124,13; 184,7-185,20; 275,12-276,5; 322,7-18; 326,1-8). Since there seems to be no essential difference in the way Mary Magdalene is treated in various parts of *Pistis Sophia I-III*, no thorough source analysis of the writing is undertaken.

In addition to Mary Magdalene, another Mary, the Virgin Mother of Jesus, is introduced as one of the interlocutors of the Risen Jesus. There is, however, no risk of confusing the two since the Virgin Mary is often introduced as the mother of Jesus and

---

[14] This version of the name appears some 159 times.

[15] The epithet ⲘⲀⲅⲆⲀⲗⲎⲚⲎ is attached to the name ⲘⲀⲣⲓⲀ 12 times.

[16] ⲘⲀⲣⲓϩⲀⲘ occurs 21 times.

[17] MacDermot (Schmidt & MacDermot 1978b, XIV) has suggested that inconsistencies in the names of Mary Magdalene "support the view that the text is a compilation."

[18] In several places the text seems to be supplied with redactional expansions and reinterpretations. It is also possible that the material used by the author derives from various sources. The repentances of Pistis Sophia related by Jesus and their interpretations may have formed a separate collection (40,4-120,10). This may also be true with an alternative version of Pistis Sophia's rescue from chaos reported by the First Mystery (129,7-184,6) as well as with the part in which Mary Magdalene and John pose questions (184,7-352,20).

always so, when she appears in a new passage for the first time
(13,18-19; 116,21-22; 120,14; 124,14). Furthermore, in those
instances, when the two occur in the same context Mary Magdalene is referred to as "the other Mary" (ΤΚΕΜΔΡΙΔ).

2.1 *The Position of Mary Magdalene Among the Disciples*

In terms of mere statistics, Mary Magdalene is unequivocally the
most prominent interlocutor of Jesus.[19] Out of a total of 115
questions and interpretations of Jesus' speeches presented by those
accompanying him, she alone is responsible for 67.[20] Some sections of *Pistis Sophia I-III* are almost entirely controlled by her. In
the latter part of Book II (184,7ff.) and in Book III, besides Mary
Magdalene only John, Peter, and Salome voice questions or interpretations of Jesus' speeches. John does it 5 times, Peter and
Salome once each, whereas Mary Magdalene speaks 53 times.[21]
This statistical supremacy over the other interlocutors of Jesus is
further underlined by Mary Magdalene's own words: "My Lord,
my mind is understanding *at all times* that I should come forward
at any time and give the interpretation of the words she (Pistis
Sophia) spoke..." (162,14-16; italics mine). These words suggest
that she could open her mouth even more frequently unless, from
time to time, she preferred to remain silent out of consideration for
or fear of the others.

Not only are Mary Magdalene's interpretations and questions
the most numerous, they are also extraordinarily well received by
Jesus. To be sure, most interpretations of Jesus' speeches, and not
only those presented by Mary Magdalene but also those of other

---

[19] Other interlocutors of Jesus are: Philip, Peter, Martha, John,
Andrew, Thomas, Matthew, James, Salome, and Mary, the Virgin Mother
of Jesus.

[20] These numbers do not include those remarks, in which a person
asks for permission to present a question or an interpretation of a speech.

[21] Harnack (1891, 71-85) calls the section on pages 262-352 "the
Questions of Mary." In earlier scholarship, some were even of the opinion that *Pistis Sophia I-III* is identical with the "Lesser Questions of
Mary" mentioned by Epiphanius, *Pan.* 26.8,2 (e.g. Harnack 1891, 108-
109; Schmidt 1892, 597; for further references, see Puech & Blatz 1987,
312). In later times, this view has not found much support. Contrary to
his earlier opinion, for example Schmidt has abandoned it (see Schmidt
& Schenke 1981, XXII).

interlocutors, are praised by Jesus with a positive remark, such as
єує, καλωc. Similarly, not only Mary Magdalene but also
John, who is the only other one whose questions are commented
on,[22] pose their questions, according to Jesus, with assurance and
certainty (e.g. 34,3-4; 191,4-6; 204,10-11). In fact, Mary herself
states that this concerns all the disciples even though she and
sometimes John function as their spokespersons (184,8-10).[23]
Taken as a whole, all the disciples who engage themselves in
conversation with Jesus seem to understand Jesus' instruction
well.[24] Like Mary, the other disciples are called "blessed beyond
all men" (352,3-5;[25] 15,15-17); likewise, both Mary and the other
disciples are told that they are pneumatic (200,4; 84,2), they will
inherit the kingdom of the light (120,12-13; 253,5-8),[26] they all
will be fulfilled in every pleroma (28,22-24; 60,8-11), and they
will be completed in all the mysteries of the height (26,16-18;
77,6-16).[27] The twelve are even entrusted with the task of saving

---

[22] In 32,14-20 Philip asks a question but Jesus' answer contains no
special commendation of his question.

[23] The same thing is confirmed by Jesus in 205,3-4; in that context,
it is John who asks a question on behalf of all the disciples.

[24] Only once is a statement put forward which raises Jesus' indignation. In 248,4-14, Andrew says that he cannot understand how the souls
having left their bodies can pass all the powers and inherit the Kingdom
of the Light. Jesus cannot but be resentful at the ignorance the remark
displays. Thereafter, he instructs the disciples concerning the matter, and
Andrew and the rest of the disciples come to fully understand his teaching. They also ask for forgiveness of Andrew's sin of ignorance. This is
mercifully granted by Jesus. Nevertheless, one should not overemphasize
Andrew's personal failure to understand (as Malvern [1975, 49] does);
it is also problematic to see the text in light of *Gos. Mary* 17,10-15
(Schmid 1990, 17). Andrew is not opposing anybody here. He acts as
representative of all the disciples who are all at this point ignorant and
need further instruction (248,14-18; 253,6-8). The others give him only
the role of a scapegoat (253,8-12).

[25] Mary Magdalene is also called "blessed among all generations"
(56,12-13).

[26] In 252,11-12, it is even stated that the male disciples will become
rulers in the eternal kingdom of the light (cf. also 90,1-7). In 68,5-6 the
same is said about John alone.

[27] When Koivunen (1994, 177-178) emphasizes the great difference
in the way Mary Magdalene and the male disciples are described in *Pistis
Sophia*, she overlooks the fact that many positive characterizations of
Mary Magdalene are ascribed to the male disciples as well.

the world.[28] Yet some remarks, either presented by the narrator or placed in the mouth of Jesus, clearly indicate that although all the disciples have understanding and are pneumatic, Mary Magdalene has special standing among the interlocutors.

While introducing other interlocutors with no extra words, the narrator of the text characterizes Mary Magdalene as "the beautiful in her speech" (33,17-18). After one special interpretation Mary Magdalene gives of Jesus' words, the narrator states: "When she finished speaking these words, the Saviour marvelled greatly at the answers to the words which she gave, because she had completely become pure Spirit" (199,20-200,3). Twice the narrator refers to the special blessing which the Savior grants to Mary Magdalene because of her splendid perception (328,18-19; 339,8-9). Moreover, the way the narrator arranges the text points to his/her interest in emphasizing the excellence of Mary Magdalene as an interlocutor of Jesus. She is the only one who answers a question of another disciple and receives the commendation of both the questioner (Salome) and Jesus (338,1-339,4). Furthermore, she explains the words of Jesus directed to another disciple, Philip (72,5-22), and presents questions on behalf of her male colleagues (201,8-25; 296,7-12; 311,17-24). It is also worth noting that in 218,1-219,22 she speaks on behalf of the male disciples who have been made so scared by Jesus' reference to his most important revelation that they cease to perceive what he is talking about.

---

[28] In 15,17-18, Jesus says to his disciples: "... it is you who will save the whole world." In the section before that text, Jesus mentions that when he came to the world he brought with him twelve powers from the twelve saviors of the treasury of the light, which are able to save the whole world, and cast these powers into the unborn bodies of the twelve in order that they may be able to accomplish their task (11,1-8). In this way, the disciples "are not from the world" but belong to the realm of the light (11,17-19; 14,7-9; 280,3-6; cf. also Schmidt 1892, 449-450). Certainly, what the twelve in the context of *Pistis Sophia* actually means is not fully clear. It is at least obvious that nowhere is it connected with the twelve male apostles of Jesus. Whether its purpose is to give the exact number of the disciples participating in the dialogue with Jesus and thus to indicate that the twelve also include women: Mary Magdalene, Martha, Salome, and Mary, the mother of Jesus, is possible (so Schmid 1990, 47) but not very likely. Actually, only seven male disciples are mentioned by name (Schmid indeed insists that there are eight male interlocutors but one of them, Bartholomew, whom she lists as the eighth, appears only in *Pistis Sophia IV*, not in *Pistis Sophia I-III*). It is more probable that the twelve is simply a traditional term which no longer has any clear function in *Pistis Sophia I-III* (see e.g. 232,21-26).

The superiority of Mary Magdalene among the interlocutors of Jesus appears most clearly in his remark in 26,17-20 where he states: "Mariam, thou blessed one, whom I will complete in all the mysteries of the height, speak openly, thou art she whose heart is more directed to the Kingdom of Heaven than all thy brothers." The meaning of directing the heart to the kingdom of heaven is disclosed in 28,16-19. It does not reflect a penitent mind or a new moral consciousness or a correct cultic behavior but an ability to hear and perceive the mysteries Jesus is revealing. In this respect Mary Magdalene is the most capable one among the disciples. Therefore, she asks the most questions and gives the best interpretations of Jesus' discourses. In addition, Mary Magdalene is also pictured as the most courageous one among the disciples. When all the disciples begin to despair that the most important mysteries Jesus is relating to them cannot be understood by anyone, it is she who comes forth, expresses their fear, and seeks Jesus' consolation (218,9-219,8).

Another passage which underlines the prominence of Mary Magdalene within the circle of the most intimate followers of Jesus is 232,26-233,2. Having said that the disciples and all the others who receive the mysteries of the Ineffable will reign with him in his future kingdom, Jesus states here: "But Mary Magdalene and John the Virgin will be superior to all my disciples."[29] Thus, the superiority of Mary Magdalene and John to the rest of

---

[29] According to MacDermot, the sentence ends here and the following ⲁⲩⲱ begins a new section which speaks about "all men who will receive mysteries in the Ineffable." According to Schmidt (Schmidt & Schenke 1981, 148), the text is to be punctuated so that Mary Magdalene and John the Virgin are not only superior to all the disciples but also to all the other people who receive mysteries. Consequently, the continuation of the text is seen as relating to Mary Magdalene and John the Virgin. The problem with Schmidt's solution is that he must assume that the following text is corrupt and he is forced to emend the possesive pronouns in 233,6-8. Otherwise, the text reads in such a way that Mary Magdalene and John rank lower than the rest of the disciples. With MacDermot's punctuation, this emendation proves needless, and the text only states that in the future kingdom of the Savior the authority of the Savior is greater than that of the disciples and the authority of the disciples is greater than that of the other people who receive the mysteries of the Ineffable. The purpose of the comment about Mary Magdalene and John is to show that the group of the disciples is in fact divided into two: Mary Magdalene and John are of the highest rank, and the rest of the disciples constitute the second, inferior category.

the disciples is not confined to the present age but is extended to the future as well.[30] It is noteworthy how the author of *Pistis Sophia I-III* modifies the promise granted to the twelve in Matt 19,28. On the one hand, the text contains a kind of democratization. It is not only the twelve who reign with Jesus in his future kingdom but all who receive the highest mystery.[31] On the other hand, among the fellow-rulers of Jesus two, Mary Magdalene and John, are singled out and they are given an extraordinary eschatological status. Nowhere else in a Gnostic or any other text, is either Mary Magdalene or John granted a similar role.

In light of these observations, there is one surprising feature in the description of Mary Magdalene in *Pistis Sophia I-III*. Even if she is depicted as the most understanding and courageous among the disciples, she does not seem to belong to those disciples who are going to preach and transmit the mysteries to the whole world after the departure of Jesus. To be sure, as a member of the circle of disciples she also receives Jesus' commandment to preach, collectively addressed to all the disciples (256,2-3; 280,11-14; 309,2-3; 314,22-23; 316,20; cf. also 232,21-24; 266,17-19; 272,21-24; 349,10-12). When she speaks about performing a mystery and preaching she can even use the inclusive language: "...we perform a mystery...we are preaching the words of the all..." (279,6-7). Yet there are some texts which show that even if preaching and transmitting mysteries are tasks which the disciples are jointly responsible for, it is apparently not Mary Magdalene but the male disciples who are supposed to participate actively in accomplishing them.

In 201,21-25 Mary Magdalene states: "...we question all things with assurance, for my brothers preach them to the whole race of men, so that they come not into the hands of the harsh archons of the darkness, and are saved from the hands of the harsh paralemptai of the outer darkness." In 296,10-12 Mary Magdalene asks: "...my Lord, be compassionate to us and reveal to us all things about which we will question thee, for the sake of the manner in which my brothers will preach to the whole race of mankind."

---

[30] Schmidt 1892, 452.

[31] A similar idea of those ruling together with Christ is found in 2 Tim 2,12 and Rev 3,21.

Giving or performing a mystery[32] also seems to be a duty of the male disciples. This is suggested by the remarks of Mary Magdalene and the Savior in 311,21-22 and in 312,5-6 (cf. also 310,1-21). Thus, Mary Magdalene's leading role among the disciples is confined to her superiority as the dialogue partner and the interpreter of Jesus, while transmitting these teachings as well as performing mysteries, especially ritual acts, seems to be entrusted to her male colleagues.[33] This raises the following questions: Is the author of *Pistis Sophia I-III* dependent on a tradition which presupposes this limitation in the role of Mary Magdalene or does the author create it personally? And if the latter is the case, does this redactional emphasis reflect somehow the concrete situation of the audience of *Pistis Sophia I-III*? Being closely related to the theme of rivalry between Mary Magdalene and her male colleagues these questions will be taken up in the following section.

2.2 *Mary Magdalene as Rival of the Male Disciples*

There are two texts in *Pistis Sophia I-III* which actualize the theme of rivalry between Mary Magdalene and the male disciples. In 58,11-14, after Mary Magdalene has presented an interpretation of the first repentance of Pistis Sophia as well as five other interpretations of Jesus' discourses, and Jesus has asked the disciples to interpret the second repentance of Pistis Sophia, Peter says to Jesus: "My Lord, we are not able to suffer this woman who takes the opportunity from us, and does not allow anyone of us to speak, but she speaks many times." Later on during the dialogue, Peter's indignation at Mary Magdalene seems to continue. This is shown by the remark of Mary Magdalene in 162,14-18, as she answers the request of the First Mystery (= Jesus) to give an interpretation of the words Pistis Sophia had spoken: "My Lord,

---

[32] In *Pistis Sophia I-III* there seem to be two kinds of mysteries: first, a special revelation (226,12-228,23); second, a ritual act, such as baptism (300,12-13).

[33] Schmid (1990, 58-61) has also noticed the extraordinary character of the passages presented in the text above. Nevertheless, she refuses to take their wording seriously and thinks that these words of Mary Magdalene cannot mean that she was not supposed to participate in the preaching activity together with her brothers "auch wenn die Formulierungen dieser drei Kapitel dies zunächst nahelegen."

my mind is understanding at all times that I should come forward
at any time and give the interpretation of the words which she
spoke, but I am afraid of Peter, for he threatens me and he hates
our race (ΓΕΝΟϹ)."

The hostile reaction Peter adopts towards Mary Magdalene
seems to have two reasons. First, the superior capacity of Mary
Magdalene to enter into a dialogue with Jesus and to give interpretations of his discourses excites jealousy in Peter. Clearly, Peter
sees her as a rival with regard to the favor of the Savior.[34] Mary
Magdalene, for her part, experiences Peter's hostility as a threat
and turns to Jesus in order to seek support from him in the face of
Peter's aggression.

The second reason why Mary Magdalene irritates Peter is the
ΓΕΝΟϹ she represents. How is this to be understood? The Greek
word ΓΕΝΟϹ may assume several meanings. In the context of
Pistis Sophia, it most commonly denotes the human race in its
entirety. It is clear that the word cannot have this meaning in
162,17-18. There is another use of the word in the fourth repentance of Pistis Sophia in 65,11. There it refers to the race "which
will be born." This is a designation of those persons who are "in
the places below" but who show repentance. Obviously, the Pistis
Sophia is anticipating an appearance of a Gnostic race. Could
Mary Magdalene's reference to "our race" be understood along
these lines, in other words, as a self-designation of the Gnostics?[35]
Before this question can be answered a third alternative interpretation of the word ΓΕΝΟϹ must be introduced.

While the editors of *Pistis Sophia,* Schmidt and MacDermot,
have rendered ΓΕΝΟϹ ambigiously as "Geschlecht" and "race,"
other interpreters of the text are of the opinion that ΠΕΝΓΕΝΟϹ in

---

[34] A further indication of competitiveness among the disciples is
Thomas' remark to Jesus in 81,18-20, as he feels himself sober in pre-
senting his interpretation of a repentance of Pistis Sophia: "Nevertheless
I have suffered my brothers up till now lest I cause anger in them. But
I suffer each one of them to come before thee to say the interpretation
of the repentance of the Pistis Sophia."

[35] This is suggested as an alternative interpretation of the word
ΓΕΝΟϹ by Parrott (1986, 205). It is interesting that some Gnostic writings
use the terms ΠΙΓΕΝΟϹ ΜΠΠΝΕΥΜΑΤΙΚΟϹ (*Tri. Trac.* 118,28-29; cf. also
Epiph. *Pan.* 31.7,5) and ΠΜΑϨϤΤΟΟΥ ΝΓΕΝΟϹ (*Orig. World* 125,5-6) as
self-designations of the Gnostics.

the mouth of Mary Magdalene refers to the female race or sex.[36] Although ΓΕΝΟΣ does not have this meaning anywhere else in *Pistis Sophia*, this interpretation of the word is lexically fully possible.[37] Actually, in light of many texts, which betray a misogynous Peter,[38] this understanding of the text appears quite likely. The closest parallels are of course *Gos. Mary* 18,8-10 and *Gos. Thom.* 114. To see in the word ΓΕΝΟΣ a reference to the Gnostic race is improbable here since there is nothing in *Pistis Sophia*, unlike the *Gospel of Mary*, which would indicate that Peter and Mary Magdalene would represent different theological stands. In the texts cited above, Peter does not oppose Mary Magdalene because she represents Gnostic and he non-Gnostic, ecclesiastical views.[39] They both are portrayed as disciples to whom Jesus is imparting gnosis. Peter's problem with Mary Magdalene is that she is spiritually more advanced than his male colleagues and that she is a woman.

When Peter appeals to Jesus in order that he and the other male disciples might get more opportunities to participate in the dialogue with Jesus, Jesus points out that the only criterion by which one gains a right to speak is that the power of the Spirit enables her or him to understand what Jesus is talking about (58,15-17). Indeed, if somebody is filled with the Spirit, no one is able to prevent him or her (162,19-21). This is true regardless of the sex of a disciple. Therefore, Mary Magdalene may assume a leading role among the interlocutors of Jesus. She is the one whom the Spirit fills with understanding time after time. She is a "pure, spiritual one," as Jesus himself states (200,4; 303,12-13). It is no wonder that when Jesus begins to reveal to the disciples the things, "which have not arisen in the hearts of men, which all the gods which are among men also do not know" (296,17-21), it is Mary Magdalene who functions as his dialogue partner. For Jesus

---

[36] So already Harnack (1891, 16-17) and Schmidt (1892, 455); see also Malvern 1975, 48; Pagels 1981, 78; T.V. Smith 1985, 106; Price 1990, 59; Schmid 1990, 55; Koivunen 1994, 176; Good 1995, 685.

[37] Liddell & Scott 1968, 344.

[38] For the references, see Berger 1981, 313-314.

[39] Earlier I held the same view (Marjanen 1992, 149); cf. also Zscharnack 1902, 161; Wilson 1968, 102-103; Perkins 1980, 141; Krause 1981, 57; Pagels 1981, 77-78; T.V. Smith 1985, 106; Price 1990, 62; Schmid 1990, 56; Koivunen 1994, 176; Good 1995, 685.695-696.

of *Pistis Sophia* and, thus, for the author of the text, the woman-hood of Mary Magdalene is no barrier to spiritual understanding.

One important question remains to be asked. What is the meaning of the conflict passages to their audience? Does the conflict between Peter and Mary Magdalene say anything about the situation in which *Pistis Sophia* was written and its first readers lived? Or is the rivalry theme simply a part of traditional lore inherited in a rather unreflected manner from earlier oral or written material?[40] There are some factors which speak against the assumption that the author of the text has simply received it as a tradition without using it to address the actual situation of the audience. As stated above, in contrast to the *Gospel of Mary*, the controversy between Peter and Mary Magdalene does not seem to involve doctrinal issues which would indicate that Peter and some other male disciples represented a religious stand radically different from that of Mary Magdalene. The debate centers on the internal spiritual hierarchy within the group of disciples and on the position of Mary Magdalene in it. Likewise, if one compares the conflict motif in *Pistis Sophia I-III* with that in the *Gospel of Thomas* it is easy to see that it has been used differently in these writings. While in the latter it motivates the discussion about the possibility of women to gain salvation, in the former it is tied to the question of Mary Magdalene's right to act as a spiritual authority.

The fact that the conflict motif is used in *Pistis Sophia* with a specific purpose different from other texts where the same theme is reflected suggests that it has a function not only in the fictive text world of *Pistis Sophia* but also in the real world of its readers. In other words, the use of the motif reflects the questions and the problems with which the readers of the text are struggling. But in which way exactly? Peter's attacks on Mary Magdalene described in *Pistis Sophia* may at least intimate that the position of Mary Magdalene as the most important interpreter of fundamental spiritual revelations was questioned, even by some Gnostics, because of her sex. By emphasizing the superior spirituality of Mary Magdalene and defending everybody's right, also a woman's, to reveal spiritual truths if he or she is filled with the Spirit, the author of *Pistis Sophia* seeks to counter this opposition. At the same time, the author tries to strengthen the religious identity of

---

[40] The latter is suggested by Perkins 1980, 140.

those readers who want to remain loyal to the traditions for which Mary Magdalene is the guarantor. The reason Peter is selected to be her opponent is not clear since here he does not represent a non-Gnostic, ecclesiastical Christianity. Perhaps, this is a feature which is received from tradition. At any rate, the misogyny reflected in the text is easily attached to Peter since that characteristic is also linked with Peter elsewhere.

But is it only the credibility of Mary Magdalene as a transmitter of authoritative traditions which is at stake here? Or do the conflict passages address themselves even more directly to the situation of the readers? In other words, do they presuppose the existence of such women among the readers of *Pistis Sophia* whose attempts to establish their position as spiritual authorities in Gnostic groups are denied by some male leaders symbolized by Peter?[41] Certainly, the text can be used very well to side with such women, since it underlines so strongly that the only qualification a person needs for revealing spiritual truths is that he or she be moved by the Spirit. The experience of Mary Magdalene could easily be generalized to apply to any woman. Yet there is very little concrete evidence in the text to indicate that what was used as an apology for Mary Magdalene was meant to defend the rights of her later female colleagues as well.[42] Actually, the emphasis that Mary Magdalene is the supreme spiritual authority in the dialogue between the Risen Jesus and his disciples but her male colleagues (and their followers?) are later responsible for preaching and giving the mysteries may even suggest the opposite. The ambiguous evidence of *Pistis Sophia I-III* may in fact show that while the writing serves to defend the traditional role of Mary Magdalene as the most important transmitter and interpreter of Jesus' revelations, still the author of the text feels no desire nor need to claim that each woman should have the same prerogative. The increasing marginalization of women in roles of leadership in the third and

---

[41] This is suggested by Pagels 1981, 78-79; Schüssler Fiorenza 1983, 305-306; Schmid 1990, 56; Koivunen 1994, 174.

[42] Mary Magdalene's generalizing remark "Peter...hates our race" may imply that the aggressive attitude which in the text world of *Pistis Sophia* is directed towards Mary Magdalene has in the real world as its object the women who aspire to positions of authority in Gnostic groups. On the other hand, the remark need not mean more than an emphasis on Peter's misogynous stand.

fourth centuries as compared with the first and second centuries may thus not be limited to ecclesiastical Christian writings, but has an influence on Gnostic writings as well.

3. *Mary Magdalene in Pistis Sophia IV*

3.1 *The Position of Mary Magdalene Among the Disciples*

With regard to the number of times various interlocutors participate in the dialogue in *Pistis Sophia IV*, Mary Magdalene[43] does not have a similar supremacy over the other disciples as she does in *Pistis Sophia I-III*. In the extant part of *Pistis Sophia IV*, she presents four questions to Jesus, whereas the other interlocutors ask eight questions altogether.[44] In addition, the whole crowd of disciples speak collectively nine times (353,3-5; 355,9; 357,18; 366,14-15; 367,20-21; 369,9; 372,15; 374,4-5; 384,15). Nevertheless, this statistical picture does not do full justice to Mary Magdalene, since the eight pages of the manuscript which are missing between 374,5 and 374,6[45] probably contained questions put by Mary Magdalene. This is implied by the phrase ⲁⲥⲟⲩⲱϩ ⲟⲛ ⲉⲧⲟⲟⲧⲥ̄ ⲛ̄ϭ1 ⲙⲁⲣⲓϩⲁⲙ ⲡⲉⲭⲁⲥ in 375,1 as well as by Peter's indignant words in 377,14-15: "My Lord, let the women cease to question, that we also may question." At any rate, although Mary Magdalene is also the most active interlocutor in this part of *Pistis Sophia*, the number of her questions is not so much greater than that of the others to support the conclusion that she has a clearly superior position among the disciples.

---

[43] The name appears 8 times in the extant part of *Pistis Sophia IV* (for the condition of the manuscript, see below). In all the occurences it is spelled ⲙⲁⲣⲓϩⲁⲙ. This form of the name is used of Mary Magdalene in *Pistis Sophia I-III* as well (cf. also *Soph. Jes. Chr.* BG 90,1; 117,13; *Dial. Sav.* 126,17-18; 134,25[?]; 139,8; 143,6; 144,5-6; 144,22; 146,1[?]) but in Coptic texts it is not employed when the mother of Jesus is indicated.

[44] Thomas (379,23; 381,6) and John (381,21; 383,17) twice; Salome (376,11), Peter (377,17), Andrew (378,22), and Bartholomew (380,16) once.

[45] Since the page numbers follow those of Schmidt & MacDermot's edition, not those of Codex Askewianus, the lacuna of the manuscript does not come forth in these references to the text.

Unlike *Pistis Sophia I-III*, neither Jesus' nor the narrator's comments betray anything special about the perception of the individual interlocutors or about the quality of the questions[46] presented by them. In *Pistis Sophia IV*, Jesus' positive statements, promises, and actions are exclusively directed to the disciples as a whole. To all the disciples he makes the promise that they will rule over all things and receive the keys of the kingdom of heaven (367,1-8). On all of them Jesus bestows his special blessing, and all of them are made capable of seeing extraordinary things (367,14-19). All the disciples are made worthy of the kingdom of his father by Jesus, and to all of them he gives the right to forgive sins and to perform the mysteries of the kingdom of heaven (369,12-372,14). It is to all the disciples that he speaks about the name which gives the soul admittance beyond the powers of darkness (373,8-14).

In the extant part of *Pistis Sophia IV*, the only passage which may intimate that Mary Magdalene has a special capacity to understand the mysteries Jesus introduces is 360,2-5. There she makes a special request: "My Lord, reveal to us in what manner the souls are carried off by theft, so that *my brothers also understand*." Mary Magdalene's statement implies that she does not need this information for herself but asks here on behalf of her brothers who do not comprehend the mysteries as easily as she does. This feature,[47] combined with the fact that she is statistically the most active interlocutor in *Pistis Sophia IV*, suggests that Mary Magdalene is also known here to have an important role among the disciples. Yet it is clear that in *Pistis Sophia IV* Mary Magdalene is not elevated above other disciples in the same way she is in *Pistis Sophia I-III*. It is of course possible that the discovery of the missing pages between 374,5 and 374,6 might modify this impression, but that is in no way certain. In fact, in the extant passage where the opportunity to underline the superiority of Mary Magdalene invites itself, the author of the text does not do it. When Peter requests Jesus to silence the women so that he and

---

[46] In *Pistis Sophia IV* the individual interlocutors mentioned by name mainly pose questions to Jesus. The whole group of disciples also make other kinds of utterances.

[47] To be sure, this feature appears more frequently and much more emphatically in *Pistis Sophia I-III* (see above).

other male disciples may ask questions (377,14-15), Jesus does it without indicating in any way, contrary to *Pistis Sophia I-III*, that Mary Magdalene is specially equipped by the Spirit and therefore asks the most questions in the dialogue.

The fact that Mary Magdalene is granted a relatively unpretentious status in *Pistis Sophia IV* compared with that in *Pistis Sophia I-III* is well in line with the way all the disciples are presented. Although the disciples are described as having a privileged position as the receivers of Jesus' revelations and mysteries, they are not considered to own extraordinary spiritual power. They are not moved by the Spirit to offer revelatory interpretations of Jesus' discourses, and their questions do not seem to presuppose any special enlightenment. Their questions only serve to show that it is Jesus alone who acts as the revelator. His answers and actions give the disciples the mysteries necessary for salvation. The disciples, including Mary Magdalene, are indeed given the keys to the kingdom of heaven but still *Pistis Sophia IV* ends with a prayer by the disciples in which they ask to be saved from the punishments of the sinners (384,15-24).

3.2 *Mary Magdalene as Rival of the Male Disciples*

In *Pistis Sophia IV*, conflict between the male and the female disciples appears only in one passage (377,14-17). After the women have asked several questions,[48] Peter becomes indignant and requests Jesus to silence the women so that he and the other male disciples can have their turns as well. At first sight the situation described in this passage resembles that of *PS* 58,11-21 and 162,14-21. Actually, Peter does not attack Mary Magdalene personally here. Nevertheless, she is singled out in the narrator's introduction to Jesus' comment. This shows that in 377,14-17 also the tension between Mary Magdalene and Peter is the underlying

---

[48] The lacuna of eight pages between 374,5 and 374,6 makes it impossible to know exactly how many questions the women asked before Peter's comment. In the extant pages, there are at least the two questions of Mary Magdalene (375,1-4) and Salome (376,11-13). In addition, the introduction to Mary Magdalene's question reveals that she had just spoken before at least once (375,1). On the basis of Peter's comment, the questions of these women (and perhaps those of others too) have been even more numerous.

motif of the text, even though Peter's misogyny is less obvious in 377,14-17 than in 162,14-21.

It is conspicuous, however, that in contrast to *PS* 58,11-21 and 162,14-21, Jesus does not here in any way vindicate the right of Mary Magdalene and the other women to participate in the dialogue. No reference is made to an extraordinary inspiration of the Spirit which would grant Mary Magdalene special prerogatives over against the other interlocutors. On the contrary, Jesus finds Peter's demand reasonable and says to Mary Magdalene and the other women: "Give way to the men, your brothers, that they may question also" (377,15-17). How is this to be understood? Does the author want to undermine the spiritual authority of Mary Magdalene and to carry on a controversy against those readers who, in his opinion, rely too strongly on the traditions attached to her? This is unlikely. As noted above, Mary Magdalene is the most active interlocutor in *Pistis Sophia IV*, and even after the confrontation with Peter she does not fall silent but still asks one question (383,12-14).

Furthermore, the author of the text does not appear to be particularly interested in picturing individual disciples as spiritual heroes. There is no attempt to defend or question anyone's position. Differently from the rivalry passages of *Pistis Sophia I-III*, the conflict in *PS* 377,14-21 is not a result of the disciples' competition to exhibit their spiritual power in revealing the mystery of the repentances of Pistis Sophia. Rather, it has to do with the equal opportunity for the disciples to ask relatively simple questions which provide Jesus with a chance to give them "all mysteries and all knowledge" (358,14-15). To put it plainly, it is not the spiritual ranking of the disciples which is at stake here but the general order in the conversation. This aligns well with the overall tendency in *Pistis Sophia IV*, where the disciples are collectively granted a special position by Jesus. It is no single disciple, but all of them who are made "rulers over all these things (= mysteries and knowledge)" (367,3-4) and "blessed ... beyond all men" (357,19-20).

When *Pistis Sophia IV* was attached to *Pistis Sophia I-III* the way it was read probably changed. The prominence of Mary Magdalene in *Pistis Sophia I-III* was projected into *Pistis Sophia IV* as well, and the conflict between Peter and Mary Magdalene in 377,14-17 was seen as an attack against the superior spirituality of

Mary Magdalene.[49] This harmonization was facilitated by the fact that although Mary Magdalene does not have a superior role in *Pistis Sophia IV* she was still the most active among the interlocutors of Jesus.

---

[49] A similar reading of the text is also found among modern scholars. See Schmid (1990, 55) who reads 377,14-17 fully in light of *PS* 58,11-21 and 162,14-21; so also Berger 1981, 313-314.

CHAPTER NINE

MARY MAGDALENE
IN THE GREAT QUESTIONS OF MARY

1. *Introductory Remarks*

In his extensive heresiological work, *Panarion*, Epiphanius refers to a writing called the *Great Questions of Mary*, in which it is related how Jesus took a woman, a Mary, aside on a mountain for special, private instruction (*Pan.* 26.8,1-3). Epiphanius does not explicitly state that she is Magdalene but it is likely that she is meant.[1] The only other Mary whom the text could allude to, the mother of Jesus, is mentioned just above (26.7,5), but Epiphanius does not make any effort to connect the *Great Questions of Mary* with her. The fact that the instruction takes place on a mountain points to the possibility that the passage has to do with a post-resurrection appearance. If this be the case, it is more natural to attribute the experience of that event to Mary Magdalene than to the mother of Jesus. The fact that the epithet Magdalene is not mentioned is no problem. The same is true with *Pan.* 26.15,6 where Epiphanius explicitly refers to Mary Magdalene.

Epiphanius ascribes the *Great Questions of Mary* to a libertine group whose identification leaves a lot to be desired. In the heading of the twenty-sixth chapter of his work, Epiphanius claims to write this part of his book against Gnostics or Borborites. Elsewhere in this chapter, he states that this sect can also be called Koddians, Stratiotics, Phibionites, Zacchaeans, and Barbelites (26.3,6-7), depending on the geographical locality where they appear.[2] In the proemium of the entire work, where he presents the sects which he treats in various chapters of his work, he still adds to these names Secundians and Socratists (Proemium I 4,3). The readers of Epiphanius are also given to understand that this particular libertine group is closely associated with the Nicolaitans

---

[1] So also Holl 1915, 284; Dummer 1965, 202; Benko 1967, 104; Puech & Blatz 1987, 312.

[2] See also the post-Epiphanian Anacephalaeosis II 26,1-2.

whom he introduces in his preceding chapter. Yet it seems apparent that Epiphanius does not describe here one particular existent Gnostic group or school but has collected in this chapter information he has to offer about obscene habits of libertine Gnostics in general.[3] To what extent his description corresponds to the actual behavior of some Gnostic groups is strongly debated.[4] Nonetheless, there is no reason to doubt that libertine Gnostics did exist.[5] It is apparent that within one of these groups the writing which Epiphanius freely quotes was composed.

Since Epiphanius' citation is the only known evidence for the existence of the *Great Questions of Mary*, nothing certain can be said about its origin[6] and its extent and contents beyond this one

---

[3] Chapters 25 (Nicolaitans), 27 (Carpocratians), and 32 (Secundians) also contain references to Gnostic groups with libertine practices.

[4] For the discussion, see Benko 1967, 103-119; Gero 1986, 287-307; Goehring 1988, 338-339.

[5] Most recently this has been advocated by Dummer 1965, 191-219; Benko 1967, 103-119; Gero 1986, 287-307; Goehring 1988, 338-344 (see also his footnote 43 on page 339) and with some reservations by Wisse 1975, 71-72. The view is contested by Kraft 1950, 78-85; Koschorke 1978, 123-124. They argue against the possible existence of libertine Gnostic groups by pointing out that no libertine tendencies are revealed by authentic Gnostic sources. They only appear in the writings of the heresiologists which serve religious polemics and which are often based on scanty and obscure evidence. To be sure, an accusation against obscene practices is a feature typical of religious polemics, and it has not only been directed against Gnostic Christians but against ecclesiastical groups as well (see e.g. Origen, *Contra Cels*. 6,27; Minucius Felix, *Octavius* 9; Mandaeans accuse Christians of consuming both bodily emissions and aborted infants; for references, see F. Williams 1987, 86). It is equally true that very often the only evidence of debauchery of a given group is the firm conviction of the heresiologists that a false doctrine automatically leads to immoral behavior (see Wisse 1975, 66). Nevertheless, not all the information given by the heresiologists can be explained away as a sheer expression of religious polemics. Goehring (1988, 339) has rightly emphasized that e.g. Epiphanius' account (*Pan*. 26) is too detailed, complex, and personal to be a mere literary fiction. In addition, the inner consistency between theology and ritual as well as sometimes rather ingenious scriptural support of the religious practices presented in the text suggest that in his description of libertine Gnostic groups Epiphanius does not simply give a free rein to his imagination but depends on his personal experiences and some authentic literary or oral sources.

[6] The fact that Epiphanius met libertine Gnostics while being in Egypt (for the location of these Gnostics, see Dummer 1965, 191-192.211 n. 4) does not necessarily mean that all the writings he is referring to in *Pan*. 26 must originate from Egypt. Gero (1986, 286-307) has

passage. It is even unclear whether *Pan.* 26.8,4–26.9,2 is derived from the writing or if it presents proof texts which come from other libertine writings but which Epiphanius has included here in order to illustrate the quote from the *Great Questions of Mary.* The dating of the *Great Questions of Mary* is furthermore almost a mere guess because of the brevity of Epiphanius' quotation.[7] *Panarion* of course provides a *terminus ad quem,*[8] but there is very little in the passage itself which would tell how much earlier the *Great Questions of Mary* was composed than Epiphanius' heresiological work. However, the fact that the topic of cosuming one's emission is also dealt with in *2 Book of Jeu* (100,18-22) and *Pistis Sophia IV* (381,6-20) might suggest that these writings date approximately from the same period, i.e., from the third century.

2. *Analysis of Panarion 26.8,1–9,5*

Epiphanius does not give the excerpt of the *Great Questions of Mary* verbatim but cites it freely as we shall see below when the text is quoted. It is also unclear where his quotation ends. Irrespective of whether *Pan.* 26.8,4–9,5 was part of the writing or not, it is included here since it is clearly meant to illustrate what is going on between Jesus and Mary Magdalene in the previous passage. Epiphanius' text runs as follows:[9]

(8,1) καὶ τὰ μὲν βιβλία αὐτῶν πολλά. ἐρωτήσεις γάρ τινας Μαρίας ἐκτίθενται, ἄλλοι δὲ εἰς τὸν προειρημένον Ἰαλδαβαώθ εἰς ὄνομά τε τοῦ Σὴθ πολλὰ βιβλία ὑποτίθεν-

---

convincingly shown that there were libertine groups in the Syro-Mesopotamian area as well. Nevertheless, the thematic connections between the *Great Questions of Mary* and the *Books of Jeu* as well as *Pistis Sophia,* which most probably have been produced in Egypt, may point to the Egyptian origin of the former too.

[7] Without giving any reasons, Bovon (1984, 56) dates the *Great Questions of Mary* to the second or third century.

[8] *Panarion* was probably written between 375 and 378 (F. Williams 1987, XIII; see also Dummer 1965, 191).

[9] The text is taken from the critical edition of Holl (1915, 284-286). The use of the inverted commas follows Holl's practice and they are supposed to indicate biblical quotations. The translation and other later translations of *Panarion* come from F. Williams (1987, 88-89) unless otherwise advised.

ται. ἀποκαλύψεις δὲ τοῦ Ἀδὰμ ἄλλα λέγουσιν, εὐαγγέλια
δὲ ἕτερα εἰς ὄνομα τῶν μαθητῶν συγγράψασθαι τετολ-
μήκασιν, αὐτὸν δὲ τὸν σωτῆρα ἡμῶν καὶ κύριον Ἰησοῦν
Χριστὸν οὐκ αἰσχύνονται λέγειν ὅτι αὐτὸς ἀπεκάλυψε
ταύτην τὴν αἰσχρουργίαν. (2) ἐν γὰρ ταῖς ἐρωτήσεσι Μαρίας καλουμέναις μεγάλαις (εἰσὶ γὰρ καὶ μικραὶ αὐτοῖς
πεπλασμέναι) ὑποτίθενται αὐτὸν αὐτῇ ἀποκαλύπτειν,
παραλαβόντα αὐτὴν εἰς τὸ ὄρος καὶ εὐξάμενον καὶ ἐκβα-
λόντα ἐκ τῆς πλευρᾶς αὐτοῦ γυναῖκα καὶ ἀρξάμενον αὐτῇ
ἐγκαταμίγνυσθαι, καὶ οὕτως δῆθεν τὴν ἀπόρροιαν αὐτοῦ
μεταλαβόντα δεῖξαι ὅτι "δεῖ οὕτως ποιεῖν, ἵνα ζήσωμεν,"
(3) καὶ ὡς τῆς Μαρίας ταραχθείσης καὶ πεσούσης χαμαὶ
αὐτὸν πάλιν αὐτὴν ἐγείραντα εἰπεῖν αὐτῇ "ἵνα τί ἐδίστα-
σας, ὀλιγόπιστε;"

(4) καί φασιν ὅτι τοῦτό ἐστι τὸ εἰρημένον ἐν τῷ εὐ-
αγγελίῳ, ὅτι "εἰ τὰ ἐπίγεια εἶπον ὑμῖν καὶ οὐ πιστεύετε,
τὰ ἐπουράνια πῶς πιστεύσετε;" καὶ τό "ὅταν ἴδητε τὸν υἱὸν
τοῦ ἀνθρώπου ἀνερχόμενον ὅπου ἦν τὸ πρότερον," τουτέστιν
τὴν ἀπόρροιαν μεταλαμβανομένην ὅθεν καὶ ἐξῆλθεν, (5)
καὶ τὸ εἰπεῖν "ἐὰν μὴ φάγητέ μου τὴν σάρκα καὶ πίητέ μου
τὸ αἷμα" καὶ τῶν μαθητῶν ταρασσομένων καὶ λεγόντων
"τίς δύναται τοῦτο ἀκοῦσαι;" φασὶν ὡς περὶ τῆς αἰσχρότητος ἦν ὁ λόγος. (6) διὸ καὶ ἐταράχθησαν καὶ ἀπῆλθον εἰς
τὰ ὀπίσω, οὔπω γὰρ ἦσαν, φησίν, ἐν πληρώματι ἐστερεωμέ-
νοι. (7) καὶ τὸ εἰπεῖν τὸν Δαυίδ "ἔσται ὡς τὸ ξύλον τὸ
πεφυτευμένον παρὰ τὰς διεξόδους τῶν ὑδάτων, ὃ τὸν καρπὸν αὐτοῦ δώσει ἐν καιρῷ αὐτοῦ" περὶ τῆς αἰσχρότητος
τοῦ ἀνδρός, φησί, λέγει. "ἐπὶ τὴν ἔξοδον τῶν ὑδάτων" καὶ
"ὃ τὸν καρπὸν αὐτοῦ δώσει" τὴν τῆς ἡδονῆς ἀπόρροιαν,
φησί, λέγει, καὶ "τὸ φύλλον αὐτοῦ οὐκ ἀπορρυήσεται," ὅτι
οὐκ ἐῶμεν, φησίν, αὐτὸ χαμαὶ πεσεῖν, ἀλλὰ αὐτοὶ αὐτὸ
ἐσθίομεν.

(9,1) Καὶ ἵνα μὴ τὰς μαρτυρίας αὐτῶν ἐν μέσῳ φέρων
βλάψω μᾶλλον ἤπερ ὠφελήσω, τούτου χάριν τὰ πολλὰ
ὑπερβήσομαι, ἐπεὶ ἂν τὰ πάντα παρ' αὐτοῖς λεγόμενα
κακῶς ἐνταῦθα παρατιθέμενος διηγόρευον. (2) τὸ γὰρ εἰπεῖν, φησί, τεθεικέναι τὴν Ῥαὰβ κόκκινον ἐν τῇ θυρίδι οὐκ
ἦν, φησί, κόκκινον, ἀλλὰ τὰ μόρια τῆς γυναικείας φύσεως
καὶ τὸ κόκκινον αἷμα τῶν καταμηνίων λέγει, καὶ τὸ εἰπεῖν
"πῖνε ὕδατα ἀπὸ σῶν ἀγγείων", περὶ τοῦ αὐτοῦ λέγει. (3)
φασὶ δὲ εἶναι τὴν σάρκα ἀπολλυμένην καὶ μὴ ἐγειρομένην,

εἶναι δὲ ταύτην τοῦ ἄρχοντος. (4) τὴν δὲ δύναμιν τὴν ἐν
τοῖς καταμηνίοις καὶ ἐν ταῖς γοναῖς ψυχὴν εἶναί φασιν, ἣν
συλλέγοντες ἐσθίομεν, καὶ ἅπερ ἡμεῖς ἐσθίομεν, κρέα ἢ
λάχανα ἢ ἄρτον ἢ εἴ τι ἕτερον, χάριν ποιοῦμεν ταῖς
κτίσεσι, συλλέγοντες ἀπὸ πάντων τὴν ψυχὴν καὶ μεταφέ-
ροντες μεθ᾽ ἑαυτῶν εἰς τὰ ἐπουράνια. διόπερ καὶ πάντων
μεταλαμβάνουσι κρεῶν λέγοντες, ἵνα ἐλεήσωμεν τὸ γένος
ἡμῶν. (5) φάσκουσι δὲ τὴν αὐτὴν ψυχὴν εἶναι, ἔν τε τοῖς
ζῴοις καὶ ἐν κνωδάλοις καὶ ἰχθύσι καὶ ὄφεσι καὶ ἀνθρώ-
ποις ἐγκατεσπάρθαι καὶ ἐν λαχάνοις καὶ ἐν δένδρεσι καὶ
ἐν γεννήμασι.

(8,1) And they too have many books. They exhibit certain "Questions
of Mary;" but others proffer many books about the Ialdabaoth we
spoke of, and in the name of Seth. They call others "Apocalypses of
Adam". And they have ventured to compose other Gospels in the
names of the disciples, and are not ashamed to say that our Savior
and Lord himself, Jesus Christ, revealed this obscenity. (2) For in the
so-called "Great[10] Questions of Mary" — they have forged "Little"
ones too — they suggest that he revealed it to her after taking her
aside on the mountain,[11] praying, producing a woman from his side,
beginning to have intercourse with her, and then partaking of his
emission, if you please, to show that "Thus we must do, that we may
live." (3) And when Mary was alarmed and fell to the ground, he
raised her up and said to her, "O thou of little faith, wherefore didst
thou doubt?"

(8,4) And they say that this is the meaning of the saying in the
Gospel, "If I have told you earthly things and ye believe not, how
shall ye believe the heavenly things?" and so with, "When ye see the
Son of Man ascending up where he was before" — in other words,
when you see the emission partaken of where it came from. (5) And
when Christ said, "Except ye eat my flesh and drink my blood," and
the disciples were disturbed and replied, "Who can hear this?" they
say the statement was about the dirt. (6) And this is why they were

---

[10] F. Williams (1987, 88) translates "Greater Questions" and "Lesser
Questions," but the use of comparative degree is not necessary here; the
Greek uses the positive degree of the adjectives. The most common
translation of the names of the writings is "Great Questions of Mary" and
"Little Questions of Mary" (see e.g. Schneemelcher & Wilson 1991, 390-
391).

[11] The rendering follows that of F. Williams (1987, 88); the text
could be translated "after taking her along to the mountain" as well.

disturbed and fell away; they were not firmly established in perfection yet,[12] they say.

(8,7) And by the words, "He shall be like a tree planted by the outgoings of water that will bring forth its fruit in due season," David means the man's dirt. "By the outgoing of water," and, "that will bring forth his fruit," means the emission at climax. And "Its leaf shall not fall off" means, "We do not allow it to fall to the ground, but eat it ourselves."

(9,1) And I am going to omit most of their proof-texts, lest I do more harm than good by making them public — otherwise I would give all their misstatements here in explicit detail. (2) When it says that Rahab put a scarlet thread in her window, this was not scarlet thread, they tell us, but the female organs. And the scarlet thread means the menstrual blood, and "Drink water from your cisterns" means the same.

(9,3) They say that the flesh must perish and cannot be raised, but belongs to the archon. (4) But the power in the menses and semen, they say, is soul "which we gather and eat. And whatever we eat — meat, vegetables, bread or anything else — we do creatures a favor by gathering the soul from them all and taking it to the heavens with us." Hence they eat meat of all kinds and say that this is "to show mercy to our race." (5) But they claim that the soul is the same, and has been implanted in animals, wild beasts,[13] fish, snakes, men — and in vegetation, trees, and the products of the soil.

2.1 *The Consuming of Bodily Emissions*

Before the role of Mary Magdalene in the *Great Questions of Mary* is more closely examined it is necessary to see how the central element of the text, the consuming of bodily emission, is viewed elsewhere by Epiphanius. In his description of the Nicolaitans (*Pan.* 25) and the Gnostics or Borborites (*Pan.* 26), Epiphanius refers several times to the consuming of male and female

---

[12] F. Williams (1987, 89) translates: "they were not entirely stable yet,..." The Greek phrase ἐν πληρώματι can hardly be rendered into a non-technical adverb "entirely." Rather, it is to be understood in light of Epiph., *Pan.* 26.10,7, where ἐν πληρώματι τῆς γνώσεως γίνεσθαι is to be translated "to be perfect in the knowledge"; see F. Williams himself (1987, 90).

[13] F. Williams (1987, 89) translates "vermin"; however, κνωδάλον denotes any wild creature (see Liddell & Scott *et al.* 1968, 965).

emissions (*Pan.* 25.3,2; 26.3,1; 26.4,1-8; 26.5,7; 26.8,2-4; 26.9,4; 26.10,8-9; 26.11,1; 26.11,8; 26.13,2-3). According to him, this ritual takes place in various contexts and with different motivations. The great variety in its description as well as a rather ingenious theological motivation not infrequently attached to the ritual suggest that Epiphanius' reports are not a product of sheer literary fiction but they are dependent on several and sometimes also authentic sources of information.[14] This does not mean, however, that everything he relates is historically reliable. Certainly, rituals such as this easily invite an antagonist to exaggerations in his descriptions. Nevertheless, based on Epiphanius' reports central features of the ritual and its theological significance can be reconstructed.

It is often presupposed that the ritual of consuming one's bodily emission is to be seen as a version of the Eucharist.[15] A careful reading of Epiphanius does not confirm this assumption. Apart from *Pan.* 26.8,5 which is either part of the *Great Questions of Mary* or at least a proof-text used by those reading the writing, there is only one other passage in *Panarion* 26 where Epiphanius explicitly links the ritual with the Eucharist. In *Pan.* 26.4,1-8 we are told that during a communal gathering a husband asks his wife to make love (τὴν ἀγαπὴν ποιῆσαι[16]; 26.4,4) with a brother. However, their intercourse is not consummated but the woman and man receive the male emission on their own hands. Semen gained through *coitus interruptus* is thus offered to the actual Father of all with the words: "We offer thee this gift, the body of Christ." Likewise, the menses are presented as the other element of the Eucharist with the saying: "This is the blood of Christ." After these ritual prayers both male and female emission are consumed together. Epiphanius' report does not make explicit what is the actual reason for consuming semen and menstrual blood in this ritual. Yet he refers to a cryptic saying which indicates that semen is the reason why "bodies suffer" (26.4,7). This may suggest that

---

[14] In *Pan.* 26.17,4-18,3 Epiphanius refers to his own experiences with a libertine sect.

[15] So e.g. Dummer 1965, 197; Benko 1967, 115-116; Goehring 1988, 340.

[16] This is clearly a technical term which however is not used elsewhere in *Pan.* 26.

the consuming of semen and menses is considered to provide a possibility to overcome suffering. For Epiphanius himself, the peculiar way to celebrate the Eucharist has no motivation other than shameful enjoyment. However, it is of interest that Epiphanius too knows that these Gnostics forbid procreation (26.5,2; cf. also 26.11,10; 26.16,4), although this, in his view, evidently only underlines the obscenity of the act.

The other texts which speak about the consuming of bodily emissions do not place the act in the context of the Eucharist.[17] Even so, they are useful to the interpretation of the excerpt of the *Great Questions of Mary* since they include clear reflections on the motives for the act. The conspicuous feature in these passages is that although the reasons for the consuming of semen and menses are manifold they all are soteriological in their character. In *Pan.* 25.3,2 the gathering of semen and menses which evidently takes place through consuming is meant to reverse the process which the imprudent activity of Sophia, i.e., Prunicus, occasioned. The text seems to reflect an ancient view, represented by Aristotle for example, according to which semen contains soul.[18] Even if one could think the result is the exact opposite, according to libertine Gnostics, by gathering and consuming the male emission they rescue the soul element from the material world. That the same procedure can be applied to the female emission as well is an interesting modification of the Aristotelian theory whose significance will be discussed below. In *Pan.* 26.9,4 it is even said that by eating anything — meat, vegetables, bread — Gnostics free the soul implanted in these products and take it to the heavens with them.[19] *Pan.* 26.10,9 states that it is explicitly by gathering oneself through male and female bodily emissions which besides gnosis makes a Gnostic capable of getting up above the archons. In *Pan.*

---

[17] *Pan.* 26.5,7 may be an exception, since there it is said: "... whenever they go wild for themselves, they soil their own hands with their own ejaculated dirt, get up, and pray stark naked with their hands defiled." The reference to prayer may hint at a Eucharistic context of the description.

[18] For references in Aristotle's writings, see R. Smith 1988, 346. To be sure, there were other conceptions as well, but Aristotle's view had a strong influence on later anthropological thinking.

[19] A similar idea is found in Manichaean texts; for references see Böhlig 1980, 141.293; F. Williams 1987, 89.

26.5,7 the gathering of semen guarantees a ready access to God through such a practice.

In the ritual act which Epiphanius sees as a mere gratification of one's shameful desires there are thus deeper theological motives.[20] If the soul is transmitted into the prison of a material body as a result of a sexual intercourse during which a man ejaculates his semen into a woman and ultimately into the body of an infant which is going to be born, it is natural from the vantage point of the Borborites that the prevention of this process is of utmost importance. This is accomplished by gathering and consuming semen before it is implanted for procreation. Through this act the Gnostic also receives the power which is necessary for his/her own deliverance from the material world and transfer back to the pleroma beyond the archontic realms.

According to Epiphanius, the gathering of semen did not only take place through *coitus interruptus* (*Pan.* 26.4,5), but also through masturbation (26.5,7; 26.11,1) and homosexual activity (26.11,8). Whether the consuming of aborted fetuses also belonged to the religious practices of the Borborites, is difficult to say. The assertion could be a product of Epiphanius' polemical imagination, but logically this idea could be derived from their theology too. If the prevention of procreation has not succeeded by gathering semen, a brother's blunder can be repaired by eating an embryo, τὸ τέλειον πάσχα (26.5,6).

2.2 *Mary Magdalene and the Consuming of Bodily Emissions*

The excerpt which Epiphanius has taken from the *Great Questions of Mary* is clearly meant to be an aetiology of the consuming of the male semen.[21] Jesus himself shows what his followers are supposed to do, and the significance of the act is stressed by its salvific and life-giving character (*Pan.* 26.8,2). The fact that Mary Magdalene is chosen to receive this revelation is apparently an indication of her prominent role in the writing. Her fear and doubt

---

[20] This is especially emphasized by Benko (1967, 109-117) and Goehring (1988, 340-341).

[21] The *Gospel of Eve* is another writing excerpted by Epiphanius in *Pan.* 26 which appears to provide an aetiology for gathering (and consuming) of bodily emissions (*Pan.* 26.3,1).

mentioned in *Pan.* 26.8,3 are not probably her only and last reactions to Jesus' deed and words. Rather, they mirror the first bewilderment which is a typical characteristic of any account that tells
about a special revelation of (the Risen) Jesus to his disciples.[22]

Jesus' act represents a kind of reenactment of Eve's creation.[23]
As in Gen 2, a woman is molded out of man's rib. The essential
difference is that the first creation of woman was bound to lead to
procreation of the human race in the material world, whereas in
the *Great Questions of Mary* Jesus' deed is meant to set an example how that process is reversed. The purpose of the gathering and
consuming of semen is to stop the subjection of human beings
under the power of death and to help them to find life. In *Pan.*
26.9,4, which clearly interprets the encounter between Jesus and
Mary Magdalene, the gathering and consuming of bodily emission
is explicitly linked with gathering the soul (cf. also 26.10,8-9). In
its own mythical way the excerpt of the *Great Questions of Mary*
demonstrates how the imprisonment of the souls can be terminated. At the same time, it also implies that the consuming of bodily
emission provides life, i.e., makes a Gnostic capable of returning
to the pleroma where he/she came from as the proof-text from
John 6,62 illustrates (*Pan.* 26.8,4). *Pan.* 26.8,5 indicates that this
takes place in the context of the Eucharist. The passage seems to
imply that, according to the writer or the interpreters of the *Great
Questions of Mary*, the real contents and meaning of the Eucharist
was not entrusted to the twelve apostles during the Last Supper of
Jesus, but to Mary Magdalene on the mountain, probably after the
resurrection.

It is noteworthy that in *Pan.* 26.9,4 (cf. also 25.3,2; 26.10,9;
26.4,7) it is not only semen that contains the soul, as is maintained
by Aristotle, but the same is said about the menses. Since this
notion does not occur only in the text where the consuming of
bodily emissions takes place in the context of the Eucharist (*Pan.*
26.9,4; 26.4,7-8), the inclusion of the menstrual blood in the ritual
act need not only be due to the Eucharistic pattern of "body and
blood." By offering a correction of the Aristotelian stance, at least
some libertine groups emphasize that woman "too contains a part

---

[22] Benko (1967, 104-105) calls attention to the similarity between *Ap.
John* II/1 1,30-2,13 and *Pan.* 26.8,2-3.
[23] So Bovon 1984, 55-56.

of the divine which must and can be gathered!"[24] The fact that it is a woman, Mary Magdalene, who appears to be the first to receive a central revelation of Jesus, shows that the egalitarian breeze reflected in the ritual of consuming of bodily emissions is not a mere coincidence.

It is also important to recognize that in Epiphanius' report of his encounter with a libertine Gnostic group women are not only active in trying to seduce him — this part of the description certainly reflects as much his own view on women as that of the group itself — but also in introducing him to the teachings of the group (*Pan.* 26.17,4; 26.17,8). The importance of the feminine for libertine Gnostic groups Epiphanius describes is further seen in the titles of the books they are using according to *Pan.* 26. Out of the eight books Epiphanius mentions by name five are attributed to a female figure:[25] *Noria* (26.1,3), the *Gospel of Eve* (26.2,6), the *Great Questions of Mary* (26.8,2), the *Little Questions of Mary* (26.8,2), and the *Birth of Mary* (26.12,1).[26] Thus, the visible role Mary Magdalene has in the *Great Questions of Mary* seems to have a correspondence in the socio-historical reality of its readers and interpreters.

2.3 *The Relationship of the Great Questions of Mary to Pistis Sophia IV*

It is conspicuous that in the *Great Questions of Mary* Mary Magdalene is the guarantor of a Christian Gnostic tradition which finds salvation in the ritual of gathering and consuming of bodily emis-

---

[24] Goehring 1988, 342.

[25] Epiphanius refers also to books about the Yaldabaoth, books which are written in the name of Seth, and to gospels which were composed in the names of the disciples (*Pan.* 26.8,1), but does not give precise names of these writings. The (*Book of*) *Prophet Barkabbas* (26.2,4), the *Gospel of Perfection* (26.2,5), and the *Gospel of Philip* (26.13,2) are the books not clearly attributed to women.

[26] Similarly Goehring (1988, 342), although he suggests that the *Questions of Mary* (*Pan.* 26.8,1) could be a separate writing and not simply a combination of the *Great* and *Little Questions of Mary*.

sions, whereas in *Pistis Sophia IV* she is one of the disciples who
question Jesus (381,6-10):[27]

ⲀⲚⲤⲰⲦⲘ̄ ⲬⲈ ⲞⲨⲚ̄ ϨⲞⲒⲚⲈ ϨⲒⲬⲘ̄ ⲠⲔⲀϨ ⲈϢⲀⲨϤⲒ Ⲙ̄ⲠⲈⲤⲠⲈⲢ-
ⲘⲀ ⲚⲚϨⲞⲞⲨⲦ ⲘⲚ̄ ⲦⲈϢⲢⲰ ⲚⲦⲈⲤϨⲒⲘⲈ ⲚⲤⲈⲦⲀⲀⲨ ⲈⲨⲀⲢϢⲒⲚ
ⲚⲤⲈⲞⲨⲞⲘϤ ⲈⲨⲬⲰ Ⲙ̄ⲘⲞⲤ ⲬⲈ ⲈⲚⲠⲒⲤⲦⲈⲨⲈ ⲈⲎⲤⲀⲨ ⲘⲚ̄ ⲒⲀ-
ⲔⲰⲂ. ⲀⲢⲀ ϨⲎ ⲞⲨϨⲰⲂ ⲈϢϢⲈ ⲠⲈ ⲬⲚ̄ Ⲙ̄ⲘⲞⲚ.

We have heard that there are some upon the earth who take male
sperm and female menstrual blood and make a dish of lentils and eat
it, saying: 'We believe in Esau and Jacob.' Is this then a seemly thing
or not?[28]

Jesus answer is blunt and harsh (381,11-20):

ϨⲀⲘⲎⲚ ϮⲬⲰ Ⲙ̄ⲘⲞⲤ ⲬⲈ ⲚⲞⲂⲈ ⲚⲒⲘ ϨⲒ ⲀⲚⲞⲘⲒⲀ ⲚⲒⲘ ⲠⲈⲒ̈ⲚⲞⲂⲈ
ⲞⲨⲞⲦⲂ̄ ⲈⲢⲞⲞⲨ. ⲚⲀⲒ̈ ⲚⲦⲈⲒ̈ⲘⲒⲚⲈ ⲈⲨⲚⲀⲬⲒⲦⲞⲨ ⲚⲤⲀ ⲦⲞⲞⲦⲞⲨ
ⲈⲠⲔⲀⲔⲈ ⲈⲦϨⲒⲂⲞⲖ ⲞⲨⲀⲈ Ⲛ̄ⲚⲈⲨⲦⲤ̄ⲦⲞⲞⲨ ⲈⲦⲈⲤⲫⲀⲒⲢⲀ
ⲚⲞⲨⲰϨⲘ̄.

Truly I say that this sin surpasses every sin and every iniquity. (Men)
of this kind will be taken immediately to the outer darkness, and will
not be returned again into the sphere.

No doubt, *PS* 381,6-20 is highly critical of those who practice
the consuming of bodily emissions. The disciples' question appears in the context where they question Jesus about the judgments
of various sinners. The punishment which is given to those consuming bodily emissions is extremely severe and compares with
that of a murderer, a blasphemer and a pederast who also get no
chance of return and are completely destroyed. As a matter of fact,
the beginning of Jesus' answer indicates that the sin of those
consuming bodily emissions is worst of all.

It is not easy to determine what the purpose of the polemics
is in *Pistis Sophia IV*. Does the writing criticize a Gnostic group
such as the one reading the *Great Questions of Mary* and other

---

[27] Thomas is the one who voices the question but as the form of the
question indicates he does it on behalf of all the disciples.

[28] The text and its translation as well as the following text and the
translation are taken from Schmidt & MacDermot 1978b, 762-763.

writings cited by Epiphanius in *Pan.* 26[29] or is the target somewhere else? Or does *PS* 381,6-20 simply serve to prove that at
least those Gnostics who read *Pistis Sophia IV* are not guilty of
such obscene behavior as that of which some other Gnostic and
orthodox Christians are accused? It is at least unlikely that *PS*
381,6-20 is meant to be a direct attack against a text which derives
its teaching about the gathering and consuming of bodily emissions from a revelation imparted to Mary Magdalene. In that case,
the author of the passage would not have made Thomas voice the
question to Jesus, but this task would have been assigned to Mary
Magdalene in order to remove all doubts that a debauched practice
such as this could have originated from her encounter with the
Risen Jesus.

The introduction to Jesus' reply (*PS* 381,10-11: ⲁ ⲓ̅ⲥ̅ ⲇⲉ
ϭⲱⲛⲧ̅ ⲉⲡⲕⲟⲥⲙⲟⲥ ⲙ̅ⲡⲛⲁⲩ ⲉⲧⲙ̅ⲙⲁⲩ; "Jesus however was angry
with the world at that time.") appears to suggest that it is a
"worldly" habit he is talking about. This does not mean, however,
that the writer of the text did not think that the ritual could not
have been religious in its character. In fact, Thomas' question
presupposes that the people observing this ritual have a religious
— Jewish or Christian — conviction. Nevertheless, for the author,
those kind of religious people belong in fact to the cosmos. It is
of utmost importance for him/her to draw a clear line between
their views and the beliefs he/she represents. The same is true in
the *Second Book of Jeu* where the practice of consuming one's
bodily emissions is attributed to those who do not know the true
God but whose God is wicked (100,16-23). In the case of the
Second Book of Jeu, the target of the polemics is most likely —
right or wrong, it is impossible to tell — ecclesiastical Christians,[30]
i.e., "those who serve the eight powers of the great archon ...
saying: 'We have known the knowledge of truth, and we pray to
the true God.'"[31] That the god of these people is later on identified
with Taricheas, the son of Sabaoth, who is the enemy of the
Kingdom of Heaven, implies that ecclesiastical Christians are
meant (*2 Book of Jeu* 100,24-101,3).

---

[29] So Schmidt 1892, 580-582.
[30] Pace Schmidt 1892, 524.580-582.
[31] For the translation, see Schmidt & MacDermot 1978a, 100.

Whatever the precise object of the polemics in *PS* 381,6-20 is, it is of interest to note that the figure of Mary Magdalene can be linked with two very different religious convictions. On the one hand, she is an authority in the writing which was read by a libertine group seeking to solve the problem of the soul's imprisonment in matter by rescuing it through a sexual act (*Great Questions of Mary*). On the other hand, she is an important figure in a writing where the very same practice is heavily criticized. In fact, *Pistis Sophia IV* is clearly encratic in its nature (*PS IV* 355,10-356,7). These two ways of looking at Mary Magdalene have developed separately and show that the interest in her elicited a wide response.

CHAPTER TEN

MARY MAGDALENE
IN THE MANICHAEAN PSALM-BOOK

1. *Introductory Remarks*

There are three psalms in the Gnostic[1] *Manichaean Psalm-book II*[2] which make reference to Mary Magdalene. All of them belong to the *Psalms of Heracleides*.[3] One is a hymnic dialogue taking place in the context of Jesus' appearance to Mary Magdalene after his resurrection (187). The other two contain a catalogue of Jesus' male and female disciples among whom Mary Magdalene is mentioned (192,21-22; 194,19).

The *Manichaean Psalm-book* was discovered together with other Coptic Manichaean manuscripts[4] sometime at the end of the 1920s in Medinet Madi near the Fayyum oasis.[5] The manuscripts have been copied in the Subachmimic or Lycopolitan dialect.[6] The

---

[1] Although Manichaeism can be considered a religion in its own right it is generally characterized as Gnostic or as an offspring of Gnosticism. For a general presentation of Manichaeism, see Böhlig 1980, 5-70; Rudolph 1990, 352-379; Lieu 1992, 7-32; Mirecki 1992, 502-511.

[2] The second part of the text (= *Man. Ps. II*) has been edited and translated by Allberry (1938). In the present study, all references are made according to this work. The first number gives the page number of the Coptic text, the second number refers to the line.

[3] There are four collections and one single psalm attributed to Heracleides in the Coptic *Manichaean Psalm-book* (Richter 1992, 248; cf. also Nagel 1967, 124). Of the collections only two are edited and translated so far (Allberry 1938; for the facsimile edition of the entire *Manichaean Psalm-book*, see Giversen 1988). The latter of the two includes psalms where Mary Magdalene occurs.

[4] The same find contained e.g. *Kephalaia* (= *Keph.*; for the text, see Polotsky & Böhlig 1940; Böhlig 1966) and the so-called *Manichaean Homilies* (= *Man. Hom.*; for the text, see Polotsky 1934). In the present study, all references to these works are made according to the editions mentioned in this note. The first number gives the page number of the Coptic text, the second number refers to the line.

[5] For the report of the discovery and the contents of the manuscripts, see Schmidt & Polotsky 1933.

[6] Schmidt & Polotsky 1933, 10-11; for a more precise classification (L4), see Funk 1985, 124-139.

Coptic version of the *Manichaean Psalm-book* has been dated to
the second half of the fourth century.[7] Since the text was not
originally composed in Coptic but either in Greek or in Syriac, the
Psalm-book must have been written earlier,[8] between the end of
the third and the middle of the fourth centuries. Whether the
psalms were really composed by Heracleides, who according to a
curse formula against the Manichaeans was known to be a close
disciple of Mani as well as a transmitter and an exegete of his
teachings,[9] is impossible to say. Yet there is no doubt that the
author of the psalms was well-educated and not only familiar with
Manichaean theological emphases but with various Christian
traditions — both canonical and extra-canonical — as well.

In the *Psalms of Heracleides* there is no clear indication of
their provenance. If the psalms were written in Syriac the most
probable place of composition is Mesopotamia or Palestine. If the
original language was Greek other locations are also possible.

2. *Analysis of Man. Ps. II 187*

2.1 *Text and Translation*

The first psalm where Mary Magdalene appears begins one of the
four collections of the *Psalms of Heracleides*. It is shown by the
title which precedes the psalm itself: ψⲁⲗⲙⲟⲓ ⲕ[ⲩ] ⲏⲣⲁⲕⲗⲉⲓ-
ⲁⲟⲩ (187,1). The end of the psalm is marked by a doxology
(187,36), as is often the case with the psalms of the *Manichaean
Psalm-book II*. The entire text runs as follows:[10]

---

[7] Schmidt & Polotsky 1933, 35.

[8] Schmidt & Polotsky (1933, 12) regard Greek as the original language while Allberry (1938, XIX) thinks it is Syriac.

[9] Böhlig 1980, 300; for other similar references, see Richter 1992,
249 n. 5.

[10] The text and its restorations are taken from Allberry (1938). The
length of the lines conforms to the manuscript. The translation follows
that of Allberry with the following exceptions: the proper noun ⲙⲁⲣⲓ-
Ⲓⲁⲙⲙⲏ is spelled Mariamme instead of Mariam; ⲡⲉⲩⲱⲛⲉ on line 10
is translated "thy weakness" and not "thy grief" (for the meaning of the
word, see Crum [1939, 570-571] and the discussion below); ⲛⲓⲟⲣ[ⲫⲁ-
ⲛⲟⲥ ⲉⲧⲥⲁ]ⲣⲙⲉ on line 12 is translated "these lost orphans" rather than
"these wandering orphans," which does not convey clearly enough the

(2) ΜΑΡΙ̣ϩΑΜ]ΜΗ ΜΑΡΙϩΑΜΜΗ ϹⲚ̄ΟΥⲰⲚⲦ̄ ΜΠⲰΡⲦⲰ
ϬΕ ΑⲢⲀⲒ]
ⲬⲰⲖ] Ⲧ̣ΡΜ̣ΙⲎ Ⲛ̄ⲚΕΒΕⲖ Ⲛ̄ⲦΕϹⲚ̄ΟΥⲰⲚⲦ̄ ⲬⲈ ⲀⲚⲀⲔ ⲠⲈ
(5) ϹⲀϩ Μ̄ΠⲰΡⲦⲰϬⲈ Μ̄ΜⲈⲦⲈ ⲀⲢⲀⲒ ⲬⲈ Μ̄ΠⲀⲦⲚⲈⲨ ⲀⲠ
ϩⲞ Μ̄ΠⲀⲒⲰⲦ
Μ]ΠⲞΥⲂⲒ ΠⲈⲚⲞΥⲦⲈ Ⲛ̄ⲬⲒⲞΥⲈ ⲔⲀⲦⲀ Μ̄ΜⲈⲨⲈ Ⲛ̄ⲦⲈΜⲚ̄ⲦⲔⲞΥ
1. Μ̄ΠⲈ ΠⲈⲚⲞΥⲦⲈ ΜⲞΥ Ⲛ̄ⲦⲀϥⲢ̄ⲬⲀⲒϹ Ⲛ̄[Ⲧ]Ⲁϥ ⲀⲠ[ΜⲞ]Υ
ⲀⲚⲀⲔ ⲈⲚ ⲠⲈ ΠⲔΗΠΟΥΡⲞϹ. ⲀⲒⲦ̄ ⲀⲒⲬⲒ ΠⲰⲈ .. [Μ̄Π]ⲒⲞΥⲰⲚϩ̣
(10) ⲀⲢⲞ. ϢⲀⲚⲦⲚⲈⲨ ⲀⲦⲈⲢΜⲒⲎ ΜⲚ̄ ΠⲈϢⲰⲚⲈ .[..]. ϩⲀⲢⲀⲒ
Ⲧ]ⲈⲔ ΠⲒⲰⲔΜⲈ ⲀⲂⲀⲖ Μ̄ΜⲞ. Ⲛ̄ⲦⲈϢⲘϢⲈ Ⲛ̄[ⲦⲖⲈⲒ]ⲦⲞΥⲢ
ⲄⲒⲀ. ϢⲰΠⲈ ⲚΗⲒ̄ Ⲛ̄ⲂⲀⲒϢⲒⲚⲈ ϢⲀ ⲚⲒⲞⲢ[ⲪⲀⲚ]ⲞϹ ⲈⲦϹⲀ]ⲢΜⲈ.
Ϭ]ⲈⲠⲎ Μ̄Μ[Ⲟ] ⲈⲢⲈⲢⲀⲨⲦ̄ Ⲛ̄ⲦⲈⲂⲰⲔ ϢⲀ ΠⲒΜ̄[Ⲛ̄ⲦⲞΥ]ⲎⲈ. Ⲉ
ⲢⲀϬⲚ̄ⲦⲞΥ ⲈΥϹⲀΥϩ ⲀϩⲞΥⲚ ϩⲒⲬⲚ̄ ΠⲔⲢⲞ Μ̄ΠⲒ[ⲞⲢ]ⲆⲀⲚΗϹ
(15) ⲀΠ̄ΠⲢⲞⲆⲞⲦΗϹ ΠⲈⲒⲐⲈ Μ̄ΜⲀΥ ⲀⲦⲢⲞΥⲢⲟ̄ΟΥⲰ[ϩⲈ ⲚⲦ]ⲞΥ
ϩⲈ Ⲛ̄ϢⲀⲢⲠ̄. Ⲛ̄ϹⲈⲔⲰ ⲀϩⲢ̄ⲎⲒ̄ Ⲛ̄ⲚⲈΥϢⲚⲎΥ [ⲈⲦⲀ]ΥϬⲀⲠ
ⲢⲰΜⲈ Ⲛ̄ϨⲎⲦⲞΥ ⲀⲠⲰⲚϩ
ⲬⲞⲞϹ ⲀⲢⲀΥ ⲬⲈ ⲦⲰⲚ ΜⲀⲢⲀⲚ ΠⲈⲦⲚ̄ϹⲀⲚ ΠⲈⲦΜⲞΥⲦⲈ
ⲀⲢⲰⲦⲚ̄. ⲈΥϢⲀⲂⲀⲂⲈ ⲦⲀΜⲚ̄ⲦϹⲀⲚ. ⲬⲞⲞϹ ⲀⲢⲀΥ ⲬⲈ
(20) ΠⲈⲦⲚ̄ϹⲀϩ ΠⲈ
ⲈΥϢⲀⲚⲀΜⲈⲖⲎ ⲀⲦⲀΜⲚ̄ⲦϹⲀϩ. ⲬⲞⲞϹ ⲀⲢⲀΥ ⲬⲈ ΠⲈ
ⲦⲚ̄ⲬⲀⲒϹ ΠⲈ Ⲣ̄ⲦⲈⲬⲚⲎ ϩⲒ ϹⲂⲰ ⲚⲒΜ ϢⲀⲚⲦⲈⲚ̄ ⲚⲈϹⲀΥ
ⲀΠϢⲰϹ
Ⲉ]ΡϢⲀⲚⲚⲈΥ ⲬⲈ ⲀΥⲦⲰΜⲦ̄ ⲀⲂⲀⲖ ϹⲀⲔ ϹⲒΜⲰⲚ ΠⲈⲦⲢⲞϹ
(25) ⲀⲦⲞΥⲰ. ⲬⲞⲞϹ ⲀⲢⲀϥ ⲬⲈ ⲀⲢⲒⲠΜⲈⲈΥ Μ̄ⲠⲈⲦⲀⲒⲦⲈⲞΥ
Ⲁϥ ⲞΥⲦⲰⲒ̄ ⲚⲈΜⲈⲔ
Ⲁ]ⲢⲒⲠΜⲈⲈΥ Μ̄ⲠⲈⲦⲀⲒⲬⲞⲞϥ ⲞΥⲦⲰⲒ̄ ⲚⲈΜⲈⲔ ϨⲚ̄ ΠⲦⲀΥ
Ⲛ̄ⲚⲬⲀⲒⲦ ⲬⲈ ⲞΥⲚ̄ⲦⲎⲒ̄ ΠⲈⲦⲚ̄ⲀⲬⲞⲞϥ. ΜⲚ̄ⲦⲎⲒ̄ ΠⲈⲦ̄
ⲚⲀⲬⲞⲞϥ ⲀⲢⲀϥ
(30) ⲢⲀⲂⲂⲒ ΠⲀϹⲀϩ Ⲧ̄ⲚⲀⲆⲒⲀⲔⲞⲚⲎ Ⲛ̄ⲦⲔ̄ⲈⲚⲦⲞⲖⲎ ϨⲚ̄ ΠⲞΥ
ⲢⲀⲦ Μ̄ΠⲀϨⲎⲦ ⲦⲎⲢϥ̄
ⲚⲒⲦ̄ ϨⲢⲀⲔ Μ̄ΠⲀϨⲎⲦ. ⲚⲒⲦ̄ ϨⲒⲚΗⲂ Ⲛ̄ⲚⲀⲂⲈⲖ. ⲚⲒⲦ̄ ϨⲢⲀⲔ
Ⲛ̄ⲚⲀΟΥⲢΗⲦⲈ ϢⲀⲚⲦⲚ̄ ⲚⲈϹⲀΥ ⲀⲦϢⲈⲒⲢⲈ
ⲞΥⲈⲀΥ Μ̄ΜⲀⲢⲒϩⲀΜΜⲎ ⲬⲈ ⲀϹϹⲰⲦΜⲈ ϹⲀ ΠⲈϹϹⲀϩ.
(35) ⲀϹⲆⲒⲀ]ⲔⲞⲚⲎ Ⲛ̄ⲦϥⲈⲚ̣ⲦⲞⲖⲎ ϨⲚ̄ ΠⲞΥⲢⲀⲦ Μ̄ΠⲈϹϨⲎⲦ
             ⲦⲎⲢϥ̄
(36) ΟΥⲈⲀΥ ΜⲚ̄] ΟΥϬⲢⲞ Ⲛ̄ⲦⲮΥⲬⲎ Ⲛ̄ⲦΜⲀⲔⲀⲢ Μ̄ΜⲀⲢⲒⲀ

(2) Mariam]me, Mariamme, know me: do not
touch me].
Stem] the tears of thy eyes and know me that I am thy
(5) master. Only touch me not, for I have not seen the
face of my Father.
Thy God was not stolen away, according to the thoughts of thy
littleness: thy God did not die, rather he mastered death.

---

technical meaning of the verb ϹⲀⲢΜⲈ (see the discussion below).

(9) I am not the gardener: I have given, I have received the ...., I
appeared (?) [not]
(10) to thee, until I saw thy tears and thy weakness ... for (?) me.
Cast this sadness away from thee and do this service:
be a messenger for me to those lost orphans.
Make haste rejoicing, and go unto the Eleven. Thou
shalt find them gathered together on the bank of the Jordan.
(15) The traitor persuaded them to be fishermen as they were
at first and to lay down their nets with which they caught
men unto life.
Say to them, 'Arise, let us go, it is your brother that calls
you.' If they scorn my brotherhood, say to them,
(20) 'It is your master.'
If they disregard my mastership, say to them, 'It
is your Lord.' Use all skill and advice until thou hast brought
the sheep to the shepherd.
If thou seest that their wits are gone, draw Simon Peter
(25) unto thee; say to him, 'Remember what I uttered
between thee and me.
'Remember what I said between thee and me in the Mount
of Olives: "I have something to say, I have none to whom
to say it." '
(30) Rabbi, my master, I will serve thy commandment in the
joy of my whole heart.
I will not give rest to my heart, I will not give sleep to my eyes, I
will not
(33) give rest to my feet until I have brought the sheep to the fold.
Glory to Mariamme, because she hearkened to her master,
(35) she] served his commandment in the joy of her whole heart.
Glory and] victory to the soul of the blessed Mary.

2.2 *The Identity of Mary*

Once again a Gnostic text refers to a Mary without specifying
clearly her identity. There are two reasons to believe that Mary
Magdalene is meant. First, the form of the name, i.e., ΜΑΡΙϨΑΜ-
ΜΗ,[11] is the one which in Coptic Gnostic texts is most often used

---

[11] The ΜΑΡΙΑ of line 36 cannot refer to the ΜΑΡΙϨΑΜΜΗ of the
hymn, because the two names are spelled differently. In addition, the
doxology of line 36 is clearly secondary since it is preceded by another
doxology (lines 34-35) attributed to ΜΑΡΙϨΑΜΜΗ (34-35). Similar

of Magdalene, but for example never of the Virgin Mary when she is explicitly identified as the mother of Jesus.[12] Second, numerous similarities between *Man. Ps. II* 187 and John 20,11-18 — this is true not only as to the general plot of the passages[13] and their form,[14] but also with respect to the details of the texts[15] — point not only to an obvious Johannine influence[16] on the composition

---

secondary doxologies, in which homage is paid to ⲘⲀⲢⲒⲀ or to other inviduals (e.g. Apa Pshai, Apa Panai, Cleopatra, Eustephios, Jmnoute, Plousiane, Pshai, Theona), appear frequently at the end of the psalms in the *Psalms of Heracleides* (e.g. *Man. Ps. II* 191,16-17; 197,8) and elsewhere in the *Manichaean Psalm-book II*. Since the names are either Graeco-Egyptian or Egyptian, it is likely that these doxologies have been added to the hymns in Egypt. Allberry (1938, XX) has suggested that the persons who are commemorated were local Manichaean martyrs. As evidence he points to two doxologies where Mary and Theona seem to be called martyrs (*Man. Ps. II* 157,13; 173,12). Allberry's suggestion has been contested by Coyle (1991, 51-53); however, Coyle's claim that the figure of Mary Magdalene is somehow mirrored in the Mary of the doxologies remains unfounded.

[12] See pp. 63-64.

[13] In both texts two persons are involved: the Risen Jesus and his female adherent. In both instances the woman is a Mary and she is assigned the job of delivering a special message to the male disciples.

[14] With regard to its form, *Man. Ps. II* 187, although it has a poetic structure (for an analysis of the structure of the psalm, see Richter [1992, 262-263] who has sought to show that the text can be divided into 13 strophes), it is related to the recognition legends (for the form-critical definition, see Becker 1981, 615) of the New Testament (Luke 24,13-35; John 20,11-18; John 21), in which the Risen Jesus appears to his disciples, is gradually identified by them, and may also entrust them with a task.

[15] E.g. the weeping of Mary (lines 4-5; John 20,13), the master's prohibition to touch him since he has not yet seen the Father or gone to his Father (line 5; John 20,17), Mary's fear that her master's body has been taken away (line 7; John 20,15), the motif that Mary confuses Jesus with a gardener (line 9; John 20,15), the terms "brother" (line 18; John 20,17) and "Rabbi" (line 30; John 20,16).

[16] To be sure, there are also significant differences between *Man. Ps. II* 187 and John 20,11-18 which represent a Gnostic reinterpretation of the Johannine account. Mary Magdalene's special assignment to approach Peter has no equivalent in John 20,11-18 but rather reminds one of Mark 16,7. The contents of the message, which Mary is supposed to convey to the eleven, as well as her response to her master (lines 18-33) have no parallel in the Johannine story either. A further difference between *Man. Ps. II* 187 and John 20,11-18 has to do with one of the basic aims of the recognition legends. While the purpose of the Johannine passage is to confirm the reality of Jesus' resurrection, the composer of the Manichaean psalm wants to stress the irreality of Jesus' death. The Risen Jesus declares to Mary Magdalene: "Thy God was not stolen away ... thy

of *Man. Ps. II* 187,[17] but also to the fact that the ⲘⲀⲢⲒϨⲀⲘⲘⲎ of *Man. Ps. II* 187 is meant to be the same person as Mary Magdalene in John 20,11-18. As is frequent in Gnostic writings, so also here in *Man. Ps. II* 187, the adjective "Magdalene" is simply omitted.

Although Mary Magdalene of John 20,11-18 has been the obvious model of ⲘⲀⲢⲒϨⲀⲘⲘⲎ in *Man. Ps. II* 187, it does not necessarily mean, however, that the psalmist was able to distinguish between various Maries of the New Testament. This appears to be suggested by *Man. Ps. II* 192,23, where ⲘⲀⲢⲒϨⲀⲘⲘⲎ[18] is introduced as Martha's sister. If the statement can be taken as an indication of consanguinity between the two women, as it seems,[19] the *Psalms of Heracleides* derive from the period when at least the figures of Mary Magdalene and Mary of Bethany begin to be fused together.

2.3 *The Encounter of Mary Magdalene with the Risen Jesus*

As in John 20,11-18, so also in *Man. Ps. II* 187 Mary Magdalene is filled with grief and sorrow before the appearance of the Risen Jesus (lines 4.10). Yet it is not only a mourning woman whom the psalm portrays for the readers. She is also characterized by having ⲘⲘⲈⲨⲈ ⲚⲦⲘⲚⲦⲔⲞⲨⲒ ("thoughts of littleness"; lines 7-8) and ⲠϢⲰⲚⲈ ("weakness"; line 10). Mary Magdalene's ⲘⲚⲦⲔⲞⲨⲒ prevented her from realizing what actually took place — according to the Manichaean conception — in the death of Jesus.[20] It is thus

God did not die, rather he mastered the death" (lines 7-8). The statement contains an evident docetic emphasis. As Richter (1992, 253-254) has pointed out, a similar view of Jesus' death is found in another psalm of the same collection (*Man. Ps. II* 196,20-26).

[17] So also Böhlig 1968, 215.

[18] The manuscript reads ⲘⲀⲢⲒϨⲀⲘⲀ. This is either a spelling error or a variant of the name. In *Man. Ps. II* 194,19 the name is spelled ⲘⲀⲢⲒϨⲀⲘⲘⲎ in a corresponding list of women where she is similarly followed by Martha, Salome, and Arsenoe.

[19] For the use of "sister" in this particular text, see however also pp. 131-132.

[20] It is worth noting what a different interpretation the motif of taking away Jesus' body in John 20,11-18 gains in *Man. Ps. II* 187. In the Johannine account Mary Magdalene is deeply troubled that she no longer can honor the memory of Jesus at his grave since his body has been

to be interpreted here in terms of spiritual immaturity and inadequacy.[21] A similar condition is described by the word ϣⲱⲛⲉ. It may have a concrete meaning "sickness," but here it obviously stands for spiritual sickness or weakness. In many other Manichaean texts the word is used metaphorically to signify the weakness which characterizes the life lived under worldly conditions and in bodily lusts.[22] In *Man. Ps. II* 153,3 the cure is provided by divine protection and in *Keph.* 195,10-13 by the knowledge of truth.

Before her encounter with the Risen Jesus, Mary Magdalene is thus seen as spiritually immature and weak. Her weakness is nevertheless removed by the appearance of Jesus, and she is called to do a service to her master. The Greek word ⲗⲉⲓⲧⲩⲣⲅⲓⲁ (lines 11-12)[23] does not appear anywhere else in *Man. Ps. II*, but the continuation of the text shows what connotation it has. Mary Magdalene's ⲗⲉⲓⲧⲩⲣⲅⲓⲁ is to be a messenger to the eleven disciples in order that she might bring them back to Jesus. The assignment of Mary Magdalene raises inevitably the question about her relationship to the male disciples.

2.4 *Mary Magdalene and the Eleven Male Disciples of Jesus*

The situation of the eleven pictured in *Man. Ps. II* 187 is that of the lost souls. Their characterization as "lost orphans" (line 12)[24] who are "gathered together on the bank of the Jordan" (line 14) as

---

removed. In *Man. Ps. II* 187 Mary Magdalene appears to have been afraid that Jesus (or his soul?) had been stolen by the hostile powers through the very act of death. The destiny of the body seems to be of no concern in that text.

[21] Elsewhere in the *Manichaean Psalm-book II* the word stands for early age (e.g. 56,17; 57,25; 58,11; 83,9; 86,15).

[22] See e.g. *Man. Ps. II* 152,10-153,5; Richter (1992, 252-253) refers also to *Keph.* 107,2-4; 209,31-210,9.

[23] Only the last six letters of the word (ⲧⲩⲣⲅⲓⲁ) are visible in the manuscript. The reconstruction made by Allberry is most likely after the verb ϣⲙ̄ϣⲉ.

[24] At this point the manuscript has a lacuna of approximately nine letters (ⲛⲓⲟⲣ[.........]ⲣⲙⲉ). In light of *Man. Ps. II* 192,21-22 (ⲟⲩϩⲁⲩϣⲛⲉ ⲧⲉ ⲙⲁⲣⲓϩⲁⲙⲁ ⲉⲥϭⲱⲣϭ ⲁⲡⲕⲉⲙⲛ̄ⲧⲟⲩⲏⲉ ⲉⲧⲥⲁⲣⲙⲉ; "A net-caster is Mariamme, hunting for the eleven others that were lost.") Allberry's restoration of the text (ⲛⲓⲟⲣ[ⲫⲁⲛⲟⲥ ⲉⲧⲥⲁ]ⲣⲙⲉ) is reasonably certain.

a result of deceptive persuasion (line 15) makes this evident. The metaphor of the orphans suggests that through the assumed death of Jesus the eleven have lost their shepherd and the contact to their Father.[25] The relative qualifier ЄТСᴚ ΡΜЄ confirms this impression. In the *Manichaean Psalm-book II* the verb ϹѠΡΜЄ, both in its intransitive meaning and in its qualitative form Ϲᴚ ΡΜЄ, describes almost as a technical term the condition in which a soul has been lead astray and has lost its sense of where it belongs.[26] The verb can for example characterize some religious groups (ᴚΟΓΜᴚ) which the Manichaeans should avoid (86,10-15) or the world which has been misled by the god of this aeon (172,26-27). The latter text is especially interesting since it also states that the god of this aeon is the one that eats sheep (cf. 187,23), the word sheep being obviously one of the metaphors used as a self-identification of the Manichaeans.

The reference to the banks of the Jordan (187,14) as the location of the lost disciples after the death of Jesus is surprising. This notice is unparalleled in early Christian literature. Unless it reflects an enormous misconception, it may not represent a concrete geographical reference at all. In some writings of antiquity the Jordan is given a metaphorical meaning.[27] In a Nag Hammadi tractate, *Testimony of Truth*, the water of the Jordan is a symbol of sexual desire (31,2-3). Similarly, the Naassenes taught that the Jordan stands for sexual intercourse which imprisons humankind in the human body (Hipp., *Ref.* 5.7,41). Philo does not connect the Jordan with sexual desire alone, but sees it as an allegory of "the nature that is down below, earthly, corruptible ... all that is done under the impulse of vice and passion" (*Leg. all.* 2,89).[28] There is no explicit indication in *Man. Ps. II* 187 that the lostness of the eleven on the banks of the Jordan should be seen as pointing to a failure in the area of sexual behavior, e.g. giving up the dedication to sexual continence, which, to be sure, did belong to the virtues of the Manichaean elect. Yet "being gathered on the banks of the

---

[25] Similarly Richter 1992, 255.

[26] Cf. also *Man. Hom.* 47,12-13. The verb is employed in the same sense in other Gnostic texts as well; see e.g. *Tri. Trac.* 127,7-8; *Ap. John* II/1 26,32-27,1.

[27] The references are found in Chadwick 1980, 10.

[28] The translation follows that of Colson *et al.* (1929-62, I 281).

Jordan" may symbolize more generally a condition in which people allow themselves to be led by their inferior, earthly, and corruptible vices and passions, to use the language of Philo.

All the metaphorical expressions which describe the situation of the eleven in *Man. Ps. II* 187 seem to suggest that instead of seeking to be freed from the world of darkness and to exhort others to do the same the disciples have been lured back to their earlier worldly life (lines 15-17). Nevertheless, when one looks at the negative portrait painted of the eleven in the text, one should realize that their situation does not in fact differ very much from that of Mary Magdalene, namely before her encounter with the Risen Jesus.[29] The assumed death of Jesus has meant both for Mary Magdalene and for the eleven a return under the domination of the cosmos. But does the encounter of Mary Magdalene with Jesus and the assignment given to her change the situation? Does her role as the first witness to the appearance of the Risen Jesus and as the messenger to the eleven give her a privileged position compared with the male disciples?[30]

The temporal priority as the witness to the appearance of the Risen Jesus granted to Mary Magdalene in the *Psalms of Heracleides*[31] does not appear to have affected the way the disciples are presented elsewhere in the collection. In the two catalogues of the disciples in *Man. Ps. II* 192,5-193,3 and 194,7-22 the order of the male and female disciples suggests that Peter being the first one in the lists is regarded as the leading figure among the disciples. After him come all the other male disciples and only then the female ones, Mary Magdalene in both cases as the first one of them.

The leading role of Peter among the disciples seems to be reflected also in *Man. Ps. II* 187 itself. In addition to a general call to all the male disciples, Mary Magdalene has a special mes-

---

[29] This is also emphasized by Richter (1992, 255).

[30] This question is answered in the affirmative by Coyle (1991, 54).

[31] Nowhere else in Manichaean writings is Jesus' first appearance to Mary Magdalene mentioned. In *Keph.* 13,6-7 we are told that after his resurrection Jesus appeared to all his disciples. It is possible that in *Man. Ps. II* 187 it is also assumed that after the first appearance to Mary Magdalene the eleven also met the Risen Jesus. Mary Magdalene's successful accomplishment of her assignment to which the doxology of lines 34-35 refers may imply this (cf. also 190,31).

sage to Peter (lines 24-29). According to it, Jesus wants Peter to recall a conversation which they had privately in the Mount of Olives. The conversation appears to anticipate the very post-resurrection situation where Peter and the other disciples have left for the Jordan and the Risen Jesus cannot under those circumstances speak the important message he has to say. Jesus' word to Mary Magdalene implies that Peter, evidently as the leading figure of the disciples, is the one who should receive this important message.[32] Mary Magdalene who is present is not the one to hear it. Her task is to transmit the master's call. In fact, this feature is characteristic of the entire description of Mary Magdalene in *Man. Ps. II* 187.

The thrust of *Man. Ps. II* is not to use the role of Mary Magdalene as the first witness to Jesus' resurrection to make a claim that she was the most prominent and authoritative person within the circle of the disciples. The focus of the text is not on her position among the disciples but on the faithfulness with which she carries out the task entrusted to her. This is not only shown by her own three-fold promise in her reply to Jesus (lines 30-33) but also by the doxology on lines 34-35. These parts of the psalm constitute the actual climax of the text. The purpose of the psalm is thus to present Mary Magdalene as the paragon of a faithful believer.[33]

The fact that there is no tension or rivalry between Mary Magdalene and the eleven further indicates that the psalm was not intended to be an instrument of polemics. Unlike some polemical Gnostic writings, the *Psalms of Heracleides* present Mary Magdalene and the male disciples as being on the same side, first as spiritually weak and lost in the world, then as objects of the Risen Jesus' interest. Finally, they all become models for Manichaean believers and missionaries.[34] As noted above, for Mary Magdalene this happens already in the first psalm of the collection, for the

---

[32] A similar saying appears in the *Acts of John* 97-98 (cf. Schneemelcher 1989, 168-169) where simultaneously(?) as Jesus is being crucified he appears to John in the Mount of Olives and says to him that he has a word to speak which needs to be heard by somebody. John as the hero and the authority of the writing is the one selected to hear it. In the *Acts of John* 100 Jesus further states that if John hears the word he will become like Jesus.

[33] So also Richter 1992, 260-261.

[34] This is emphasized by Nagel 1973, 176-177.

eleven in the catalogues of disciples preserved in *Man. Ps. II* 192,5-193,3 and 194,7-22. These lists contain the names of the male and female disciples as well as a brief characterization of their person and activities. Mary Magdalene is also included. Therefore, we turn to these texts to see whether their description of Mary Magdalene adds anything to the picture *Man. Ps. II* 187 gives of her.

3. *Analyses of Man. Ps. II 192,21-22 and 194,19*

As noted above, in both catalogues the female disciples are listed after the male ones. The following women are mentioned: Mary Magdalene, Martha, Salome, Arsenoe, Thecla, Maximilla, Iphidama, Aristobula, Eubula, Drusiane, and Mygdonia. The first four appear in both lists (cf. also *1 Apoc. Jas.* 40,25-26). The seven others occur only in the first catalogue (*Man. Ps. II* 192,21-193,3). Their names derive from the five second and third century apocryphal acts attributed to Peter, Paul (and Thecla), John, Andrew, and Thomas.[35]

In both catalogues Mary Magdalene is introduced as the first of all the women. Probably this indicates that she was considered the leading figure, if not among all these women, at least among those four women who were regarded as disciples of the earthly Jesus. In the first catalogue (192,21-22), Mary Magdalene's characterization is a summary of the assignment given to her in *Man. Ps. II 187* and reads as follows: ⲟⲩϩⲁⲩϣⲛⲉ ⲧⲉ ⲙⲁⲣⲓϩⲁⲙⲁ ⲉⲥϭⲱⲣϭ ⲁⲡⲕⲉⲙⲛ̄ⲧⲟⲩⲏⲉ ⲉⲧⲥⲁⲣⲙⲉ ("A net-caster is Mariham, hunting for the eleven others that were lost"). The text contains an interesting change of roles. The eleven male disciples, who have laid down nets with which they have caught men unto life and become once again ordinary fishers, are now hunted for by Mary Magdalene who has been made a net-caster by the Risen Jesus. The text underlines the faithfulness and the skill with which Mary Magdalene went about the task Jesus had entrusted to her. Yet there is no implication that the successful accomplishment of the assignment would have given her a special position of authority over against the male disciples.

---

[35] Cf. Nagel 1973, 152-173.

The second list of women portrays Mary Magdalene as ⲡⲡⲛⲁ
ⲛ̄ⲧⲥⲟⲫⲓⲁ (*Man. Ps. II* 194,19). Based on this identification,
Coyle has suggested that Mary Magdalene in Manichaean thought
serves a dual capacity: on the one hand she personifies Sophia, on
the other hand, she stands for a feminine complement to the
Christ-Savior figure who is often identified as Wisdom.[36] To be
sure, Wisdom plays an important role in Manichaean writings, as
an aspect of the four-faced God, for example.[37] Likewise, there are
some cases in Manichaean texts where wisdom is more or less
identified with Jesus.[38] Yet in several instances wisdom simply
stands for a human quality which although sometimes explicitly
characterized as god-given[39] can even be taught and learned.[40]
Certainly, wisdom gives its owner a special ability to act as a
spiritual guide. This is especially true in Mani's and his disciples'
case.[41] It is most likely in that last sense that wisdom is used as
characterization of Mary Magdalene. This is suggested by two
factors. First, this interpretation corresponds best to the use of
ⲥⲟⲫⲓⲁ in the portrayal of James in the very same list. He is introduced as ⲧⲡⲏⲅⲏ ⲛ̄ⲧⲥⲟⲫⲓⲁ ⲛ̄ⲃⲣ̄ⲣⲉ. In that phrase ⲥⲟⲫⲓⲁ can
hardly be anything other than a human quality. Second, the expression ⲡⲡⲛⲁ ⲛ̄ⲧⲥⲟⲫⲓⲁ is probably derived from the Letter to
the Ephesians (1,17) where it is said that in getting to know Jesus
(or God?) one may receive the spirit of wisdom. In light of *Man.
Ps. II* 187, which says that Mary Magdalene was the first to know
the Risen Jesus, it is quite natural that of all the disciples it is
exactly she who is called ⲡⲡⲛⲁ ⲛ̄ⲧⲥⲟⲫⲓⲁ.[42] The fact that ⲡⲛⲉⲩ-
ⲙⲁ thus denotes a person is by no means surprising in the context
of the *Psalms of Heracleides*. The very psalm where the list of
disciples appears begins by referring to the Son of God as the
Savior of Spirits, i.e. the disciples (193,14; cf. also 190,21).

---

[36] Coyle 1991, 54-55.

[37] Coyle (1991, 47 n. 52) refers to the following passages in the
Manichaean Psalm-book II: 134,6; 186,9; 190,20.

[38] Cf. e.g. Böhlig 1980, 247.290.

[39] *Man. Hom.* 47,7-10; see also Böhlig 1980, 207.

[40] *Man. Hom.* 12,24; 28,8-10; cf. also Böhlig 1980, 101.

[41] See e.g. Böhlig 1980, 82.89.93.177.222.

[42] I owe this suggestion to Siegfried Richter who made it in a private
letter. The suggestion is included in his dissertation which unfortunately
was not available to me.

In the *Psalms of Heracleides* Mary Magdalene is thus seen as a paragon for faithful Manichaean believers and missionaries. In addition, she is the spirit of wisdom, because she was the first one to recognize the real character of the Risen Jesus. Yet this does not mean that the writer of the text would want to place her above the other disciples. They all share the same function of being models of Mani's later disciples. Neither has Mary Magdalene's role affected the possibilities for women to gain authoritative positions in Manichaean communities. They were able to be part of the electi, the spiritual group of the Manichaeans, but they had no access to the most prominent roles of authority in the Manichaean church. They could not become apostles, bishops, and presbyters.[43]

---

[43] Rudolph 1990, 366; Mirecki 1992, 508.

CHAPTER ELEVEN

CONCLUSION

A common feature in the Gnostic writings which contain and use Mary Magdalene traditions is that in all of them she is given a significant position among the most intimate adherents of Jesus. She is not always the most central figure of the work (*Gospel of Thomas, Psalms of Heracleides*) or she shares this position with others (*Sophia of Jesus Christ, Dialogue of the Savior, Pistis Sophia IV*), but in none of the writings is she shown in a negative light.

Another characteristic trait in Gnostic Mary Magdalene texts is that in most of them she is introduced together with other disciples of Jesus. The number and the names of the disciples may vary but usually she is not presented alone. The only real exception seems to be the excerpt of the *Great Questions of Mary* whose real character and contents remains somewhat vague, however, since only part of the writing is available to us. Admittedly, in *Man. Ps. II* 187 a private encounter between the Risen Jesus and Mary Magdalene is described and in the *Gospel of Mary* it is presupposed, but in both cases the instruction received through these meetings is shared with all the disciples.

A further feature typical of Mary Magdalene texts is that in most of the texts the events portrayed are situated in the period after the resurrection. Several of the texts, in fact, represent the genre of the Gnostic post-Easter revelation dialogue (*Sophia of Jesus Christ, Dialogue of the Savior, Gospel of Mary, First Apocalypse of James, Pistis Sophia*) or a sort of appearance story (*Man. Ps. II* 187, *Great Questions of Mary*). Even one of the two exceptions, *Gospel of Thomas*, does not actually have its setting in the life of the historical Jesus but it is rather a "timeless" collection of Jesus' sayings. The only text which in this respect really differs from the others, is the *Gospel of Philip*, in which Mary Magdalene has a special role explicitly in the life of the historical Jesus. She is the only one of his disciples who already during his earthly life understands his real character and message.

Having stated the common features in these Gnostic pictures of Mary Magdalene, I shall summarize the various, often differing presentations found in the Gnostic writings analyzed in this study. This is done not only by paying attention to most central elements of the Mary Magdalene's role in each writing, but also by considering how the description of Mary Magdalene is related to feminine gender language used by the authors and to the way the other disciples are depicted. Finally I present what my findings can say about the origins of Mary Magdalene traditions and the position of women among the Gnostics.

In the *Gospel of Thomas* Mary Magdalene is presented in logion 21 as a disciple who is in need of a deeper understanding of Jesus' teaching in order to reach the level of a "masterless, Jesus-like" disciple in the manner of Thomas. In logion 114 another, probably later situation is reflected. The figure of Mary Magdalene is used to illustrate the debate about the role of women among Thomasine Christians. With the help of Jesus' words the editor of the text tries to settle the dispute. The message of the text is that Mary Magdalene and thus all women of the community not only have the right to stay as members of the community, but that their role is equal to that of the male members.

In the *Sophia of Jesus Christ* Mary Magdalene together with four male disciples act as the main interlocutors of Jesus during a revelation dialogue and later on as the preachers of the new gospel of God. In the *Dialogue of the Savior*, which is a revelation dialogue as well, the situation is very similar. Along with Judas (Thomas) and Matthew, Mary Magdalene is imparted a special instruction. Clearly, both writings describe Mary as a Gnostic disciple, from whom, together with the other disciples mentioned by name, the traditions utilized in these books are claimed to derive.

There are two writings which clearly give Mary Magdalene the superior position among the followers of Jesus. In the *Gospel of Mary* she is the most beloved disciple. As in the *Gospel of Philip* there is no evidence that Jesus' love for Mary would involve a sexual relationship. As an indication of Mary's special status she receives a secret vision from the Risen One, which reveals how a soul after having departed from the body finds its way to the ultimate rest. On the whole, she betrays a far greater understanding of Jesus' teaching than the other (male) disciples, including Peter.

Clearly, the author of the text wants to show that after the ascension of the Savior Mary Magdalene takes his role as comforter and instructor of the other disciples. In *Pistis Sophia I-III* the dominant role of Mary Magdalene among the disciples is also obvious. In the dialogue between the Risen Savior and the disciples, which the writing describes, she presents more questions and interpretations of Jesus' words than the others altogether. Her preeminence is explicitly acknowledged by the Savior, who states that her "heart is more directed to the Kingdom of Heaven" than all her brothers. Together with John, she also receives the promise that in the eschatological kingdom they are superior to all the other disciples. The only dissonance in the highly praiseworthy description of Mary Magdalene is the fact that the proclamation of Jesus' instruction after his ascension is not entrusted to her but to the male disciples. In *Pistis Sophia IV* Mary Magdalene is not as dominant as in the three first books of the work, although even there she is the most active interlocutor of Jesus. In that writing the disciples on the whole are given a lesser status and attention is mainly focused on Jesus whose function as the only revelator is emphasized.

In the *First Apocalypse of James* the role of Mary Magdalene is given less attention because she is only a subsidiary character in the writing. Yet the small window which the *First Apocalypse of James* opens into her life shows that together with some other women she has a significant role in her own context. Even in the text world of the *First Apocalypse of James* she becomes a reference person to whom the protagonist of the writing, James the Just, is advised to turn (40,22-26) as he seeks to understand how to preach the gospel.

The role Mary Magdalene has in the *Gospel of Philip* differs very much from what she has in all the other writings. As already noted above, she is first of all known as the favorite disciple of the historical Jesus, the companion who alone understands his real nature and teaching. Thus, Mary Magdalene is the paragon of apostleship whose spiritual maturity is reached by other disciples of Jesus only later. The companionship between Mary and Jesus has also a wider dimension. In Valentinian terms, Mary is also seen as Jesus' syzygos, i.e., she forms a spiritual consortium with Jesus. Together they provide the prototype of the union between Christ and his Church which materializes when the pneumatic elect are united with their pleromatic counterparts. The relationship between Mary and Jesus is purely spiritual. The mention of Jesus kissing Mary has no sexual implications but it is to be understood as a metaphorical expression for conveying special spiritual nourishment and power. Mary's special role engenders envy among the male disciples. After the resurrection the situation changes, however, when the male apostles also gain better understanding and become transmitters of spiritual mysteries. As a matter of fact, despite the prominent position Mary has as the companion of Jesus she is not made the guarantor of the teaching transmitted in the *Gospel of Philip* but the task is entrusted to the collective apostolic body.

The *Great Questions of Mary* is in many respects an exceptional writing among the Gnostic Mary Magdalene texts. It is the only work which is libertine in its spirit. Its main focus is to demonstrate how the imprisonment of the soul in the body can be terminated by consuming the semen and the menstrual blood in which the human soul dwells. Unlike the ascetic texts it does not therefore forbid sexual acts, although they are not practiced for procreation but for production of semen. It is significant that even this libertine Gnostic tradition may find its roots in the person of Mary Magdalene, although she is also linked with ascetic streams of Christianity, such as the ones represented by the *Sophia of Jesus Christ*, the *Dialogue of the Savior*, and *Pistis Sophia IV*. It is especially interesting that *Pistis Sophia IV* gives Mary Magdalene a central role among Jesus' disciples, although it strongly criticizes the very practice which the *Great Questions of Mary* claims to originate from the encounter between Mary Magdalene and Jesus. The explanation for this is that the author of *Pistis Sophia IV* did not obviously have any direct knowledge of the *Great Questions of Mary* or the Gnostic groups which attached the practice of eating bodily emissions to Mary Magdalene. Nevertheless, the existence of the *Great Questions of Mary* and *Pistis Sophia IV* serves to prove how the person of Mary Magdalene elicited a wide response.

Man. Ps. II 187 is a further elaboration of the appearance of the Risen Jesus to Mary Magdalene recorded in John 20,11-18. It reports how Mary, after having understood the irreality of Jesus' death and after having recovered from her spiritual weakness caused by his death, is entrusted with the task of finding the eleven lost disciples. The task given to her does not imply, however, that Mary would be superior to the eleven male disciples. The focus of the psalm is not on her position among the followers of Jesus but on the faithfulness with which she carries out the task given to her. In this way the psalm as well as the other texts of the *Psalms of Heracleides* where she appears seeks to present her as a paragon for Manichaean believers and missionaries.

It is conspicuous that despite the prominent role the Gnostic writings grant to Mary Magdalene many of them can use a language which devalues women. For example, in *Gos. Thom.* 114 Jesus does assure Mary and the other women of the community that they not only have a right to remain members of the community but that their role is equal to that of the male members. Yet the women are granted this position, only if they become "male." The implication of the statement is that they have to become more spiritual and probably also celibate.

Admittedly, there is nothing wrong with demanding that the members of a religious community should be spiritual. The problem with the statement is, however, that it was made using such language from the contemporary patriarchal culture which connects male with spiritual, perfect, transcendent, and female with sensual, incomplete, mundane. Even though it is not often noticed and reflected in earlier Mary Magdalene studies a similar phenomenon is encountered in other Gnostic Mary Magdalene texts as well. In those cases the positive impact her figure as the prominent female disciple might have had on furthering a new ideology of women's position in society and in religious life, was watered down by the use of such language which emphasizes women's inferiority and subordination. For example, in the *Sophia of Jesus Christ*, where Mary Magdalene acts as one of the main interlocutors of Jesus during a revelation dialogue and later on as a preacher of the gospel of God, it is the masculine multitude (III/4 118,6) which is supposed to be the result of her preaching. It is paradoxical that it is in the reply to Mary Magdalene's question that the Savior mentions this self-identification of the Gnostics.

Likewise, in the *Dialogue of the Savior* Mary Magdalene is the main spiritual authority together with Judas (Thomas) and Matthew. These three are said to have received a special revelation of Jesus after the resurrection. Obviously the community reading the writing believed it derived its message from these three. Still, the book referring to a woman as one of its authorities speaks about destroying the "works of womanhood," in accordance with the dominant male gender constructions typical of Mediterranean society, when it alludes to sexual abstinence. These examples show how firmly fixed the dichotomy between "male" and "female" was in the language and cultural values of the contemporary society.

It is likely that in the case of the *Sophia of Jesus Christ* and the *Dialogue of the Savior* Mary Magdalene's person hardly created any change in the attitudes towards women or their role in society and religious life. In neither case does the treatment of Mary Magdalene lead to any reflection about the position of women in general. Curiously, in the *Dialogue of the Savior* it is Mary Magdalene herself who with her question about the works of womanhood is made to undermine the positive impact which her role as a major interlocutor of Jesus might have had on advancing women's status. Even in the *Gospel of Mary*, where Mary Magdalene is an unchallengeable authority and the most beloved disciple of Jesus, salvation is described as "putting on the perfect human being (= ⲢⲰⲘⲈ)." Even though the word ⲢⲰⲘⲈ (Gr. ἄνθρωπος) does not have the same exclusive connotation as "male" in *Gos. Thom.* 114 it defines salvation in terms of male-oriented language.

Although the *First Apocalypse of James* too contains sections where feminine gender language is used pejoratively (41,15-19; 24,27-30), the way the female spiritual heroes, including Mary Magdalene, are brought into the text seems to alleviate the negative connotation attached to femaleness. To the great astonishment of James the Just women may through gnosis become strong and leave their powerlessness. Yet even in the *Apocalypse of James* femaleness describes the earthly existence with all its limitations, and even if it need not be fully left behind in the act of redemption it must be complemented with maleness.

The relationship between Mary and the other (primarily male) disciples is described in different ways in Gnostic writings. Unlike the impression one easily gets from earlier Mary Magdalene research (especially Pagels, Price, Haskins, Koivunen), Mary's relations to the disciples are by no means loaded with conflict in all the Gnostic writings. In the *Sophia of Jesus Christ* and the *Dialogue of the Savior* neither controversy, nor any rivalry can be detected between Mary and the male disciples while they are engaged in the dialogue with the Risen Jesus. On the contrary, together and without any contention they represent the whole body of Jesus' disciples. In the *Manichaean Psalm-book*, too, no traces of conflict between Mary Magdalene and the male disciples can be discerned. The *First Apocalypse of James* does indeed picture the twelve disciples in somewhat negative terms; they seem to have an insufficient conception of gnosis and faith. Yet even there no real controversy between them and Mary Magdalene is developed. Partly, this may be explained by the fact that she has a subsidiary role in this writing. Obviously the relationship between James the Just, who has good contact with Mary Magdalene, and the twelve disciples is rather tense. In the *Gospel of Philip* the male disciples do envy Mary Magdalene because of her privileged position as the companion of the Savior, but even their envy does not really lead to a conflict with her. Their dissatisfaction is more directed to Jesus. Besides, after the resurrection Mary Magdalene and the male disciples together seem to constitute the collective body of the apostles.

Nonetheless, there are three Gnostic writings which display a clear conflict between Mary Magdalene and the male disciples. Yet unlike earlier Mary Magdalene research has suggested, in each case the situation is viewed somewhat differently. Only in the *Gospel of Mary* does the usual interpretation of this conflict find support. The controversy between Mary Magdalene and Peter seems to reflect a disagreement between Gnostic and non-Gnostic, orthodox Christians over the position of women with regard to the question of spiritual authority. No doubt, the author of the writing sides with the Gnostics and thus defends women's claims for being allowed to take part in spiritual leadership. Although in *Pistis Sophia I-III* the controversy seems in the same way to center on Peter and Mary Magdalene, the situation appears to be different. The cause of the quarrel is probably not the position of women in general but the credibility of Mary Magdalene as a transmitter of authoritative traditions. In contrast to the *Gospel of Mary*, in *Pistis Sophia I-III* Peter does not seem to represent an orthodox interpretation of Christian faith but his ideas are as Gnostic as Mary's. So, the writing seems to reflect an inter-Gnostic controversy. In *Gos. Thom.* 114 the debate concerns the position of women, more precisely their right to stay among Thomasine Christians. Unless Peter's comment in logion 114 is a mere hyperbole which gives the writer or editor of the text a chance to express personal views of women, the two views found in the logion seem to represent two different models of asceticism, one wanting to keep the male and female ascetics apart and the other allowing them to stay together. The author of the logion supports the latter alternative.

The question of the nature and the origin of the Gnostic Mary Magdalene traditions is a difficult one. At least it appears likely, however, that despite some common elements which can be found in various Mary Magdalene writings no literary dependence between them can be established. When one looks for roots of the Mary Magdalene traditions two aspects are significant. First, we have the testimony of the canonical gospels that after his resurrection Jesus appeared to Mary Magdalene (John 20,14-18; Mark 16,9-11). This story has evidently made Mary Magdalene an attractive figure for a Gnostic myth-making process. The Johannine story has had direct influence at least on *Man. Ps. II* 187, more indirectly on the other writings as well. Second, *Gos. Thom.* 21, the *Sophia of Jesus Christ*, and the *Dialogue of the Savior* provide evidence for an emergence of a tradition (perhaps in eastern Syria) which presents Mary Magdalene as a Gnostic disciple. It is worth noting that in its initial stage it is not connected with any kind of conflict with the male disciples, especially with Peter. Clearly, this is a matter of later development and makes impossible the attempts of Price and Koivunen to see historical reminiscences in the conflict between Peter and Mary Magdalene. The idea of a special, permanent group of Gnostic disciples, which also includes Mary Magdalene, a Philip group, to use the term coined by Parrott, is not likely either. It simply does not correspond to the information in the texts, according to which Peter and Bartolomew, for example, are in some texts in the camp of the Gnostics, in others in the camp of the orthodox Christians. So, we are left with the idea of a prominent Gnostic disciple, Mary Magdalene, showing its first signs sometime at the beginning of the second century. But can we go beyond that? Does it reflect a historical figure who besides having been known to have experienced an appearance of Jesus had a leadership function among early Christians? It may, but there is no real evidence for it.

Finally, what do the Gnostic Mary Magdalene traditions say about the concrete situation of women among second and third century Gnostics? Many of the writings analyzed in this study reveal no direct interest in the concrete reality women experienced in Gnostic communities. In the *Sophia of Jesus Christ*, the *Dialogue of the Savior*, the *Gospel of Philip*, and the *Manichaean Psalm-book* Mary Magdalene seems to be an ideal heroine from the distant past. She is acknowledged as an important transmitter of the Gnostic tradition, but there is no explicit indication that the women of the contemporary Gnostic groups using and reading these writings would or could claim the same or similar status. As a matter of fact, the pejorative feminine gender language in the *Sophia of Jesus Christ* and the *Dialogue of the Savior* suggests that the authors of the writings would not necessarily be even aware of such strivings. In the Manichaean communities we even know that women had no access to any leadership functions.

It is difficult to say whether *Pistis Sophia I-III* should be placed together with the previous writings or not. In other words, it is not really clear whether the controversy between Mary Magdalene and Peter concerns only the validity of the tradition connected with Mary Magdalene or also the legitimacy of women's spiritual authority in general. The first alternative may be more likely because the author of the work seems to suggest that after the ascension of Jesus it was not Mary Magdalene but the male disciples who were responsible for proclaiming his message and performing the mysteries. This may mirror an increasing marginalization of women in roles of leadership in the third and fourth centuries as compared with the first and second centuries not only in non-Gnostic, orthodox circles but among Gnostics as well.

Gos. Thom. 114 probably shows that there were women ascetics among Thomasine Christians in the mid-second century and that their position as members of the community was threatened. The logion only reveals that the author bolsters their right to stay as members but it does not say anything about the concrete status of women. The casualness with which the "powerless vessels capable of becoming strong through the gnosis" are mentioned in the *First Apocalypse of James* may very well be taken as an indication of an authentic reflection of strong and perceptive women who taught and proclaimed the Christian message among the Gnostics the author of the writing knew.

There are at least two works among the Gnostic Mary Magdalene writings in which the significant position of Mary Magdalene in the text world seem to have a clear correspondence in the socio-historical reality of women. Those texts are the *Gospel of Mary* and the *Great Questions of Mary*. The *Gospel of Mary* was at least partly written as a defence of the women wanting to take part in spiritual leadership but being prevented by those who regarded it as an illegitimate enterprise. This is shown by the concreteness of the controversy between Mary and Peter. It is not only the role of Mary as a transmitter of a visionary revelation which is at stake but the spiritual authority of women in general. With regard to the *Great Questions of Mary* it is not only the prominent position the writing gives to Mary Magdalene which suggests a strong female participation in the leadership of the Gnostic group which read that work. Moreover, the information Epiphanius offers of powerful women leaders within the group as well as the occurrence of several female names in the titles of the other writings used by the group speak for a significant influence women had in this libertine Gnostic group which claimed to derive its origin from an encounter between the Risen Jesus and Mary Magdalene.

BIBLIOGRAPHY

The abbreviations for journals, series and ancient literature follow the style recommended in the *Society of Biblical Literature Membership Directory and Handbook 1994*, pp. 223-240. The four abbreviations not mentioned in the *Handbook* are frequently used: *Gos. Mary* (= *Gospel of Mary*), *PS* (= *Pistis Sophia*) and *Man. Ps.* (= *Manichaean Psalm-book*), and *CH* (= *Corpus Hermeticum*).

Primary Sources and Their Translations

Aland, K. *et al.*
1979   *Nestle—Aland, Novum Testamentum Graece*. 26. neu bearbeitete Auflage. Stuttgart: Deutsche Bibelstiftung.
Allberry, C.R.C.
1938   *A Manichean Psalm-Book. Part II.* Manichean Manuscripts in the Chester Beatty Collection, Vol. II. Stuttgart: W. Kohlhammer.
Attridge, H.W.
1977   "The Dialogue of the Savior (III,5): Translation." In: J.M. Robinson (ed.), *The Nag Hammadi Library in English*. Leiden: E.J. Brill, 230-238.
1989   "Appendix: The Greek Fragments." In: B. Layton (ed.), *Nag Hammadi Codex II,2-7 together with XIII,2*, Brit. Lib. Or. 4926(1), and P. Oxy. 1, 654, 655. Vol. One: Gospel According to Thomas, Gospel According to Philip, Hypostasis of the Archons, and Indexes.* NHS 20. Leiden: E.J. Brill, 95-128.
Attridge, H.W. (ed.),
1985a   *Nag Hammadi Codex I (The Jung Codex). Introduction, Texts, Translations, Indices.* NHS 22. Leiden: E.J. Brill.
1985b   *Nag Hammadi Codex I (The Jung Codex). Notes.* NHS 23. Leiden: E.J. Brill.
Barns, J.W.B. *et al.*
1981   *Nag Hammadi Codices. Greek and Coptic Papyri from the Cartonnage of the Covers.* NHS 16. Leiden: E.J. Brill.
Bihlmeyer, K.
1970   *Die apostolischen Väter. Erster Teil: Didache, Barnabas, Klemens I und II, Ignatius, Polykarp, Papias, Quadratus, Diognetbrief.* Neubearbeitung der funkschen Ausgabe. 3. Auflage. Tübingen: J.C.B. Mohr (Paul Siebeck).
Blatz, B.
1987a   "Der Dialog des Erlösers." In: W. Schneemelcher (ed.), *Neutestamentliche Apokryphen in deutscher Übersetzung. I. Band: Evangelien.* 5., Auflage der von Edgar Hennecke begründeten Sammlung. Tübingen: J.C.B. Mohr (Paul Siebeck), 245-253.
1987b   "Das koptische Thomasevangelium." In: W. Schneemelcher (ed.), *Neutestamentliche Apokryphen in deutscher Übersetzung. I. Band:*

Evangelien. 5., Auflage der von Edgar Hennecke begründeten Sammlung. Tübingen: J.C.B. Mohr (Paul Siebeck), 93-113.

Böhlig, A.
1966   *Kephalaia. 2. Hälfte (Lieferung 11-12).* Manichäische Handschriften der staatlichen Museen Berlin. Stuttgart: W. Kohlhammer Verlag.
1980   *Die Gnosis. Dritter Band: der Manichäismus.* Die Bibliothek der alten Welt. Zürich: Artemis Verlag.

Böhlig, A. & Labib, P.
1963   *Koptisch-gnostische Apokalypsen aus Codex V von Nag Hammadi im Koptischen Museum zu Alt-Kairo.* Sonderband, Wissenschaftliche Zeitschrift der Martin-Luther-Universität Halle-Wittenberg, 29-54.

Bury, R.G.
1973   *The Symposium of Plato. Edited With Introduction, Critical Notes and Commentary.* Cambridge: W. Heffer and Sons Ltd.

de Catanzaro, C.J.
1962   "The Gospel According to Philip." *JTS* 13, 35-71.

Charlesworth, J.H. (ed.),
1983   *The Old Testament Pseudepigrapha. Vol. I: Apocalyptic Literature and Testaments.* London: Darton, Longman & Todd.
1985   *The Old Testament Pseudepigrapha. Vol. II: Expansions of the "Old Testament" and Legends, Wisdom and Philosophical Literature, Prayers, Psalms and Odes, Fragments of Lost Judeo-Hellenistic Works.* London: Darton, Longman & Todd.

Colson, F.H. *et al.*
1929-62   *Philo.* LCL. 10 vols. and 2 sups. London: William Heinemann Ltd.

Drijvers, H.J.W.
1987   "Abgarsage." In: W. Schneemelcher (ed.), *Neutestamentliche Apokryphen in deutscher Übersetzung. I. Band: Evangelien.* 5., Auflage der von Edgar Hennecke begründeten Sammlung. Tübingen: J.C.B. Mohr (Paul Siebeck), 389-395.

Emmel, S. (ed.),
1984   *Nag Hammadi Codex III,5: The Dialogue of the Savior.* NHS 26. Leiden: E.J. Brill.

Foerster, W. (ed.),
1979   *Die Gnosis. Erster Band: Zeugnisse der Kirchenväter.* Die Bibliothek der alten Welt. Zürich: Artemis Verlag.

Funk, W.-P.
1976   *Die zweite Apokalypse des Jakobus aus Nag-Hammadi-Codex V.* Berlin: Akademie-Verlag.
1987   "Die erste Apokalypse des Jakobus." In: W. Schneemelcher (ed.), *Neutestamentliche Apokryphen in deutscher Übersetzung. I. Band: Evangelien.* 5., Auflage der von Edgar Hennecke begründeten Sammlung. Tübingen: J.C.B. Mohr (Paul Siebeck), 253-264.

Giversen, S.
1988   *The Manichaean Coptic Papyri in the Chester Beatty Library. Vol. III: Psalm Book, Part I: Facsimile Edition; Vol. IV: Psalm Book,*

Part II: Facsimile Edition. Cahiers d'Orientalisme XVI-XVII
Genève: Patrick Cramer.

Goodspeed, E.J.
1914   *Die ältesten Apologeten. Texte mit kurzen Einleitungen.* Göttingen:
Vandenhoeck & Ruprecht.

Grenfell, B.P. & Hunt, A.S.
1898   *The Oxyrhynchus Papyri. Part I: Edited With Translations and
Notes.* London: Egypt Exploration Fund.
1904   *The Oxyrhynchus Papyri. Part IV: Edited With Translations and
Notes.* London: Egypt Exploration Fund.

Guerrier, L. & Grebaut, S.
1913   "Le Testament en Galilée de Notre Seigneur Jésus Christ." In: *PO*
9, 141-236.

Guillaumont, A. *et al.*
1959   *Evangelium nach Thomas. Koptischer Text herausgegeben und
übersetzt.* Leiden: E.J. Brill.

Hedrick, C.W.
1990   *Nag Hammadi Codices XI, XII, XIII.* NHS 28. Leiden: E.J. Brill.

Holl, K.
1915   *Epiphanius, Erster Band: Ancoratus und Panarion 1-33.* GCS 25.
Leipzig: J.C. Hinrichs'sche Buchhandlung.

Horner, G.
1911-1924   *The Coptic Version of the New Testament in the Southern Dialect.*
Oxford: Clarendon Press.

Howard, G.
1981   *The Teaching of Addai.* Texts and Translations 16. Ann Arbor,
Michigan: Scholars Press.

Isenberg, W.W.
1989   "The Gospel of Philip. Introduction, Translation." In: B. Layton
(ed.), *Nag Hammadi Codex II,2-7 together with XIII,2*, Brit. Lib.
Or. 4926(1), and P. Oxy. 1, 654, 655. Vol. One: Gospel According
to Thomas, Gospel According to Philip, Hypostasis of the Archons,
and Indexes.* NHS 20. Leiden: E.J. Brill, 131-217.

James, M.R.
1975   *The Apocryphal New Testament.* Oxford: Clarendon Press. [1924]

Joly, R.
1958   *Hermas le Pasteur. Introduction, texte, traduction et notes.* SC 53.
Paris: Les Éditions du Cerf.

Kasser, R.
1968   "Bibliothéque gnostique VI: Les Deux Apocalypses de Jacques."
RTP 18, 163-186.

Kasser, R. *et al.*
1975   *Tractatus Tripartitus. Partes II et III.* Bern: Francke Verlag.

Klostermann, E.
1933   *Apocrypha I: Reste des Petrusevangeliums, der Petrusapokalypse
und des Kerygma ʾPetri.* KlT 3. 3. Auflage. Berlin: Walter de
Gruyter.

Koetschau, P.
1899   *Origenes, Contra Celsum.* GCS 2-3. Leipzig: J.C. Hinrichs'sche
            Buchhandlung.
Krause, M.
1971   "Das Philippusevangelium." In: M. Krause & K. Rudolph (eds.),
            Die Gnosis. Zweiter Band: Koptische und Mandäische Quellen. Die
            Bibliothek der Alten Welt. Zürich: Artemis Verlag, 92-124.
Kytzler, B.
1993   *M. Minucius Felix, Octavius. Lateinisch-Deutsch.* Darmstadt:
            Wissenschaftliche Buchgesellschaft.
Lambdin, T.O.
1989   "The Gospel According to Thomas: Translation." In: B. Layton
            (ed.), *Nag Hammadi Codex II,2-7 together with XIII,2*, Brit. Lib.
            Or. 4926(1), and P. Oxy. 1, 654, 655. Vol. One: Gospel According
            to Thomas, Gospel According to Philip, Hypostasis of the Archons,
            and Indexes.* NHS 20. Leiden: E.J. Brill, 53-93.
Layton, B.
1987   *The Gnostic Scriptures.* Garden City, New York: Doubleday &
            Company.
Layton, B. (ed.),
1989a   *Nag Hammadi Codex II,2-7 together with XIII,2*, Brit. Lib. Or.
            4926(1), and P. Oxy. 1, 654, 655. Vol. One: Gospel According to
            Thomas, Gospel According to Philip, Hypostasis of the Archons,
            and Indexes.* NHS 20. Leiden: E.J. Brill.
1989b   *Nag Hammadi Codex II,2-7 together with XIII,2*, Brit. Lib. Or.
            4926(1), and P. Oxy. 1, 654, 655. Vol. Two: On the Origin of the
            World, Expository Treatise On the Soul, Book of Thomas the
            Contender.* NHS 21. Leiden: E.J. Brill.
Lightfoot, J.B.
1976   *The Apostolic Fathers.* Edited and Completed by J.R. Harmer.
            Grand Rapids, Michigan: Baker Book House. [1891]
Lipsius, R.A. & Bonnet, M.
1891-1903   *Acta Apostolorum Apocrypha.* 2 Vols. Leipzig: H. Mendelssohn.
Marcovich, M.
1986   *Hippolytus, Refutatio omnium haeresium.* Patristische Texte und
            Studien 25. Berlin: Walter de Gruyter.
Merkel, H.
1987   "Anhang: Das 'geheime Evangelium' nach Markus." In: W.
            Schneemelcher (ed.), *Neutestamentliche Apokryphen in deutscher
            Übersetzung. I. Band: Evangelien.* 5., Auflage der von Edgar
            Hennecke begründeten Sammlung. Tübingen: J.C.B. Mohr (Paul
            Siebeck), 89-92.
Migne, J.P. *et al.* (eds.),
1857-1866   *Patrologiae cursus completus, series Graeca.* 162 vols. Paris:
            Migne.
Parrott, D.M. (ed.),
1979   *Nag Hammadi Codices V,2-5 and VI with Papyrus Berolinensis
            8502,1 and 4.* NHS 11. Leiden: E.J. Brill.

1991   *Nag Hammadi Codices III,3-4 and V,1 with Papyrus Berolinensis 8502,3 and Oxyrhynchus Papyrus 1081: Eugnostos and The Sophia of Jesus Christ.* NHS 27. Leiden: E.J. Brill.

Parsons, P.J.
1983   "3525. Gospel of Mary." In: *The Oxyrhynchus Papyri. Volume L.* London: The British Academy, 12-14.

Pearson, B. (ed.),
1981   *Nag Hammadi Codices IX and X.* NHS 15. Leiden: E.J. Brill.

Polotsky, H.J.
1934   *Manichäische Homilien.* Manichäische Handschriften der Sammlung A. Chester Beatty. Stuttgart: W. Kohlhammer Verlag.

Polotsky, H.J. & Böhlig, A.
1940   *Kephalaia. 1. Hälfte (Lieferung 1-10).* Manichäische Handschriften des staatlichen Museen Berlin. Stuttgart: W. Kohlhammer Verlag.

Puech, H.-Ch.
1959   "Gnostische Evangelien und verwandte Dokumente." In: E. Hennecke & W. Schneemelcher (eds.), *Neutestamentliche Apokryphen in deutscher Übersetzung. I. Band: Evangelien.* 3., völlig neubearbeitete Auflage. Tübingen: J.C.B. Mohr (Paul Siebeck), 158-271.

Puech, H.-Ch. & Blatz, B.
1987   "Andere gnostische Evangelien und verwandte Literatur." In: W. Schneemelcher (ed.), *Neutestamentliche Apokryphen in deutscher Übersetzung. I. Band: Evangelien.* 5., Auflage der von Edgar Hennecke begründeten Sammlung. Tübingen: J.C.B. Mohr (Paul Siebeck), 285-329.

Rehm, B.
1953   *Die Pseudoklementinen. I. Band: Homilien.* GCS 42. Berlin: Akademie-Verlag.

Roberts, C.H.
1938   *Catalogue of the Greek and Latin Papyri in the John Rylands Library.* Vol. III. Manchester: University Press.

Roberts, A. & Donaldson, J.
1956-68   *The Ante-Nicene Fathers. Translations of the Writings of the Fathers down to A.D. 325.* Grand Rapids, Michigan: Wm. B. Eerdmans. [1885-1906]

Robinson, F.
1896   *Coptic Apocryphal Gospels.* TextsS 4/2. Cambridge: University Press.

Robinson, J.M. (ed.),
1972-84   *The Facsimile Edition of the Nag Hammadi Codices.* 11 vols. Leiden: E.J. Brill.
1988   *The Nag Hammadi Library in English.* Third, Completely Revised Edition. Leiden: E.J. Brill.

Rousseau, A. & Doutreleau, L.
1974-82   *Irénée de Lyon, Contre les hérésies. Livres I-III.* 6 vols. Sources chrétiennes 210-211, 263-264, 293-294. Paris: Les Éditions du Cerf.

Sagnard, F.-M.-M.
1948   *Clément d'Alexandrie, Extraits de Théodote. Texte grec, introduc-tion, traduction et notes.* SC 23. Paris: Les Éditions du Cerf.
Schenke, H.-M.
1959   "Das Evangelium nach Philippus. Ein Evangelium der Valentini-aner aus dem Funde von Nag Hammadi." *TLZ* 84, 1-26.
1987   "Das Evangelium nach Philippus." In: W. Schneemelcher (ed.), *Neutestamentliche Apokryphen in deutscher Übersetzung. I. Band: Evangelien.* 5., Auflage der von Edgar Hennecke begründeten Sammlung. Tübingen: J.C.B. Mohr (Paul Siebeck), 148-173.
Schermann, T.
1914   *Die allgemeine Kirchenordnung, frühchristliche Liturgien und kirchliche Überlieferung. Erster Teil: Die allgemeine Kirchenord-nung des zweiten Jahrhunderts.* Studien zur Geschichte und Kultur des Altertums. Dritter Ergänzungsband. Paderborn: Druck und Verlag von Ferdinand Schöningh.
Schmidt, C.
1919   *Gespräche Jesu mit seinen Jüngern nach der Auferstehung. Ein katholisch-apostolisches Sendschreiben des 2. Jahrhunderts.* TU 43. Leipzig: J.C. Hinrichs'sche Buchhandlung.
1925   *Pistis Sophia. Ein gnostisches Originalwerk des 3. Jahrhunderts aus dem Koptischen übersetzt.* Leipzig: J.C. Hinrichs'sche Verlag.
1936   Πράχεις Παύλου, *Acta Pauli.* Nach dem Papyrus der Hamburger Staats- und Universitäts-Biblitothek, unter Mitarbeit von W. Schubart.
Schmidt, C. & MacDermot, V.
1978a   *The Books of Jeu and the Untitled Text in the Bruce Codex.* NHS 13. Leiden: E.J. Brill.
1978b   *Pistis Sophia.* NHS 9. Leiden: E.J. Brill.
Schmidt, C. & Schenke, H.-M.
1981   *Koptisch-Gnostische Schriften. Erster Band: Die Pistis Sophia, Die beiden Bücher des Jeû, Unbekanntes altgnostisches Werk.* GCS. Berlin: Akademie-Verlag.
Schneemelcher, W. (ed.),
1987   *Neutestamentliche Apokryphen in deutscher Übersetzung. I. Band: Evangelien.* 5., Auflage der von Edgar Hennecke begründeten Sammlung. Tübingen: J.C.B. Mohr (Paul Siebeck).
1989   *Neutestamentliche Apokryphen in deutscher Übersetzung. II. Band: Apostolisches, Apokalypsen und Verwandtes.* 5., Auflage der von Edgar Hennecke begründeten Sammlung. Tübingen: J.C.B. Mohr (Paul Siebeck).
Schneemelcher, W. & Wilson, R.McL. (eds.),
1991   *New Testament Apocrypha. Vol. I: Gospels and Related Writings.* Revised Edition. Cambridge: James Clarke & Co.
1992   *New Testament Apocrypha. Vol. II: Writings Relating to the Apos-tles, Apocalypses and Related Subjects.* Revised Edition of the Collection initiated by E. Hennecke. Cambridge: James Clarke & Co.

Schoedel, W.R.
1979   "The (First) Apocalypse of James." In: D.M. Parrott (ed.), *Nag Hammadi Codices V,2-5 and VI with Papyrus Berolinensis 8502,1 and 4*. NHS 11. Leiden: E.J. Brill, 65-103.
Scott, W. & Ferguson, A.S.
1924-36   *Hermetica. The Ancient Greek and Latin Writings which contain Religious and Philosophic Teachings ascribed to Hermes Trismegistus.* 4 vols. Oxford: Clarendon Press.
Schwartz, E. & Mommsen, Th.
1903-09   *Eusebius Caesariensis, Historia ecclesiastica.* GCS 9/1-3. Leipzig: J.C. Hinrichs'sche Buchhandlung.
Sieber, J.H. (ed.),
1991   *Nag Hammadi Codex VIII.* NHS 31. Leiden: E.J. Brill.
Stroker, W.D.
1989   *Extracanonical Sayings of Jesus.* SBLRBS 18. Atlanta, Georgia: Scholars Press.
Till, W.C.
1955   *Die gnostischen Schriften des koptischen Papyrus Berolinensis 8502.* TU 60. Berlin: Akademie-Verlag.
1963   *Das Evangelium nach Philippos.* Berlin: Walter de Gruyter.
Till, W.C. & Schenke, H.-M.
1972   *Die gnostischen Schriften des koptischen Papyrus Berolinensis 8502.* 2. Auflage. TU 60. Berlin: Akademie-Verlag.
Völker, W.
1932   *Quellen zur Geschichte der christlichen Gnosis.* Sammlung ausgewählter kirchen- und dogmengeschichtlicher Quellenschriften: Neue Folge 5. Tübingen: J.C.B. Mohr (Paul Siebeck).
Williams, F.
1987   *The Panarion of Epiphanius of Salamis. Book I (Sects 1-46).* NHS 35. Leiden: E.J. Brill.
1994   *The Panarion of Epiphanius of Salamis. Books II and III (Sects 47-80, De Fide).* NHS 36. Leiden: E.J. Brill.
Wilson, R.McL. & MacRae, G.W.
1979   "The Gospel According to Mary." In: D.M. Parrott (ed.), *Nag Hammadi Codices V,2-5 and VI with Papyrus Berolinensis 8502,1 and 4*. NHS 11. Leiden: E.J. Brill, 453-471.

Secondary Literature

Arai, S.
1993   "'To Make Her Male': An Interpretation of Logion 114 in Gospel of Thomas." In: E.A. Livingstone (ed.), *Studia Patristica. Vol. XXIV.* Leuven: Peeters Press, 373-376.

Attridge, H.W. & MacRae, G.W.
1985   "The Gospel of Truth: Notes." In: H.W. Attridge (ed.), *Nag Hammadi Codex I (The Jung Codex): Notes.* NHS 23. Leiden: E.J. Brill, 39-135.

Baarda, T.
1994   "Jesus and Mary (John 20:16f.) in the Second Epistle on Virginity Ascribed to Clement." In: Tj. Baarda, *Essays on the Diatessaron.* Kampen: Kok Pharos.

Bauer, W.
1964   *Rechtgläubigkeit und Ketzerei im ältesten Christentum.* Zweite Auflage mit einem Nachtrag von Georg Strecker. BHT 10. Tübingen: J.C.B. Mohr (Paul Siebeck). [1934]
1967   *Das Leben Jesu im Zeitalter der neutestamentlichen Apokryphen.* Darmstadt: Wissenschaftliche Buchgesellschaft. [1909]

Bauer, W. & Aland, K. & Aland, B.
1988   *Griechisch-deutsches Wörterbuch zu den Schriften des Neuen Testaments und der frühchristlichen Literatur.* 6., völlig neu bearbeitete Auflage. Berlin: Walter de Gruyter.

Becker, J.
1979   *Das Evangelium nach Johannes. Kapitel 1-10.* Ökumenischer Taschenbuchkommentar zum Neuen Testament 4/1. Gütersloh: Gütersloher Verlagshaus Gerd Mohn.
1981   *Das Evangelium nach Johannes. Kapitel 11-21.* Ökumenischer Taschenbuchkommentar zum Neuen Testament 4/2. Gütersloh: Gütersloher Verlagshaus Gerd Mohn.

Benko, S.
1967   "The Libertine Gnostic Sect of the Phibionites According to Epiphanius." *VC* 21, 103-119.

Berger, K.
1981   "Unfehlbare Offenbarung. Petrus in der gnostischen und apokalyptischen Offenbarungsliteratur." In: P.-G. Müller & W. Stenger (eds.), *Kontinuität und Einheit. Für Franz Mußner.* Freiburg/Basel/Wien: Herder.

Böhlig, A.
1967   "Der jüdische und judenchristliche Hintergrund in gnostischen Texten von Nag Hammadi." In: U. Bianchi (ed.), *The Origins of Gnosticism. Colloquium of Messina 13-18 April 1966.* Numen Supplement 12. Leiden: E.J. Brill, 109-140.
1968   "Christliche Wurzeln im Manichäismus." In: A. Böhlig, *Mysterion und Wahrheit. Gesammelte Aufsätze zur spätantiken Religionsgeschichte.* Leiden: E.J. Brill, 202-221.

Bovon, F.
1984   "Le privilège pascal de Marie-Madeleine." *NTS* 30, 50-62.

Buckley, J.J.
1980   "A Cult-Mystery in the *Gospel of Philip.*" *JBL* 99, 569-581.
1985   "An Interpretation of Logion 114 in the *Gospel of Thomas.*" *NovT* 27, 245-272.

1988   "'The Holy Spirit Is a Double Name': Holy Spirit, Mary, and
            Sophia in the *Gospel of Philip*." In: K.L. King (ed.), *Images of the
            Feminine in Gnosticism*. Studies in Antiquity and Christianity.
            Philadelphia: Fortress Press, 211-227.

Burkitt, F.C.
1930-31   "Mary Magdalene and Mary, Sister of Martha." *ExpTim* 42, 157-
            159.

van Cangh, J.-M.
1992   "Miracles évangéliques — miracles apocryphes." In: F. van Seg-
            broeck *et al.* (eds.), *The Four Gospels 1992. Festschrift Frans
            Neirynck*. Leuven: University Press, Vol. III, 2277-2319.

Chadwick, H.
1980   "The Domestication of Gnosis." In: B. Layton (ed.), *The Rediscov-
            ery of Gnosticism. Proceedings of the International Conference on
            Gnosticism at Yale New Haven, Connecticut, March 28-31, 1978.
            Vol. I: The School of Valentinus*. Leiden: E.J. Brill, 3-16.

Clark, G.
1995   "Women and Asceticism in Late Antiquity: The Refusal of Status
            and Gender." In: V.L. Wimbush & R. Valantasis (eds.), *Asceticism*.
            Oxford: Oxford University Press, 33-48.

Collins, R.F.
1992   "Mary (Person), 2. Mary Magdalene." In: *ABD*, Vol. 4, 579-581.

Coyle, J.K.
1991   "Mary Magdalene in Manichaeism?" *Mus* 104, 39-55.

Crossan, J.D.
1991   *The Historical Jesus. The Life of a Mediterranean Jewish Peasant*.
            San Fransisco: Harper Collins Publishers.

Crum, W.E.
1939   *A Coptic Dictionary*. Oxford: The Clarendon Press.

Dart, J.
1978   "The Two Shall Become One." *TToday* 35, 321-325.

Davies, S.L.
1983   *The Gospel of Thomas and Christian Wisdom*. New York: The
            Seabury Press.

De Boer, E.
1988   "Maria van Magdala en haar Evangelie." In: G. Quispel (ed.),
            Gnosis. De derde component van de Europese cultuurtraditie.
            Utrecht: Hes Uitgevers.

De Conick, A.D.
1996   *Seek to See Him. Ascent and Vision Mysticism in the Gospel of
            Thomas*. Supplements to Vigiliae Christianae 33. Leiden: E.J. Brill.

Desjardins, M.R.
1990   *Sin in Valentinianism*. SBLDS 108. Atlanta, Georgia: Scholars
            Press.

1992   "Where Was the Gospel of Thomas Written?" *Toronto Journal of
            Theology* 8, 121-133.

Devos, P.
1978a   "L'apparition du Resuscité a sa mére. Un nouveau témoin copte."
             Analecta Bollandiana 96, 388.
1978b   "De Jean Chrysostome a Jean de Lycopolis. Chrysostome et Chal-
             kèdôn." *Analecta Bollandiana* 96, 389-403.
Doresse, J.
1948   "Trois livres gnostiques inédits." *VC* 2, 137-160.
1960   *The Secret Books of the Egyptian Gnostics. An Introduction to the
             Gnostic Coptic manuscripts discovered at Chenoboskion.* Translated
             from French (1959) by Philip Mairet. New York: The Viking Press.
Dornseiff, F. & Hansen, B.
1957   *Rückläufiges Wörterbuch der griechischen Eigennamen.* Berichte
             über der sächsischen Akademie der Wissenschaften zu Leipzig.
             Philologisch-historische Klasse, Band 102/4. Berlin: Akademie-
             Verlag.
Drijvers, H.J.W.
1982   "Facts and Problems in Early Syriac-Speaking Christianity."
             SecCent 2, 157-175.
Dummer, J.
1965   "Die Angaben über die Gnostische Literatur bei Epiphanius, Pan.
             haer. 26." In: *Koptologische Studien in der DDR. Zusammengestellt
             und herausgegeben vom Institut für Byzantinistik der Martin-Lu-
             ther-Universität Halle-Wittenberg.* Halle: Martin-Luther-Universität,
             191-219.
Dunderberg, I.
1994   *Johannes und die Synoptiker. Studien zu Joh 1-9.* Annales Acade-
             miac Scientiarum Fennicae, Dissertationes humanarum litterarum
             64. Helsinki: Academia Scientiarum Fennica.
Emmel, S.
1980   "A Fragment of Nag Hammadi Codex III in the Beinecke Library:
             Yale inv. 1784." *BASP* 17, 53-60.
Fallon, F.T.
1979   "The Gnostic Apocalypses." *Semeia* 14, 123-158.
Fallon, F.T. & Cameron, R.
1988   "The Gospel of Thomas: A Forschungsbericht and Analysis."
             ANRW II 25/6, 4195-4251.
Feuillet, A.
1975   "Les deux onctions faites sur Jésus, et Marie-Madeleine. Contribu-
             tion à l'étude des rapports entre les Synoptiques et le quatrième
             évangile." *RevThom* 75, 357-394.
Filoramo, G.
1990   *A History of Gnosticism.* Translated by Anthony Alcock. Oxford:
             Basil Blackwell.
Fitzmyer, J.A.
1981   *The Gospel According to Luke I-IX.* AB 28. New York: Doubleday.
Funk, W.-P.
1985   "How Closely Related Are the Subakhmimic Dialects?" *Zeitschrift
             für ägyptische Sprache und Altertumskunde* 112, 124-139.

Gaffron, H.-G.
1969   "Studien zum koptischen Philippusevangelium unter besonderer
            Berücksichtigung der Sakramente." Th.D. diss. Rheinische Fried-
            rich-Wilhelms-Universität, Bonn.
Gärtner, B.
1960   *Ett nytt evangelium? Thomasevangeliets hemliga Jesusord.* Stock-
            holm: Diakonistyrelsens bokförlag.
Gero, S.
1986   "With Walter Bauer on the Tigris: Encratite Orthodoxy and Liber-
            tine Heresy in Syro-Mesopotamian Christianity." In: C.W. Hedrick
            & R. Hodgson, Jr. (eds.), *Nag Hammadi, Gnosticism, and Early
            Christianity.* Peabody, Massachusetts: Hendrickson Publishers, 287-
            307.
Goehring, J.E.
1988   "Libertine or Liberated: Women in the So-called Libertine Gnostic
            Communities." In: K.L. King (ed.), *Images of the Feminine in
            Gnosticism.* Studies in Antiquity and Christianity. Philadelphia:
            Fortress Press, 329-344.
Good, D.J.
1987   *Reconstructing the Tradition of Sophia in Gnostic Literature.*
            SBLMS 32. Atlanta: Scholars Press.
1995   "Pistis Sophia." In: E. Schüssler Fiorenza (ed.), *Searching the
            Scriptures. Volume Two: A Feminist Commentary.* London: SCM
            Press, 678-707.
Grant, R.M.
1960   "Two Gnostic Gospels." *JBL* 79, 1-11.
1961   "The Mystery of Marriage in the Gospel of Philip." *VC* 15, 129-
            140.
1966   *Gnosticism and Early Christianity.* Revised Edition. New York:
            Harper & Row.
Grassi, J. & Grassi, C.
1986   *Mary Magdalene and the Women in Jesus' Life.* Kansas City:
            Sheep & Ward.
Haenchen, E.
1961-62   "Literatur zum Thomasevangelium." *TRu* 27, 147-178.306-338.
Hall, S.G.
1990   "Nag Hammadi." In: R.J. Coggins & J.L. Houlden (eds.), *A Dictio-
            nary of Biblical Interpretation.* London: SCM Press, 483-486.
Hallenberg, H. & Perho, I.
1992   *Heijastuksia valosta — mystikkojen islam.* Helsinki: Yliopistopaino.
Harnack, A.
1891   *Über das gnostische Buch Pistis Sophia. Brod und Wasser: Die
            eucharistischen Elemente bei Justin. Zwei Untersuchungen.* TU 7/2.
            Leipzig: J.C. Hinrichs'sche Buchhandlung.
1897   *Geschichte der altchristlichen Litteratur bis Eusebius. Zweiter Teil:
            Die Chronologie. Erster Band: Die Chronologie der Litteratur bis
            Irenäus.* Leipzig: J.C. Hinrichs'sche Buchhandlung.

1958   *Geschichte der altchristlichen Literatur bis Eusebius. Teil II: Die*
            Chronologie. Band I: Die Chronologie der Literatur bis Irenäus.
            2. erweiterte Auflage. Leipzig: J.C. Hinrichs Verlag.

Haskins, S.
1993   *Mary Magdalen. Myth and Metaphor.* London: Harper Collins
            Publishers.

Hauck, F.
1966   "κοινός κτλ." In: *TDNT* 3, 789-809.

Hills, J.V.
1991   "The Three 'Matthean' Aphorisms in the *Dialogue of the Savior*
            53." *HTR* 84, 43-58.

Holzmeister, U.
1922   "Die Magdalenenfrage in der kirchlichen Überlieferung." *ZKT* 46,
            402-422.556-584.

Jackson, H.M.
1985   *The Lion Becomes Man. The Gnostic Leontomorphic Creator and*
            the Platonic Tradition. SBLDS 81. Atlanta, Georgia: Scholars
            Press.

Kasser, R.
1965   "Textes gnostiques: Remarques à propos des éditions récentes du
            Livre secret de Jean et des Apocalypses de Paul, Jacques et Ad-
            am." *Mus* 78, 71-98.

King, K.L.
1987   "Kingdom in the Gospel of Thomas." *Foundations & Facets Fo-*
            rum 3/1, 48-97.

1992   "The Gospel of Mary." In: R.J. Miller (ed.), *The Complete Gospels.*
            Annotated Scholars Version Sonoma, California: Polebridge Press,
            351-360.

1995   "The Gospel of Mary." In: E. Schüssler Fiorenza (ed.), *Searching*
            the Scriptures. Volume Two: A Feminist Commentary. London:
            SCM Press, 601-634.

Klauck, H.-J.
1992   "Die dreifache Maria. Zur Rezeption von Joh 19,25 in EvPhil 32."
            In: F. van Segbroeck *et al.* (eds.), *The Four Gospels 1992. Fest-*
            schrift Frans Neirynck. Leuven: University Press, Vol. III, 2343-
            2358.

Klijn, A.F.J.
1972   "Christianity in Edessa and The Gospel of Thomas. On Barbara
            Ehlers, Kann das Thomasevangelium aus Edessa stammen?" *NovT*
            14, 70-77.

Koester, H.
1979   "Dialog und Spruchüberlieferung in den gnostischen Texten von
            Nag Hammadi." *EvT* 39, 532-556.

1990   *Ancient Christian Gospels. Their History and Development.* Lon-
            don: SCM Press.

Koester, H. & Pagels, E.
1984   "Introduction." In: S. Emmel (ed.), *Nag Hammadi Codex III,5: The*
            Dialogue of the Savior. NHS 26. Leiden: E.J. Brill.

Koivunen, H.
1994   *The Woman Who Understood Completely. A Semiotic Analysis of*
             the Mary Magdalene Myth in the Gnostic Gospel of Mary. Acta
             Semiotica Fennica. Imatra: International Semiotics Institute.
Koschorke, K.
1978   *Die Polemik der Gnostiker gegen das kirchliche Christentum. Unter*
             besonderer Berücksichtigung der Nag-Hammadi-Traktate "Apoka-
             lypse des Petrus" (NHC VII,3) und "Testimonium Veritatis" (NHC
             IX,3). NHS 12. Leiden: E.J. Brill.
Kraft, H.
1950   "Gnostisches Gemeinschaftsleben. Untersuchungen zu den Gemein-
             schafts- und Lebensformen häretischer christlicher Gnosis des
             zweiten Jahrhunderts." Th.D. diss. Ruperto Carola Universität.
Krause, M.
1964a   "Das Literarische Verhältnis des Eugnostosbriefes zur Sophia Jesu
             Christi." In: *Mullus. Festschrift Theodor Klauser.* JAC, Ergän-
             zungsband 1. Münster: Aschendorffsche Verlagsbuchhandlung, 215-
             223.
1964b   Review of W.C. Till, Das Evangelium nach Philippos. Berlin:
             Walter de Gruyter, 1963. *ZKG* 75, 168-182.
1977   "Der *Dialog des Soter* in Codex III von Nag Hammadi." In: M.
             Krause (ed.), *Gnosis and Gnosticism. Papers read at the Seventh*
             International Conference on Patristic Studies (Oxford, September
             8th-13th 1975). Leiden: E. J. Brill.
1981   "Christlich-gnostische   Texte   als   Quellen   für   die   Aus-
             einandersetzung von Gnosis und Christentum." In: M. Krause (ed.),
             Gnosis and Gnosticism. Papers read at the Eighth International
             Conference on Patristic Studies (Oxford, September 3rd-8th 1979).
             NHS 17. Leiden: E.J. Brill, 47-65.
Kümmel, W.G.
1976   "Ein Jahrzehnt Jesusforschung (1965-1975): II. Nicht-wissenschaft-
             liche und wissenschaftliche Gesamtdarstellungen." *TRu* 41, 197-
             258.
Leisegang, H.
1950   "Pistis Sophia." In: PW 20, 1813-1821.
Lelyveld, M.
1987   *Les logia de la vie dans l'Évangile selon Thomas. A la recherche*
             d'une tradition et d'une rédaction. NHS 34. Leiden: E.J. Brill.
Liddell, H.G. & Scott, R. *et al.*
1968   *A Greek-English Lexicon.* 9th edition. Oxford: The Clarendon
             Press.
Lieu, S.N.C.
1992   *Manichaeism in the Later Roman Empire and Medieval China.*
             WUNT 63. 2. edition, revised and expanded. Tübingen: J.C.B.
             Mohr (Paul Siebeck).
Lincoln, B.
1977   "Thomas-Gospel and Thomas-Community: A New Approach to a
             Familiar Text." *NovT* 19, 65-76.

Lucchesi, E.
1985   "Évangile selon Marie ou Évangile selon Marie-Madeleine?"
            Analecta Bollandiana 103, 366.
Lührmann, D.
1988   "Die griechischen Fragmente des Mariaevangeliums: POx 3525 und
            PRyl 463." *NovT* 30, 321-338.
Luttikhuizen, G.P.
1988   "The Evaluation of the Teaching of Jesus in Christian Gnostic
            Revelation Dialogues." *NovT* 30, 158-168.
Malvern, M.
1975   *Venus in Sackcloth. The Magdalen's Origins and Metamorphoses.*
            Carbondale/Edwardsville: Southern Illinois University Press.
Marjanen, A.
1992   "Varhaiskristillisyyden aktiivisia ja vaiennettuja naisia. Toisen
            vuosisadan gnostilaisuuden ja Pastoraalikirjeiden naiskuvan muo-
            toutuminen." In: R. Sollamo & I. Dunderberg (eds.), *Naisia Raa-
            matussa. Viisaus ja Rakkaus.* Helsinki: Yliopistopaino, 130-169.
Meeks, W.A.
1973-74   "The Image of the Androgyne: Some Uses of a Symbol in Earliest
            Christianity." *HR* 13, 165-208.
Meier, J.P.
1992   "Matthew, Gospel of." In: *ABD*, Vol. 4, 622-641.
Ménard, J.-É.
1967   *L'Évangile selon Philippe. Introduction, Texte, Traduction, Com-
            mentaire.* Strasbourg: Université de Strasbourg, Faculté de Théo-
            logie Catholique.
1975   *L'Évangile selon Thomas.* NHS 5. Leiden: E.J. Brill.
Meyer, M.W.
1985   "Making Mary Male: The Categories 'Male' and 'Female' in the
            Gospel of Thomas." *NTS* 31, 554-570.
1990   "The Youth in Secret Mark and the Beloved Disciple in John." In:
            J.E. Goehring *et al.* (eds.), *Gospel Origins and Christian Begin-
            nings. In Honor of James Robinson.* Sonoma, California: Pole-
            bridge Press, 94-105.
1992   *The Gospel of Thomas. The Hidden Sayings of Jesus.* San Fran-
            sisco: Harper.
Mirecki, P.A.
1992   "Manichaeans and Manichaeism." In: *ABD*, Vol. 4, 502-511.
Moxnes, H. (ed.),
1989   *Feminist Reconstruction of Early Christianity.* ST 43, 1-163.
Nagel, P.
1967   "Die Psalmoi Sarakoton des manichäischen Psalmbuches." *OLZ* 62,
            123-130.
1973   "Die apokryphen Apostelakten des 2. und 3. Jahrhunderts. Ein
            Beitrag zur Frage nach den christlichen Elementen im Mani-
            chäismus." In: K.-W. Tröger (ed.), *Gnosis und Neues Testament.
            Studien aus Religionswissenschaft und Theologie.* Gütersloh: Gü-
            tersloher Verlagshaus Gerd Mohn, 149-182.

Pagels, E.
1978   "Visions, Appearances, and Apostolic Authority: Gnostic and Orthodox Traditions." In: B. Aland (ed.), *Gnosis. Festschrift für Hans Jonas.* Göttingen: Vandenhoeck & Ruprecht, 415-430.
1981   *The Gnostic Gospels.* New York: Random House.
1983   "Adam and Eve, Christ and the Church: A Survey of Second Century Controversies Concerning Marriage." In: A.H.B. Logan & A.J.M. Wedderburn (eds.), *The New Testament and Gnosis: Essays in Honour of Robert McL. Wilson.* Edinburgh: T&T. Clark Ltd., 146-175.
1988   "Pursuing the Spiritual Eve: Imagery and Hermeneutics in the *Hypostasis of the Archons* and in the *Gospel of Philip.*" In: K.L. King (ed.), *Images of the Feminine in Gnosticism.* Studies in Antiquity and Christianity. Philadelphia: Fortress Press, 187-206.
1990   "NHC XI,2: A Valentinian Exposition. Introduction." In: C.W. Hedrick (ed.), *Nag Hammadi Codices XI, XII, XIII.* NHS 28. Leiden: E.J. Brill, 89-105.
1991   "The 'Mystery of Marriage' in the *Gospel of Philip* Revisited." In: B.A. Pearson (ed.), *The Future of Early Christianity. Essays in Honor of Helmut Koester.* Minneapolis: Fortress Press, 442-454.

Pagels, E. & Koester, H.
1978   "Report on the *Dialogue of the Savior* (CG III,5)." In: R.McL. Wilson (ed.), *Nag Hammadi and Gnosis. Papers Read at the First International Congress of Coptology (Cairo, December 1976).* NHS 14. Leiden: E.J. Brill.

Parrott, D.M.
1971   "The Significance of the Letter of Eugnostos and the Sophia Jesus Christ for the Understanding of the Relation Between Gnosticism and Christianity." In: SBLSP 2, 397-416.
1986   "Gnostic and Orthodox Disciples in the Second and Third Centuries." In: C.W. Hedrick and R. Hodgson, Jr. (eds.), *Nag Hammadi, Gnosticism, and Early Christianity.* Peabody, Massachusetts: Hendrickson Publishers, 193-219.
1987   "Gnosticism and Egyptian Religion." *NovT* 29, 73-93.
1992   "Eugnostos and the Sophia of Jesus Christ." In: *ABD*, Vol. 2, 668-669.

Pasquier, A.
1983   *L'Évangile selon Marie (BG 1).* Bibliothèque copte de Nag Hammadi. Section "Textes" 10. Québec: Les Presses de l'Université Laval.

Patterson, S.
1993   *The Gospel of Thomas and Jesus.* Sonoma, California: Polebridge Press.

Pearson, B.
1990   *Gnosticism, Judaism, and Egyptian Christianity.* Studies in Antiquity and Christianity. Minneapolis: Fortress Press.

Perkins, P.
1971   "The Soteriology of Sophia of Jesus Christ." In: SBLSP 2, 165-
            181.
1980   *The Gnostic Dialogue. The Early Church and the Crisis of Gnos-
            ticism.* New York: Paulist Press.
1992a   "Mary, Gospel of." In: *ABD*, Vol. 4, 583-584.
1992b   "Pistis Sophia." In: *ABD*, Vol. 5, 375-376.
1993   *Gnosticism and the New Testament.* Minneapolis: Fortress Press.
1995   "The Gospel of Thomas." In: E. Schüssler Fiorenza (ed.), *Search-
            ing the Scriptures. Volume Two: A Feminist Commentary.* London:
            SCM Press, 535-560.

Petersen, W.L.
1985   *The Diatessaron and Ephrem Syrus as Sources of Romanos the
            Melodist.* CSCO 475. Louvain: Peeters.

Polotsky, H.J.
1987   *Grundlagen des koptischen Satzbaus. Erste Hälfte.* American
            Studies in Papyrology. Decatur, Georgia: Scholars Press.

Price, R.M.
1990   "Mary Magdalene: Gnostic Apostle?" *Grail* 6, 54-76.

Przybylski, B.
1980   "The Role of Calendrical Data in Gnostic Literature." *VC* 34, 56-
            70.

Puech, H.-C.
1950   "Les nouveaux écrits gnostiques découverts en Haute-Egypte
            (premier inventaire et essai d'identification)." In: *Coptic Studies in
            Honor of Walter Ewing Crum.* Boston: The Byzantine Institute, 91-
            154.

Quecke, H.
1963   "'Sein Haus seines Königreiches.' Zum Thomasevangelium 85.9f."
            Mus 76, 47-53.

Quispel, G.
1961   "Pistis Sophia." In: *RGG*[3] 5, 386-388.

Rengstorf, K.H.
1967   "μανθάνω κτλ." In: *TDNT* 4, 390-461.
1970   "Urchristliches Kerygma und 'gnostische' Interpretation in einigen
            Sprüchen des Thomasevangeliums." In: U. Bianchi (ed.), *The
            Origins of Gnosticism. Colloquium of Messina 13-18 April 1966.*
            Numen Supplement 12. Leiden: E.J. Brill, 563-574.

Richter, S.
1992   "Untersuchungen zu Form und Inhalt einer Gruppe der Hera-
            kleides-Psalmen." In: G. Wießner & H.-J. Klimkeit (eds.), *Studia
            Manichaica. II. Internationaler Kongreß zum Manichäismus.* Wies-
            baden: Otto Harrassowitz, 248-265.

Riley, G.
1994   "The *Gospel of Thomas* in Recent Scholarship." *Currents in Re-
            search: Biblical Studies* 2, 227-252.

Rudolph, K.
1988   "Response to ' 'The Holy Spirit is a Double Name': Holy Spirit,
            Mary, and Sophia in the *Gospel of Philip*' by Jorunn Jacobsen
            Buckley." In: K.L. King (ed.), *Images of the Feminine in Gnos-*
            ticism. Studies in Antiquity and Christianity. Philadelphia: Fortress
            Press, 228-238.
1990   *Die Gnosis. Wesen und Geschichte einer spätantiken Religion.* 3.,
            durchgesehene und ergänzte Auflage. Göttingen: Vandenhoeck &
            Ruprecht.
Schaberg, J.
1992   "Luke." In: C.A. Newsom & S.A. Ringe (eds.), *The Women's Bible*
            Commentary. London: SPCK, 275-292.
Schenke, H.-M.
1962   "Nag-Hamadi Studien II: Das System der Sophia Jesu Christi."
            ZRGG 14, 263-278.
1965   "Die Arbeit am Philippus-Evangelium." *TLZ* 90, 321-332.
1966   Review of Böhlig & Labib, *Koptisch-gnostische Apokalypsen aus*
            Codex V von Nag Hammadi im Koptischen Museum zu Alt-Kairo.
            Sonderband, Wissenschaftliche Zeitschrift der Martin-Luther-Uni-
            versität Halle-Wittenberg, 1963. *OLZ* 61, 23-34.
1986   "The Function and Background of the Beloved Disciple in the
            Gospel of John." In: C.W. Hedrick and R. Hodgson, Jr. (eds.), *Nag*
            Hammadi, Gnosticism, and Early Christianity. Peabody, Massachu-
            setts: Hendrickson Publishers, 111-125.
Schmid, R.
1990   *Maria Magdalena in Gnostischen Schriften.* München:
            Arbeitsgemeinschaft für Religions- und Weltanschauungsfragen.
Schmidt, C.
1892   *Gnostische Schriften in koptischer Sprache aus dem Codex Bruci-*
            anus. TU 8. Leizig: J.C. Hinrichs'sche Buchhandlung.
1896   "Ein vorirenaeisches gnostisches Originalwerk in koptischer Spra-
            che." In: SPAW, Jahrgang 1896, zweiter Halbband. Berlin: Verlag
            der königlichen Akademie der Wissenschaften, 839-846.
Schmidt, C. & Polotsky, H.J.
1933   "Ein Mani-Fund in Ägypten. Originalschriften des Mani und seiner
            Schüler." In: SPAW, Phil.-hist. Klasse, Jahrgang 1933. Berlin:
            Akademie-Verlag.
Schoedel, W.R.
1991   "A Gnostic Interpretation of the Fall of Jerusalem: The First Apoc-
            alypse of James." *NovT* 33, 153-178.
Schottroff, L.
1980   "Frauen in der Nachfolge Jesu in neutestamentlicher Zeit." In: W.
            Schottroff & W. Stegemann (eds.), *Traditionen der Befreiung.*
            Sozialgeschichtliche Bibelauslegung. 2. Frauen in der Bibel. Mün-
            chen: Kaiser Verlag, 91-133.
Schulz, S.
1983   *Das Evangelium nach Johannes.* NTD 4. 4. Auflage dieser Fas-
            sung. Göttingen: Vandenhoeck & Ruprecht.

Schüngel, P.
1994   "Ein Vorschlag, EvTho 114 neu zu übersetzen." *NovT* 36, 394-401.
Schüssler Fiorenza, E.
1979   "Feminist Theology as a Critical Theology of Liberation." In: G.H.
            Anderson & T.F. Stransky (eds.), *Mission Trends No. 4: Liberation
            Theologies in North America and Europe*. Grand Rapids: Wm. B.
            Eerdmans Publishing Co., 188-216.
1980   "Der Beitrag der Frau zur urchristlichen Bewegung. Kritische
            Überlegungen zur Rekonstruktion urchristlicher Geschichte." In: W.
            Schottroff & W. Stegemann (eds.), *Traditionen der Befreiung.
            Sozialgeschichtliche Bibelauslegung. 2. Frauen in der Bibel.* Mün-
            chen: Kaiser Verlag, 60-90.
1983   *In Memory of Her. A Feminist Theological Reconstruction of
            Christian Origins.* New York: Crossroad.
Segelberg, E.
1960   "The Coptic-Gnostic Gospel According to Philip and Its Sacramen-
            tal System." *Numen* 7, 189-200.
1966   "The Antiochene Background of the Gospel of Philip." *Bulletin de
            la Société d'Archéologie Copte* 18, 205-223. (Reprinted in: *Gnosti-
            ca — Mandaica — Liturgica. Opera eius ipsius selecta & collecta
            septuagenario Erico Segelberg oblata curantibus Jan Bergman, Jan
            Hjärpe, Per Ström.* Uppsala: Almqvist & Wiksell International,
            1990, 31-49.)
1967-68   "The Antiochene Origin of the 'Gospel of Philip'." *Bulletin de la
            Société d'Archéologie Copte* 19, 207-210. (Reprinted in: *Gnostica
            — Mandaica — Liturgica. Opera eius ipsius selecta & collecta
            septuagenario Erico Segelberg oblata curantibus Jan Bergman, Jan
            Hjärpe, Per Ström.* Uppsala: Almqvist & Wiksell International,
            1990, 51-54.)
Seim, T.Karlsen
1995   "The Gospel of Luke." In: E. Schüssler Fiorenza (ed.), *Searching
            the Scriptures. Volume Two: A Feminist Commentary.* London:
            SCM Press, 728-762.
Sellew, P.
1991   "*Secret Mark* and the History of Canonical Mark." In: B.A. Pear-
            son (ed.), *The Future of Early Christianity. Essays in Honor of
            Helmut Koester.* Minneapolis: Fortress Press, 242-257.
Sickenberger, J.
1925   "Ist die Magdalenen-Frage wirklich unlösbar?" *BZ* 17, 63-74.
Siker, J.S.
1989   "Gnostic Views On Jews and Christians in the Gospel of Philip."
            NovT 31, 275-288.
Smith, M.
1973   *Clement of Alexandria and a Secret Gospel of Mark.* Cambridge,
            Massachusetts: Harvard University Press.

Smith, R.
1988 "Sex Education in Gnostic Schools." In: K.L. King (ed.), *Images of the Feminine in Gnosticism*. Studies in Antiquity and Christianity. Philadelphia: Fortress Press, 345-360.

Smith, T.V.
1985 *Petrine Controversies in Early Christianity. Attitudes Towards Peter in Christian Writings of the First Two Centuries*. WUNT, 2. Reihe, 15. Tübingen: J.C.B. Mohr (Paul Siebeck).

Stählin, G.
1974 "φιλέω κτλ." In: *TDNT* 9, 113-171.

Stern, L.
1971 *Koptische Grammatik*. Osnabrück: Biblio Verlag. [Leipzig 1880]

Stroud, W.J.
1990 "New Testament Quotations in the Nag Hammadi Gospel of Philip." In: D.J. Lull (ed.), *Society of Biblical Literature 1990 Seminar Papers*. Atlanta, Georgia: Scholars Press, 68-81.

Sumney, J.L.
1989 "The Letter of Eugnostos and the Origins of Gnosticism." *NovT* 31, 172-181.

Tardieu, M.
1984 *Écrits Gnostiques: Codex de Berlin*. Sources gnostiques et manichéennes 1. Paris: Les Éditions du Cerf.

Till, W.C.
1946 "Εὐαγγέλιον κατὰ Μαρίαμ." *La Parola del Passato* 1, 260-265.
1949 "Die Gnosis in Ägypten." *La Parola del Passato* 4, 230-249.
1978 *Koptische Grammatik (Saïdischer Dialekt). Mit Bibliographie, Lesestücken und Wörterverzeichnissen*. 5. Auflage. Leipzig: VEB Verlag Enzyklopädie.

Torjesen, K.J.
1993 *When Women Were Priests*. San Francisco: Harper Collins Publishers.

Trautmann, C.
1981 "La parenté dans l'*Évangile selon Philippe*." In: B. Barc (ed.), *Colloque international sur les Textes de Nag Hammadi (Québec, 22-25 août 1978)*. Bibliothèque copte de Nag Hammadi. Section "Études" 1. Louvain: Peeters.

Tuckett, C.M.
1986 *Nag Hammadi and the Gospel Tradition. Synoptic Tradition in the Nag Hammadi Library*. Edinburgh: T. & T. Clark.
1987 *Reading the New Testament. Methods of Interpretations*. Philadelphia: Fortress Press.

van Unnik, W.C.
1963-64 "Three Notes On the 'Gospel of Philip.' " *NTS* 10, 465-469.

Uro, R.
1995 *Jeesus-liikkeestä kristinuskoksi*. Helsinki: Yliopistopaino.

Veilleux, A.
1986   *La première apocalypse de Jacques (NH V,3). La seconde apoca-*
            lypse de Jacques (NH V,4). Bibliothèque copte de Nag Hammadi.
            Section "Textes" 17. Québec: Les Presses de l'Université Laval.
Vielhauer, P.
1964   "ΑΝΑΠΑΥΣΙΣ. Zum gnostischen Hintergrund des Thomasevange-
            liums." In: *Apophoreta. Festschrift für Ernst Haenchen zu seinem*
            siebzigsten Geburtstag. Berlin: Verlag Alfred Töpelmann, 1964,
            281-299.
Vogt, K.
1985   "'Männlichwerden' — Aspekte einer urchristlichen Anthropologie."
            Concilium 21, 434-442.
Vööbus, A.
1958   *History of Asceticism in the Syrian Orient. A Contribution to the*
            History of Culture in the Near East. Part I: The Origin of Asceti-
            cism. Early Monasticism in Persia. CSCO 184. Louvain:
            Secrétariat du Corpus SCO.
Welburn, A.J.
1978   "The Identity of the Archons in the 'Apocryphon Johannis.' " *VC*
            32, 241-254.
Williams, M.A.
1985   *The Immovable Race. A Gnostic Designation and the Theme of*
            Stability in Late Antiquity. NHS 29. Leiden: E.J. Brill.
1986   "Uses of Gender Imagery in Ancient Gnostic Texts." In: C.W.
            Bynum *et al.* (eds.), *Gender and Religion: On the Complexity of*
            Symbols. Boston: Beacon Press, 196-227.
Wilson, R.McL.
1956-57   "The New Testament in the Gnostic Gospel of Mary." *NTS* 3, 236-
            243.
1960   *Studies in the Gospel of Thomas.* London: A.R. Mowbray & Co.
1962   *The Gospel of Philip. Translated from the Coptic Text, with an*
            Introduction and Commentary. London: A.R. Mowbray & Co.
1968   *Gnosis and the New Testament.* Philadelphia: Fortress Press.
Wisse, F.
1975   "Die Sextus-Sprüche und das Problem der gnostischen Ethik." In:
            Zum Hellenismus in den Schriften von Nag Hammadi mit Beiträgen
            von Alexander Böhlig und Frederik Wisse. Wiesbaden: Otto
            Harrassowitz, 55-86.
1988   "Flee Femininity: Antifemininity in Gnostic Texts and the Question
            of Social Milieu." In: K.L. King (ed.), *Images of the Feminine in*
            Gnosticism. Studies in Antiquity and Christianity. Philadelphia:
            Fortress Press, 297-307.
Zandee, J.
1991   *The Teachings of Sylvanus (Nag Hammadi Codex VII,4). Text,*
            Translation, Commentary. Leiden: Nederlands Instituut voor het
            Nabije Oosten.

Zscharnack, L.
1902   *Der Dienst der Frau in den ersten Jahrhunderten der christlichen Kirche.* Göttingen: Vandenhoeck & Ruprecht.

INDEXES

1. Ancient Texts and Authors

1.1 Old Testament

1.2 Jewish Apocrypha and Pseudepigrapha

1.3 New Testament

63,34-37	95,101,156, 158
63,37-64,5	16
64,1-10	110
64,2.4	95
64,3	152
64,31-65,1	155
65,1-26	156
65,3-5	153
65,20	154
65,23-36	153
66,29	165
67,24-25	165
69,1-4	155
70,5-9	118
70,9-22	153
70,19	154
70,24.29	154
71,13-15	165
73,2	169
73,8	117
73,8-19	165
73,12.15	152
74,12-14	148
74,17-18	165
75,13-14	164
75,14-21	118
75,21-24	118
76,6-9	153,154
76,17-22	164
76,22-23	118
77,6-7	164
78,18	153
78,25	153
79,33-80,23	164
80,9-10	166
81,1-14	165
81,34-82,7	153
82,1	154
82,4-8	155
85,24-27	118
86,18-19	118

Orig. World
109,16-25	90
125,5-6	180

Thom. Cont.
138,2-3	69,75,88
144,8-10	144
144,9	89

Eugnostos
III/3
70,1-85,9	62
70,15	60
71,13-83,2	63
84,4-5	61
85,8-9	60
85,8	56
90,4-11	58

V/1
17,9-15	58

Soph. Jes. Chr. III/4
90,14-92,5	57,61
90,14-91,12	167
90,16-18	64,65
90,17-18	71,126
91,18-20	74
91,20-23	61
92,4	65
94,1	65
95,19	65
96,14	65
97,16-99,12	56
97,23-24	65-66
98,10	57,63
100,17	65
101,13-15	61
103,22	65
105,3-4	65
106,9	65
106,24-108,16	64,65
108,4	73
108,11-13	73
108,17	65
108,19-23	66
112,19-20	65
114,8-119,18	57
114,8-12	41
114,9	57,63
114,11-12	81
114,14-15	75
118,6-8	58,220

2. Modern Authors

NAG HAMMADI AND MANICHAEAN STUDIES

FORMERLY

NAG HAMMADI STUDIES

1. SCHOLER, D.M. *Nag Hammadi bibliography, 1948-1969.* 1971. ISBN 90 04 02603 7
2. MÉNARD, J.-E. *L'évangile de vérité.* Traduction française, introduction et commentaire par J.-É. MÉNARD. 1972.
   ISBN 90 04 03408 0
3. KRAUSE, M. (ed.). *Essays on the Nag Hammadi texts in honour of Alexander Böhlig.* 1972. ISBN 90 04 03535 4
4. BÖHLIG, A. & F. WISSE, (eds.). *Nag Hammadi Codices III, 2 and IV, 2. The Gospel of the Egyptians.* (The Holy Book of the Great Invisible Spirit). Edited with translation and commentary, in cooperation with P. LABIB. 1975.
   ISBN 90 04 04226 1
5. MÉNARD, J.-E. *L'Évangile selon Thomas.* Traduction française, introduction, et commentaire par J.-É. MÉNARD. 1975. ISBN 90 04 04210 5
6. KRAUSE, M. (ed.). *Essays on the Nag Hammadi texts in honour of Pahor Labib.* 1975. ISBN 90 04 04363 2
7. MÉNARD, J.-E. *Les textes de Nag Hammadi.* Colloque du centre d'Histoire des Religions, Strasbourg, 23-25 octobre 1974. 1975. ISBN 90 04 04359 4
8. KRAUSE, M. (ed.). *Gnosis and Gnosticism.* Papers read at the Seventh International Conference on Patristic Studies. Oxford, September 8th-13th, 1975. 1977. ISBN 90 04 05242 9
9. SCHMIDT, C. (ed.). *Pistis Sophia.* Translation and notes by V. MACDERMOT. 1978. ISBN 90 04 05635 1
10. FALLON, F.T. *The enthronement of Sabaoth.* Jewish elements in Gnostic creation myths. 1978. ISBN 90 04 05683 1
11. PARROTT, D.M. *Nag Hammadi Codices V, 2-5 and VI with Papyrus Berolinensis 8502, 1 and 4.* 1979. ISBN 90 04 05798 6
12. KOSCHORKE, K. *Die Polemik der Gnostiker gegen das kirchliche Christentum.* Unter besonderer Berücksichtigung der Nag Hammadi-Traktate 'Apokalypse des Petrus' (NHC VII, 3) und 'Testimonium Veritatis' (NHC IX, 3). 1978.
    ISBN 90 04 05709 9
13. SCHMIDT, C. (ed.). *The Books of Jeu and the untitled text in the Bruce Codex.* Translation and notes by V. MACDERMOT. 1978. ISBN 90 04 05754 4
14. McL. WILSON, R. (ed.). *Nag Hammadi and Gnosis.* Papers read at the First International Congress of Coptology (Cairo, December 1976). 1978.
    ISBN 90 04 05760 9
15. PEARSON, B.A. (ed.). *Nag Hammadi Codices IX and X.* 1981.
    ISBN 90 04 06377 3
16. BARNS, J.W.B., G.M. BROWNE, & J.C. SHELTON, (eds.). *Nag Hammadi Codices.* Greek and Coptic papyri from the cartonnage of the covers. 1981.
    ISBN 90 04 06277 7
17. KRAUSE, M. (ed.). *Gnosis and Gnosticism.* Papers read at the Eighth International Conference on Patristic Studies. Oxford, September 3rd-8th, 1979. 1981. ISBN 90 04 06399 4
18. HELDERMAN, J. *Die Anapausis im Evangelium Veritatis.* Eine vergleichende Untersuchung des valentinianisch-gnostischen Heilsgutes der Ruhe im Evangelium

Veritatis und in anderen Schriften der Nag-Hammadi Bibliothek. 1984.
ISBN 90 04 07260 8

19. FRICKEL, J. *Hellenistische Erlösung in christlicher Deutung.* Die gnostische
Naassenerschrift. Quellen, kritische Studien, Strukturanalyse, Schichtenschei-
dung, Rekonstruktion der Anthropos-Lehrschrift. 1984. ISBN 90 04 07227 6

20-21. LAYTON, B. (ed.). *Nag Hammadi Codex II, 2-7, together with XIII, 2* Brit. Lib.
Or. 4926(1) and P. Oxy. 1, 654, 655.* I. Gospel according to Thomas, Gospel
according to Philip, Hypostasis of the Archons, Indexes. II. On the origin of
the world, Expository treatise on the Soul, Book of Thomas the Contender.
1989. 2 volumes. ISBN 90 04 09019 3

22. ATTRIDGE, H.W. (ed.). *Nag Hammadi Codex I* (The Jung Codex). I.
Introductions, texts, translations, indices. 1985. ISBN 90 04 07677 8

23. ATTRIDGE, H.W. (ed.). *Nag Hammadi Codex I* (The Jung Codex). II. Notes. 1985.
ISBN 90 04 07678 6

24. STROUMSA, G.A.G. *Another seed. Studies in Gnostic mythology.* 1984.
ISBN 90 04 07419 8

25. SCOPELLO, M. *L'exégèse de l'âme.* Nag Hammadi Codex II, 6. Introduction,
traduction et commentaire. 1985. ISBN 90 04 07469 4

26. EMMEL, S. (ed.). *Nag Hammadi Codex III, 5.* The Dialogue of the Savior. 1984.
ISBN 90 04 07558 5

27. PARROTT, D.M. (ed.) *Nag Hammadi Codices III, 3-4 and V, 1 with Papyrus
Berolinensis 8502,3 and Oxyrhynchus Papyrus 1081.* Eugnostos and the Sophia of
Jesus Christ. 1991. ISBN 90 04 08366 9

28. HEDRICK, C.W. (ed.). *Nag Hammadi Codices XI, XII, XIII.* 1990.
ISBN 90 04 07825 8

29. WILLIAMS, M.A. *The immovable race.* A gnostic designation and the theme of
stability in Late Antiquity. 1985. ISBN 90 04 07597 6

30. PEARSON, B.A. (ed.). *Nag Hammadi Codex VII.* 1996. ISBN 90 04 10451 8

31. SIEBER, J.H. (ed.). *Nag Hammadi Codex VIII.* 1991. ISBN 90 04 09477 6

32. SCHOLER, D.M. *Nag Hammadi Bibliography.* (in preparation)

33. WISSE, F. & M. WALDSTEIN, (eds.). *The Apocryphon of John.* Synopsis of Nag
Hammadi Codices II,1; III,1; and IV,1 with BG 8502,2. 1995.
ISBN 90 04 10395 3

34. LELYVELD, M. *Les logia de la vie dans l'Evangile selon Thomas.* A la recherche
d'une tradition et d'une rédaction. 1988. ISBN 90 04 07610 7

35. WILLIAMS, F. (Tr.). *The Panarion of Epiphanius of Salamis.* Book I (Sects 1-46).
1987. ISBN 90 04 07926 2

36. WILLIAMS, F. (Tr.). *The Panarion of Epiphanius of Salamis.* Books II and III (Sects
47-80, De Fide). 1994. ISBN 90 04 09898 4

37. GARDNER, I. *The Kephalaia of the Teacher.* The Edited Coptic Manichaean Texts
in Translation with Commentary. 1995. ISBN 90 04 10248 5

38. TURNER, M.L. *The Gospel according to Philip.* The Sources and Coherence of an
Early Christian Collection. 1996. ISBN 90 04 10443 7

39. VAN DEN BROEK, R. *Studies in Gnosticism and Alexandrian Christianity.* 1996.
ISBN 90 04 10654 5

40. MARJANEN, A. *The Woman Jesus Loved.* Mary Magdalene in the Nag Hammadi Library and Related Documents. 1996. ISBN 90 04 10658 8